THE JEWISH EXPERIENCE

Third Edition

Jay A. Holstein

University of Iowa
Iowa City, Iowa

BURGESS INTERNATIONAL GROUP INC
Bellwether Press Division

Printed in the United States of America.
J   I   H   G   F   E   D

Address orders to:

BURGESS INTERNATIONAL GROUP, Inc.
7110 Ohms Lane
Edina, MN 55435
Telephone 612/831-1344
EasyLink 629-106-44
Fax 612/831-3167

Bellwether Press

A Division of BURGESS INTERNATIONAL GROUP, Inc.

Contents

For

Sarah Abigail
and
Joshua Saul

Preface

This is a book about the Hebrew Bible. It is my intention that this book serve to introduce the reader to both the problems and delights of biblical study. The problems are legion: the Hebrew Bible is an ancient book written in an ancient tongue; it consists of thirty-nine books which appear to differ widely both in form and content; and it is considered by the adherents of three world religions to be sacred literature, which for many implies that it is not to be read as one would read any other book. These and other problems will be discussed in this book with the goal in mind of formulating a method for beginning to read the Hebrew Bible. More than anything else, this book is about how to read the Hebrew Bible.

It is my belief that once one learns to approach the Hebrew Bible with neither pietistic devotion nor condescension, the delights of reading the Bible can be as numerous as the problems. Not without reason has the Hebrew Bible had an immense influence on the growth and development of Western civilization. The religions, the legal codes, the literature, the music and art of Western man are suffused with biblical motifs because few books have gripped the imagination of mankind as has the Hebrew Bible.

This book is intended for use in a course called "Judeo-Christian Tradition" at the University of Iowa. This course is meant to provide a basic introduction to these two great religions, both of which venerate the Hebrew Bible. The ideal typical student I have in mind is, while largely ignorant about the Hebrew Bible, intelligent and eager to learn. Therefore, this book seeks to provide some rudimentary information in the opening chapters before it introduces the reader to some of the complexities of biblical studies. I have been a part of this course for fifteen years and, in the greatest number of cases, the students have proven to be both intelligent and eager to learn. They have been a pleasure to teach.

The University of Iowa kindly granted me two summer fellowships and a semester's leave to research and write this textbook. It is a pleasure to thank former president Willard Boyd and President James O. Freedman and the Dean of Liberal Arts, Howard Laster.

I would like to thank my colleagues Professors George Forell and John Boyle, with whom I teach this course, for seeing to it that in a setting in which the overwhelming majority of our students are Christians, the Jewish experience is in no way slighted. Professor Forell, a Lutheran minister, and Professor Boyle, a Roman Catholic priest, have sought always to insure that our presentation of the material is in conformity with the highest academic standards. That is, those of us who teach this course are guided by our setting, which is a state university.

I would like also to thank the graduate students who, over the years, have been teaching assistants in our course. Their work in teaching the discussion sections, in preparing the exams, and in meeting with students is of central importance to the effectiveness of our course. I cannot overstate my gratitude to them.

Finally, I would like to thank Professor Herbert Brichto of Hebrew Union College. He taught me how to read the Bible, and whatever is of value in this work is due to him.

Preface to the Second Edition

Chapters seven through twelve complete *The Jewish Experience* in the sense that the story of the Jewish people is carried into the present. The reader of these chapters will note that there are three main themes: the tracing of a pattern of anti-Semitism which culminates in the Holocaust; the description of the emergence of two vital Jewish communities, one in Israel and the other in the United States; and the elucidation of three theoretical stances toward the Hebrew Bible in the postbiblical Jewish experience.

This last theme (which, for the most part, is found in Chapter Eight), will require a good deal of attention from the reader. It is expected that the student will be guided through this chapter both in lecture and in discussion, but even then, it will not be easy going. My respect for the material and the typical student whom we teach in "The Judeo-Christian Tradition" led me to include this chapter.

This book ends with some speculations on the nature of Jewish identity. Since the Jewish experience has been bound up with the Hebrew Bible, both in terms of its creation and its interpretation, it seemed appropriate to end the last chapter with an analysis of a biblical book. Thus does the book come full circle: it begins and ends with speculations about the Hebrew Bible.

This book appears on the occasion of Professor George Forell's last semester of teaching at the University of Iowa. This course was his creation and he has been its guiding spirit. It was he who invited me into "The Judeo-Christian Tradition" and it is fair to say that I have learned more about the art of teaching from him than from anyone else. Above all, he has demonstrated that a competent and critical exposition of complex issues need not be weighted down with pedantic gobbledygook. I cannot imagine what the course will be like without him.

Preface to the
Third Edition

This is the third and, I think, last reworking of this book. Nine of the twelve chapters have been rewritten, but what I wrote at the beginning of the first Preface remains true: "This is a book about the Hebrew Bible." To the extent that the third edition is an expansion of the second, it is due to the inclusion of more material from the Hebrew Bible. The reader of this volume will soon become aware of its primary preachment, *viz.*, that the Hebrew Bible is so much at the center of the Jewish experience that without this great corpus of literature there can be no Judaism.

As I also wrote in the first Preface, this book is designed for use in a course called "The Judeo-Christian Tradition" at the University of Iowa. Those of us who teach this course would like to think that its popularity (some 800 students take the course each fall) is due to the course's quality. It is a fact that we work hard to see that "The Judeo-Christian Tradition" is worthy of the material it seeks to transmit. And it is a fact that no one in the course works harder than the graduate teaching assistants. Thus, it is a pleasure to thank them, for without their devotion to this course it could not be offered. Apart from those undergraduates who have responded so positively to "The Judeo-Christian Tradition," my most enduring memories of my eighteen year involvement in the course is of graduate teaching assistants who, almost without exception, have been outstanding colleagues.

1

The Bible and History

The Hebrew Bible is virtually our only source of information on the origin and early development of the Israelite people. According to the Hebrew Bible, Abraham (the first Israelite) migrated from Mesopotamia, the verdant area between the Tigris and Euphrates rivers, to the land of Canaan (today's Israel). Canaan, unlike the lush region of Abraham's forebears, was a small, barren territory whose largest river, the Jordan, grew progressively more salty as it flowed southward and thus was of marginal value for irrigation. Canaan, therefore, was a land whose vegetation depended on rainfall; however, for six months of the year there was little or no rain. Accordingly, in Abraham's day (c. 1700 B.C.E.), the land of Canaan was unable to sustain many people.

What then impelled Abraham to leave the fertile plain between the two rivers of his ancestors? And once having left, why did Abraham not continue his southward migratory path down into the land of Egypt with its great river Nile? The beginning of the story of Abraham gives an unambiguous answer to this question (Gen. 12:1ff.):

> The Lord said to Abram [for so he was called before his name was changed by God Himself in Gen. 17:5]: 'Go forth from your ancestral land and from your father's hegemony [indicative of a change in emphasis: Abraham will no longer be the son of his father so much as he will be the father of his sons] to the land which I will show you....' So Abram took his wife Sarai [her name becomes Sarah in Gen. 17:15] and his nephew Lot, and all the wealth they had acquired...and they made their way to the land of Canaan....Then the Lord appeared to Abram and said, 'to your progeny I will give this land.'

The beginning of the story of Abraham, therefore, shows the progenitor of the people Israel journeying to Canaan at the behest of the biblical God. Moreover, as Abraham's story unfolds, divine revelations continue to play a pivotal role. For instance, the biblical God repeatedly assures the patriarch that his descendants will one day inhabit Canaan (Gen. 13, 15, 17, 22) and in Gen. 18 Abraham and his God engage in a colloquy concerning the nature of divine justice.

So much do these revelations control mood and theme that when a purely natural motive (hunger) drives Abraham to go down to Egypt, the biblical narrator utilizes Abraham's stay in Egypt to relate a strange tale in which the patriarch has his wife tell the Egyptians that she is Abraham's sister so no harm will befall him. As Abraham puts it (Gen. 12:11f.):

> 'I know that you are a fine looking woman. Thus when the Egyptians lay eyes on you, they will say, "She is his wife," and they will kill me but let you live. So tell them that you are my sister so that it may go well with me because of you, and so that I survive because of you.'

In short order, Sarah is taken into Pharoah's harem and things do go "well" for Abraham until the Lord devastates the Pharoah's household with plagues. When the Pharoah learns that Sarah is Abraham's wife he expels Abraham and Sarah "and all that Abraham possessed" from Egypt.

Now however one interprets this episode (and what are clearly sequels to it in Gen. 20 and 26; our interpretation will follow in a later chapter), it is abundantly clear that the biblical storyteller does not chart the socioeconomic causes and effects of Abraham's stay in Egypt. Which is to say that on one of the few occasions when a biblical writer provides information which is the stuff of historical reporting (a natural event like a famine followed by a natural human response to search out food), it is to relate an episode which turns on a supernatural event (the overwhelmingly destructive plagues sent by the Lord) and which focuses on what seems to be a spiritual crisis in the life of Abraham.

Consider, for example, that part of Abraham's story which tells of Lot's separation from his uncle. The stated reason for the break appears to involve the distribution and consumption of wealth (Gen. 13:6–7):

> ...the land could not support the two of them living in close proximity; for their possessions were simply too great to allow for that. And there was strife between the herdsmen of Abram's cattle and those of Lot's cattle.

One can imagine that if an historian like Thucydides were relating this incident he would trace this quarrel between Abraham and his nephew to the problems attendant to the growth of clans and the utilization of resources. And in fact when the great sociologist Max Weber sought to reconstruct the patriarchal period [see his *Ancient Judaism* (New York: The Free Press, 1952)] he filtered the stories of the patriarchs through such theoretical constructs as nomadism, semi-nomadism, and peasantry in order to get at the material conditions which he believed were then present.

In the biblical account, however, the breaking apart of Abraham's family serves not to point to the stuff of history and sociology (i.e., facts of one kind or another) but to the "stuff" of which metaphors are made. In the biblical story we see Abraham, clearly the leader of the familial group, graciously granting his nephew first choice in the matter of habitation. And it appears that Lot chooses wisely (Gen. 13:10–13):

> Lot surveyed the area and saw how verdant the whole plain of the Jordan was, all of it—this was before the Lord had destroyed Sodom and Gomorrah—
> ...it was [then] like the Garden of Eden, like the land of Egypt. [The reader will do well to keep this simile in mind for it points both backward and forward in the biblical narrative; but in whichever direction, the point is the same: places rich in material sustenance are sometimes desolate spiritually. This is akin to our expression that you cannot judge a book by its cover.] So Lot chose the Jordan plain and he traveled eastward. Thus did they part

company. Abram remained in the land of Canaan, while Lot settled in the cities of the Plain, setting up a campsite near Sodom. Now the inhabitants of Sodom were very wicked indeed, sinners from the perspective of the Lord.

Lot's choice is not the first human choice with which the reader of Genesis has been presented. The reader has seen:

— first man and first woman choose to leave the Garden of Eden;

— Cain choose to kill his brother Abel;

— humankind choose to befoul the earth;

— humankind choose to build a skyscraping tower;

— Abram choose to obey the Lord's command to migrate southward to Canaan;

— Abram choose (in the absence of any command from God) to go down to Egypt, where he seeks to protect himself at his wife's expense.

In later pages we will have occasion to examine these choices, but for the present let us limit ourselves to one question: why does Lot choose as he does?

The answer is as obvious as it is clear: because the Jordan plain was then lush and prosperous. While perhaps not as obvious, it is clear that Lot's choice of what was then the verdant area around Sodom reverses God's priorities for Abraham. For we saw that God directed the patriarch to leave the well-watered area of his forebears for the materially desolate land of Canaan.

From the outset, however, Abraham is assured by God (an assurance the patriarch, in the absence of the fulfillment of the promise, must accept on faith) that Canaan will be, both for him and his progeny, spiritually productive (Gen. 12:1ff.):

'And you will be a blessing; I will bless those who bless you, and curse him that curses you; all the families of the earth shall be blessed through you.'

Lot's reversal consists in his choice of the material splendor of the spiritually desolate Sodom. Given the reversal it is not surprising that it will be Abraham who will plead with God to spare Sodom (Gen. 18:23 ff.). As a result of this experience as well as his harrowing test in Gen. 22 when God commands the patriarch to burn his son Isaac to a crisp, Abraham begins to grasp what is entailed in the service of God. It is a lesson never learned by his nephew who when last seen (Gen. 19:30–38), is in such a drunken stupor that he does not realize that his two daughters cohabit with him.

In none of these contexts does the biblical narrator weave into the complex intersections of the tapestry of his narrative the sociological ramifications of semi-nomadism. In none of these contexts does the narrator present a bare factual recitation. Rather, it is a relationship between human beings and a supernatural Being which ramifies his tales.

Hence, while the first Israelites may have been historical personages, and while some of the events related about them may, however imperfectly, mirror historical reality, the individuals who wrote and compiled the book of Genesis did not attempt to produce a historical chronicle. And what is true of Genesis is true of the rest of the Hebrew Bible.

Most modern biblical scholars regard 2 Sam. 11–20 as the most historically accurate section in the Hebrew Bible. These chapters relate a series of episodes in the public and private lives of David, the most illustrious of biblical Israel's monarchs. Let us now consider the opening episode with the goal of demonstrating how little it too is like historical reporting.

This episode follows a series of decisive successes in David's reign which place him at the highest point of his power and popularity. The episode begins as follows:

> At the time of year when it was the custom for kings to lead their troops out to battle, David sent Joab [his trusted military chief of staff] forth with his officers and the whole Israelite army and they laid waste Ammon and besieged Rabbah. David, however, remained in Jerusalem [the capital city which was conquered by David and which was not only the location of the king's palace but the site to be of the Lord's Temple].

The question raised by this opening is this: why does David, the greatest of biblical Israel's warrior kings, whose very ascent to the throne is made possible by military heroics (beginning with the famous slaying of the Philistine giant, Goliath), not lead his troops out to battle at precisely that time of year when, as the narrator takes pains to note, kings normally do so? The reader of this passage may recall that the onset of monarchy in Israel is marked by the firm resolve of the people to "...be like all the other nations: let our king govern us and lead our troops out to battle." (1 Sam. 8:20)

In the next five verses, which are packed with information, we learn that:

— a restless King David, walking on his palace rooftop, sees a beautiful woman bathing;

— David inquires as to her identity and learns that she is Bathsheba (literally: "the daughter of Sheba"), wife of one of his mercenary soldiers, one Uriah the Hittite;

— the king nonetheless has Bathsheba brought to his bedchamber;

— later, Bathsheba sends word to David that she is pregnant, whereupon the king summons Uriah back from the battlefront.

Clearly, the reader is meant to infer that a battle weary David (but are his troops not battle weary too?) has stayed in Jerusalem for rest and relaxation. The narrator, proceeding at a breakneck pace, shows David's attraction to Bathsheba, his determination of her identity, his having intercourse with her, his learning that she has conceived, and his summoning of Uriah—in the space of six short verses.

There are enough details in these opening verses to form the basis of an extended novel, to say nothing of a t.v. miniseries. The biblical narrator, however, uses these particulars only as a prelude to his main theme: the laying bare of the enormously complex personality of David the king. Thus the narrator, who has glossed over so much so quickly (as, for instance, answers to questions like: what about Bathsheba attracts the king? how does Bathsheba feel about her encounter with David both before and after intercourse? how many in the palace, apart from the messengers the king sends to fetch her, know of David's perfidy? what are his feelings for this woman after intercourse and after being informed that he has impregnated her?), slows down markedly when he depicts the meeting between David, the most powerful of all of biblical Israel's kings, and the non-Israelite husband of the daughter of Sheba, Uriah the Hittite.

It is well to consider the meeting in detail. It reads as follows:

When Uriah came to him David inquired as to how Joab and the troops were and as to how the war was going. Then David said to Uriah: 'go home and warm your feet.' [cf. Gen. 18:4 and 19:2 where the washing of feet is part of a metaphor for hospitality] And when Uriah left the king's presence, a present from the king followed him. But Uriah spent the night at the entrance to the palace along with all the officers of Joab [who for one reason or another were on leave in Jerusalem]; Uriah never went to his own home. When David was told that Uriah never went home [he had Uriah summoned] and said to him: 'have you not returned from the front? Why have you not gone home?' Uriah responded to David: 'The Ark and all the troops of Israel and Judah [the north and the south] are sleeping [at best] in makeshift dwellings as well as my master Joab and your Majesty's men some of whom are bivouacked out in the open; how then can I go home to eat and drink and lay with my wife. As you live, by your very life [an oath formula which underlines the depth of Uriah's resolve], I will not do such a thing!' David then said to Uriah: 'Stay here one day more and then I will send you [back to the front].' So Uriah stayed on in Jerusalem that day and the next. Then did David call for him and Uriah ate [at the king's table] and David saw to it that Uriah became drunk. Even so however when Uriah bedded down for the night, it was again with his fellow soldiers; to his home he did not go.

The most important interpretive question to ask of the above context concerns Uriah's reaction to what we would call "the royal treatment." He surely must have wondered why he had been called back from the front by the king himself (which is to say that this was not a part of any furlough program). And then when David wines and dines him his wonderment certainly must have taken on a suspicious cast.

At that point Uriah would have had to have been a complete fool not to question the king's sincerity. Uriah's carefully worded replies to the powerful king (whose bodyguards, it must be remembered, are never out of sight) reveal the relatively helpless Hittite mercenary to be anything but a fool. Uriah's responses to the king display not only his unwillingness to cover David's tracks but also his absolute awareness of what David has been up to. When Uriah notes that the king's troops are encamped "in the open," he reminds the king in as direct a fashion as any commoner (and non-Israelite commoner at that) can remind his sovereign that at the very time when it is expected that kings will be in the field with their troops, David has stayed behind in his securely enclosed capital city. Perhaps it was some such feeling of guilt that impelled the king to seek out the open sky of his palace's roof.

The open sky, however, leads not to loyalty to his troops but to an act of supreme disloyalty: he takes to bed the wife of one of his soldiers. Thus the import of Uriah's reference to the Ark of the Covenant which is also in the field. That it is Uriah, a non-Israelite, who invokes the Ark of Israel's God in which was placed the Decalogue (i.e., the Ten Commandments, one of which, of course, prohibits adultery), and that it is Uriah, a mercenary soldier, who pays homage to the value of loyalty to his comrades-in-arms, only deepens the reader's awareness of the enormity of David's wrongdoing.

There are more references to David in the Hebrew Bible than to any other character, while Uriah's role begins and ends with this episode. (Uriah is mentioned in 1 Kings 15:5: "For David had done what was pleasing to the Lord...except in the matter of Uriah the Hittite" and in two listings of soldiers in 2 Sam. 23:39 and 1 Chronicles 11:41). Nonetheless, Uriah makes an indelible impression. He acts with dignity, sobriety, and great courage while David breaks two of the Ten Commandments: he has coveted his neighbor's wife and he has committed adultery.

In short order David proceeds to violate a third Commandment when he orders Uriah back to the front with a dispatch instructing Joab "...to place Uriah in the front line where the fighting is fiercest" and "...to then fall back so that he may be wiped out."

Thus, as if coveting, adultery, and murder by proxy were not crimes enough, David compounds his malfeasance by forgetting about the whole matter. We see this when Joab sends a battle report to the king which relates a large loss of life. Joab knows that this will anger his king so he instructs the messenger to note that one of those who fell in battle was Uriah the Hittite. Joab knows his master well. When David hears that Uriah is dead, his indignation dissolves and he tells the messenger:

> 'Give Joab this message: "Do not be upset about the matter. The sword kills one way or the other. Press your attack and level the city to the ground." Encourage him!'

It is to be noted that the narrator points out that other soldiers died so that Uriah could be liquidated: "So it was that when Joab lay siege to the city that he stationed Uriah where he knew the [enemy's] ablest soldiers would be. When the men from the city came out to meet Joab's force there fell in battle Israelite soldiers and counted among them was Uriah the Hittite."

To top it all off, David is not at all remorseful. In fact, after waiting for Bathsheba's mourning period to end (David is thus seen as a follower of little rules and a breaker of big ones!) he sends for her and makes her his wife. So one can therefore add brazenness to his having coveted, committed adultery, and murdered.

From David's perspective, the matter has been brought to a successful conclusion. He adds a beauty to his royal harem and, for good measure, she bears him a son which, as we shall see, was a great blessing in biblical Israel.

Since, however, point of view in the narrative is that David's perspective is twisted out of shape, the matter is far from concluded.

> From the Lord's perspective that which David had done was evil. So the Lord sent Nathan [a prophet] to David. When Nathan came to the king he said to him: 'Once there were two men, residents of the same town, the one rich and the other poor. The rich man had many sheep and cattle, while the poor man had but one little ewe which he had bought and raised and which grew up with him and his children; it would share his food, drink from his cup, and nestle in his bosom; [in short] it was like a daughter to him. One day a traveler visited the rich man and rather than take from his own cattle and sheep for a meal for his guest, the rich man appropriated the poor man's lamb and prepared it for his visitor.'

Nathan's parable begins the second part of the episode involving David and Uriah's wife. Unlike the first part where the narrator uses few words to express much, here he seems wordy to the point of redundancy. Surely the reader already knows that King David, with a bevy of women at his disposal, chose instead to take the one women of Uriah. Why, that is, does the narrator have Nathan relate what is already obvious to the reader?

Part of the reason for the slow, deliberate pace of the second part becomes evident when the narrator describes David's reaction to the parable:

David exploded in [righteous] indignation at the rich man's behavior and said
to Nathan: 'As the Lord lives [underlining his seriousness as had Uriah by
taking an oath], the man that did this deserves to die! He shall pay fourfold
damages for the lamb, because he did such a pitiless thing.' Nathan responded: 'You are the man! Thus says the Lord the God of Israel [we see now
that the parable was merely the introduction to the prophecy Nathan will
now deliver]: 'It was I who anointed you as king over Israel; and it was I who
rescued you from the clutches of Saul [the first king who determined, and for
good reason, that the young David was a threat to Saul's dynasty]. Did I not
give you your master's [i.e., Saul's] house [as in position] as well as his harem;
and I gave you the northern and southern sections of Israel [so that David
ruled over a united Israel] and if all that were not enough I would have added
to it in other ways. Why then have you spurned the Lord's command by doing
that which displeases Him? You have put Uriah the Hittite to the sword and
his wife you have taken as yours.... Therefore the sword will not depart from
your house....Thus says the Lord: "I will see to it that trouble rises against
you from within your own house; I will take your wives and give them to another man before your very eyes and he shall lay with your wives in the broad
light of day. You acted in secret, but I will make this happen in the sight of all
Israel and in bright sunlight." ' Then David said to Nathan, 'I stand guilty before the Lord!' Nathan said: 'You shall not die for the Lord has remitted your
sin. However, since you spurned the Lord, the child about to be born to you
shall die.'

We see now that as Nathan was relating the parable David was
growing ever more angry until he explodes with "...that man deserves
to die!" That exclamation, of course, lays bare the king's callousness:
ever ready to condemn another, he is unable, until now, to judge
himself. Nathan's "You are the man" induces David to recognize not
only what he has done but against Whom he has done it. The Ten
Commandments are enjoined on biblical Israel by Israel's God. Thus
when David responds to Nathan it is to acknowledge the Lord, God of
Israel, as the source of morality: "David said to Nathan, 'I have
sinned against the Lord.' "

It requires only a moment's reflection to appreciate the intricate
way in which the parable not only exposes David but also presages
what is to come in his story. David's assertion that a fourfold payment is required is a reference to Exod. 21:37: "If a man steals an ox
or a sheep, and kills it or sells it, he shall pay five oxen for an ox, and
four sheep for a sheep." There is a strong undercurrent of irony in
David's reference. David wants to be understood as having a fine
moral sensitivity: the letter of the law calls for a rich man to

compensate the poor man fourfold; David hyperbolically declares that the rich man deserves death. The deeper irony, of course, is that David has in fact committed what in the Hebrew Bible are two capital crimes: murder and adultery.

While David's confession wins for him a reprieve, he clearly is not pardoned. 2 Sam. 13 and 18:14f. describe the killing of Amnon by Absalom (both sons of the king) and of Absalom (David's favorite son) by Joab. And 2 Sam. 16:21f. tells of Absalom's breaking into (before witnesses) his father's harem. Moreover, David is in fact deprived of four sons: Bathsheba's first born, Amnon, Absalom, and Adonijah.

This then is the opening episode of a section which is said to reflect more of a historical tendency than any other part of the Hebrew Bible. Carefully crafted it is, but is it history? I have observed that the goal of historical reporting is to get at the "facts." To appreciate how little the biblical writer of 2 Sam. 11–12 was interested in conveying factual information, let us consider what he chooses *not* to do:

— he chooses not to stimulate the reader's sexual curiosity; encounter, intercourse, and conception are (in the Hebrew) covered in fewer than sixty words;

— he chooses not to shed light on Bathsheba's character; the reader is never explicitly informed as to how Bathsheba feels about David or, for that matter, about her husband Uriah. In fact, Bathsheba may be the most opaque character in the story of David the king;

— he chooses not to engage the reader's attention in battle sequences, troop deployments, and military strategy. Such matters are brought into the narrative only to highlight David's treachery. The narrator is not concerned to explain why kings went out to battle at a certain time of the year and what may be the social, economic, and military consequences of this custom (if in fact custom it was). The detail is introduced to make the reader ponder David's choice to stay in Jerusalem when he should have been with his army. And the account of the battle (such as it is), which results in Uriah's death, is a prelude to what is the focal point of the episode: the king's moral insensitivity.

If historical reporting this account was meant to be, then it is blinkered reporting indeed. However, the power which springs from this episode suggests that our author was a writer of sufficient competence (to say the least) who, had he wished, could have presented a register of facts.

But if not a chronicle, then what is this episode? Which is to say, if the biblical narrator did not think of himself as a historian, what was his main concern in his presentation of the encounter between David and Bathsheba? At the core of this episode is the intricate web of lust and love, ruthlessness and fear, and shamelessness and remorse which is at the center of the inner life of Israel's most famous king.

The complexity of the man David is underscored by the content of Nathan's parable and by David's reaction to it. As noted, David serves only to emphasize his own callous behavior by his self-righteous exclamation: " 'the man who did this deserves to die!' " The reader, even the casual reader, has little difficulty recognizing the analogues in the parable:

— the rich man is David

— the poor man is Uriah

— and the ewe is Bathsheba.

Still, for all of the obviousness there are some interesting differences which serve, I think, to shed more light on what David did and on the David who did it. To begin with, Bathsheba, the "one ewe" of Uriah, is not slaughtered; rather it is the "poor man" Uriah who is murdered. Also, Bathsheba is not the "daughter" of Uriah (the ewe "...was like a daughter" to the poor man). Both of these differences accentuate David's culpability: his treachery does not end with the appropriation of Uriah's "one ewe." The poor man survives while Uriah is snuffed out and his wife will one day bear Solomon, the next king of Israel. Furthermore, just compensation is at least theoretically possible in the case of the poor man. And David's reaction brings home to the reader the fact that it is the king who, in biblical Israel, is ultimately responsible for the dispensation of justice.

It is precisely the matter of justice which reverberates throughout this episode, The parable, as noted, is the introduction to Nathan's prophetic deliverance. We note now that the parable itself has a one line proem: "From the Lord's perspective, that which David had done was evil." In the parable justice requires a just king; ironically, David the king is only too willing to be the judge. But what is to be done when the judge not only is not just but is himself enmeshed in the crime? As the proem makes explicit, and as many another biblical context will suggest, there is a Judge who is absolutely reliable. As we will see, however, the working out of this Judge's justice will sometimes require decades, if not centuries (in the Hebrew Bible justice delayed is not necessarily justice denied), and the working out of this justice does not do away with suffering which sometimes partakes of the pit of despair. While the biblical author is careful to indicate the depth and extent of David's punishment, in a very real sense the human king gets away with adultery and murder. Since the reader is consistently denied access to Bathsheba's feelings, one can only guess at the depth of the pathos of her situation. As for Uriah, no more need be said than that his death is all the more poignant because the afterlife model for biblical Israel (and for her pagan neighbors to the east and to the north) stipulated that if one died without sons there was little chance of "resting in peace." In a later chapter I will spell out in detail this afterlife model.

It is David who is the center of this narrative. David assuredly did rule as king over a united Israel. He is as much a historical figure as Shakespeare's Henry V. And like Shakespeare, the biblical narrator here makes use of historical people not to relate facts but to create a fictional universe in which, in this case, values are seen colliding within the soul of one human being. Understand that it does not necessarily follow that because it is fiction it is therefore not "true." This fictional world can, in fact, be more meaningfully true than any historical chronicle if the author can infuse into his tale elements of the reality we all experience as human beings.

The anonymous genius who wrote this episode not only reveals the complicated make-up of David's persona, but infers that all of us as human beings partake of this complexity. For our author the world is not simply to be divided into good and evil people. Rather, the line separating good and evil goes through the heart of every human being. And this line shifts back and forth. The best of human beings are capable of the worst behavior and vice versa. Moreover, in the blink of an eye a man who has ruthlessly manipulated the lives of others can be touched by the death of an animal belonging to a man he has never met.

Also to be noted, if only briefly, is that the episodes which follow in 2 Sam. 11–20 are not given over to historical reporting either. These episodes, in keeping with the mood and theme of the David and Bathsheba context, display the extreme range of behavior of which humans are capable. The narrator deals with such matters as incest, rape, the murder of brother by brother, heartbreaking estrangement of son from father, and civil war between David and forces led by his favorite son, Absalom.

Additionally, these episodes are marked by what makes the David and Bathsheba story so breathtaking: the narrator's unrelenting objectivity in his depiction of David the king and David the man. What makes this objectivity so remarkable is that in the folk imagination of biblical Israel, King David was George Washington, Abraham Lincoln, and the poet laureate all wrapped up in one.

In the biblical story of David, good and evil are shown clashing in the soul of this great man, and since David is alternately censured and praised, one moral of the story is that since the human being is free to choose between that which is good and that which is evil, we are responsible for our behavior. As we shall see, this is one of, if not *the* most basic propositions of the entire Hebrew Bible.

The chapters which follow will deal with the following questions:

— What kind of book is the Hebrew Bible?

— How and under what circumstances was it written, compiled, and edited?

— How are its various books and sections arranged and why?

— How has it been interpreted?

— What are its major themes and how are these themes explicated?

— What relationships exist between the Hebrew Bible and the various forms of
    postbiblical Judaism?
    early Christianity?

— How did three of the greatest personalities in the postbiblical experience of the Jews (Halevi, Maimonides, and Spinoza) advise one to read the Hebrew Bible?

— What factors led to the Holocaust? And how did Jews and Judaism respond to this disaster?

— What types and distinguishes the two greatest centers of Judaism today (in Israel and the United States)?

— What does it mean to be a "Jew"?

Before we proceed, however, I will present a survey of the major events of the biblical period. Although this book is not intended as a history of Jews and Judaism, the reader will note that a sequential chronology is present in chapters two, six, seven, nine, and ten. This material is included to give the reader some sense of the history, so far as it can be determined, of the people Israel.

2

A Historical Survey of the Biblical Period

In the light of my remarks in the first chapter, one must proceed cautiously in reconstructing the history of biblical Israel. For if the Hebrew Bible is almost the only source of information for this period and if the Hebrew Bible manifestly is not a history book, then only in a very limited way are we able to sketch the configurations of the biblical era. What is visible to us is even less than what is visible of an iceberg.

The first Israelites sojourned in the land of Canaan some 1700 years before the birth of Jesus. Canaan was no more than 150 miles long and 30–80 miles wide. To the west the land was bounded by the Mediterranean Sea. To the east was a geological fault through which coursed the river Jordan. Growing progressively salty as it flowed southward, the Jordan emptied into the Dead Sea, some 1300 feet below sea level.

Unlike Egypt (to the southwest) where it almost never rained and where the Nile made the land habitable, and unlike Mesopotamia (to the northeast; today's Iran and Iraq) where life was sustained both by irrigation (of the Tigris and Euphrates rivers) and by rainfall, the population of Canaan had to depend for its water entirely on rainfall.

During the rainy season (from October to May), sections of the coastal plain as well as portions of the north-central region bloomed with vegetation. But during the long dry season, most of Canaan was almost as desolate as the wilderness which made up its southern region.

And unlike Egypt whose natural boundaries (the sea, wilderness, a mountain range, the cataracts of the Nile) provided protection against foreign intrusion, Canaan was wide open from the north and from the east. Accordingly, there were frequent clashes between the settled populations of Canaan and nomads and semi-nomads in search of better living conditions.

In the book of Genesis the first Israelites are depicted living a semi-nomadic existence in and around the area of Canaan. There seems to have been an uneasy tension between them and the native population. Although Abraham is able to purchase a grave site for his wife Sarah (Gen. 23), and although both he and his descendants enter into a series of mutually beneficial treaties with settled clans (so, e.g., Gen. 21), the so-called patriarchal period (named after Abraham, Isaac, and Jacob, the patriarchs of the people Israel) is not without fighting and pillaging (Gen. 14, 34).

The Hebrew Bible relates that Jacob, the third and last patriarch, settled with his family in Egypt because of the rise to prominence there of Joseph, his favorite son. Apparently, many in Jacob's group became herdsmen after being given a royal grant to some of Egypt's best grazing land: "Then Pharoah said to Joseph: 'Now that your father and your brothers have joined you, the land of Egypt is before you [i.e., what we have is yours]: settle your kin in the best land available, settle them in the region of Goshen; and if there are among them some capable men, put them in charge of my flocks.' " (Gen. 47:5 f.)

Thus begins the story of Israel in Egypt. According to the Hebrew Bible, the people Israel stayed in Egypt for some 400 years. However, except for the initial and final stages, the Bible relates nothing of what happened during those 400 years. At the end of the 400 years, it is clear that Jacob's clan had increased greatly in numbers and that it continued to retain its ethnic identity. Then, in the words of the biblical narrator:

A new king came to the throne in Egypt who did not know Joseph [i.e., did not choose to continue treating the Israelites as a tolerated minority]. The king said to his people: 'The people Israel is more numerous than we are. Let us therefore deal wisely with them, lest they increase further and, in time of war, join with our enemies and thereby gain control of our country.' (Exod. 1:8 ff.)

The Egyptians proceeded to put into force a series of repressive decrees which led finally to the departure of Israel from Egypt.

Future generations of Israelites interpreted the exodus from Egypt and the subsequent years of wandering in the wilderness as being conclusive in shaping the religion of biblical Israel. Certain it is that the writers of the Hebrew Bible attach special significance to these events and to the individual who stands at their center. This individual, *the* prophet Moses, is quite simply pictured as the dominant character in the entire Hebrew Bible. Moses is depicted not simply as prophet but also as military leader, judge, and administrator. It is, however, his prophetic status which sets Moses apart. For Moses is described, and unambiguously so, as biblical Israel's greatest prophet: "Never again did there arise in Israel a prophet like Moses...." (Deut. 34:10). In one biblical context (Num. 12:6 ff.), God asserts that He communicates with Moses not through dreams and visions (as, presumably, is the case with all other biblical prophets), but "...mouth to mouth, plainly and not in riddles."

The story of the people Israel is not understandable without the complex of events which gave to the people a set of norms made distinctive by their having been given by a God who used Moses as an intermediary. In a later chapter we will examine parts of the story of Moses.

After a sojourn in the Sinai peninsula that, according to the Hebrew Bible, lasted a generation, the people Israel, under the command of Joshua, invaded Canaan. In the books of Joshua and Judges the invasion proceeds first in the form of a concerted push which saw the Israelite army take control of parts of the hill country of central Canaan. Then, individual Israelite tribes, and at times several confederated tribes, gradually gain control of the rest of the land.

The Hebrew Bible portrays this period (c. 1200–1000 B.C.E.) as one in which the national unity, achieved under Moses and maintained by Joshua, disintegrated. While individual tribes apparently retained a common religious ideology, social, political, and military factionalism was the order of the day. Indeed, the book of Judges records instances of internecine conflict set off by and resulting in atrocities (see, for example, the last three chapters of Judges).

The appearance of the Philistines in the area changed everything. Biblical historians speculate that the Philistines migrated from the Greek islands. Apparently the Philistines first tried to conquer Egypt, and only after being driven away did they set up enclaves along Canaan's southwestern coastal plain. These enclaves were garrisoned city-states from where their influence radiated northward and eastward, bringing the Philistines into conflict with Israelite settlements. The singleness of purpose which this conflict brought to the Israelites came to overwhelm the fragmentation.

The Philistine threat forced a difficult choice on the fragmented Israelite tribes: either to retain their individual tribal freedoms and thereby risk being picked off one by one by the Philistines, or to centralize and thereby be forced to swear allegiance not simply to a transtribal God but to a transtribal human ruler as well.

In the end the instinct for survival proved stronger than a concern for what today we would call states' rights. Under pressure from the people, Samuel, a powerful and respected leader, chose as king Saul of the tribe of Benjamin. While Saul was able to blunt the Philistine advance, he was never able to place the fledgling nation on a secure footing. Saul died in battle (c. 1000 B.C.E.), and it was left to David (of the tribe of Judah), Saul's eventual successor, to complete the task of building a nation.

Whatever doubts remained about the legitimacy of the monarchical system dissipated during the 40 year reign of King David. While future generations would sometimes argue over who was to be king, there was general agreement that biblical Israel was to be ruled by a king. It is instructive that the future hopes of many of biblical Israel's prophets take the form of depictions of an ideal state ruled by a descendant of the house of David.

David did more than break the Philistine hold on Canaan. He also conquered the city of Jerusalem and made it his capital city;

henceforth it would often be called "the city of David." No reader of this volume needs to be told of Jerusalem's subsequent importance in the traditions of Judaism, Christianity, and Islam. David's army, most often with the great warrior king at its head, crossed the Jordan river and subjugated the kingdoms of Edom, Moab, and Ammon. His forces also pushed northward and subdued Syria. Twenty years into his reign, David's kingdom was the most powerful and prosperous nation state in the immediate area.

Our review of aspects of David's story in the first chapter is sufficient testimony that this great king is not depicted as an ideal human being. But his status as a king is higher than that accorded any other Israelite monarch. David's reign marked the high water point in biblical Israel's political history. But though long remembered, this political golden age was of short duration.

When the people are pictured demanding from Samuel that he designate a king, the biblical narrator has Samuel warn the people as follows (1 Sam. 8:11–18):

> 'This is what the king will do who will rule over you: He will conscript your sons into the chariot force and the cavalry, and the infantry; he will have your sons plow his fields, reap his harvest, and make them into weapons' makers.... He will make your daughters perfumers, cooks, and bakers. He will confiscate the best of your fields, vineyards, and olive groves.... He will tithe your grain and vintage.... He will tithe your flocks and enslave you. The day will come when you cry out because of this king you want; but the Lord will not answer you on that day.'

The process described above was already in motion when David died. During the reign of David's son Solomon, Samuel's prophecy was fulfilled in toto. Initially, Solomon was able to maintain economic and cultural prosperity by virtue of extensive building projects and by putting in place a royal bureaucracy which numbered in the thousands. Solomon also divided his realm into administrative districts in order to more expeditiously conscript an army of workers which built military fortresses, royal palaces, and a resplendent Temple in Jerusalem. Not incidentally, this division also enabled Solomon to levy more taxes. Although Solomon seems not to have expanded his country's territory, he was able to exploit his nation's trade routes and natural resources. And he solidified relations with many of the surrounding nations through treaties which were sometimes sealed by royal marriages.

Some biblical narratives describe Solomon's regime as one of peace and prosperity and, moreover, depict Solomon as the wisest of kings. Other biblical narratives, however, furnish one with a different perspective. In these Solomon is shown overextending his country's resources in order to finance his many commercial ventures; at one point he is even forced to cede some Israelite territory to a neighboring state to meet a debt obligation. Moreover, Solomon's policy of building shrines for the gods and goddesses worshipped by his many foreign wives apparently led to widespread polytheistic practices as many Israelites also worshipped at these temples. One biblical narrator shows Solomon himself succumbing to the lure of apostasy: "In his old age, his wives turned Solomon's heart to the worship of other gods so that he was no longer completely devoted to the Lord his God as his father David had been. Solomon worshipped Ashteroth the goddess of the Phoenicians, and Milcom the abomination of the Ammonites." (1 Kings 11:4–5)

Two elements were added to this already volatile mix of economic dislocation and religious syncretism. First, the northern tribes, by far the more numerous and powerful, believed that the southerner Solomon was bleeding them dry. Second, a powerful new dynasty in Egypt pursued an aggressive foreign policy which threatened the southern borders of Israel.

By the end of Solomon's reign, his kingdom was cracking wide open. Jeroboam, a former official in Solomon's bureaucracy, led the northern tribes in a successful civil war against Solomon's son Rehoboam. Jeroboam became the king of the north (now called Israel) which had more people, territory, and resources than Rehoboam's southern kingdom (now called Judah, after the name of the largest tribe and the tribe to which David's family belonged).

In the years that followed, the north was beset by one bloody overthrow after another; only two of its first six kings were sons of previous kings. In the south, with the southern tribes remaining loyal to the Davidic line, there was much greater political stability.

The split in the nation state hastened the dismantling of David's empire. To the north, Syria gained her independence. To the east, the

Transjordanian kingdoms threw off Israel-Judah's yoke. To the south, Egypt exerted ever-increasing pressure. And to the northeast, in the area between the rivers, Assyria gained control and undertook frequent military forays in order to exact tribute from both Israel and Judah.

The external difficulties besetting Israel and Judah were compounded by frequent skirmishes between the two of them. Repeatedly one or the other aligned itself with a foreign country in order to make war against the other. For the first forty years after the secession of the south, the north and south were almost continually at war.

The situation changed, for a time, in 876 B.C.E. when Omri, an army officer, seized the throne in the north and began an illustrious twelve year reign. He established economic and military ties, not only with Judah, but with the Transjordanian kingdoms in order to better protect his own country from Syria and Assyria. Omri's son, Ahab, continued his father's policy of peaceful coexistence with Judah. In fact, during Ahab's reign the northern kingdom, with the exception of Egypt and Assyria, was the dominant nation state in the area.

As we will see in a later chapter, the Bible's interest in Ahab lies not in his political and military successes (no more with him than with David), but rather in his spiritual failures. In particular, we will examine Ahab's struggles with the great prophet Elijah.

After Ahab's heroic death in battle (he dies face to foe), an army officer named Jehu brought a bloody end to the Omride dynasty. The destruction of the Omride dynasty brought to an end the fragile alliance among Israel, Judah, and the Transjordanian kingdoms. The result was that by 841 B.C.E. Assyria dominated most of the area.

In the years that followed, Israel and Judah often tried to break Assyrian dominance. Two factors apparently persuaded Israel and Judah to challenge the far superior might of Assyria: first, there was the relatively great distance separating Assyria from Israel and Judah; and second, Assyria often had to deal with uprisings elsewhere in its extensive empire. Sometimes Israel and Judah did in fact succeed in freeing themselves, for a time, from Assyrian rule. During the reign of Jeroboam II (801–746), for example, the borders of Israel approximated those of the glory days of David's rule. The biblical narratives about Jeroboam—consistent with the Hebrew Bible's singular interest in the realm of the spirit—detail not the socio-economic side of his rule but present a prophetic critique of Jeroboam's misuse of power.

By the middle of the eighth century, Assyria was once more poised to come down from Mesopotamia to re-establish its control over Syria, Israel, and Judah. In the face of this Assyrian threat, Israel and Syria put aside their differences and demanded that Judah join their alliance. When Judah refused, Syria and Israel made ready to attack. Judah was saved when Assyria intervened and soundly defeated Syria and Israel.

Probably because Assyria only deployed a garrison force in Syria and Israel, in a few years they tried once more to shake off the Assyrian yoke. Once again Assyria came down in force and this time, in order to put an end to insurrections, exiled some 40,000 Israelites up into Mesopotamia. Thus did the political independence of the northern kingdom come to an end. At the present state of our knowledge it is not possible to know what became of the exiled Israelites. Whether it was the result of persecution, assimilation, or something else again, these Israelites disappeared from history.

Judah just barely avoided Israel's fate. Egypt, fearing the rising tide of Assyrian power, induced Judah to rebel against Assyria on the promise of Egyptian aid. But when the Assyrians invaded, Egypt sent no troops. As a result, Judah was crushed and deprived of virtually all political independence. Judah was now little more than a vassal state in the sprawling Assyrian empire. Judah's borders did not much exceed the city of Jerusalem and its immediate environs. Judah's kings were in no sense independent rulers.

For most of the seventh century Assyria remained in control of the area. But toward the end of that century widespread revolts broke out in the Assyrian empire. Most significant was the increasing pressure that the Babylonians put on Assyrian control of Mesopotamia. In 621 B.C.E., the Assyrian capital fell to the Babylonians, and the Egyptians, fearing that Babylon would one day threaten them, sent a force northward to aid the faltering Assyrians. Josiah, the very able king of Judah, decided that Assyria in federation with Egypt constituted more of a threat than Babylon alone. Therefore, he placed his army in the path of the advancing Egyptian force. Although he succeeded in delaying the Egyptian push northward, and thereby insured the defeat of Assyria, Josiah, perhaps Judah's most resourceful king since the days of David and Solomon, was killed in battle. Moreover, to punish Judah, Egypt left a garrison force there.

However, it took Babylon but a few years to break Egyptian control of Judah and to replace it with that of her own. For only a brief time did the Judeans submit to Babylonian rule. But when, in 597 B.C.E., the Judeans did revolt, the Babylonians responded swiftly and decisively. They crushed the revolt and deported to Babylon the Judean king, much of the nobility, and perhaps as many as ten thousand Judeans. In several years, however, those Judeans who were left in Judah, perhaps emboldened by promises of Egyptian aid, once more defied Babylonian authority. The Babylonians leveled the city. And they exiled most of Jerusalem's inhabitants to Babylon. Apparently, only the poor and the dispossessed were left in Judah.

And so it came about that the exiled Judean community in Babylon became the one remaining bearer of the traditions of the people called Israel. Had the exile continued for a long time, the Judeans, like the northern kingdom before them, might also have disappeared. But the exile ended after less than 75 years because the Babylonians were conquered by the Persians (present day Iran). In 539 B.C.E. the Persians, under the leadership of Cyrus, took control of Mesopotamia. The Persians reversed the Assyrian and Babylonian policy of the forced deportation of subject peoples. Accordingly, the Persians encouraged the Judean exiles to return to Judah and once there to rebuild the Jerusalem Temple.

At the end of the biblical period, Judah was a small province in the Persian empire. Its population was probably no more than 50,000. For certain, at the end of the biblical period there was little indication that the traditions created and preserved by the people Israel, traditions which one day would constitute the Hebrew Bible, would have such a profound impact on the future history and destiny of humankind.

3

The Books of the Hebrew Bible

The Jews usually refer to their Bible as the Hebrew Bible, or sometimes as the *Tanak*. "Hebrew Bible" is a self-evident title: a book written in Hebrew. The term *Tanak* is a Hebrew acronym whose consonants represent the three main divisions of the Hebrew Bible:

— the *Torah:* the books of Genesis, Exodus, Leviticus, Numbers, and Deuteronomy;

— the *Neviim* (Prophets): the books of Joshua, Judges, 1 and 2 Samuel, 1 and 2 Kings, Isaiah, Jeremiah, Ezekiel, Hosea, Joel, Amos, Obadiah, Jonah, Micah, Nahum, Habakkuk, Zephaniah, Haggai, Zechariah, and Malachi;

— the *Ketuvim* (Writings): the books of Psalms, Proverbs, Job, The Song of Songs, Ruth, Lamentations, Ecclesiastes, Esther, Daniel, Ezra, Nehemiah, 1 and 2 Chronicles.

We possess no detailed, straightforward account as to how and why these books came to be included in the Hebrew Bible. Scholars conjecture that the process of canonization (that is, accepting certain books as sacred or authoritative) proceeded in three main stages. In the first, perhaps as early as the 5th century B.C.E., the Palestinean Jewish community set apart the 5 books of the Torah as holy. Then, perhaps in the 3rd century B.C.E., the books of the Prophets were added. The books comprising the Writings were probably included sometime in the 1st century of this era.

However, even were we able to date precisely the canonization process, many questions would still remain. Why, for instance, were these 39 books and no others included in the sacred canon? That is, what criteria were employed by those who were in charge of including some books and of excluding others? Also, why were books like Ecclesiastes (with its pessimistic world view), Esther (with its questionable moral tone), and Song of Songs (with its overt sensuality) included?

We do not even know why the Hebrew Bible is arranged as it is. In fact, Christians order the books of the Hebrew Bible differently than do the Jews. For most Christians the Hebrew Bible is the "Old Testament." This name is used in order to indicate a relationship between the Hebrew Bible and the New Testament. Christians believe that the Old Testament prefigures the New Testament. The Christian Bible differs from the Jewish Bible in three important ways:

1. The order of the books is different. In the Christian Bible the book of Ruth follows the book of Judges; 1 and 2 Chronicles, Ezra, and Nehemiah follow 1 and 2 Kings, and most of the books of the Prophets follow the books of the Writings. Ruth was put after Judges since the story is set in the time of the Judges. And 1 and 2 Chronicles, Ezra, and Nehemiah were placed after Samuel and Kings as the former books retell much of the material in Samuel and Kings. It is probable that the Christian community placed the prophets at the end because these books are presumed to most closely anticipate the major themes of the New Testament.

2. Catholics and Protestants do not agree on the canonical status of the books of the Apocrypha. Catholics include the books of the Apocrypha in the Old Testament; Protestants either omit them or place the books of the Apocrypha between both Testaments. Catholics and Protestants disagree about the status of the books of the Apocrypha because their two traditions used two different Old Testaments. When Christianity began to spread throughout the Greek-speaking world it adopted a Greek translation of the Hebrew Bible which had been completed by the Alexandrian Jewish community several

centuries before the birth of Jesus. This Greek translation of the original Hebrew is known as the Septuagint. The title, which is Latin for 70, derives from a legend that 72 scholars labored for 72 days (72 was apparently rounded off to 70) and miraculously produced identical translations. The Septuagint, which was the Bible of many Greek-speaking Jewish communities, contained books and sections of books not included in the Hebrew Bible of the Palestinean Jewish community. As noted above, the Septuagint became the Bible of the early Church. The Catholic Church continues to regard the Apocrypha as part of the sacred canon. The following books comprise the Apocrypha: The First Book of Esdras; the Second Book of Esdras; Tobit; Judith; the Rest of the Chapters of the Book of Esther; The Wisdom of Solomon; Ecclesiasticus or the Wisdom of Jesus Son of Sirach; Baruch; A Letter of Jeremiah; The Song of the Three; Daniel and Susanna; Daniel, Bel, and the Snake; The Prayer of Manasseh; The First Book of the Maccabees; The Second Book of the Maccabees. Later, the Septuagint was translated into Latin (the vulgate). However, Reformation Protestants, who used the Old Testament of the Palestinean Jewish community, did not (and do not) regard the books of the Apocrypha as sacred.

3. The third major difference between the Christian and Jewish Bibles is an obvious one: the Christian Bible includes the books of the New Testament; the Jewish Bible does not.

Since the focus of this book is the Bible used by the Jews, we will deal only with the Jewish or Hebrew Bible. As we saw, the Hebrew Bible has three major sections consisting of 39 books. We turn now to a descriptive survey of these books before we proceed to some reflections on how to read the Hebrew Bible.

As we noted, the first major section of the Hebrew Bible has been called the Torah. It is no simple matter to translate the Hebrew term into English. Torah is a feminine noun which comes from a verb stem meaning "to throw" or "to shoot." In a few biblical contexts the verb means to teach or instruct. The noun Torah seems based on this sense of the verb. The noun controls the following meanings in the Hebrew Bible:

1. human instruction; e.g., of parents, sages, poets;

2. divine instruction; e.g., through prophets or priests;

3. a body of priestly instruction;

4. a body of legal decisions; e.g., those given by Moses;

5. custom, manner.

When the term Torah is used to designate the first major section of the Hebrew Bible it controls the meaning of Torah (or instruction) of Moses since, as we will see, it is Moses who is the dominant human figure in the first major section. And since the preeminence of Moses derives from his unique relationship with the biblical God, it can be said that the title of the first major section of the Hebrew Bible intends to convey the sense of "God's Instruction."

GENESIS

Genesis, the first book of the Hebrew Bible, can be divided into two main sections. The first (as the title of the book suggests) deals with the beginnings of things; how the universe as we experience it came to be and how mankind is to function in this universe. In regard to mankind, the book of Genesis seems to describe a series of failures:

— first man and first woman fail to follow the only divine command in Eden and are evicted from that idyllic garden;

— the progeny of the first human couple so violate the most basic of moral norms that eventually the biblical God engulfs the world and the many families of man are reduced to one (that of Noah);

— after the flood the descendants of Noah spread out over the earth. However, their misdeeds bring down punishment again from the biblical God. This time the punishment is in the form of a separation of mankind into national and ethnic groupings.

This separation leads to the second main section of the Book of Genesis: the description of the origin and development of one people—the people Israel—from among the units of mankind. The first

Israelite is Abraham who separates himself from both his native land and his father's clan, and, at God's command, begins sojourning in the land of Canaan. The biblical God tells Abraham that his descendants will one day occupy this land. The son and grandson of Abraham (Isaac and Jacob) continue to live a semi-nomadic existence in and around the land of Canaan until circumstances draw the clan to Egypt. In Egypt, one of the sons of Jacob, Joseph—who had been sold as a slave by his envious brothers—rises to a position of great power and is eventually reunited with his brothers and aged father who come to Egypt in search of food. Jacob's clan settles in Egypt and the Book of Genesis ends with the death of Joseph.

EXODUS

The book of Exodus continues the narratival story of Genesis. In Egypt the Israelites greatly increase in numbers and the Egyptians take repressive measures to check their growth. Moses is born to an Israelite family but grows to manhood in the palace of the Egyptian ruler. Moses is forced to flee from Egypt after killing an Egyptian. He settles in the wilderness of Midian where he remains until he is commissioned by God to return to Egypt in order to liberate the Israelites. Aided by plagues of supernatural force which rake Egypt, Moses leads the people out of Egypt up into the wilderness of Sinai. There he receives a series of revelations from the biblical God. In conformity with these revelations—to which the people at first respond enthusiastically—Moses begins to establish the legal, social, and religious institutions of biblical Israel. However, the initial enthusiasm of the Israelites turns to rebellious dismay in the face of the wilderness existence. The people fight Moses at virtually every turn.

LEVITICUS

The book of Leviticus does little to continue the narratival flow of the story of Moses. Instead it is made up of a series of laws, norms, and rules. Most of these relate directly or indirectly to the sacrificial cult. The book lays down rules governing sacrifice, the installation of the priests who are to oversee the cult, and the proper way to bring certain sacrificial offerings. There are also regulations in regard to "clean" and "unclean" animals (i.e., animals which the Israelites may and may not eat), and regulations concerning the distinction between the ritually pure and impure, and some of the ways men and women may cleanse themselves of various impurities. The principle upon which these distinctions are based is "You shall be holy, for I, the Lord your God, am holy." (Lev. 19:2) Flowing from this principle is the supreme value of human life and, accordingly, interspersed in Leviticus are laws calling for fair and equal treatment of non-Israelites.

NUMBERS

The book of Numbers picks up the narrative again and, like the book of Exodus, interweaves narrative and law. The book describes events which begin thirteen months after the exodus from Egypt and carries on the story of the wilderness experience to the fortieth year after the exodus. As the title suggests, one of the book's concerns is a census which numbers the males over twenty in the Israelite people at 603,550. The census, which probably functioned as a military draft, coupled with regulations about the positioning of the tribal groupings when the Israelites make and break camp, is designed to prepare the Israelites for combat. Included in the book of Numbers are rules in regard to the priesthood and its helpers, the treatment of certain diseases, the program for one who takes a vow to become a Nazirite, and the institution of the holiday of Passover. Most of the narratival episodes in the book depict rebellions from within the ranks of the people against Mosaic authority. Typical (Num. 16–18) is the story of the rebellion of Korah, Dathan, and Abiram. Directed against Moses' secular leadership and Aaron's [the brother of Moses] priestly authority, the revolt is put down with the help of divine intervention. Repeatedly segments of the people rebel against Moses and repeatedly the biblical God intervenes to reaffirm Mosaic authority. The obstinacy of the people leads to years of disaffected wandering in the wilderness. The book of Numbers closes with depictions of the idolatrous ways of the Israelites and with further preparations for the invasion of and settlement in the land promised by God to Abraham's progeny.

DEUTERONOMY

Deuteronomy, the fifth and last book of the *Torah*, records the events of the last month of the 40 years' wilderness experience. The Israelites are bivouacked on the eastern side of the Jordan River. Most of the book concerns the last speeches of Moses. The prophet reiterates the legal framework which the people are to adopt once they settle in Canaan. Moses also outlines the moral principles which concretize what is meant by loyalty to the God of Israel. In no uncertain terms Moses warns the people of the disasters which will befall them if they forsake their God-given destiny. Moses then commissions Joshua to lead the assault on Canaan and the book ends with a description of the death and burial of Moses.

In this way does the first section of the Hebrew Bible end. The Torah's chronological framework encompasses events from the Creation to the death of Moses. Except for the book of Genesis, huge chunks of legal material are interspersed into the narratival flow. In a subsequent chapter we will examine some of the major themes of the Torah. For the present, however, we merely raise the following questions which will guide our later discussion:

1. Who wrote the Torah?

2. When was the Torah written?

3. Why was the Torah written?

4. What are the major themes of the Torah?

5. How does the Torah anticipate what is to come in the rest of the Hebrew Bible?

JOSHUA

The book of Joshua opens the Prophets, the second major section of the Hebrew Bible. Joshua can be divided into two parts. In the first part the conquest of Canaan is described. Chronological details are sketchy in the book, but it would appear that the war of conquest lasted some seven years. Joshua's forces win one victory after another. In the second part of the book, Joshua allots the Promised Land to the tribes of Israel. Then, in two closing addresses, Joshua urges the people to follow the legal framework put in place by Moses and to refrain from adopting the ways of the Canaanites. Finally, Joshua reviews the saving acts of God (Joshua 24:2 ff.):

> Then Joshua said to all the people: 'Thus says the Lord, the God of Israel: "In bygone days your ancestors, Terah, Abraham's father and father of Nahor, lived along the Euphrates and worshipped other gods. I took your ancestor Abraham from there and led him through the length and breadth of Canaan and I gave him many descendants. I gave him Isaac, and to Isaac I gave Jacob and Esau. I gave Esau the hill country of Seir as his inheritance, but Jacob and his sons went down to Egypt. Then I sent Moses and Aaron and I smote the Egyptians and then I brought your ancestors from Egypt and you came to the Sea. And the Egyptians chased after your ancestors with chariots and cavalry to the Sea. Then your ancestors cried out to the Lord and He put darkness between you and the Egyptians whereupon He brought the Sea down upon them so that it engulfed them. Your own eyes saw what I did to the Egyptians. Then you stayed a long time in the wilderness. And I brought you to the land of the Amorites who lived on the east side of the Jordan. They battled you but I delivered them into your hands; I wiped them out for you, and you were able to take possession of their land.... Then you crossed the Jordan and you came to Jericho. The people of Jericho and the Amorites, Perizzites, Canaanites...fought you, but I delivered them into your hands. I sent a plague ahead of you, and it drove them out.... I have given you a land for which you did not work and towns which you did not construct, and you have settled down in them. You are enjoying vineyards and olive groves which you did not plant. Therefore, worship the Lord and serve Him with undivided loyalty; put away the gods that your ancestors worshipped beside the Euphrates and in Egypt and worship the Lord." ' The people agreed that they worship only the Lord.

The book ends with Joshua's death and burial, "buried [unlike Moses] on his own property."

JUDGES

The narratives of the book of Judges span some 410 years: from the first months of the Israelite presence in Canaan to the time immediately preceding the establishment of the monarchy. Unlike the book of Joshua, which describes a unified thrust into Canaan, Judges depicts a drawn out struggle between individual tribes or groups of several tribes and the native population. The book describes some of these battles as well as the activities of military leaders called "Judges" (hence the name of the book) who appear in perilous times and who deliver the Israelites from foreign domination. The chaotic nature of this period is typified both by Israel's continual backsliding from their exclusive worship of God and by internecine conflicts among many of the tribes. The conflicts within the Israelite people are so severe as to require the establishment of a transtribal system of government which could impose unity and order on the scattered, warring tribes. In this fashion does the book prepare for the events recounted in the first chapters of the next biblical book which describe the crowning of Israel's first king.

THE BOOKS OF SAMUEL

The two books of Samuel, like the two books of Kings, formed originally a single book. 1 and 2 Samuel cover events from the birth of Samuel to the close of King David's active role in public life. Samuel, the last of the so-called Judges, displays a multi-faceted authority ranging from his roles as prophet, judge (in a juridical sense, unlike the previous "judges" who were mostly military leaders), and king-maker. Near the end of his public life the people urge Samuel to appoint a king who will lead them in battle against the Philistines. With great reluctance Samuel agrees and anoints Saul as Israel's first king. Saul does manage to blunt the Philistine threat. Samuel breaks with Saul when the king disobeys him. Samuel secretly anoints David as Saul's successor. Ironically, Saul's own counselors, not knowing of David's high destiny, recruit David to calm their mercurial king and there begins a love-hate relationship between

Saul and David. David becomes Saul's military chief of staff and gains great public support. Saul comes to view David as a threat to his dynasty and seeks to kill him. For years David is forced to live as an outlaw, until, upon Saul's heroic death in battle, he is publicly crowned king over first the southern part of the kingdom and then, when Saul's son is murdered, over the north as well. David's reign is marked by territorial and economic prosperity which make Israel the preeminent power in the area. However, palace intrigue and discontent within certain factions of the Israelite people lead to a series of revolts against David. Although he is able to quell them, it is clear that there are centrifugal forces at work within the Israelite body politic.

KINGS

The two books of Kings begin with David's nomination of his son Solomon as his successor and end with the release of King Jehoiachin from prison in Babylon in 562 B.C.E. The opening chapters show Solomon securing his throne by neutralizing the opposition to his rule (often by having them killed). Solomon then embarks on a series of ambitious building projects which enhance his reputation but which also produce some bitterness because of the huge numbers of workers he drafted to work on these structures and because of the increased taxes he levied to pay for them. Disaffection was strongest in the northern part of the kingdom, and at Solomon's death the kingdom of Israel split into two. The narrative concerning the political destinies of the northern and southern kingdoms is punctuated by a number of tales about the prophets Elijah and Elisha. These stories have as a common theme the idolatrous behavior of both the people and their rulers. The political independence of the northern kingdom is terminated by the Assyrians in the 8th century and the southern kingdom experiences a similar fate in the 6th century at the hands of the Babylonians.

The rest of the books of this second section deal with the teachings and activities of individuals who are known as prophets.

ISAIAH

This book purports to record the preachments and actions of an 8th century prophet named Isaiah. Since, however, much of the latter part of the book deals with events in the 7th, 6th, and 5th centuries, most biblical scholars are of the opinion that at least from chapter 40 onward, the book of Isaiah deals with at least one other prophet. In the opening chapters of this first biblical book devoted to a prophet, a recurrent theme of biblical prophecy is introduced: the unfaithfulness of the people Israel will bring on dire punishment. Moreover, the reaction of the prophet's listeners to his warning is also a typical motif in the books of the prophets: they spurn the prophet's advice to mend their ways. The closing chapters have to do with the bright future which will rise Phoenix-like out of the ashes of disaster. This bright future is made possible not simply by the repentant behavior of the people but by the Lord's mercy. The notion that the biblical God is more than fair is everywhere apparent in the books of the prophets and, in fact, in virtually every book in the Hebrew Bible. The most explicit formulation of this principle can be found in what are perhaps the two most famous contexts in the Hebrew Bible (Exod. 20 and Deut. 5); famous because the so-called Ten Commandments are listed in them. God's magnanimity is defined as follows (Exod. 20:5 f., Deut. 5:9 f.):

> '...I the Lord your God am a zealous God, visiting the iniquity of the ancestors on the progeny, upon the third and upon the fourth generations of those who hate Me, but keeping faith to the thousandth generation of those who love Me and keep My commandments.'

Which is to say that bad deeds have short-term effects unlike those of good deeds, which are credited to man by God for a long duration.

The book of Isaiah concludes with the vision of a redeemed people Israel instructing the nations of the world in the true religion in which not might but justice is glorified.

JEREMIAH

The book of Jeremiah, the longest book in the Hebrew Bible, recounts the prophetic career of a prophet who participated in the events leading to the collapse of the southern kingdom in 586 B.C.E. Jeremiah was convinced that the whole area would soon be overwhelmed by the Babylonians and he called on the Judean leadership not to resist this inevitability. But the Judeans did not listen and, as Jeremiah predicted, Jerusalem was besieged. During the siege Jeremiah was arrested on a charge of treason. After the Babylonians conquered the city Jeremiah was released only, in a short time, to be carried against his will down into Egypt by a group of Judeans still intent on fighting Babylonian hegemony. No short summary can convey the intelligence and passion the prophet infused into his mission. Certain that the violation of the moral norms would lead to his nation's ruin, he knew keen disappointment when his calls for repentance went unheeded. And not only were his warnings ignored; according to his testimony he was a "laughingstock" among his people. (Jer. 20:7) And when not ignored he was persecuted. Little wonder then that he did not relish his prophetic role. Nonetheless, he is unable to desist (Jer. 20:8 ff.):

> ...The word of the Lord causes me constant disgrace and contempt. I said to myself, 'I will not remember Him, No more will I speak anymore in His name'—But His word is like a raging fire in my heart, Shut up in my bones; And I could not hold it in, I was helpless.

EZEKIEL

The prophet Ezekiel was apparently one of the exiles carried off by the Babylonians in 597 B.C.E. In exile he predicted the fall of Jerusalem because of its inhabitants' idolatrous ways. Like the messages of Isaiah and Jeremiah his words met indifference at best and hostility at worst. And like Jeremiah he asserted that the coming disaster was inevitable. In line with the beliefs of Isaiah and Jeremiah, Ezekiel predicted a brighter future. Unlike them, however, he describes the reconstituted state in some detail.

All three of these prophetic books envision a future in which all nations recognize the majesty of the God of Israel. And all three of these prophetic books were certain that the biblical God's majesty was in no way threatened by the fall of Judah. And, most importantly, all three of these biblical books affirm that the distinguishing characteristic of devotion to God is moral behavior.

The twelve books which follow the books of Isaiah, Jeremiah, and Ezekiel have been called the "Minor Prophets" because of their short length in comparison with the first three prophetic books. These twelve books reaffirm the basic themes of the first three books. The one book which, stylistically at least, separates itself from the others is the Book of Jonah. Unlike the other prophetic books, Jonah consists almost entirely of prose narrative. Also, the prophet Jonah, far from being an exemplar of the prophetic role, seems to be everything a prophet should not be:

— he seeks to avoid his mission; when ordered east by land to Assyria's capital Nineveh he heads west by sea.

— when forced to Nineveh by God he gets no satisfaction when the citizens of Nineveh repent; in fact, Jonah berates God for being a "softy" in letting the Assyrians off the hook. Jonah confesses that it was the knowledge that God would wind up forgiving the Assyrians which led him to seek to avoid his mission.

We will discuss Jonah in a later chapter. For the present it is enough to note two things. First, once the reader understands that the prophet Jonah points the way with the back of his neck, the book's teachings conform to the other prophetic books. Second, since the prophet is directed by God to speak to the Assyrians, who were among the most hated and feared of biblical Israel's enemies, there is the indication that God's graceful concern is not limited to the people Israel.

Those books of the second major section of the Hebrew Bible which deal with prophets and prophecy raise in a reader's mind a series of related questions:

— how does one become a prophet?

— what does it mean to "hear" the word of God?

— how does one distinguish between a "true" and a "false" prophet?

In a later chapter we will attempt to answer these questions.

The title of the last major section of the Hebrew Bible is simply descriptive—"Writings"—and appropriately so since this section contains books which vary greatly both thematically and formally.

The first book of this last section is the book of Psalms, a collection of 150 poems. It should be noted that biblical Hebrew poetry depends not on rhyming but on a relationship between successive lines in which the second line of a couplet either repeats, completes, or contradicts the first line. This is called "parallelism." The most frequent form of parallelism is that in which the second line reinforces the thought of the first by repeating it:

> Why are the nations in an uproar?
> And why do the peoples mutter in vain?

A less common form of parallelism is that in which the second line is in contrast to the first:

> They [my enemies] confronted me the day of my calamity;
> But the Lord was a support for me.

Still another form of parallelism is that in which the second line of a couplet supplements or completes the first:

> Yet I have set my King upon Zion.
> My holy hill.

It is impossible to categorize the psalms except in the most general way. Ideally, each psalm should be interpreted on its own terms. Overall, the Psalms deal with the following kinds of subjects, concerns, and themes:

— the ways in which God relates to man, usually emphasizing God's majesty and man's inadequacies;

— the ways in which man can serve God properly, usually emphasizing moral conduct;

— the kinds of feeling evoked in individuals who speculate about the ways of God (reverence, piety, submission, anger, confusion, etc.);

— descriptions of the dire circumstances the psalmist feels himself or his people to be in and the corresponding appeals to God for help;

— descriptions of certain periods in the past history of the people with the usual purpose of drawing morals or lessons which are relevant to the present circumstances;

— hymns of praise and thanksgiving for either the mortal or divine king or both.

Seventy three (of the 150) psalms are attributed to David, who in other sections of the Hebrew Bible is renowned as a musician and poet. Other psalms are attributed to Moses, Solomon, and some lesser known personages. At the present state of our knowledge it is impossible to know if those to whom a psalm is attributed in fact wrote that psalm.

PROVERBS

The second book in the Writings is Proverbs. This book appears to be a compilation of several collections of sayings. The first such collection deals with the theme of wisdom: praise of it, how to acquire it, its power, etc. It is asserted that although ultimate wisdom is the possession of God, there is much that man can know, especially when it comes to discerning the difference between the good and the bad. The second collection is composed of almost 400 sayings, maxims, aphorisms, which do not appear to conform to any one pattern. Many of them rest on the principle that justice is rewarded and injustice punished. Some of them describe the ways of the good/wise man and contrast them to the ways of the bad/foolish man. Another group of sayings commends the life of moderation in which one is cognizant of both his inadequacies when compared with God and of his obligations to one's fellow man. In sum, these collections touch upon many aspects of everyday life:

— how to conduct one's business affairs;

— how to treat one's servants;

— how to enjoy life;

— how to bear up under sorrows, etc.

Several of the collections are attributed to King Solomon, who, in the books of Kings and Chronicles, is sometimes praised for his wisdom.

JOB

The book of Job may be the most complicated and baffling book in the Hebrew Bible. The book may be divided into the following five parts:

— a prose prologue (chpts. 1–2)

— a series of discussions between Job and Eliphaz, Bildad, and Zophar (chpts. 3–31)

— the speeches of Elihu (chpts. 32–37)

— the speeches of God (chpts. 38–42:6)

— the prose epilogue (ch. 42:7–17)

The opening of the book introduces us to Job who is described as pious and prosperous. It seems clear that the book revolves around this question: does disinterested piety exist? That is, is Job pious because piety is worthwhile in and of itself (as God claims), or is Job pious because it is profitable to be pious (as Satan, one of God's ministering angels, claims)? In pursuit of an answer to this question God allows Satan to strip Job of his possessions and his children and then to afflict him with leprosy. Although Job does not understand the reason for his suffering, he refuses to renounce God; that is, he remains

THE JEWISH EXPERIENCE   43

pious. The question remains in his mind, however, as to why he is suffering. Eliphaz, Bildad, and Zophar try to convince Job that he is suffering because he has sinned. While Job does not know why he is suffering, he knows (as does the reader) that he has not sinned. Neither side is able to convince the other. Elihu then intrudes, seeming to repeat many of the arguments of Eliphaz, Bildad, and Zophar. Finally, God Himself appears to Job, and through a series of striking images seems to demonstrate that man is in no position to judge God. Job grants the truth of God's position and, in effect, apologizes to God for having questioned His ways. The book ends with a restoration of Job's prosperity and God's commendation of Job and condemnation of the friends.

In a later chapter we will discuss the book of Job; for the present we note several questions that the book of Job raises:

— is Job pious for the right reasons?

— is there a connection between suffering and sinning; that is, does God reward the good and punish the wicked?

— how important is man to God?

— why does God prefer Job to Eliphaz, Bildad, and Zophar?

— is there a retributive afterlife where the good are rewarded with the wicked punished?

We also note that scholars, for two thousand years and more, have disagreed as to how the Book of Job answers these questions.

THE SONG OF SONGS

The Song of Songs is a love poem, but critics have for a long time debated whether it is a sensuous or an allegorical treatment of love. There seem to be two or three characters in the book: the so-called "Shulamite woman," her shepherd lover, and perhaps King Solomon. If there are but two characters then this poem would appear to describe the transition from immature to mature love. If there are three characters the book would seem to describe a conflict between the shepherd and Solomon for the affections of the Shulamite woman. This conflict is resolved when Solomon allows the two lovers to remain together. Those scholars who have interpreted the Song of Songs allegorically believe it is a poem symbolizing the love between God and Israel. But whether read allegorically or not, it is certain that the Song of Songs is replete with sensuous imagery.

RUTH

The book of Ruth, set in the days of the "Judges" (1200–1020 B.C.E.), tells how the Israelite Elimelech, along with his wife Naomi and their two sons Mahlon and Chilion, immigrated to Moab because of famine in their native Israel. In Moab, Mahlon and Chilion wed Moabite women (Ruth and Orpah). Shortly thereafter, however, Elimelech, Mahlon, and Chilion died. Naomi decided to return to Israel, and urged her daughters-in-law to remain in Moab. Orpah did so, but Ruth accompanied Naomi back to Israel. Once in Israel, Ruth supported the two of them by gleaning in harvested fields. By chance, a kinsman of Elimelech, one Boaz, learned of their plight and agreed to redeem Elimelech's land and to marry Ruth for the purpose of saving Elimelech's line. The book ends with a note to the effect that a son was born to them from whose line eventually came King David. The story of Ruth, though simply and beautifully told, concerns a serious theme: the obligations of the living to the dead. Assumed in the story is the duty of a kinsman to provide one who dies without male offspring with a son by having intercourse with his widow. This duty was bound up with the belief that one's status in the afterlife was adversely affected if no such son was provided. We will have more to say about the book of Ruth in a later chapter, as well as about the various afterlife models found in the Hebrew Bible.

LAMENTATIONS

The book of Lamentations consists of five independent poems on a common theme: the disasters which befell the Judeans as a result of the Babylonian invasion in the sixth century. The poems describe the desolation of Judah's capital city Jerusalem and how the city with a long, proud history was reduced to rubble. The book ends with an appeal for God's compassion.

ECCLESIASTES

The book of Ecclesiastes has for a recurrent theme the notion that human life lacks substance; in the famous words of the book: "vanity, vanity, all is vanity." The Hebrew term which is rendered "vanity" means a puff of wind, i.e., something without substance. The author believes there is nothing a man can do to overturn the essential meaninglessness of life. The author asserts, in no uncertain terms, that man cannot overcome his finitude and that, moreover, much that happens to man on his journey to the grave is outside his control. According to the author, it is not simply that death is inevitable, or that, perhaps, man's fate was fixed long ago, but also that even in the few years granted to man "the race is not always to the swift, nor the battle to the strong," which is to say that many aspects of life lack purpose and meaning. In the face of this pessimistic assessment of the human condition, the author advises the reader to make the best of a bad lot: to enjoy one's youthful vigor because the unrelenting weakness of old age will rob one of all such pleasure. He tells his reader to work well at the task one is assigned and to enjoy the product of one's labor. And perhaps, above all other things, he counsels his reader to seek out a good mate for help and companionship in a frequently harsh world. The author of Ecclesiastes (tradition has ascribed this book to Solomon) wants his reader to limit his expectations. While wisdom about the highest matters and immortality are not achievable, more limited goals such as companionship and bodily pleasures are.

It is by no means clear how the book of Ecclesiastes came to be a part of the sacred tradition of Israel. Was it included because the canonizers wanted to include diverse positions? Was it included because the canonizers could not pass up such a masterpiece even though its teaching would appear to be at variance with the other biblical books?

Was it included because of the several "pious" glosses (e.g., "The sum of the matter, when all is said and done: revere God and observe His commandments")? At the present state of knowledge it is impossible to know why this pessimistic (life is meaningless), decidedly materialistic (eat, drink, and be merry) book was included in the sacred literature of the Jews.

ESTHER

The book of Esther tells how Esther, a Jewish resident in Susa, the Persian capital, came to be queen of the Emperor Xerxes (485–465 B.C.E.) and how she saved her Jewish brethren from destruction which one of the emperor's officers (Hamen) had prepared for them. The Jews were then given free rein to kill their enemies and, when one day proved to be inadequate for the task, Esther persuaded Xerxes to grant another day so the bloodshed could continue. This victory was celebrated in the feast of Purim, which is mentioned nowhere else in the Hebrew Bible. As with Ecclesiastes, many ancient and modern critics have wondered how the book of Esther, which seems to glorify vengeance, and which never once mentions God, came to be a part of the canon. Some have conjectured that if the book of Esther is read properly it does indeed glorify God's providence; others have speculated that the book records an historical event worthy of preservation. Still others have insisted that the book of Esther is an ironic satire in which the author intended to poke fun at overly zealous nationalists, whether Persian or Jewish.

In spite of all these and other suppositions, Esther's canonization (like that of Ecclesiastes and Song of Songs) remains a mystery.

DANIEL

The book of Daniel is set in 605 B.C.E. The Babylonian Emperor Nebuchadnezzar is besieging Jerusalem. Daniel, along with some other Jews, is taken captive. When Daniel interprets a dream of Nebuchadnezzar which had befuddled his own experts, Daniel is rewarded with a powerful position within the Babylonian bureaucracy. However, when the companions of Daniel refuse to bow before an image of Nebuchadnezzar, the emperor has them thrown into a [blast] furnace. When they survive miraculously, Nebuchadnezzar acknowledges the power of their God and publishes an edict which praises the God of Israel. Later when Daniel is tossed into a lion's den by Darius, the Persian Emperor, there is again a miraculous escape. The second half of the book describes some visions of Daniel concerning both the near and the far futures.

THE BOOKS OF EZRA AND NEHEMIAH

The books of Ezra and Nehemiah were probably originally one book and may in fact have been part of a larger work which included 1 and 2 Chronicles. Ezra and Nehemiah describe the return of the Judeans to their homeland from exile in Babylon. Of central concern is the rebuilding of Solomon's Temple, which had been destroyed by the Babylonians. This project is both sanctioned and urged by Cyrus, Emperor of Persia. Ezra and Nehemiah are Judeans in the employ of the Persians. They seek to resolve some of the problems faced by the returning Judeans. In addition to the task of rebuilding the Temple, the Judean community in Jerusalem faced the problem of defining its relationship to non-Judeans in the land. Ezra and Nehemiah, for example, condemn marriages between Judeans and non-Judeans and, furthermore, urge a religion based on the ancient laws of Moses.

1 AND 2 CHRONICLES

These two books (which, again, like Ezra and Nehemiah were at first one book) close the Hebrew Bible, even though in terms of chronology they end where Ezra and Nehemiah begin. With a minimum of narratival detail, 1 and 2 Chronicles cover a time span from Abraham to the fall of Jerusalem and the decree of Cyrus permitting the return and rebuilding of Jerusalem. In the course of this narration Chronicles often presents a far different picture than did the books of Samuel and Kings. There is, for instance, a strong emphasis on priestly matters (the maintenance of the sacrificial cult), and on the depiction of the ideal rather than the real. In terms of its emphasis on the ideal, one need only consider how the narrators of Chronicles describe David. They omit many of the most important episodes found in Samuel and Kings; e.g.,

— the disputes between Saul and David;

— the David-Bathsheba story;

— the rebellion against David by his son Absalom.

4

Some Thoughts on
How to Read the Bible

A variety of problems confront one who attempts to understand the Hebrew Bible. In the first place, the Hebrew Bible is an ancient book written in an ancient tongue. We have noted already that while most of what we know about the biblical period comes from the Hebrew Bible, the biblical authors were manifestly not trying to communicate factual information. There are huge gaps, therefore, in our knowledge regarding the societies which produced, compiled, and canonized the biblical record. It is a foregone conclusion that many of the biblical narratives assume knowledge of customs, beliefs, and laws which the modern reader lacks.

To give but one example which I will expand on in the next chapter, the prevailing view of afterlife in biblical Israel is no longer a part of Judaism nor is it explicitly described anywhere in the Hebrew Bible. Thus, very few readers of the Hebrew Bible have any awareness of an afterlife model which one biblical author after another incorporates, albeit implicitly, into the texture of their tales.

Let me give but one instance. In chapter 38 of the book of Genesis the author interrupts the narrative flow of the story of Joseph to tell us something about Judah, one of Joseph's older brothers. This divagation is by no means irrelevant to the story of Joseph as Judah will play a decisive role in the resolution of Joseph's story; and since the material contained in chapter 38 casts doubt on Judah's loyalty, it frames in bold relief his future moment of truth when he is called upon to exhibit loyalty both to his younger brother Joseph and to his aged father Jacob.

In any case, in chapter 38 Judah is pictured leaving his brothers and setting off on his own, settling in the Canaanite lowlands to the south where he marries the daughter of a Canaanite named Shua. Judah and Bathshua (i.e., "the daughter of Shua") have three sons, Er, Onan, and Shelah.

After Er grows to manhood, Judah arranges a marriage for him with a woman named Tamar. Shortly thereafter, Er dies: "But Er, Judah's first-born was evil in the eyes of the Lord, so the Lord killed him."

It is at this point that the story becomes obscure for many readers. Judah orders Onan to copulate with his sister-in-law in order "...to provide offspring for your brother." Judah's order is related to a custom (did it ever achieve the status of a law?) which is explicated in Deuteronomy 25:5 ff. This context stipulates that if a man dies without sons, his "brother" (it turns out that in the absence of a brother a relative will do) is to have intercourse with the dead brother's widow in order to provide a son for the dead man. If the brother refuses, he is released from this act of loyalty to the dead, but not without shame (see Deut, 25: 9–10).

While Deut. 25 may make intelligible Judah's order, it does not tell us the why of the legislation. Nor does it cast light on Onan's action. Here is how the biblical narrator describes Onan's action: "Since Onan knew that the seed [i.e., offspring] would not count as his, he ejaculated on the ground whenever he had intercourse with the wife of his brother, so as not to provide offspring for his brother." While Onan's behavior seems unclear, the Lord's response is clarity itself: "What Onan did was evil in the eyes of the Lord, so the Lord took his life as well."

If, as the narrative assumes, it is crucial to have sons, then Judah's action in withholding Shelah makes sense, for he now has but one son left. But why does he not tell Tamar the truth? And why does he not free her from her obligation to her dead husband? Remember that he instructed her to return to her father's house and remain as a widow. Tamar, too, is without sons, so by not letting her pursue her destiny with another man, is Judah not being cruel to her? And why was it so necessary to have sons that biblical Israel was apparently willing to violate its own sexual code of conduct (see Lev. 18:16), a code which was nothing if not austere?

Let us return to the story. A long time passes during which Shelah grows to maturity, Judah never communicates with Tamar, and Judah's wife dies. Judah waits for the period of mourning to pass and then he takes off with a friend to a sheepshearing festival. Tamar learns that her father-in-law will be passing her way and she removes her widow's garb (so she *has* remained loyal to her dead husband) and, covering her face with a veil, she stations herself by the road on which Judah will pass.

Ironically, when Judah sees her not only does he not recognize her but he takes her (of all people!) for a whore. He propositions her and she demands payment beforehand. He promises to send a kid from his flock when he returns home, but she wants a token that he will in fact do so. Who better than Tamar should know, by the way, that Judah is one who promises to do things without delivering on the promise? Judah hands over his "seal, cord, and staff," which is probably the equivalent of one's driver's license and Visa card.

After they have intercourse and Judah goes on his way, Tamar immediately puts on her widow's garb. Judah eventually sends the kid in order to redeem his pledge but, of course, no prostitute can be found. Judah decides to drop the matter: " 'Let her keep them, lest we become a laughingstock....' "

Three months later Judah is forced to bring Tamar to mind when he is told that she is pregnant. Since he had commanded her to remain a widow (i.e., in effect still married to her dead husband Er), she in effect has committed adultery. Judah, therefore, has no difficulty evaluating her behavior: " 'Bring her out...and let her be burned.' " (In biblical Israel the institution of marriage was protected by a categorical prohibition against adultery).

But as she is brought out Tamar produces the pledge and Judah understands what has happened and why: " 'She is more in the right than I am, since I did not give her to my son Shelah.' " And he did not have intercourse with her again. The episode concludes with Tamar giving birth to twin boys.

The writer of this story assumes, apparently as a matter of course, that the reader will understand what motivates Judah, Onan, and Tamar to act as they do so that the reader can appreciate the difference between Judah and Onan on the one hand and Tamar on the other. As we shall see, biblical Israel's regnant view of afterlife consisted of the following:

— at death the imperishable part of one goes to Sheol, the abode of the dead;

— in Sheol, one would "rest in peace" if one had living males in the family and if the land on which one was buried remained in the family's possession.

As Deut. 25 makes clear, a process was set in place whereby the family could provide a son for one who died without one.

In the light of the above, much of what transpires in Genesis 38 is clear. Each of the characters, in fact, can only be comprehended by the manner in which he or she "relates" with the dead Er. And these relationships make sense only if one understands that Er cannot "rest in peace" unless and until his family provides for him what he cannot provide for himself.

At first Judah seems determined to help Er. But as soon as he has reason to fear for his own rest or security in Sheol, i.e., when Onan dies, Judah can neither bring himself to turn his back on his first born nor expose himself to more risk by sending Shelah to Tamar. So what does he do? In a way he does, figuratively speaking, exactly what Onan had done. Rather than risk public censure Onan, as it were, went through the motion of helping his brother but at the same time he saw to it that there would be no conception. If at this point you ask why Onan should care at all if he produces a son for his dead brother Er the answer is that his son, though biologically Onan's, will stand in for Er and inherit from Judah's estate what would have come to Er and thereby leave less for Onan. Though Judah's concern comes from a different direction, i.e., that he may be left with no sons at all, his behavior imitates Onan's (albeit unknowingly; it is improbable that Onan let it be known that he was practicing "onanism"). For Judah sends Tamar to her father's house with the assurance that he will send Shelah to her when his last son matures. Thus publicly he exhibits loyalty to Er, his first born. But he is never able to bring himself to send Shelah, nor is he able to forthrightly tell his daughter-in-law whom, by the way, he consigns to a life of loneliness and barrenness.

Of course, Judah's behavior with Tamar, whom he believes to be a prostitute, is in no sense flattering to him. He clearly is not overwhelmed by grief over the loss of Bathshua; like King David who waited for the appropriate period of mourning to pass before marrying Bathsheba, Judah reveals himself to be a follower of the law's letter and a violator of the spirit which undergirds all of biblical Israel's norms: both are disloyal to the extreme. Note, too, that Judah's concern in tracking down the "prostitute" so that he can redeem his pledge is based solely on what others will think: " 'Let her keep them, lest we become a laughingstock.' " Concern for the public's attitude is behind David's eradication of Uriah as well.

Then, too, Judah is only too ready to have Tamar executed when he learns that she is pregnant. Having consigned her to a living death by virtue of his unwillingness to deliver Shelah despite his public posture of loyalty, he now self-righteously calls for her to be burned. His exclamation is akin to David's " 'The man who did that deserves to die.' " In both cases, Judah and David want to underline their piety; both succeed, however, only in emphasizing their disloyalty.

This brings us to Tamar, a Canaanite woman who is destined to begin a line which will produce none other than King David (see Ruth 4:17–21). This Canaanite woman exhibits extraordinary loyalty to her dead husband, and she does so under very difficult circumstances. She clearly is bound to Er until Judah frees her from that obligation. But Judah wants his cake (i.e., public concern for Er's welfare) and he wants to eat it too (i.e., never providing Shelah). Tamar can only wait. When her chance comes she acts with a single-minded devotion that exposes Judah not only to the public (" 'She's more right than I, inasmuch as I did not give her to my son Shelah' ") but to himself as well. When we meet him next in the Joseph story he is a far different character, one who is willing to expose himself to the greatest of risks to protect an aged father who, for different reasons, is as helpless as was Tamar.

Without some sense of the reason for the concern for Er's well-being which permeates Gen. 38, the story remains almost a complete cipher. And we can only guess how much we have yet to learn about the beliefs, norms, and conventions which ramified biblical Israel's society. Although the archaeological finds of this century in the Middle East have, to be sure, shed considerable light on the biblical period (especially on biblical Israel's pagan neighbors), the fact remains that the Hebrew Bible continues to be virtually our only source of information in regard to biblical Israel itself.

Yet another problem is the great diversity of the Hebrew Bible. The Hebrew Bible is not so much one book as a library of some thirty nine books. Had these books, which run to well over a thousand pages, been written by one individual whose ideas and beliefs remained constant, it would still be no small matter to read and comprehend the Hebrew Bible. It seems, however, that not one but many were involved in the production of the Hebrew Bible. It is possible that these individuals had differing temperaments, interests, and abilities.

It might help if we could know who these individuals were, but in the greatest number of instances the Hebrew Bible is completely silent about authorship. While modern scholarship is filled with conjectures about when, where, by whom, and under what circumstances a particular biblical text was written, these remain just that, i.e., conjectures. It is perhaps significant that when a biblical text does seem to identify its author as, for example, the book of Ecclesiastes (which begins, "The words of the Preacher, son of David, King in Jerusalem," i.e., Solomon) or some of the Psalms (which begin "A Psalm of David"), the great majority of modern biblical scholars do not accept the explicit testimony of the text.

Still, it must be admitted that no matter how much information one accumulates about how, by whom, when, and under what circumstances a biblical text achieved its present form, still unanswered is the all-important question of what that text means. Knowledge, for example, about the probable date of composition and/or compilation of the opening chapters of Genesis is of real value only is it enables the reader to better understand these chapters.

Whether such historical knowledge is of substantial help is an interesting and complex question. The process of trying to answer such a question would perforce require one to speculate not only about the origin and development of ideas but also to ponder the question of whether and to what extent thought processes are conditioned and/or determined by environment.

To say the least, these are not very easy problems to solve. To know with any precision what the relationship may have been between an individual's thought and his environment would seem to require more knowledge than any mortal could possibly bring to bear on the problem. Who, that is, could possibly acquire such knowledge about both history and the history of thought?

Because of what is noted in the previous paragraph, to many modern biblical scholars the Hebrew Bible seems to be not a work which is ordered coherently but rather one which is fanciful and haphazard. It is therefore not surprising that the great majority of modern biblical scholars give priority to the formulation of a method which can render coherent that which is incoherent rather than to careful, painstaking, word by word exegesis of the biblical text.

Perhaps the following quotation from an essay by Professor Leo Strauss on Spinoza, the man generally acknowledged to have been the progenitor of the way in which modern biblicists read the Bible, will help elucidate the difference between bringing to bear on a text a method which is foreign to that text and trying to understand a text on its own terms:

> To understand the words of another man, living or dead, may mean two different things which...we shall call interpretation and explanation. By interpretation we mean the attempt to ascertain what the speaker said and how he actually understood what he said, regardless of whether he expressed that understanding explicitly or not. By explanation we mean the attempt to ascertain those implications of his statements of which he was unaware. Accordingly, the realization that a given statement is ironical...belongs to the interpretation of the statement, whereas the realization that a given statement is based on a mistake, or is the unconscious expression of a wish, an interest, a bias, or a historical situation, belongs to its explanation. It is obvious [to Strauss and to me but not to the great majority of modern biblical

scholars] that the interpretation has to precede the explanation. If the explanation is not based on an adequate interpretation, it will be the explanation, not of the statement to be explained, but of a figment of the imagination of the historian. [Leo Strauss, *Persecution and the Art of Writing* (Glencoe, Illinois: The Free Press, 1952), p. 143.]

The reader is urged to reread the above citation for it represents the approach to the Hebrew Bible adopted in this book. My primary concern is with *interpretation* and not with *explanation* (as Strauss uses these words).

Let us understand where we have arrived. The Hebrew Bible is made up of thirty nine books which exhibit great diversity. There are legends, parables, allegories, fables, prophetic and perhaps philosophic discourses, law codes, hymns, lamentations, religious poetry, love poetry, and so on.

Although many biblical contexts involve historical people and events, the Hebrew Bible does not read like a history book. I am not referring simply here to modern historians. The reader is urged to consult Thucydides' account of the Peloponnesian War to understand how little the Bible reads like any kind of historical reporting, ancient or modern. I direct the reader to Thucydides because in his work he sometimes inserts speeches which are clearly composed by him (that is, he does not pretend that these words were actually spoken), but even here the reader will note that Thucydides' primary concern is to get at what *was* rather than (as in the case of the Bible) what *ought* to have been. Perhaps it will help to say that whereas Thucydides seems always to want to understand the universal by scrutinizing the individual (i.e., he devotes himself to the study of one war), the biblical writer introduces the universal (which in the biblical metaphor is God) on virtually every page. To say the least, it is hard to imagine a character like the biblical God being at the center of any historical work. While it is accurate to state that we first see the biblical God at work in creating the ordered universe, *it must never be forgotten* that the biblical God is Himself a creation, a character—albeit the central character—in the biblical corpus of literature.

The question we ask now is: how does one begin to read such a vast piece of literature? In the spirit of Professor Leo Strauss' use of the word interpretation, we propose to take as a starting point the hypothesis that those who produced the biblical record (whoever they were and wherever they lived) were competent writers and editors. We will assume that they wrote and edited the Hebrew Bible precisely the way they wanted. We will therefore confront the biblical text on its own terms. We will not look outside of the Bible, unless a biblical author forces us to by using a literary allusion to a non-biblical work. We will acknowledge that to speculate about authorship of a biblical text which does not itself divulge authorship is not within the scope of our interpretive endeavor.

All of the above can be summed up in the notion that we will always be guided by the modest assumption that the biblical text under examination is intelligible; that is, that it is understandable because the writer and/or editor knew what he wanted to convey and had the artistic resources to convey it.

We turn now to three biblical texts which are related by a common theme and which have bewildered generations of exegetes. In three different contexts in the book of Genesis, a patriarch (twice Abraham and once his son Isaac) counsels his wife to tell the people of the locale in which they are sojourning that she is his "sister."

These contexts have been the subjects of innumerable comments and speculations. I chose these contexts not because I can solve all the interpretive problems which they pose but because they hopefully will demonstrate some of what is involved in the interpretation of biblical literature.

Our first text, Gen. 12:10–20, reads as follows:

There was a famine in the land [of Canaan] so Abram went down to Egypt to sojourn there, for the famine was very severe. When he was about to enter Egypt he said to his wife Sarai, 'Look, I know I have for a long time known that you are a beautiful woman. When the Egyptians see you they will say, that is his wife, and they will kill me, but you they will let live. So tell them that you are my sister so that it will go well with me because of you.' When Abram arrived in Egypt the Egyptians saw that his wife was very beautiful. Pharoah's courtiers saw her and praised her to the Pharoah and she was taken into the Pharoah's palace. And because of her, it went well with Abram; he acquired sheep, oxen, asses, male and female slaves, she-asses and camels. However, the Lord smote the Pharoah and his household with mighty plagues because of Sarai the wife of Abram. Pharoah summoned Abram and said, 'What have you done to me! Why did you say, "She is my sister" so that I took her as my wife? Now, here is your wife. Take her and get out.' And Pharoah put men in charge of him and sent him away with his wife and all that he possessed.

The second text comes eight chapters later (Gen. 20):

Abraham journeyed from there southward and he settled between Kadesh and Shur. While residing in Gerar, Abraham said of his wife Sarah, 'She is my sister.' So Abimelech, the king of Gerar, sent for her and took Sarah. And God came to Abimelech in a dream by night and He said to him: 'Behold you are a dead man because of the woman you took for she is a married woman.' Now Abimelech had not gone near her. Abimelech said, 'O Lord, will you destroy an innocent nation? He himself said to me, "She is my sister." And she said, "He is my brother." When I did this I was innocent.' Then God said to him in the dream, 'I knew that you were innocent and so I kept you from sinning against Me. That was why I did not let you touch her. But now return this man's wife for he is a prophet and he will pray for you, to save your life. If you do not return her, know that you and all that are yours will certainly die.' Early next morning Abimelech summoned all of his servants and told them what had happened, and they were very frightened. Then Abimelech summoned Abraham and said to him, 'What have you done to us? What sin have I committed against you that you should bring so great a guilt upon me and my kingdom? You have done things to me which should not be done. Why,' Abimelech demanded of Abraham, 'did you do such a thing?' 'I thought,' said Abraham, 'that there was no fear of God in this place, and that they [the inhabitants of Gerar] would kill me because of my wife. And besides, she is in fact my sister, my father's daughter though not my mother's, and she became my wife. Then when God caused me to travel from my father's house, I said to her, "Let this be the loyalty that you shall show to me; whatever place we come to, say there of me: He is my brother." ' Abimelech took sheep and oxen and male and female slaves, and gave them to Abraham; and he returned his wife Sarah to him. Then Abimelech said, 'Settle wherever you please in my land.' And to Sarah he said, 'I give your brother a thousand pieces of silver; this will serve as a covering of the eyes before all who are with you, and you will be completely vindicated.' Abraham then prayed to God and God healed Abimelech, his wife, and his slave girls so that they were able to conceive; for the Lord had shut tight every womb of the household of Abimelech on account of Sarah the wife of Abraham.

Finally, here is our third text (Gen. 26: 1–16):

There was a famine in the land, not the earlier famine in Abraham's time, and Isaac went to Abimelech, king of the Philistines, in Gerar. The Lord had appeared to him [Isaac] and said, 'do not go down to Egypt; stay in the land which I will point out to you; I will give all these lands to you and your offspring, in keeping with the oath I swore to your father Abraham. And I will make your descendants as numerous as the stars of heaven, and give to your descendants all these lands, so that all the nations of the earth shall bless themselves by your offspring, because Abraham obeyed Me and followed My commands, My laws, and My teachings.' So Isaac stayed in Gerar. When the men of the place asked him about his wife, he said, 'She is my sister,' for he was afraid to say, 'my wife,' thinking, 'the men of the place might kill me because of Rebekkah, for she is beautiful.' After some time had passed, Abimelech, king of the Philistines, looked out the window and saw Isaac caressing [literally "playing, laughing," a pun on Isaac's own name] his wife Rebekkah. Abimelech sent for Isaac and said, 'so she is your wife! Why then did you say, "she is my sister?"' Isaac said to him, 'I thought I might lose my life because of her.' Abimelech said, 'look what you have done to us! One of the people might have slept with your wife, and you would have brought guilt upon us.' Abimelech then ordered all the people as follows: 'Anyone who bothers this man or his wife shall be put to death.' Isaac sowed in the land and harvested a hundred fold the same year. The Lord blessed him, and the man grew richer and richer until he was very wealthy; he had acquired flocks and herds, and a large household, so that the Philistines envied him. The Philistines stopped up all the wells which his father's servants had dug in the days of his father Abraham, filling them with earth. And Abimelech said to Isaac, 'Go away from us, for you have become too strong for us.'

These are the three episodes which make up what has been called "the sister-wife" story in Genesis. Not without reason these episodes not only have attracted attention but have resisted definitive interpretation for two thousand years and more. A series of questions comes to mind almost immediately:

— What are these episodes meant to convey?

— Why is the same motif repeated three times in the space of 14 chapters?

— How could Abraham and Isaac have made such requests of Sarah and Rebekkah?

— And what do Sarah and Rebekkah think and feel about their husbands' behavior?

To put some of the interpretive problems in perspective, let us begin by considering the manner in which a great scholar sought to explain these episodes. The scholar is E. A. Speiser, who was a brilliant exegete of ancient texts, both pagan and biblical. In an article entitled "The Wife-Sister Motif in the Patriarchal Narratives" (in *Biblical and Other Studies*, 1963), Professor Speiser claimed to have uncovered a legal fiction in Mesopotamia (the area of Abraham's beginnings) whereby a woman from an important family could assume sister status in marriage in order to give her more legal protection.

Professor Speiser conjectured that the three Genesis narratives were originally intended to underline the nobility of Sarah and Rebekkah by showing them to be worthy of the lofty sister-wife status. To understand what he then did we must take a brief detour into what is called "source analysis." It must be understood from the outset that source analysis partakes of what Professor Strauss called "explanation" rather than "interpretation."

In the 18th century a French physician named Astruc made what he thought was an extraordinary discovery:

> In the Hebrew text of Genesis, God is regularly designated by two different names. The first which presents itself is that of Elohim ["God"].... The other name of God is that of YHWH ["Lord"].... It might be thought from these remarks, that these two names, Elohim and YHWH, are employed without distinction in the same places in Genesis, as synonymous terms, and appropriate for varying style; but this would be an error. These names are never confounded; there are whole chapters, and the greater portions of chapters, where God is always Elohim, and never YHWH; there are others at least as numerous, where the name of YHWH alone is given to God, and never that of Elohim.

In short order scholars were attempting to demonstrate that there were substantive and stylistic differences between the *YHWH* and *Elohim* portions of Genesis. A third "source" was said to be discovered which also used the term *Elohim* but which, it was believed, had its own peculiar characteristics. These sources were subsequently named; there was the J source which used *YHWH*, the E source which used *Elohim*, and a P source which also avoided using *YHWH* in Genesis and which is distinguished from the E source by virtue of its supposed emphasis on cultic matters (thus "P" for priestly).

Then, early in the 19th century, another source, this one called D (for Deuteronomy), was identified. Efforts were made to date these sources by connecting the ideas and institutions found in the first five books of the Hebrew Bible with events recounted in the so-called historical books, i.e., Judges, Samuel, Kings, Ezra, Nehemiah, and Chronicles. It was presumed that most of the legal contexts in the Torah were pious frauds in that the laws were in fact formulated long after the time of Moses (the time frame for Moses was said to be c. 1300 B.C.E.). From this presumption it was only a small step to the conclusion that virtually the entire story in which the greatest of biblical Israel's prophets is featured was a delusion.

These studies led to the following general conclusions about the compilation of the sources:

— P, in the 5th century B.C.E.;

— D and E, in the 7th century B.C.E.;

— J, in the 8th century B.C.E.

Although there is much disagreement nowadays among source critics as to when to date a particular source or even as to where one source ends and another begins, there is widespread agreement that it is of paramount importance to identify and date the putative sources. Since the Hebrew Bible does not divide itself into sources this is tantamount to asserting that the Hebrew Bible is not intelligible. Not intelligible in that the biblical authors and editors do not provide the kinds of information needed to understand it properly.

If it is asked why so much effort is expended in the search for answers to questions the biblical authors seem not even to ask (as, e.g., who wrote a text, when was it written, what was the author's and/or editor's society like), the answer is as clear as it is simple: it is a virtual faith axiom in modern biblical scholarship that environmental conditions determine the texture and scope of an individual's thought.

For instance, if it could be determined that the first chapter of Genesis (the story of creation) was written in the 5th century B.C.E. while the two chapters which follow (the story of Eden) were written in the 8th century B.C.E., then the seeming differences between the two stories could be explained by the supposed differences which existed between the two societies.

At this point we return to part of what I previously quoted from Professor Leo Strauss: "It is obvious that the interpretation has to precede the explanation. If the explanation is not based on an adequate interpretation, it will be the explanation, not of the statement to be explained, but of a figment of the imagination of the historian." Which is to say that even if a biblical scholar could separate a biblical text into sources and then date the sources (at best, a very doubtful supposition), it hardly follows that the process of interpretation is completed. Even if we are willing to grant the highly unlikely possibility that there are sources in the biblical text which can be separated and dated accurately, still to be determined is that text's meaning. No matter how much information one thinks one has accumulated about how, by whom, when, and under what circumstances a text like Gen. 1–3 achieved its present form, one still has to confront that text as it presents itself. Knowledge about the probable date of composition and/or compilation of the opening chapters of Genesis is of real value only if it enables the reader to better interpret these chapters.

Whether such historical knowledge is of substantive help is an interesting and profoundly complex question. Seeking an answer to such a question would of necessity require one to inquire not only into the origin and development of ideas but to ponder as well whether and to what extent the processes of thought are determined by environmental conditions.

To say the least, these matters are not easily solvable. To know with any precision what the relationship may have been between an individual's thought and his environment would seem to require more knowledge than any human being could possibly have.

We return now to Professor Speiser's attempt to unravel what he perceived to be the twisted yarns of the sister-wife story. Here is how his argument proceeded:

— Chapters 12 and 26 belong to the so-called "J" source which uses the term *YHWH* (usually translated as "Lord") for God.

— Chapter 20 is part of the so-called "E" source which uses the term *Elohim* (usually translated as "God") for God.

— Thus two sister-wife episodes involved Abraham and Sarah because both the J and the E sources tell such a tale. Accordingly, Abimelech, who appears once in each source, is duped twice.

— Since it is one of the conclusions of source critics that the E source is more "pietistic" than J, it is to be expected that chapter 20 goes to great lengths to free Abraham from blame. The narrator there has Abraham assert that Sarah is, in fact, his sister and, moreover, the narrator himself states that there had been no sexual contact between Sarah and Abimelech.

Professor Speiser knew, of course, that the three contexts unambiguously show the patriarchs introducing their wives as their sisters for ulterior motives. In regard to this Speiser noted: "Something is obviously wrong there." His *explanation* is very instructive (p. 27):

> It should be borne in mind that the accounts before us were committed to writing several centuries after the events and hundreds of miles away from the center where the wife-sister institution was immediately understood and appreciated. The underlying concept could not have long retained preserved, its original significance on foreign soil. When the memory of an incident is preserved, but its import has been lost, a new interpretation is likely to be substituted, an interpretation in keeping with local conditions and in conformance with common human instincts. In the present instance, traditions had to deal with certain incidents the meaning of which had been lost in the course of centuries. In due time a new explanation was bound to emerge.

Professor Speiser's solution depends on the assumption that those who compiled the Genesis narratives sometimes preserved traditions they themselves did not understand. According to Professor Speiser, when the sister-wife episodes were first related they had as their purpose the glorification of Sarah and Rebekkah. It is Professor Speiser's claim that with the passage of time this original intent was obscured. To recover it, Professor Speiser felt that he had to understand these episodes differently than did those who wrote and preserved them. From Professor Leo Strauss' perspective, Professor Speiser was engaged not in interpretation at this point but in explanation. Professor Speiser brought external criteria and information to bear on the text in order to make the text intelligible. According to this line of inquiry, some biblical contexts, as here in the case of the sister-wife episodes, cannot be understood on their own terms.

Let us return to the sister-wife episodes in order to attempt to interpret them rather than to explain them. We will thus assume that those who created and preserved the biblical record had a clear idea of what they were doing. In specific, we will assume that the sister-wife episodes are understandable as they stand because the author of these tales both knew what he wanted to say and how he wanted to say it. That is, we will accept as a hypothesis the notion that our anonymous author was not only a first-rate thinker but a first-rate writer as well. The evidence which will either validate or invalidate this hypothesis consists of the texts themselves. If the proof of the pudding is in the eating, then our hypothesis will stand or fall on whether these texts exhibit not only coherence but levels of meaning which we can only begin to plumb.

In regard to Professor Speiser's explanation, it is now apparent that he did not understand the Mesopotamian texts. More recent studies have demonstrated that to the extent such an adoption procedure existed, it applied only to the economically disenfranchised (such as widows and orphans) rather than, as Professor Speiser believed, to the aristocratic class.

Also, Professor Speiser's source analysis, which like all such analysis depends on separating texts based on the different names for God, cannot explain how in the "E" source (which it is said uses *Elohim* for God), the name YHWH appears in Gen. 20:18. In his splendid commentary on the book of Genesis, Professor Speiser can only write that "...the YHWH of the M. T. [the Hebrew manuscript] must be a copyist's error influenced by YHWH in the next line." [See Speiser's *The Anchor Bible Genesis* (New York: Doubleday, 1964), p. 150.]

Is it not true, however, that once a text, be it ancient or modern, is presumed to be unintelligible (so that, as is the case with the Hebrew Bible, it is believed that it is necessary to divide it into sources), then an apparent lack of clarity in the text will be blamed on a haphazard writer or editor rather than on a careless reader? The hypothesis that we have accepted demands that we make every effort to interpret the received text. In the words of another: "In the end, we should remember a good old philological rule: when one does not understand something, one should first mistrust oneself and not the text." [H. S. Nyberg, quoted in Walter Kaufmann's *Critique of Philosophy and Religion* (New York: Doubleday Anchor Books, 1961), p. 385].

We begin our interpretation of the sister-wife episodes with a straightforward observation: whatever the differences among them (and, as we shall see, there are important differences), all these episodes *apparently* portray a patriarch in less than honorific terms. In chapter 12 the narrator has Abram say:

> '...I know that you are a beautiful woman. When the Egyptians see you they will say, that is his wife, and they will kill me and let you live. So tell them that you are my sister so that it will go well with me because of you.'

In chapter 20, Abraham is shown justifying his behavior to Abimelech by declaring:

> 'I thought that there was no fear of God in this place, and that they [the inhabitants of Gerar] would kill me because of my wife.'

Chapter 26 is equally explicit:

> When the men of the place asked him about his wife, he said, 'She is my sister,' for he was afraid to say 'my wife' thinking, 'the men of the place might kill me because of Rebekkah for she is beautiful.'

One could say, and it has in fact been said, that in biblical days such behavior was not viewed as contemptible. However, in the light of the unambiguous prohibition against adultery in the Hebrew Bible, it could be said that not only was such behavior considered contemptible, it was deemed so offensive that it was punishable by death. Adultery is proscribed in the Decalogue (Exod. 20:14; Deut. 5:17) and Leviticus 20:10 spells out the punishment: "If a man commits adultery with a married woman, committing adultery with a kinsman's wife, both the adulterer and adulteress shall be killed." Deuteronomy 22:22 describes what will happen if the perpetrators are caught in the act:

If a man is caught having intercourse with a married woman, both that man—who had intercourse with the woman—and that woman shall die. You must destroy evil from Israel.

You will note that the Hebrew Bible's definition of adultery has as its essential component a married woman, so that a married man cohabiting with a single woman would not have been considered an adulterer. In our texts, of course, both Sarah and Rebekkah are married.

Thus, if we are willing to agree that both Abraham and Isaac appear to act dishonorably, the question that needs to be asked is why the biblical narrator chose to impart this kind of information about the first two patriarchs. And why, by the way, is there no such episode in Jacob's story?

One could answer these questions and any others like them by asserting that these episodes were preserved because they happened, while Jacob, the third and last patriarch, was involved in no such incident. But even if one is inclined to believe that some biblical narrators viewed themselves as transmitters of factual information (no matter how little these accounts resemble factual reporting), one still has to inquire as to why they included some "facts" and excluded others.

There are huge gaps, for example, in the stories of Abraham and Isaac. When first met, in Gen. 12, Abraham is already 75 years old, and when he dies, in Gen. 25, he is 175 years old. Since all of chapter 24 is given over to a description of how Rebekkah came to be Isaac's wife, the whole Abraham story encompassing some 100 years in the patriarch's life, is recounted in less than twelve chapters. As for Isaac, who dies at age 180: his story takes up no more than four chapters. Thus, even if we accept what I believe is the dubious hypothesis that the biblical writers viewed themselves as chroniclers, they were highly selective chroniclers.

So we repeat our question: why does the Hebrew Bible have these episodes which seem to cast the patriarchs in a negative light? A plausible, though very general, answer is that almost all characters in the Hebrew Bible are depicted as having feet of clay. Not even the best of individuals is free from fallibility. Recall, e.g., the episode involving David and Uriah's wife.

While on the one hand it is clear that Abraham is an exemplary figure (he leaves the land of his ancestors at the Lord's command; he takes on the role of moral partner with God when he argues, in Gen. 18:22 ff., that the innocent not perish with the guilty; and he so loves the Lord that he is ready to sacrifice his future in the service of God in Gen. 22); on the other hand the two sister-wife episodes in which he participates do not appear to be to his credit.

This is especially so in the first episode wherein the narrator makes no attempt to soften his apparently harsh verdict. Abraham is shown acquiring sheep, oxen, asses, male and female slaves (this is probably when he acquires Hagar who will play such a crucial role in his story), she-asses, and camels as a result of what can only be called his duplicity. Moreover, the patriarch is kicked out of Egypt by an angry Pharoah who is so determined to rid himself of Abraham that he sends him off with an armed escort. It is very much unclear whether the escort is meant to protect Abraham or to insure that he leaves, or both. The second episode is much more oblique in its treatment of Abraham. Of course, much has happened to the patriarch in the interim. Abraham has graciously allowed his nephew to choose what was then the lush area around Sodom. He has, in chapter 14, deployed his forces in a night attack to rescue Lot. He agreed to cohabit with Hagar, at Sarah's request, in an episode which as we shall see, has striking parallels with the sister-wife story. And his relationship with his God continues to strengthen as he receives reassurances from God that his progeny will one day occupy the land in which he is sojourning.

In a general sense, then, it can be said that the chapters which intervene between the two sister-wife episodes in Abraham's story certainly enhance his stature. His generosity, loyalty, and bravery speak well for him. It is thus possible that the differences between the two episodes are to be viewed in the light of Abraham's development. Some of the most obvious differences between the two episodes are these:

— In chapter 12 Abram's motive is stated immediately: he apparently not only lies to save himself but also to gain a measure of prosperity. In chapter 20 Abraham divulges his motive only after God reveals the truth to Abimelech. And whereas the Pharoah, in chapter 12, expels Abraham from Egypt, in chapter 20 Abimelech tells the patriarch to settle wherever he wants in Abimelech's domain.

— In chapter 12 it is left unclear as to whether the Pharoah had intercourse with Sarah (see v. 18). In chapter 20, however, it is made explicit that there had been no sexual contact. First the narrator makes this clear in his own voice (v. 4) and then the narrator has God repeat the same information (v. 6).

— Perhaps most significant is that while no one has a good word to say about the patriarch in chapter 12, in chapter 20 God Himself calls Abraham "a Prophet" (the first individual so named in the Hebrew Bible), a status the patriarch utilizes to heal Abimelech's household.

There is, of course, no denying that even in chapter 20 Abraham seems to protect himself at the expense of Sarah. Still, the differences may epitomize Abraham's growth as a character. If the most obvious differences between these episodes are integrated into the general pattern of the Abraham story then perhaps the differences between these two episodes on the one hand and the last sister-wife tale (in Gen. 26) on the other may tell us something by way of a contrast about differences between Abraham and Isaac.

The notice of a famine ("aside from the previous famine that had occurred in the days of Abraham") begins the third and last sister-wife episode. The Lord directs Isaac not to go down to Egypt (as his father Abraham had done) but to remain in the land which one day the people Israel will call their own. Sojourning in the area of Gerar (just to the southwest of Beersheba near that territory along the southwestern coast which is the enclave of the Philistines), he tells the men of the locale that his wife Rebekkah is his sister.

The narrator tells us exactly what Isaac has in mind: "...[he thought] that the men of the place might kill me on account of Rebekkah, for she is beautiful." After some time has passed, Abimelech ("king of the Philistines") learns that Isaac and Rebekkah are husband and wife (v. 8). He summons Isaac and demands to know why Isaac lied. Again, the reason is explicated clearly: "Because I thought I might lose my life on account of her." Abimelech's response makes it clear that no one has had sexual contact with Rebekkah, and he commands his subjects, on pain of death, to leave Isaac and Rebekkah alone. Isaac remains in Gerar and is so successful that he arouses the ire of the native Philistines, and Abimelech orders Isaac to leave the area. But when Isaac encamps to the north he once again comes into conflict with the Philistines, this time over water rights. Finally, he encamps in the area of Beersheba where the Lord reaffirms the promise made to his father Abraham. Abimelech and his highest military and civilian advisers come to Isaac and ask that there be a treaty for " 'We now see that the Lord is with you.' " The treaty is negotiated and sealed.

On the surface, the most dramatic difference between this third telling of the sister-wife tale and the first two is the lack of direct involvement by God in uncovering the deceit. In the first episode the Lord afflicts the Pharoah's household with unspecified plagues. In the second telling God appears to Abimelech in a dream. In the Isaac-Rebekkah sister-wife story the Lord's direct involvement consists of the following:

— He orders Isaac not to go down to Egypt.

— After Abimelech discovers the truth, Isaac's prosperity is attributed to the Lord's blessing: "The Lord blessed him and he grew ever richer until he was very wealthy."

It is to be noted that the Lord's command to Isaac to stay out of Egypt is followed by His reaffirmation of the promise made to Abraham. It is made clear that the Lord's blessing on Isaac ("...all the nations of the earth shall bless themselves by your offspring") is a result not of Isaac's worth or lack thereof but of Abraham's merit ("...inasmuch as Abraham obeyed Me and followed My commandments, My laws, and My teachings"). The Abraham story makes it clear that biblical Israel's ideal destiny is to be a moral exemplar and in this sense will "all the nations of the earth...[be] bless[ed] by your offspring" (see Gen. 18:16–19).

Perhaps the lack of direct involvement by the Lord in the third episode is related to the apparent fact that Isaac (whose story is by far the shortest of the three patriarchs) has not the close kind of relationship with God which both his father and son have. To be more precise, Isaac, alone of the three patriarchs, is what we today would call a flat character in that he does not exhibit growth, certainly not spiritual growth. Is only one sister-wife episode recounted about him (you will note that in Gen. 20:13, Abraham indicates to Abimelech that he tells Sarah to identify him as her brother in "...whatever place we come to") because he does not need much cutting down to size?   •

Isaac, moreover, is the only one of the patriarchs who does not receive a name change. Isaac's name comes out of the ironic laughter with which his parents greet God's announcement that in spite of their advanced years they will yet have a son (see Gen. 17:17 and 18:12). Their ironic response is, however, as nothing in the face of the fact that the Lord, Who is depicted as the source of all life and blessing, has decided to continue Abraham's line at this time in this way. Thus does it come about that Isaac (whose very name comes from the root "to laugh") is born. Is it stretching things too far to say that the final irony is that Isaac is a bit of a "joke"? Perhaps. And perhaps not. For while Abram becomes Abraham, a name which adumbrates the destiny of the people he will sire, and while Jacob becomes "Israel," the very name of this people, a name which is interlocked with Jacob's extraordinary spiritual growth, Isaac takes his name with him to the grave. What seems most noteworthy about Isaac is that he is the (weak?) link between two spiritual titans.

But why then no sister-wife story about Jacob? Does it have to do with the fact that for the first twenty years of his married life Jacob is not, as were his father and grandfather, in the exposed position of being a stranger in a strange land? For Jacob is living with his wives' clan in their homeland. And by the time he does return to Canaan, his story is virtually over; the narrator's focus has begun to shift to one of Jacob's sons (Joseph). Also, as we shall see, Jacob is, as it were, cut down to size at the very beginning of his story.

It is possible that one purpose of the sister-wife episodes is to underline the necessity for a homeland for the people Israel. As resident aliens they are always at the mercy of the host population. Perhaps that is why the sister-wife motif disappears once the patriarchal period ends. For the patriarchal period is followed by the 400 year Egyptian experience in which the Israelites are not only given title to some of the best grazing lands in Egypt but in which they become so powerful that the host population fears for *its* life. And when the Egyptians turn on the Israelites so that the children of Abraham are forced to leave Egypt, their numbers and strength are such that in the wilderness they are not at the mercy of any host population. After the forty or so years in the wilderness the Israelites invade and conquer the land of Canaan and they themselves become the host population.

This brings us to another facet of these sister-wife episodes. In each of the three episodes, fear, deceit, material acquisitions, and involvement by God are interwoven. However, in each of the episodes the emphases shift and the various shiftings do not seem to be haphazard. But what does not change from episode to episode is a complex of issues which would appear to comprise the core elements of the sister-wife motif. In the first place, the patriarchs find themselves in what we could call enemy territory. In chapter 12 it is Egypt, and it is no exaggeration to state that the ways of Egypt are consistently rejected by the biblical writers. In chapters 20 and 26 Abraham and Isaac sojourn among the Philistines, and we have already noted that it was the Philistines who forced biblical Israel to turn to a monarchical form of government. It was only in the time of David that the Philistines ceased to be a potent enemy of Israel.

Fear of the ways of Egypt and Philistia force Abraham and Isaac to the desperate measure of seeking to purchase their safety by passing their wives off as sisters. What Abraham says explicitly in chapter 20:11, " 'I thought...surely there is no fear of God in this place, and they will kill me because of my wife' " is present implicitly in chapter 12. Abraham says as much in 20:13 when he indicates that this is what Sarah was asked to do in "whatever place we come" and in 26:7 Isaac repeats the same rationale for the deceit. However many times this deceit may have been put into practice, it is a fact that we see it in operation only in Egypt and Philistia.

There is also the fact that in each of the three episodes the patriarchs' material possessions increase and increase dramatically. While chapter 12 is the shortest of the episodes, the biblical narrator takes time to list what the patriarch gained because of Sarah (12:16). And in the second episode virtually the same list of possessions is repeated (20:14); this time, however, instead of being expelled Abraham is given *carte blanche* to settle where he wants in Philistia. In the third episode, Isaac's possessions increase at what can only be called a supernatural rate (26:12–14): "Isaac sowed in that land [i.e., Philistia] and reaped a hundredfold the same year! For the Lord blessed him, and he grew richer and richer until he was very wealthy: he acquired flocks and herds, and a large household, so that the Philistines envied him."

Thus, each of the three episodes ends well. It is true that Abraham is expelled from Egypt and not only is he unharmed but none of his possessions is taken from him. It is possible that the armed escort Pharoah sends along with him is more to protect Abraham's impressive caravan than to see to it that he leaves Egypt. In any case, Egypt in no sense represents the geographical future of Abraham's family, so a safe exodus from Egypt, whether here on a small scale or later on a large scale, is all to the good. Philistia, however, is part of the territory promised by the biblical God to Abraham's progeny. Thus the second two episodes make it clear that treaty agreements between Abraham and Isaac and the Philistines make it possible for the patriarchs to sojourn more safely in the promised land. It is also worth noting that when the Philistine representatives enter into a treaty with both Abraham and Isaac the reason they do so is in both cases the same, viz, that the Philistines see that " 'God is with you in anything you do.' " (This to Abraham in 21:22) and " 'We now see plainly that the Lord has been with you...' " (to Isaac in 26:28).

What the Pharoah of Egypt and Abimelech, king of the Philistines, "see" is yet another feature which forms an important, perhaps *the* important, part of each of the sister-wife episodes. I am referring to God's providential care for Abraham and his son Isaac. There is a measure of dramatic justice involved in this care, for according to Abraham, when the patriarch is explaining his rationale for subterfuge, it is God who stirred Abraham to move from the land of his forebears.to face the inevitable uncertainties and conflicts of life in a land not yet his own.

Thus while the beginning of Abraham's story unambiguously proclaims Abraham's exalted destiny (Gen. 12:1–9), the vagaries of the fulfillment of the promise are made immediately evident in the first telling of the sister-wife motif which follows the promise.

It is not that the narrator is telling us that all is well which ends well (which is clearly, if you think about it, either a deeply ironic assertion or clearly absurd), but that while the biblical God sees the big picture, his human creatures, having to deal with bits and fragments of that picture, often despair that what God promises will come to pass.

But do Abraham and Isaac have to do what they do in these sister-wife episodes? This is not a question which the biblical narrators make it easy for us to answer. On the one hand, the unnamed Pharoah and Abimelech express outrage when they discover the truth, and in each case it is plainly moral outrage (Gen. 12:18; 20:5–6; 26:10). But on the other hand, their words seem undercut by what they do. They do take a beautiful woman when all is said and done because they have the power to do so. It is not a question of right; it is a question of might. And when they surrender Sarah and Rebekkah they do so because of God's might, which as God makes clear in His revelation to Abimelech, has only to do with right (26:3–7). Moreover, when Abimelech enters into treaty agreements, first with Abraham and then with Isaac, it is because, as he explicitly acknowledges, of God's might which is revealed in the incredible success of the patriarchs. The second instance could not be more clear since Abimelech first expels Isaac (26:16) and then is forced, because of Isaac's increasing power, to enter into an accommodation (26:28–29).

Perhaps it is accurate to say that the actions of the Pharoah and Abimelech are as difficult to evaluate as are those of Abraham and Isaac. But if the ambiguity is equal then the advantage lies clearly with the pagan rulers because the whole point of this new beginning in chapter 12 is to initiate a quest by Abraham and his line whose parameters will, or at least, should, be determined by doing what is right in the eyes of God.

Now one thing that is certainly not "right" in the eyes of God is sexual licentiousness. Witness, for example, the fate of Sodom: the very name screams out its sin (to be considered too is Gen. 19:30–38). Moreover, the introduction to the flood story (Gen. 6:1–8) intimates that interspecies breeding was the overriding factor in God's decision to wipe the slate clean and to begin again with the "righteous" Noah. Biblical Israel's sexual code of conduct, which is spelled out in a concrete legal setting in Leviticus 18, is austerity itself.

Let me finish this discussion of the sister-wife episodes by pointing out two ironies whose meaning is captured by our metaphor "what goes around comes around." It is striking that neither Sarah nor Rebekkah is given a word of dialogue in these episodes. They are spoken to but they do not speak. This fact is all the more startling not only because dialogue makes up such a great part of biblical narrative but also because Sarah and Rebekkah are anything but passive characters. Indeed, it is Rebekkah and not her husband Isaac who determines correctly which one of her children is the child of destiny and who acts forcefully in that child's behalf. Even a casual reading of those contexts in which Sarah and Rebekkah take part will suffice to show the passion, the power, and the intelligence which the writers invest in the first two matriarchs.

For our purposes, and this is the first irony of which I wrote above, it will have to suffice to point to the first words of dialogue which are given to Sarah. They occur in Gen. 16:2. Sarah, desperate because she is unable to conceive, is driven to the following measure: "And Sarai said to Abram, 'See, the Lord has kept me from bearing. Have intercourse with my maidservant [who turns out to be Hagar the Egyptian, almost certainly one of the "female slaves" acquired by Abraham in Egypt by virtue of his deceit]; perhaps I shall be built up [a pun on the word son] through her.' " Sarai, growing older and in despair over her barrenness; Sarai, seeing only bits and fragments of the big picture, means to adopt Hagar's child as her own. Abram complies and impregnates Hagar but even before the son, who will be named Ishmael by the Lord Himself (see Gen. 16:11 ff.), is born, Sarai tries to banish her from the kinship group because of Hagar's increased stature. The Lord gentles Hagar back to the clan armed with a promise that Ishmael too will have a grand future. But when, in

Gen. 21, Sarah sees Ishmael "playing" (a pun on Isaac's name) with her own son Isaac, she—this time with God's approval—sends her Egyptian maidservant packing. As 21:17 makes clear, the Lord delivers on His promise.

You will note that Sarah asks no more of her husband (when she sends him to Hagar) than he on at least two occasions asked of her: that she have intercourse with another for the wellbeing of Abraham (or: what is good for the gander is good for the goose!). And you will note that the straw which broke the back of her plan (a plan, to be sure, made less pressing because of the birth of Isaac) is the sight of Ishmael "playing," the very same verb used when Abimelech sees Isaac "playing" with Rebekkah (26:8–9).

The second irony is much more corrosive. It is prepared for by what seems to be an incidental notice at the end of Gen. 26, which contains the last of the sister-wife episodes. The notice reads as follows: "When Esau [the twin brother of Jacob] was forty years old, he took to wife Judith daughter of Beeri the Hittite, and Basemath daughter of Elon the Hittite; and they were a source of bitterness to Isaac and Rebekkah." Esau, more sinned against than sinning, shut out of the family's destiny by virtue of the manipulations of his mother and brother, marries at the same age as had his father (see Gen. 25:20) but outside of the clan (see Gen. 27:46–28:9).

Of what relevance is this notice to the sister-wife episodes? I am asking not only why the author included this notice but why he placed it here. We saw that the sister-wife episodes were precipitated by Abraham's and Isaac's fear that they were sojourning among people whose rulers were willing to remove any obstacles which stood in the way of what they wanted. Thus did Abraham and Isaac seek to remove themselves as obstacles in the way of acquiring their desirable wives. We saw that it is difficult to determine whether and to what degree Abraham and Isaac were altogether right about the Egyptian and Philistine rulers.

We also saw that the sister-wife episodes are part of a larger story in which the people Israel are given a destiny by the one God of the Heavens and the Earth to be a moral exemplar to the nations. As that story unfolds one of its central characters, a character mentioned more times than any other in the Hebrew Bible, a character who is

remembered as the greatest of Israel's kings and one of its great poets, is held up for the most strenuous of rebukes concerning precisely
that matter about which the biblical author exhibited such reticence
in regard to an Egyptian Pharoah and a Philistine king.

I am referring, of course, to the episode of David and Bathsheba.
But whereas the Pharoah and Abimelech took women they thought
were unmarried, David takes a woman he knows to be married. And
David, moreover, clearly does have intercourse with her and just as
clearly has her husband murdered in cold blood. And whereas the actions of Abraham and Isaac are clouded by ambiguity, what Uriah
does is unambiguously honorable. And Uriah, of course, as the narrator never tires of telling us, is a non-Israelite. And finally, Uriah is a
Hittite, that nation according to the Hebrew Bible which is descended
from the line of Canaan, the very complex of peoples which make up
the indigenous population of the land which one day will be called
Israel. Now Israel, as we have seen, is the name given to the third
patriarch Jacob. And we saw that Jacob's twin brother Esau was excluded from the clan's high destiny and in a fury married two Hittite
women, for "...he realized that the Canaanite women displeased his
father Isaac" (28:8).

Talk about disinterested objectivity! The greatest king in Israel's
history is held up to scorn for sexual impropriety while a Hittite is
praised for refusing to cohabit with his wife while the Ark of the
Covenant is in the fields. And as if that were not enough, this king's
behavior is contrasted to that of Egyptian and Philistine rulers and it
is the Israelite's behavior which is found wanting.

It will be remembered that we approached these episodes with
the assumption that they were understandable on their own terms.
Since the text of Genesis offers not the slightest indication as to
when, by whom, and under what circumstances it was written, we did
not concern ourselves with such matters. While we certainly did not
solve all the interpretive problems, we did uncover some of the layers
of meaning in these episodes. While we are uncertain as to the co-
gency of the interpretation, of this we are fairly certain: the more
closely one examines a text in the Hebrew Bible, the more likely it is
that the text will reveal its meaning.

5

A Thematic Overview
of the Hebrew Bible

Many books, especially modern ones, begin with prefaces or introductions in which the author conveys his intentions. Spinoza, for instance, in the preface to his *Theological-Political Treatise* indicates that his remarks are directed to the "philosophical reader." He goes on to say: "To the rest of mankind I care not to commend my treatise, for I cannot expect that it contains anything to please them: I know how deeply rooted are the prejudices embraced under the name of religion; I am aware that in the mind of the masses superstition is no less deeply rooted then fear; I recognize that their constancy is mere obstinacy, and that they are led to praise or blame by impulse rather than reason. Therefore the multitude, and those of like passions with the multitude, I ask not to read my book; nay I would rather that they should utterly neglect it, than that they should misinterpret it after their wont." (Elwes translation, p. 11). Such prefaces not only indicate what the reader should expect from a particular book; they can guide the reader to ask the questions which the text was designed to answer. In the case of *The Theological-Political Treatise,* for example, the preface makes it clear that Spinoza's approach to the biblical text will be guided by the rules of rational inquiry. These rules will dictate the way Spinoza interprets the biblical text, and Spinoza will follow them even if they lead him to conclusions diametrically opposed to traditional views and beliefs about the Bible. As a matter of historical fact, that is exactly what happened and in spite of Spinoza's warning in his preface many non-philosophical readers did read his *Treatise* and were so offended that the book was taken off the market. In any case, prefaces and introductions would certainly be useful in preventing a reader from asking historical questions of a non-historical work or scientific questions of a non-scientific text and so on.

There is, of course, no introduction or preface to the Hebrew Bible. And, as we have seen, there is not even a title. In fact, the names for the various books derive from the LXX (the Greek translation), and purport to describe the book's contents; so, e.g., Genesis for beginnings, Exodus for departure, Leviticus for priestly things, Numbers for the census which that book describes, and Deuteronomy for the second telling of the Law. Nor, in the Hebrew Bible, is there any identification of author, compiler, or editor.

How is one to know then how to begin to read the biblical text? Which is to say, how is one to determine which are the proper questions to ask of the biblical text? It would seem that the reader should endeavor to see what questions the biblical text itself raises and then to see how the text goes about answering these questions.

Let us begin at the beginning, at the first chapters of Genesis, to see what questions emerge. We noted in our descriptive overview that the first biblical book begins with an account of how the universe came to be. However restricted the focus will come to be, in the beginning at least, the biblical author chooses for himself a comprehensive theme. As will become evident, he does so because however much he will telescope his focus, his agendum is always comprehensive because the author's God is God of both the Heaven and the Earth.

The creation account in Genesis is divided into seven parts, each part corresponding to a day. The account proceeds as follows:

Day one: light is created;

day two: Heaven is created;

day three: the primordial waters are massed, dry land appears and on the land, perennial vegetation;

day four: the sun, moon, and stars are created;

day five: sea life and sky life appear;

day six: land life is created, capped by the appearance of the human creature;

day seven: God ceases creating and declares the seventh day holy.

Among the most obvious difficulties in the biblical creation account is this: according to the account itself, no human being could have witnessed the events he is describing since mankind was not created until the sixth day. Certainly, the account makes no claim, not explicitly, not implicitly, that the creator God authored the account. When the Hebrew Bible introduces sayings of the Lord, the biblical narrator will say "the Lord said...." In Genesis 1, God is Himself a created character. The text does not read: "In the beginning when I began creating...", but "In the beginning when God created...."

We are left then with some intriguing possibilities in regard to the origin of this creation account. Does our author want us to understand that God revealed what He had done in His creating to some human being? If so, who was that human being? Since Moses was the greatest of the biblical prophets, many have ascribed authorship to him. But neither this text nor any other text in the Hebrew Bible makes such an identification. Perhaps we are meant to surmise that the author heard the account from the human, whoever he or she was, to whom God revealed His activities on the days of creation. But again, no biblical text gives even a clue as to whom, when, and under what circumstances such a communication process took place.

There is, of course, another possibility; a possibility which in the light of what the creation story itself says, is the most likely one. For does not the manner and order of the creation story lead one to the conclusion that the anonymous author simply made up the account? The last and, in my opinion, most likely possibility leads, inevitably, to the conclusion that our author was not presenting a historical account of how things came to be. Our author, rather, is presenting a speculation, and given the nature of the account, one could only say that it is a sheer speculation. But it is by no means a haphazard speculation.

Although we do not know who wrote this account, and where or when this author lived, it is evident that our anonymous author dealt with his subject with great care. The creation story, which describes how God imposed order, itself proceeds in an orderly fashion. The account divides itself neatly into two parts. On the first three days, the created entities (Light, the Sky, the Seas, Earth, and Vegetation) cannot move from their places. On the second three days of creation, the created entities (Sun, Moon, Stars, Sea Life, Sky Life, and Earth Life) possess the ability to move from their places. The author appears to have arranged his material by using motion as a paradigm.

With this in mind, let us look more closely at the days of creation. On day one Light slashes the darkness. On day two, God puts in place the Heavenly firmament (the Hebrew term suggests a plate of pounded out metal) which separates the primordial water into upper waters which are held back by the arched vault of the Heaven and the lower waters which run freely and unbounded beneath the firmament. On day three, the lower waters are gathered together and bounded and land, which had previously been submerged, appears. The dry land then brings forth vegetation. From the author's perspective, the perennial vegetation is the fixed covering of the fixed earth. The problem of how vegetation could have preceded the sun is disposed of by the observation that the author is interested not in making a scientific point (surely he must have known that plant life requires sunlight) but a metaphorical point. That is, our author has organized his material in order to contrast mankind's extraordinary ability to "move" to that of other created entities. For while the sun, moon, and stars (from our author's perspective) move across the domed ceiling of the firmament, they cannot change their courses as can the various life forms. And, as we will see, man has a freedom of movement which goes beyond that of the animals. Man, of all created things, has the capacity to be Godlike.

Another indication that the author used great care in the ordering of his material is the manner in which the days in the two parts of creation correspond to each other. Consider the following:

— on day four the light created on day one is concretized in the Heavenly light givers;

— on day five the locales made possible by the creation of the firmament on day two (the space under the domed ceiling and the lower waters) are filled with living creatures;

— on day six the earth, which appeared on day three when the lower waters are gathered into bounded areas, is occupied by life.

What is the chief concern of this author who invested so much care in the ordering of his creation story? Some have conjectured that the author intended to present a factual account of how the universe was created. We have already noted, however, that according to the creation story itself, no human eyes could have witnessed what transpired and that, moreover, there is no claim in the story for divine authorship. To be noted as well is the fact that the creation story does not read like a scientific text, ancient or modern. Consider that in less than a thousand words the author places before us his creation account. If his concern was scientific would he not have provided his reader with more facts? Would he not have stipulated, for instance, how the sun, moon, and stars were placed in/on the two-dimensional firmament? Would he not, in reference to the Heavenly light givers, have written about their relationship to the light created on day one? Would he not, moreover, have speculated about the kinds of sea life, sky life, and earth life? As a matter of fact, such scientific concerns are never discussed in any of the thirty-nine books of the Hebrew Bible.

What then is our author's focal concern? It would seem that the manner in which he proceeds emphasizes the uniqueness of the human creature. Man is the last to be created; only man is created in the "image" of God; and man is made the overlord of the earth and the denizens of the earth. While man's place in the scheme of things is lower than that of God (what human could have set the universe in order as God is described as having done?) it is clearly higher than that of any of the other creatures.

Let us begin to understand man's uniqueness by quoting in full the creation of mankind (vv. 26–28):

> And God said, 'Let us make man in our image, after our likeness. They shall rule over the fishes of the sea, the birds of the sky, the cattle, the whole earth, and all the creeping things that creep on earth.' And God created man in His image, in the image of God He created him, male and female He created them. Then God blessed them, and God said to them, 'be fruitful and multiply and fill the earth and master it, and rule the fishes of the sea, the birds of the sky, and all the living things that creep on earth.'

In addition to what is obviously unique about man's status (being created in the image of God, his rule over the earth and its creatures) is the hint of multiplicity in God. Only in regard to mankind's creation does this happen: " 'Let *us* create man in *our* image after *our* likeness.' " (emphasis added). Also, only in the case of man does our author specify that God created man "male and female." Since these two irregularities occur in the same context, it is reasonable to assume that they are somehow connected.

Why the explicit specification of male and female in regard to mankind? Surely the biblical narrator knew that the animal kingdom too is divided into male and female. One need only consider the fact that the narrator has God bless creaturedom with the command to "...be fruitful and multiply," a command which certainly implies sexual intercourse.

It is possible that the biblical author is indicating that, unlike the animals for whom the distinction between maleness and femaleness is not crucial, for man this distinction goes to the heart of what it means to be human. That is, for mankind, the roles of marrying and parenting are absolutely crucial. As we proceed, we will see repeatedly that the relationships between husband and wife, parent and child are again and again featured by the biblical narrators. And we will see that the most prevalent view of afterlife in the Hebrew Bible is inextricably connected with these relationships. Unlike the animals (who, of course, also meet in sexual congress), man's sexual activities mark off the boundaries of the human experience. To cite an example with which we have already dealt, the story of King David, the greatest of biblical Israel's kings, is for the most part given over not to David's public life but to his successes and failures as a son, father, brother, and husband.

The matter of plurality in reference to God is more complicated. The Hebrew term which the author uses for God *(Elohim)* is itself a masculine plural. However, in Gen. 1 and in most other biblical contexts where *Elohim* refers to the God of Israel, this term controls a masculine singular verb. In three contexts in the opening chapters of Genesis, however, a plural form is used both with *Elohim* and with *YHWH.* Here is how these contexts read:

— And God said, 'Let us make man in our image, after our likeness.' (Gen. 1:26)

— And the Lord God said, 'Now that man has become like one of us, knowing good and bad, what if he should put forth his hand and also take from the Tree of Life and eat and live forever.' (Gen. 3:22)

— [The Lord]: 'Let us go down and confound their speech, so that they will not understand each other's speech.' Gen. 11:7)

The first context, as we have seen, concerns the creation of man. The second context deals with man's expulsion from the Garden of Eden, and the third occurs in the Tower of Babel story where the Lord intervenes to stop mankind from building their great tower. We will have occasion to examine these latter two contexts; for the present, we deal with that which these three contexts appear to have in common. Each of the occurrences involves a comparison and a contrast between mankind and God. The first context emphasizes man's uniqueness by asserting that man alone is created in the image of God. But the first context also points to a basic dissimilarity between the divine and human realms. For while mankind is created "male and female," the implication is that the creator God is above such distinctions. Only in the case of man (created in the image of God) could one think that a similar sexual distinction exists in God; therefore, the writer introduces the unexpected plural form to direct the reader's attention to this contrast between God and man.

The same pattern is repeated in the second and third contexts. In the second context (" 'Now that man has become like one of us, knowing good and bad, what if he should put forth his hand and also take from the Tree of Life and eat and live forever.' "), the comparison and contrast are seemingly more evident. Man and the Lord God both possess the Tree of Knowledge of the Good and the Bad, but the Lord God alone has the Tree of Life. Shortly, we will examine what these trees are. For the present it is enough to indicate that the plural form again involves a basic comparison and contrast between God and man: man does not "live forever" while the Lord God does. The third context denotes yet another critical distinction between God and man: God's inherent singularity is contrasted to the disunity in the human community (at Babel the Lord divides mankind into different units), even though man, like God, is by nature one (i.e., all men remain "brothers").

Before we return to our discussion of the creation story, we note that in the Garden of Eden story when the serpent tries to convince the first woman to take of the Fruit of the Tree of the Knowledge of the Good and the Bad, it says: " 'God knows that, as soon as you eat of it, your eyes will be opened, and you will be like the gods who know good and bad.' " (Gen. 3:5). Note again the plural form in the divine realm; and note again that it occurs in the context of a comparison between God and man. As we will see, it is no simple matter for the biblical narrators to talk of a God who:

— is asexual;

— possesses both the Tree of Knowledge and the Tree of Life;

— is unalterably unified.

After the creation of man, God looks on all that He had created and finds it to be "very good." This evaluation by the Creator leads to this question: where, then, does evil come from? This question is the central concern of the second story in the Hebrew Bible. This story, set in a fabulous garden, begins as follows: "When the Lord God made Earth and Heaven, there was neither shrub nor plant growing wild because the Lord God had not sent rain upon the earth and there was no man to till the soil." (Gen. 2:4b–5). The phrase "Heaven and Earth" appeared in the creation story to signify the created universe. The Eden story begins by transposing these terms to indicate, perhaps, a change of emphasis. Whereas the Creation story focuses on "Heaven" in the sense that it is God who is directing events, the Eden story emphasizes "Earth" by giving prominence to the activities of man. This change in emphasis remains in effect for the rest of the Hebrew Bible. From Gen. 2:4b onward, in most biblical narratives the activities of man hold center stage.

The plot outline of the Eden story is relatively simple. The Lord God forms man out of clay and, with a divine breath, activates him to life. The Lord God then places man in a well-watered and bountiful garden. In the middle of this garden are two special trees: the Tree of the Knowledge of the Good and the Bad and the Tree of Life. The Lord God either warns or commands (the Hebrew can be read either way) man not to eat of the fruit of the Tree of the Knowledge of the Good and the Bad on pain of death: " '...as soon as you eat of it, you shall be doomed to die.' " Then the Lord God decides that it is not "good" for man to be alone in the garden. The Lord God creates the beasts of the field and parades them before man. But from among them man finds no counterpart. The Lord God then causes a deep sleep to fall upon the man whereupon He extracts from man a female. When, upon awakening, the man sees the woman, he declares: " 'This one at last is bone of my bones and flesh of my flesh.' " The narrator adds: "Hence a man leaves his father and mother and joins with his wife, so that they become one flesh." The narrator also observes that though the two of them were naked, they felt no sense of shame.

Thus is the stage set for the so-called "fall" of first man and woman. The wily serpent seemingly entices the woman to eat of the fruit of the Tree of the Knowledge of the Good and the Bad and she in turn offers it to the man who also eats it. They feel shame and improvise loin cloths for themselves. When confronted by the Lord God the man and woman unsuccessfully seek to evade responsibility for their act. The first human couple is expelled from the paradise-like setting of Eden. The end of the story makes it clear that there will be no return, for the approaches to the garden are guarded by fantastic creatures wielding weapons of fantasy: "The Lord God drove the man out, and put east of the garden of Eden the *cherubim* and the fiery ever-turning sword, to guard the approaches to the Tree of Life."

The Eden story is full of perplexities. In our treatment of the story we will address the following problems:

— What distinguishes life in Eden from life outside of Eden?

— What is the Tree of the Knowledge of the Good and the Bad?

— What is the Tree of Life?

— What induced the snake to act as it did?

— What induced first man and first woman to act as they did?

— What is the Lord God's role in the story?

What characterized life in Eden? In Eden there was a nutritious and varied diet for which man had only to reach. The climate was ideal, so that neither clothing nor shelter was required. In short, there was no need in Eden. As the punishments meted out by the Lord God make clear, life outside of Eden is both needy and harsh. Man will have to work hard in order to sustain himself and his family. Woman will be locked into a cycle in which her need for her man will result in the painful bearing of children.

It is clear that it was the taking of the fruit of the Tree of the Knowledge of the Good and the Bad which led to man's expulsion from Eden. When the Tree of Knowledge is introduced, it is in the company of that other special tree, the Tree of Life. However, it is only about the Tree of Knowledge that the Lord warns man. In that context (Gen. 2:9), not a word is said about the Tree of Life. From this silence we can infer that in Eden, before man took of the fruit of the Tree of the Knowledge of the Good and the Bad, he had access to the Tree of Life. And the whole point of the expulsion from Eden is to ensure that now that man has partaken of the Tree of Knowledge he will not also partake of the Tree of Life. We can conclude, therefore, that man was permitted access to either one or the other of these two special trees, but not both.

It would seem then that what really demarcates life in Eden from life outside of Eden is that in Eden man had access to the Tree of Life but not to the Tree of Knowledge while outside of Eden he had access to the Tree of Knowledge but not to the Tree of Life. Since in Eden man was not subject to death (thus the Lord God's warning to man that if he takes from the Tree of Knowledge he will surely die), we can conclude that the Tree of Life was like a fountain of youth. And since life outside of Eden is marked not simply by death but by complicated choices, we can conclude that the "knowledge" gained from the Tree of Knowledge allows man to chart his destiny outside of Eden. Also, as is evident from the man and woman's "shame" after having taken from the Tree of Knowledge, that tree also imparts sexual awareness. In fact, the very verb "to know" in biblical Hebrew can mean "to have sexual intercourse with." In this regard, consider Gen. 4:1 which reads, "And the man knew his wife Eve, and she conceived and bore Cain...."

It becomes apparent, therefore, why the acquisition of the Tree of Knowledge would be both unnecessary and impossible in Eden. The knowledge which the Tree of Knowledge imparts is unnecessary in Eden because no choices of consequence (apart from whether to take of the fruit of the Tree of Knowledge) face man and woman. Also, since there is no death in Eden, the Tree of Knowledge would be an impossibility because deathlessness combined with the ability to procreate would result in a chaotic world of overcrowding and starvation. The Tree of Knowledge equips man to face a world of need, complexity, and death. In regard to death, the Tree of Knowledge, in activating man's sexual capacities, provides the antidote to death: while individuals come and go the human race will endure.

The following context in 2 Samuel gives one a feel for that which the Tree of Knowledge imparts. In the Samuel passage an old man named Barzillai, who had befriended King David, is asked by the King to accompany him to Jerusalem where David will provide for him. Barzillai replies (2 Sam. 19:35 ff.):

'How many years are left to me that I should go up with Your Majesty to Jerusalem? I am now eighty years old. Do I any longer know the difference between the good and the bad? Can your servant taste what he eats and drinks? Can I any longer listen to the singing of men and women? Why then should your servant continue to be a burden to my Lord the King.... Let your servant return, and let me die in my own town, in the ancestral sepulcher.'

Barzillai declines King David's offer because of his advanced age. His refusal is framed in terms which stress his inability to pursue actively his destiny. Therefore, it makes little difference where he lives, for no longer enjoying the delights of the body, he can only wait for death. In effect then, Barzillai's simple, functional existence is one which does not require the fruit of the Tree of the Knowledge of the Good and the Bad.

We are now ready to look more closely at plot development in the Eden story. When the Lord God places man in Eden, man is apparently content with his simple existence. There is no indication whatsoever in the story that man cannot tolerate his loneliness. It is the Lord God who decides that " '...it is not good for man to be alone: I will make a fitting helper for him.' " This leads to the extraction of the woman from the man. Later, after having eaten of the fruit of the Tree of Knowledge, man is confronted by the Lord God who poses this question: " 'Did you eat of the tree which I warned you against eating?' " The man has a ready response: " 'The woman You put at my side, she gave me of the tree, and I ate.' " The man, then, blames not the woman but God who provided the woman without being asked. The woman, when confronted by the Lord God, follows the man's lead. " 'The serpent duped me, and I ate.' " Since the snake's shrewdness was apparently congenital, the woman also endeavors to place the blame on the Lord God. The Lord God dismisses their contentions out of hand by ignoring them. He goes on to list the consequences of man's, woman's, and the snake's behavior, consequences which, in effect, define aspects of life outside of Eden.

But do not first man and first woman make a valid point? Man did not ask for the woman who, after all, offers the so-called forbidden fruit to him. And as for the snake, the text indicates that it is what it is by virtue of having been so created by the Lord God: "Now the serpent was the most wily of all the wild creatures made by the Lord God."

Who or what is responsible for man's expulsion from Eden? In order for man and woman to be responsible for their behavior they would have to be free both to abstain from eating the fruit of the Tree of Knowledge and to understand the consequences of eating from it.

Man surely was not without all knowledge before he partook of the Tree of Knowledge. He knew enough, for instance, to name the beasts which the Lord God paraded before him. He certainly knew that the woman was "bone of my bones, flesh of my flesh." But did the man (and woman) understand what was entailed in taking of the fruit of the Tree of Knowledge? The logic of the story dictates that man and woman both had a choice and understood the consequences of their choice. The Lord God holds them responsible and presumably He was in a position to know whether and to what extent the first human couple was responsible. And Adam and Eve do not deny responsibility so much as they indicate that the Lord God Himself wanted them to eat of the fruit of the Tree of Knowledge.

If one looks at some of the details provided by the narrator it seems that man and woman make a valid point. Consider the following:

— The Lord God placed the Tree of Knowledge in the middle of the garden and within man's reach;

— the Tree of Knowledge "...was good for eating and a delight to the eyes...and the tree was desirable as a source of wisdom.";

— moreover, it is the Lord God who decides that it is not good for man to be alone, and who extracts the woman from the man. It is, of course, the woman whom the snake approaches. And the snake's shrewdness is traced by the narrator to God.

It would seem that the Lord God is gently nudging man toward taking of the fruit of the Tree of Knowledge. However that may be, one should not refer simply to what happens to man and woman as a result of their acquisition of the Tree of Knowledge as a "fall." For according to the Lord God (Who, be it noted, thereby corroborates part of what the serpent had told Eve), man has become in some sense divine by virtue of having eaten of the fruit of the Tree of Knowledge. This godlike capacity, as we have seen, will enable man to create his destiny outside of Eden.

We can conclude that the first man and first woman, with a little help from God, found the lack of meaningful choices in Eden unendurable. Adam and Eve willingly chose the dynamism of life outside of Eden even though that choice carried with it not only the ability to create but also pain, suffering, and death.

While one should be cautious about generalizing about a story as complex as the Eden tale, a story, moreover, which has been interpreted in a wide variety of ways, two conclusions seem clear enough. First, the choice to take of the fruit of the Tree of Knowledge was unalterable. The end of the story makes it clear that there is no way back to Eden with its Tree of Life. Nowhere, in fact, in the Hebrew Bible is a return to Eden ever projected as a possibility. Second, human life outside of Eden, while circumscribed by vicissitude, is characterized by exhilarating freedom. First man and first woman now have the capacity not simply to continue the human story by procreating; they and their children have the power to "write" (create) that story.

The next story in Genesis relates how man uses his newly won freedom. This story begins with high expectation (Gen. 4:1): "Now the man knew his wife Eve, and she conceived and bore Cain saying, 'I have gained a male child with the help of the Lord.' " However, the narrator goes on to relate how Cain, despite having been warned by God Himself against sinning, chooses to commit an ultimate sin: he murders his brother Abel, and without just cause. God's warning had been unequivocal:

> 'Surely, if you do right
> There is uplift.
> But if you do not do right,
> Sin is a demon crouching at the door,
> Whose urge is toward you,
> Yet you can be its master.'

There is nothing mysterious about this revelation. Cain, who is downcast because God preferred his brother Abel's more generous offering, is told in no uncertain terms that his disgruntlement is of his own making (since he did not bring a generous offering) and that better behavior in the future will bring an end to his displeasure. In spite of the fact that Cain responds to God's warning by murdering his brother, God punishes him in what seems to be a relatively mild fashion: Cain is banished from the agricultural lifestyle of his kinship group and will instead have to endure a nomadic existence. Cain responds to this sentence by saying that it might as well be death since he will be deprived of kinship protection so that anyone coming across him could kill him without fear of kinship retribution. God promises to protect him: "The Lord said to him, 'Therefore, if anyone kills Cain, sevenfold vengeance shall be taken on him.' "

Why, however, does the Lord want to keep Cain alive? The lines which follow the Cain-Abel story provide the answer (Gen.4:17 ff.):

> Cain knew his wife, and she conceived, and bore Enoch. And he then built a city and named the city after his son Enoch. To Enoch was born Irad, and Irad begot Mehujael, and Mehujael begot Methushael, and Methushael begot Lamech. Lamech took two wives; the name of the one was Adah, and the name of the other was Zillah. And Adah bore Jabel; he was the father of those who dwell in tents and amidst herds. The name of his brother was Jubal; he was the father of all who play the lyre and the pipe. As for Zillah, she bore Tubalcain, who made all implements of copper and iron. And the sister of Tubalcain was Naamah. And Lamech said to his wives, 'Adah and Zillah, listen to me; O' wives of Lamech, hear my speech. I have killed a man for wounding me, and a boy for simply bruising me. If Cain is avenged seven fold, then Lamech will be avenged seventy seven fold.' Adam knew his wife again, and she bore a son and named him Seth, meaning, 'God has provided me with another offspring in place of Abel,' for Cain had killed him. And then to Seth a son was born, and he named him Enosh. It was then that men began to invoke the Lord by name.

In the very next chapter the line of Seth is recorded. In that genealogy two individuals stand out. One is Enoch who "walked with God" and the other is Noah, who was a "righteous" man. The most noteworthy individual in Cain's line is Lamech who brags that he is a more ferocious avenger than God. Also, out of Cain's line come the artisans and craftsmen who make city life possible. There is not one artisan or craftsman in Seth's line.

The reason, then, that Cain is left alive is to contrast his line to that of Seth. The Cainite genealogy indicates that the roots of urbanized life are in fratricide, the murder of brother by brother. Since the most noteworthy individuals in Seth's line are the pious Enoch and the righteous Noah, we can infer that, from the biblical perspective, civilization and piety may be two very different things.

As the biblical narrative continues there is little doubt that it is Cainness and not Sethness that prevails. That is, man's craving for power and vengeance takes precedence over man's inclination to be pious and just. In terms of the Eden story, it is the "bad" which overwhelms the "good."

So widespread does evil become on earth that (Gen. 6:6) "...the Lord regretted that He had made man on earth, and His heart was saddened." The story of Noah begins with God's decision to wipe mankind off the face of the earth. In this story God decides to reinitiate the human story with a righteous man. Thus Noah and his family are saved from the flood waters in order to parent a new race of man. When the flood waters abate the Lord God promises to never again devastate the earth because of man. The Lord God is pictured lowering His expectations regarding man (Gen. 8:2): " 'Never again will I doom the world because of man, since the imaginings of man's mind are evil from his youth....' " Henceforth the Lord God will no longer expect man to prefer the good over the bad without compulsion. In the first covenantal agreement between the biblical God and man, murder is expressly forbidden (Gen. 9:6):

'Whoever sheds the blood of man,
By man shall his blood be shed,
For in the image of God
Was man created.'

From the time of the flood onward, it is incumbent on man (" 'By *man* shall his blood be shed...' ") to establish a system of justice. The punishment of man will be left to man. A Cainlike act will henceforth be punished in kind.

What are we to make of mankind's new status after the flood? In the Eden story we saw that although man was cut off from the Tree of Life, he had also acquired the godlike capacity to create. But man, for the most part, chose to create a destiny not in the image of God but in the image of Cain. After the flood it is clear that man is to live under some constraint. Man's evil bent must be checked. The first chapters of Genesis indicate that a mankind which is unbridled is by far the most dangerous species on earth.

But while, after the flood, man's freedom to act like Cain will be held in check, from another perspective man's freedom to act is increased. After the flood man is given permission by God to eat flesh (Gen. 9:3):

'Every creature that lives shall be yours to eat;
as with the green grasses. I give you all these.

With this new privilege, however, comes responsibility (Gen. 9:4):

'You must not, however, eat flesh with its lifeblood in it.'

That is, when man kills an animal for food he is not to partake of that animal's blood which, according to this biblical passage, contains the life force of that creature.

What is Scripture's intent here? How is one to eat flesh without blood? Even overcooked meat "bleeds" when it is cut. Other biblical contexts which assume this same taboo shed light on this context in Genesis. We will consider two of them. The first is Leviticus 17 which reads as follows:

The Lord spoke to Moses as follows: 'Speak to Aaron and to his sons and to all the Israelite people and say to them: this is what the Lord has commanded: If any Israelite slaughters an ox or sheep or goat in the camp, or does so outside the camp and does not bring it to the entrance of the Tent of Meeting [the sanctuary] to present it as an offering to the Lord before the Lord's Tabernacle, bloodguilt shall be attributed to that man: he has shed blood; that man shall be cut off from among his people.... And if any Israelite or if the resident alien who lives among them partake of any blood, I will set My face against the person who partakes of the blood, and I will cut him off from among his kin. For the life of the flesh is in the blood, and I have assigned it to you for making expiation for your lives upon the altar; it is the blood, as life, that produces expiation. Therefore, I declare to the Israelite people: no one shall partake of blood, not even the resident alien who lives with you. Also if any Israelite or resident alien who lives among them hunts down an animal or a bird that may be eaten, he shall pour out its blood and cover it with earth. For the life of all flesh—its blood is its life. Therefore I say to the Israelite people: you shall not partake of the blood of any flesh, for the life of all flesh is its blood. Anyone who partakes of it shall be cut off. Any person, whether citizen or stranger, who eats what has died or what has been ripped apart by beasts, shall wash his clothes, bathe in water, and remain unclean until evening; then he shall be clean. But if he does not wash [his garments] and bathe his body, he shall bear his guilt.'

Each of the cases in this Leviticus passage assumes the taboo against eating flesh with its blood. In the first, the command is to bring the slaughtered animal to the entrance of the Tent of Meeting. There the priest dashes the blood against the altar. Anyone who does otherwise is deemed a murderer who is to be executed. The rationale for the commandment is clearly stated: " 'For the life of the flesh is in the blood...it is the blood, as life, that produces expiation.' " A slaughtered animal, then, must be brought to the Tent of Meeting where the priest, by dashing its blood against the altar, makes the killing licit.

The second case concerns hunting; in specific, one who hunts down an animal too far from the camp to bring the freshly killed animal to the Tent of Meeting. In that case the hunter is to cover the bloody spot, where the animal fell, with dirt. Why? The same rationale is given: " '...for the life of all flesh—its blood is its life.' "

The last instance involves the eating of the flesh of an animal one has not slaughtered. In that case there is no ritual at all regarding the blood. The person who eats the flesh of an animal that "has died or has been torn by beasts" is to remain ritually unclean until he washes his garments (in case the animal carried some disease); if he does not do so he is to bear an unspecified guilt.

What emerges from the Leviticus context is the same reverence for life expressed at the end of the Noah story where the taking of human life is prohibited because all men are created in the image of God. The "guilt" man incurs by taking animal life is atoned for by returning, as it were, the animal's blood to God who is the Creator of all life. The ritual to effectuate this "return" varies according to the circumstances of the taking of the life. The variation suggests that it is not so much a specific ritual which accomplishes the "return" so much as the intent to do so by the one who will eat the flesh. The different rituals have as their goal the thanking of God for the privilege of being able to take life which one did not create in order to eat its flesh.

That it is not so much what one does but that one does something to "return" the blood to God is made clear by a context in 1 Sam. 14. The episode there recorded tells of a battle between the Israelites and the Philistines. Before the battle begins King Saul adjures his troops not to eat before nightfall. When the day's fighting is over, Saul's famished troops pounce on the animals left by the retreating Philistines. They take the sheep and the cows and slaughter them "...on the ground, and the troops ate with the blood." The text continues:

> When it was told to Saul that the people were sinning against the Lord by eating on the blood, Saul said, 'You have acted treasonously. Roll a great stone in place.' He then said, 'Spread out among the troops and tell them that everyone must bring me his ox or his sheep and slaughter it here [on the great stone], and then eat. You must not sin against the Lord by eating on the blood.' ... Thus Saul set up an altar to the Lord, it was the first altar Saul put in place to the Lord.

In the Samuel passage the taboo not to eat meat with the blood is violated when ravenous soldiers eat on the very spot where they slaughtered the animals. After Saul has his make-shift altar put in place and the soldiers slaughter the animals on it, the blood has, in effect, been "returned" to God. Saul's altar effectuates the "return" symbolically. Since this was Saul's first altar we cannot conclude that previously when he ate meat he sinned. Saul's altar serves to remind his troops that with the privilege of eating flesh comes the responsibility of acknowledging God as the Lord of Life. That is, though the biblical God permits man to become a carnivore, each time that man eats flesh he must somehow sanctify the process by which he acquires and consumes the flesh. It matters not so much what is done to sanctify as it matters that something be done. In the wilderness the Israelites brought the slaughtered victim to the priest so that he could sprinkle some blood on the altar in order to symbolize the "return." A hunter, some distance from camp, could simply cover the animal's blood with dirt. In the Samuel passage, Saul has the animals slaughtered on the "altar."

In terms of our own conventions an approximate symbolic "return" would be the saying of grace. Of course, a casual muttering of the prayer so that one simply says the words to get the ritual out of the way, or no grace at all, would be, from the biblical perspective, eating flesh with its blood.

We saw that in the first chapter in Genesis mankind is separated from animalkind by virtue of having been created in the image of God. In the Eden story man can find no helpmate from among the animals and, moreover, man names the animals as they parade by him. By doing so he takes on the role God had played in the first chapter when God names the various parts of His creation. In the two opening stories of the Hebrew Bible, mankind clearly is more than simply an animal. But while more than animal, man is less than God. God's asexuality, His possessing both the Tree of Knowledge and the Tree of Life, and God's ability to create the Heaven and the Earth, distinguish the divine from the human realm.

In the Noah story the lines between God and man on the one hand and man and the animals on the other remain clearly defined: since man is something less than God, He will no longer expect man to act Godlike without a measure of compulsion; since man is something more than an animal, man is permitted to kill animals for food, but he must not do so in a beastlike fashion.

A pattern of sorts can now be discerned in these opening stories in the Hebrew Bible. We find in these stories a series of Divine experiments which ends in failure. Initially, the Lord God places man in Eden but man willingly forsakes it. Then God allows man to live in history without legal constraint. However, lawlessness leads to extreme disobedience. After the Flood, God requires man to take life for life; that is, a most basic law is to restrain man. This restraint combined with Noah's righteousness leads to the expectation of a more successful start by mankind.

However, the first episode following the flood is not at all encouraging. Noah plants vineyards, drinks wine, and passes out naked in his tent. One of his sons sees his father's nakedness (which was a violation of a powerful taboo in biblical Israel) and tells his brother what he saw. This son brings down upon himself and upon some of his progeny his father's curse. This is the first act in the new drama of mankind.

This conflict within Noah's family is repeated on a larger scale in the Tower of Babel story (Gen. 11:1–9). In the Babel story the mankind sired by Noah and his sons resolves to build a skyscraping tower in order "to make a name" for itself. Mankind, that is, has decided to make a reputation for itself without recourse to God. No divine command initiates the building. The Lord frustrates mankind's plans and scatters man across the face of the earth. Thus is a decisive change effected in the community of man.

Let us put this change which takes place at Babel in perspective. In Eden, man, free of pain and suffering, and not subject to death, was limited only by the Lord God's warning to stay away from the fruit of the Tree of the Knowledge of the Good and the Bad. Once outside Eden, man is limited by his mortality and by the necessity to toil for a food supply. With the murder of brother by brother and the general depravity of mankind, man, after the devastating Flood, learns that God will require life for life. This limitation, too, proves insufficient as once more man abuses the freedom graciously granted him by God: he places his trust in the work of his own hands in order to increase his own power. Man's actions in the Tower of Babel story are yet another variation on Cainness.

So once again the Lord intervenes. This time He places new limits on man by sundering the natural unity of mankind into conventional divisions. Racial, national, linguistic, and ethnic differences will henceforth limit unified man's propensity to exploit his Cainlike predisposition. Whereas before Babel there had been one mankind, now there will be Egyptians, Moabites, Edomites, Assyrians, Babylonians, and so on. The divisions in the human community limit severely the ability of mankind to exercise his freedom. Man, after Babel, is faced with the prospect of defending what is his from the encroachments of others. Though still unified by common characteristics which are rooted in nature, man will now turn against his fellow man to preserve by force what is merely conventional. Strife arising out of national, cultural, and religious differences will be unavoidable. Understand that the natural unity of man is not erased at Babel. Ideally, all men remain "brothers," created in the image of God, who trace their ancestry back to the first human couple.

While the division of mankind at Babel is a milder punishment than the ravaging Flood, it is a punishment nonetheless. For almost all practical purposes the essential unity of man is submerged and it is no exaggeration to state that since Babel the planet Earth has been awash in human blood which has been shed for country, for religion, for race; that is, for conventional ends.

The punishment at Babel is in keeping with the biblical God's promise near the end of the Flood story (Gen. 8:21): " 'Never again will I doom the world because of man, since the imaginings of man's mind are evil from his youth....' "

The division in mankind prepares for the emergence of one people to become the focal point of the biblical perspective. The rest of the Hebrew Bible concentrates on the people Israel. However, the selection of the Israelites by the biblical God has, from the beginning, universal implications. The Lord says to Abram, the father of the people Israel, " 'All the families of the earth shall bless themselves by you.' " This means that the Israelites are to be moral exemplars for mankind. This selection of one people from among the peoples of the earth marks yet another attempt by the biblical God to make it easier for man to restore symmetry to God's creation. And once again we see that God has limited His expectations in regard to man's ability to be godlike. Initially, God allowed man to live without law; then, after the Flood, God circumscribed human freedom by imposing certain basic laws; now, after Babel, God enters into a covenant with one people, Israel, whose task it will be to serve as a moral beacon to the other peoples of the Earth.

While we do not know the identity of the individuals who wrote and compiled the biblical record, it is reasonable to suppose that the writers and editors were Israelites. It is not to be wondered at, then, that in a work produced by Israelites the people Israel is proclaimed as the "chosen" people. However, the Hebrew Bible rarely indulges in vainglorious boasting in regard to the Israelites. We will see that as the story of biblical Israel unfolds, the writers have almost nothing good to say about the behavior of the people Israel. And since it is Israel who, according to the biblical testimony, has entered into a convenantal agreement with God, Israel is responsible in ways in which others are not.

Unlike Noah, who was apparently chosen by God because of his righteousness ("Noah found favor with the Lord.... Noah was a righteous man; he was the one blameless man of his time.... The Lord said to Noah, 'Go into the ark, you and all your household, for you alone have I found righteous before Me in this generation' "), the biblical narrator gives no indication as to why God chooses Abram. Moreover, Abram's excursion down into Egypt where he has his wife Sarai tell the Egyptians that she is his sister hardly casts the patriarch in a favorable light. And we saw, too, that his father Terah had already begun the migratory trek toward Canaan. Thus, Abram's readiness to continue the journey now that God offers him great reward (" 'I will make of you a great nation, and I will bless you; I will make your name great, and you shall be a blessing: I will bless those who bless you, and curse him that curses you; all the families of the earth shall bless themselves by you.' ") is hardly an indication of great faith.

However, as the story of Abraham continues, it is evident that Abraham stands head and shoulders over Noah. Keeping in mind that Noah accepted the destruction of his generation without question, let us consider the following context in the Abraham story (Gen. 18:17 ff.):

The Lord thought: 'Shall I conceal from Abraham what I plan to do; for Abraham will become a great and numerous nation and all the nations of the Earth are to be blessed through him? For I have selected him, that he may teach his sons and his posterity to keep the way of the Lord by doing what is just and right, so that the Lord may bring about for Abraham what He has promised him.' Then the Lord said, 'The outcry concerning Sodom and Gomorrah is very great; and their sin is very grave! I will go down and see if the outcry about them corresponds to their deeds; if not I will know it.'... Abraham came forward and said, 'Will You sweep away the evil and the good together? What if there are fifty innocent people in the city; would You not forgive the city for the sake of the innocent fifty? Far be it from You to do such a thing, to kill the innocent as well as the guilty, so that the two groups meet the very same fate. Far be it from You! Does not the Judge of all the Earth deal justly?' And the Lord answered, 'If I find fifty innocent human beings in the city of Sodom, then I will, for their sake, forgive the entire place.' Abraham answered as follows: 'May I presume to speak to the Lord even though I am but dust and ashes? What if there should be forty five innocent people? Will you destroy the entire city for only five?' And the Lord answered, 'I will not destroy it if I find forty five there.' And Abraham spoke to Him again, What if forty should be found there?' And He answered, 'I will not destroy it for the sake of forty.' And he said, 'Please do not be angry if I speak once more: what if thirty should be found there?' And He answered, 'I will not do it if I find thirty there.' And he said, 'I resolve to speak again to my Lord, what if twenty should be found there?' And He answered, 'I will not destroy for the sake of twenty.' And he said, 'Please do not be angry if I speak once more: what if ten should be found there?' And He answered, 'I will not destroy for the sake of ten.' The Lord departed when he had finished speaking to Abraham; and Abraham returned to his place.

Let us begin our analysis of this episode by asking this question: why does the Lord decide to communicate His intentions regarding Sodom and Gomorrah? The answer is simple enough: in order to determine if Abraham is worthy of his high destiny in which the nations of the earth "are to bless themselves by him." In other words, this episode begins with a test by God of Abraham.

To understand of what this test consists and how Abraham passes it, let us consider another question: on what does Abraham's high destiny depend? It depends on Abraham (and, of course, the progeny of Abraham) "doing what is just and right." Then and only then will "the Lord...bring about for Abraham what he has promised...." Abraham and Abraham's people are to quest for justice. In this episode, the narrator demonstrates Abraham's concern for justice by having the patriarch dare to question God's justice.

The Lord has decided to destroy Sodom and Gomorrah because of their extreme wickedness. The Lord's decision in this case is similar to His determination to destroy mankind in the Flood story. Unlike Noah, however, who had accepted God's judgment without a word of protest, Abraham questions God's decision. Abraham does so by appealing to the principle that the innocent must not be destroyed along with the guilty. It is evident that God values this principle because of His willingness to spare the cities if a small number of righteous human beings are found there. Abraham's questions assume that God, too, is concerned with justice. These questions are not so much audacious as they are reverential. Abraham knows that while no constraints whatsoever are or can be placed on the biblical God, God Himself will abide by the standards of justice in His relations with man.

In this episode Abraham demonstrates his willingness to be a kind of moral partner with God and by doing so demonstrates that he is worthy of his high destiny. In the light of this we can understand why Abraham is the first individual in the Hebrew Bible to be called a prophet (Gen. 20:7). In the Hebrew Bible, as we will see, a prophet is an individual who is preoccupied with justice. Since, in the Hebrew Bible, God "speaks" through the prophets, we can conclude that what unites God and man is a concern for justice. Thus, when Abraham displays his zeal for justice he, in effect, is acting Godlike.

It should be noted, however, that Abraham's question, " 'Will You sweep away the innocent along with the guilty?... Shall not the Judge of all the earth deal justly?' " is not really answered. It is true that God is willing to spare Sodom and Gomorrah if ten righteous individuals can be found there. Since those cities are destroyed we are led to conclude that ten could not be found. Leaving aside the question why God would not spare the cities for the sake of fewer than ten, what about the infants in Sodom and Gomorrah? This same question can, of course, be raised of the Flood story. In regard to the Flood story, a question can also be raised concerning animalkind. What did they do wrong? Since animalkind lacks the knowledge of the good and the bad, how could God have held them accountable? Certain it is that animalkind is destroyed (Gen. 6:7): "The Lord said, 'I will blot out from the earth the men whom I created, men together with beasts...for I regret that I made them.' " Some have conjectured that the sin which led to the Flood was interspecies copulation. But aside from the fact that there is no firm textual evidence for such an hypothesis, even if true, the beasts would still not be accountable since they would hardly have been the ones to initiate the sexual contact.

Now God's concern with righteousness in both the Flood and Sodom and Gomorrah stories is clear enough. The biblical God values righteous behavior in that one earthly species which is capable of distinguishing between the good and the bad. Noah is saved because of his righteousness and Abraham appeals to the standard of justice in order to try to save Sodom and Gomorrah. But it remains a fact that in both stories the innocent are swept away along with the guilty.

What then is the nature of the biblical God's justice? *The* staple of biblical faith is, perhaps, the belief that God rewards the good and punishes the bad. However, in both the flood story and the episode concerning Sodom and Gomorrah, innocents are overwhelmed by the general depravity of their time and place. What provisions are made for them?

The question of the nature of God's justice is at the very center of the climactic episode in the Abraham story. This episode, sometimes called the "Binding of Isaac," reads as follows (Gen. 22):

> It was after these things that God tested Abraham. He said to him: 'Abraham,' and he said 'Here I am.' And He said, 'Take your son, your one and only, whom you love, Isaac, and go to the land of Moriah, and offer him up there as an offering on one of the mountains which I will point out to you.' The next morning Abraham arose early and he put a saddle on his ass. He took two of his servants and Isaac and he gathered wood for the offering. Then he made for the place which God would point out to him. On the third day Abraham looked and saw the place from afar. Then Abraham said to his servants: 'Stay here with the ass, I and the boy will go over there, we will worship and then we will return to you.' Abraham took the wood for the offering and he placed it on his son Isaac, while he took the firepot and the knife. And the two of them walked on together. Then Isaac said to his father Abraham, 'Father?' And Abraham answered, 'Here I am, my son.' Isaac said, 'Behold, the fire, and the wood, but where is the animal for the offering?' And Abraham said, 'God will provide for the sacrifice, my son.' And the two of them walked on together. They came to the place which God had pointed out. And Abraham built an altar there and he arranged the wood and he bound Isaac his son and he placed him on the altar on top of the wood. And Abraham put forth his hand, took the knife in order to slaughter his son. Then an angel of the Lord cried out to him from Heaven and He said, 'Abraham, Abraham.' And he said, 'Here I am.' And He said, 'do not lay a hand on the boy, do not do anything to him for now I know that you fear God in that you did not withhold your son, your one and only from me.'

God goes on to repeat His promise to Abraham that the patriarch's seed will be numerous and blessed.

This episode raises a series of questions. For example:

— why is Abraham so willing to slaughter his own son? The very same Abraham, be it remembered, had argued for the sinful inhabitants of Sodom and Gomorrah.

— what is this test of Abraham designed to prove?

— what is Isaac's role in this episode?

— what are we to make of the ending of the episode which simply repeats God's promise to Abraham?

— how could God ask Abraham to do such a barbarous thing?

Many have interpreted this story as a biblical protest against the pagan practice of child sacrifice. The most obvious difficulty with this interpretation is the simple fact that this episode does not offer such a protest. One can think of a hundred different and better ways to object to the barbarous act of child sacrifice. Also, biblical Israel, as a matter of fact, never accuses any of its pagan neighbors of sacrificing their children. The Hebrew Bible, as we will see, has many important quarrels with paganism, but the practice of child sacrifice is not one of them. In the third chapter of 2 Kings, for example, the King of Moab, desperate not to lose his domain to the advancing Israelite army, does, in fact, offer his son up as a burnt offering in plain view of the Israelite forces. The Israelites do not, however, dismiss his act as yet another example of pagan barbarism. No, the Israelites withdraw in horror. The Israelites understand that the Moabite king is willing to sacrifice everything in order to save his domain. If the Moabites had sacrificed their children as a general practice there would have been nothing extraordinary about the king's willingness to sacrifice his son for the good of the state.

The action of the Moabite King provides an instructive contrast to the behavior of Abraham in the Binding of Isaac episode. While the Moabite King is willing to sacrifice everything for his domain, Abraham is willing to sacrifice everything only for his God. Since the predominant view of afterlife in the Hebrew Bible is one in which one's "rest" or "security" beyond the grave depends on having male heirs, Abraham is shown willing to sacrifice not simply his son but his own security for all eternity.

But how could God have asked the patriarch to do such a thing? The ending of the episode makes it clear that God stops the patriarch from slaughtering his son. However, it is also clear that God is pictured as finding Abraham's willingness to sacrifice his son praiseworthy. What are we to make of Abraham's willingness? We already know from the Sodom and Gomorrah sequence that Abraham is willing to "argue" with God and, moreover, in that episode Abraham is shown being concerned with the value of life. Why then is he so ready to sacrifice his son and his future? These and other difficulties disappear once one accepts the episode's most basic message that what God wants from man is man's willingness to sacrifice everything only to God. Since God intervenes to stay the patriarch's hand it is clear that God will never demand the sacrifice. In the story of the Moabite King, by contrast, there is no Divine intervention to stop the slaughter. The Moabite King shows a willingness to sacrifice everything for the state and he loses everything. In the Binding of Isaac episode the biblical narrator is warning his reader not to sacrifice his future for that which is less than ultimate.

Isaac's role in the episode is not altogether clear. The reader knows almost nothing about Isaac, not even his age. Isaac seems to function as a symbol for Abraham's future. The reader is meant to understand that before he feels superior to Abraham for his willingness to sacrifice his future, the reader is to ask himself how he is sacrificing his own future. It is probable that we know so little about Isaac, apart from the fact that he represents Abraham's future, so that the symbolic force of what he represents is made clear to the reader.

Isaac's story is the briefest of the three patriarchal stories. What is most noteworthy about Isaac is that he is the son of Abraham and the father of Jacob. Abraham, of course, is the father of the Israelite people, while Jacob's very name will become Israel. Jacob's name ("he supplants") signifies the manner of his birth when he is pictured clutching the heel of his twin brother Esau. The manner of his birth, where he is shown trying to prevent his brother from being first born, anticipates later efforts by Jacob to wrest from Esau his rights as first born. In biblical Israel the first born male was normally entitled to a double portion of his father's legacy. Nor is that all Jacob does, or attempts to do, to his brother. With the help of Rebekkah, Jacob is pictured duping his aged, nearly blind father into bestowing Isaac's death bed blessing on him rather than on Esau, Isaac's own choice. When Esau learns of Jacob's duplicity, he vows revenge. Jacob flees back to the land of Abraham's beginnings.

The story of Jacob's flight, his stay in Mesopotamia, and his return to the Promised Land, provides valuable information about the themes we have been tracing.

Encamped after his first day's travel, Jacob dreams that he sees a ladder stretching from Earth to Heaven. Going up and down the ladder are angels, while above the ladder stands God. The Lord speaks (Gen. 28:13 ff.):

> 'I am the Lord, the God of your father Abraham and the God of Isaac: the ground on which you are lying I will give to you and to your offspring. Your descendants shall be as the dust of the earth; you shall spread out westward and eastward, northward and southward. All the families of the earth shall bless themselves through you and your seed. Behold, I am with you; I will watch over you wherever you go, and I will bring you back to this land. I will not abandon you until I have done what I promised you.'

In this dream the Lord repeats the substance of His promise to Abraham, adding the surety that He will not abandon Jacob.

A startled Jacob awakens and concludes that he must have chanced upon a sacred area. His response to the revelatory dream is interesting: Jacob proposes to serve the Lord only if he returns safely to his homeland. The Lord's assurance that He will be with Jacob does not suffice; Jacob, in effect, says that the proof of the pudding will be the eating of it. In Jacob's words:

> 'If God stays with me, if He watches over me on this journey that I am making, and gives me food to eat and clothing to wear, and I return safely to my father's house, then the Lord shall be my God.'

The realization of God's promise lies somewhere in the future and therefore belief in the promise requires faith. Jacob, who is in flight from the consequences of his own behavior, has no such faith. The revelatory dream does not, in and of itself, give him the necessary faith. We have already seen that revelation need not compel faith in the Cain-Abel episode wherein Cain responded to God's revelation by killing his brother Abel. What these and other biblical contexts suggest is that man has the freedom to say no to God. As we shall see, those few individuals who respond positively to the biblical God are deemed worthy of praise because they have the freedom to respond negatively. These meritorious individuals are called true prophets of God.

At this early point in Jacob's story, his faith in the Lord is quite tenuous. And related to this is the fact that his character lacks substance. He has taken from Esau what rightfully belonged to him, and Jacob has done this by deceiving his father Isaac. Rather than face the consequences of his behavior, Jacob has chosen to flee. It will be more than twenty years before Jacob returns to the Promised Land.

During these years Jacob lives with the clan of Laban, his mother Rebekkah's brother. He marries Laban's two daughters (Leah and Rachel), and although he is initially bested by the cunning Laban, Jacob grows in strength of character until he is more than a match for his uncle. When Jacob resolves to return to the Promised Land, Laban is unable to stop him. Of note is Jacob's acceptance, without question, of two revelations (Gen. 31) in which God urges him to return to the land of his fathers.

One could argue that the by now prosperous Jacob obeys God's command to return to Canaan because it is easy for him to do so. We must not, however, forget about Esau. Jacob has no way of knowing whether his brother has either forgotten or forgiven him. In fact, enroute home, Jacob learns that Esau is coming out to meet him with a troop of four hundred men. But although Jacob is apprehensive, he does not flee. He divides his camp in two, thinking that if Esau attacks one the other will be able to escape. Jacob then prays to God (Gen. 32:10 ff.):

'Oh God of my father Abraham and God of my father Isaac, the Lord who said to me "return to your native land and I will deal well with you." I am not worthy of the loyalty that you have displayed to your servant; with my staff alone I crossed the Jordan, and now I have become two camps. Deliver me, I pray, from the power of my brother, from Esau; else I am afraid, he may come and strike me down, mothers and children alike. Yet you have said: 'I will deal well with you and your seed like the sands of the sea, which are countless." '

In this prayer Jacob both expresses his unworthiness (which is itself a far cry from his egocentric response to his dream revelation) and acknowledges his God given destiny. But while his destiny is God given it is dependent for its fulfillment not on God but on Jacob himself. Thus Jacob makes careful preparations as Esau approaches, including the sending of a bountiful present to placate him.

The night before the rendezvous with his brother, Jacob has one of the most peculiar experiences recorded in the Hebrew Bible (Gen. 32:25–32):

> Jacob was left alone. And a man wrestled with him until dawn. When the man saw that he could not prevail, he wrenched Jacob's hip at its socket.... And he said, let me go for it is dawn. And Jacob answered, 'I will not let you go unless you bless me.' The man said, 'What is your name?' He replied, 'Jacob.' He said, 'No longer shall your name be Jacob, but Israel, for you have striven with beings divine and human, and have prevailed.' Jacob then asked, 'Tell me, if you would, your name.' But he said, 'You must not ask my name.' And he [the divine being] took leave of him there. Thus Jacob named the place Peniel, meaning. 'I have seen a divine being face to face, yet my life has been preserved.' The sun came up as he passed Peniel, limping because of his hip. That is why the Israelites do not eat the thigh muscle that is on the socket of the hip....'

On the simplest level this revelatory encounter provides an explanation for the origin of the names "Israel" and "Peniel." Also, the account gives us the derivation of the dietary taboo about the sciatic muscle.

Of more significance is the new direction in Jacob's life this strange experience symbolizes. Twenty one years before, a sly, cowardly Jacob fled from his father's home. Now Jacob has learned to strive successfully not only with men but with a titan. This new direction is epitomized by Jacob's new name which, in time to come, will designate the children of Abraham and their Promised Land.

While this revelatory experience signifies what Jacob has become in these intervening twenty one years, it is not itself the cause of Jacob's character transformation. The revelation comes after his sojourn with Laban and after Jacob has made the decision not to flee from Esau. However mysterious the revelation (who or what is this being with whom Jacob wrestles? Why must it leave before daybreak?), it seems clear that the revelation is meant to be indicative of Jacob's increased spiritual power.

The matter of Jacob's name change is an interesting motif in the patriarchal narratives. As we may recall, Abram's name is changed to Abraham which means "father of a multitude." Abraham's name presages the hoped for future of the people Israel. Significantly, Abraham's name is changed only after the narrator has informed us that (Gen. 15:6): "...he [Abraham] had faith in the Lord which the Lord reckoned meritorious." That is to say, both Abraham and Jacob must first prove themselves worthy of the names before they are bestowed on them. For both Abraham and Jacob, the new names are tokens of their spiritual growth.

It is not by chance that Isaac, alone among the patriarchs, does not receive a new name. For Isaac is the one patriarch whose story is not connected with local motion. Abraham is shown migrating from Mesopotamia to the Promised Land and Jacob is shown traveling back to Mesopotamia. Isaac's journeys, however, are pretty much confined to the area of Canaan. In the cases of Abraham and Jacob, their journeys are intertwined with their spiritual growth. In keeping with the manner in which the paradigm of motion is employed in the Creation story, Abraham and Jacob not only change their places, they change their ways. Abraham does not simply continue the migratory path initiated by his father; he completes it in the decisive sense of breaking with his pagan past. Jacob's travels, though not prompted by any spiritual quest, nonetheless result in the ascendance of Jacob's spirit. The two revelations which frame his going from and returning to the Promised Land indicate Jacob's spiritual growth. In the first, Jacob vows to serve the Lord *if* the Lord delivers on His promise. This can be contrasted to Abraham's faith in a divine promise the fulfillment of which will not come in his lifetime. Jacob's response to his dream revelation at Bethel can also be contrasted to his revelatory experience at Peniel. At Peniel, Jacob earns his blessing.

Not very much happens, however, to Isaac. That is, Isaac is not depicted changing his ways. He is by far the most passive of the patriarchs. For example, when it is time for Isaac to marry, his father Abraham sends a servant back to Mesopotamia in order to arrange a marriage for Isaac. His very name, which means "he laughs," perhaps functions as an hyperbole: he is very close to being a laughingstock.

The last we see of him he is being hoodwinked by his wife and one of his sons into misdirecting the crucial death bed blessing.

All of this is by way of indicating that the journeys of the patriarchs are essentially spiritual ones. Abraham leaves Mesopotamia in the service of a God radically different from the gods worshipped by his pagan ancestors.

It is time to consider the differences between Abraham's God and the gods of his fathers. The essential distinction is a qualitative rather than a quantitative one. That is, it is not simply a matter of the one (monotheism) versus the many (polytheism). The essential distinction between the biblical God and the gods of paganism has to do with the fact that the biblical God is qualitatively different from that which He creates. While all created entities depend on Him for their existence, He, being uncreated, depends on nothing.

In the creation stories of Mesopotamia, the gods and goddesses emerge out of the basic "stuff" of the universe and are dependent on this "stuff." These deities are not themselves separate from matter, and as material creatures they have material needs: they gestate and give birth; they lust; they eat and drink, fight, fall sick, and require healing. Most importantly, the Mesopotamia gods are not in complete control of their destinies because they are often at the mercy of what we would call fate or chance. In the Mesopotamian creation stories fate/chance is for the most part identified with the primordial oceanic waters. This is the "stuff" out of which the gods emerge. This "stuff," which existed before any gods or goddesses, is without will or intelligence. It (the stuff) did not will to create the gods; the gods were simply generated spontaneously.

Two very different worldviews derive from biblical Israel and pagan Mesopotamia. The biblical vision proclaims that one Creator God consciously imparted meaning and purpose to His creation. Moreover, the first chapters of Genesis assign a great dignity to man, who alone is created in this God's image. The Mesopotamian vision asserts that both man and the gods are subject to an indifferent fate which is the ultimate (though mindless) arbiter in the universe.

The differences between these two venerable traditions have to do with the ways in which they seek to answer the following questions:

— how and why did God (or the gods) come to be?

— how and why did mankind come to be?

— how and why are God (or the gods) and man similar? dissimilar?

— what is man's place in the scheme of things?

As we have seen, in the Hebrew Bible God creates, but is not Himself created. And although God is described as having created mankind in His image, there is a wide gulf separating the divine from the human realm. While, in important ways, men can also create, man's power and scope are limited to the earth. And the ineluctable fact of death also demarcates the human realm from the divine. As we saw in the Eden story, the entry of death into the human condition was due not to God but to man; man was depicted as willingly choosing mortality and the world of time over the changelessness of Eden. Once outside of Eden man is free to create his own destiny within the limitations imposed by his mortality and his domain. But mortal man is not without help from an immortal source. Man enters into a series of covenants with God. These covenants give witness to God's loving concern for mankind. The biblical God does not enter into these covenants out of need but out of a grace-filled awareness of man's needs and inadequacies.

A far different arrangement is made manifest in the Mesopotamian pagan tradition. Interestingly, the physical structure of the universe as described in the Mesopotamian creation stories is identical to that found in the Genesis narrative. In both the Heaven is pictured as a solid firmament holding back part of the primordial waters, and the earth is a solid mass which appears to rest on pylons extending down into the watery depths. In both traditions, the sun, moon, and stars are shown making their ways across the vault of Heaven. And in both the Mesopotamian and the biblical stories of creation, the earth is pictured as the fixed center of the universe.

However, in the Mesopotamian tales of beginnings, it is clear, in the first place, that the first gods emerge spontaneously from the primordial waters. And the creation of the cosmos ("the Heaven and the Earth") comes about as a result of violence within the community of gods. When man is created, moreover, he is meant to serve the gods for the good of the gods by bringing sacrificial offerings so that the divine beings can eat without having to procure their own food. Not surprisingly, then, tension types the relationship between the gods and mankind. Whereas in the Eden story man is shown choosing mortality, in the Mesopotamian ethos the gods consign man to the grave so that man will not be able to threaten the gods. But both god and man, in the Mesopotamian imagination, are under the mindless sway of chance or fate. Thus tragedy stalks both the Heavenly and earthly realms. At any moment fate can level the hopes and dreams of the strongest of gods and of the best of men.

The Mesopotamian storytellers determine the worth of human behavior in light of the difficulties and fatefilled straits in which men find themselves. One of, if not the primary virtue in the Mesopotamian stories, is the willingness to risk everything. In what is perhaps the most famous creation story from Mesopotamia (*The E'numa E'lish*), warring groups of gods attempt to marshall the forces of nature in their quest for power. The hero of the tale, the god Marduk, is the one willing to risk the most. Marduk is described in Tarzan-like imagery ("Enticing was his figure, flashing the look of his eyes. Manly was his going forth, a leader from the beginning."), and he performs feats of derring-do. In what is probably the greatest of the Mesopotamian stories (*The Epic of Gilgamesh*), beings part human and divine struggle with fate, with the gods, and with their own fears not simply to eradicate evil and death from the world but to make a name for themselves. Although the hero, the mighty Gilgamesh, gains victory after victory, each victory produces another and greater challenge, until he confronts the inevitable fact of death which finally robs him of all hope.

Mesopotamian paganism is not a relic of the antique past. Consider, for instance, the following words of the twentieth century thinker Bertrand Russell (in *A Free Man's Worship*):

> That man is the product of causes which had no prevision of the end they were achieving; that his origin, his growth, his hopes and fears, his loves and beliefs, are but the outcome of an accidental collocation of atoms; that no fire, no heroism, no intensity of thought and feeling, can preserve an individual life beyond the grave; that all the labor of the ages, all the devotion, all the inspiration, all the noonday brightness of human genius, are destined to

extinction in the vast death of the solar system, and that the whole temple of man's achievement must inevitably be buried beneath the debris of a universe in ruins—all these things, if not quite beyond dispute, are yet so nearly certain, that no philosophy which rejects them can hope to stand.

You should note that all the essential elements of Mesopotamian paganism are present in the above citation:

— the unplanned, spontaneous generation of consciousness;

— the inevitability of death which is proof positive that man is at the mercy of an unjust or indifferent fate;

— the absolute inability of man and man's creations to endure.

These assertions are also present in the work of Ernest Hemingway, certainly one of the most important of twentieth century American writers. In *A Farewell to Arms*, for instance, the young hero, who is courageous, intelligent, and sensitive, has to endure the loss of the love of his life who dies giving birth to their child who also dies. The lovers are certain that death is "just a dirty trick." Bereft of the love which had given meaning to his life, the hero expresses himself in words which could have been written by the anonymous genius who wrote *The Epic of Gilgamesh* or by Bertrand Russell:

So now they got her in the end. You never get away with anything.... You did not know what it is all about. They threw you in and told you the rules and the first time they caught you off base they killed you.... They killed you in the end.... You could count on that. Stay around and they would kill you.... Once in a camp I put a log on the fire and it was full of ants. As it commenced to burn, the ants swarmed out and went first toward the center where the fire was; then turned back and ran toward the end. When there was enough on the end they fell off into the fire. Some got out, their bodies burnt and flattened, and went off not knowing where they were going. But most of them went toward the fire and then back toward the end and swarmed on the cool end and finally fell off into the fire. I remember thinking at the time that it was the end of the world and a splendid chance to be a messiah and lift the log off onto the ground. But I did not do anything but throw a tin cup of water on the log, so that I could have the cup empty to put whiskey in before I added water to it. I think the cup of water on the burning log only steamed the ants.

This excerpt from Hemingway's *A Farewell to Arms* emphasizes the tragic nature of human existence. The "they" in the citation ("They got her in the end.... They killed you...stay around and they would kill you") refers to the fateful accidents of life over which man has little or no control. The hero watches helplessly as his love and their infant die. The hero compares the plight of man to ants scurrying frantically on a burning log. When he, as potential savior, thinks about intervening to save the ants, he finally only worsens their lot. In that metaphor our hero becomes a god who could but will not save man. To the extent, then, that there is suprahuman intervention in the affairs of man, it is only to "steam" mankind.

The pagan vision emphasizes the utter helplessness of mankind. It points to the impermanence of man and man's achievements in a universe which is either indifferent or actively hostile to man's needs and aspirations. For Russell, the heroic impulse in man prompts him to search out the mysteries of a lifeless, indifferent universe. Hemingway's hero, like Gilgamesh, seeks out the unequal challenge in a battle to the death with death itself. And like Gilgamesh, the Hemingway hero can only lose.

In contrast to such tales of heroic striving against impossible odds, the stories in Genesis appear to be almost colorless. Rare are the scenes of heroic conflict. Nor does this change in the other biblical books. While books like Joshua, Judges, Samuel, and Kings sometimes describe battles and conflicts of all sorts, the focus is rarely on deeds of daring and risk. Joshua, for example, wins battle after battle as he attempts to secure the Promised Land, but the narrator emphasizes neither Joshua's physical prowess nor his military sagacity. Rather, the actions of Joshua and the people he leads are measured by the extent to which they line up to or backslide away from the laws of Moses. And it is worth noting that the narrator never gives a physical description of Moses or Joshua.

It might seem that the book of Judges is another matter altogether. Armies clash; a woman drives a tent peg through a warrior's skull; an Israelite warrior named Gideon wins an impressive victory against a numerically superior foe; an Israelite assassin disembowels an obese king; an Israelite, whose woman is raped and murdered by fellow Israelites, in desperate fury hacks her corpse into parts and sends a part to each of the Israelite tribes to induce them to avenge him.

In all of these tales, however, the emphasis is on the evaluation of human behavior in light of man's God given potential. The biblical storyteller's main concern, that is, is with the life of the spirit. Again and again the Israelites are depicted violating their covenant with God. Physical acts are evaluated by the spiritual criteria of the covenant first made with Abraham whom the Lord "...singled out, that he may instruct his children and his posterity to keep the way of the Lord by doing what is just and right...." There is a somber ring which runs through the stories in the book of Judges. The native population of Canaan is deemed unworthy of the land because of their immoral behavior; the Israelites, however, almost immediately begin acting like the Canaanites. For instance, when the Israelites view the severed remains of the aforementioned raped and murdered woman, they themselves pronounce this judgment (Judg. 19:30): "And everyone who saw it cried out, 'Never has such a thing happened or been seen from the days the Israelites came out of the land of Egypt to this day!' "

The closest the Hebrew Bible comes to a physically imposing hero is Samson, whose story is found in the book of Judges. But even apart from the fact that his strength is rooted in a vow to God made by his parents, the astonishingly strong Samson mostly acts like an impetuous, petulant dolt. His braggadocio-like nature exposes first his wife and then his kinship group to great danger. And his self-indulgent temper tantrums almost bring down full scale disaster on the members of his tribe who are only too eager to turn him over to the Philistines. Only after his imprisonment and torture (the Philistines bore his eyes out) does Samson seem to realize that real strength depends on faithfulness to the Lord. Never is Samson described in the glowing terms which are associated with such legendary Mesopotamian heroes as Gilgamesh. Also, the dark fate which stalks Gilgamesh is altogether absent in the story of Samson. In his story his character is his fate. Samson's problems are, for the most part, of his own making. To the extent that God intervenes in Samson's story, it is to help him. Gilgamesh and, of course, Hemingway's hero, are not at all befriended by the gods. Gilgamesh, in fact, displays more intelligence and courage than do any of the gods in his story. And in any case, both Gilgamesh and the gods are harassed by a fate which is not of their making and beyond their control.

There is no analogue to Gilgamesh in the Hebrew Bible. Shortly we will examine the story of Moses, who is surely the greatest hero in the Old Testament. We will see how little he is like a pagan hero. For the present, let us reconsider King David, who is perhaps the closest the Hebrew Bible comes to a character like Gilgamesh. David unquestionably is of heroic dimensions. He checkmates the imposing King Saul repeatedly; he survives on the lam as an outlaw; as a king he expands the borders of Israel by subjugating virtually all of biblical Israel's neighbors.

There are, however, two important contrasts between David and one such as Gilgamesh. In the first place, the only physical description of David provided by the biblical storyteller is, as it were, anti-heroic. In 1 Samuel 16 the prophet Samuel is sent by God to Bethlehem to anoint a king to replace Saul who has disobeyed God's directives. Samuel is directed to the family of Jesse, and there he thinks he has found his man in Eliab, David's strapping older brother. But the Lord sets Samuel straight: " 'Pay no attention to his appearance or his stature, for I have rejected him. For not as man sees [does the Lord see]; man sees only what is visible, but the Lord sees into the heart.' " When David is introduced it is as a lad who is in no way physically impressive. But early on in the story David is able to do what the robust Saul (who is repeatedly described as towering physically over those around him) will not do: he ventures forth against the Philistine giant Goliath, the most physically imposing human being in the Hebrew Bible. The narrator spares no details when it comes to Goliath's stature (1 Sam. 17:4 ff.):

> A man came forth from among the Philistine battalions, his name was Goliath from Gath. He was more than ten feet tall. And he had a bronze helmet on his head; he wore a breastplate of scale armor, a bronze breastplate weighing more than one hundred fifty pounds; he had bronze greaves on his legs, and a bronze javelin on his shoulders. The shaft of his spear was like a weaver's bar, and the iron head of his spear weighed twenty pounds, and a shield bearer marched in front of him.

This detailed recitation of Goliath's form and vast armaments, a recitation which is almost half the length of the entire Creation story, is surely ironic, for it serves only to underline his vulnerability.

This brings us to the second contrast between the biblical hero and his pagan counterpart. When Goliath sees David coming out from the Israelite battle ranks he is insulted that the Israelites have sent out an unarmed youth. Scornfully, he calls out to the advancing David that he " '...will give your flesh to the birds of the sky and the beasts of the field.' " But for all of Goliath's seeming advantage over David, it is clear that real and absolute power is with David. For, as David puts it, " 'You come against me with sword and spear and javelin; but I come against you in the name of the Lord of Hosts, the God of the battle ranks of Israel, whom you have defied.' "

Power, then, is vested in that man who is with God. And God is with that man who is worthy. Thus, when David will later abuse his power as king, in effect violating the very principle he enunciated as he sallied forth against Goliath (that might does not lie in the sword), his power disintegrates. The turning point for David comes in the Bathsheba episode. While we have already examined that episode, one aspect of the tale is relevant to our present context. When the prophet Nathan tricks David into pronouncing sentence against himself, a repentant David declares (2 Sam. 12:13), " 'I have sinned against the Lord.' " David's acknowledgment of God as the source of moral values is a crucial part of the biblical perspective. It is not the uniqueness of these values which separates the biblical and pagan traditions but rather the fact that the biblical God underwrites these values. Such values as honesty, courage, compassion, and decency are everywhere apparent in the literature of pagan Mesopotamia. But in the biblical religion the ultimate force in the universe is pictured valuing the same values as man. In *The Epic of Gilgamesh* and in the modern variations of paganism, ultimate power is vested in a chance or fate which values nothing.

Since the beginnings of the Israelite people revolve around spiritual quests, it is not surprising that Moses, the most towering figure in the Hebrew Bible, undergoes what is the most dramatic spiritual transformation. As was the case with Abraham and Jacob, this spiritual change is connected with spatial journeys.

The external details of the story of Moses are not complicated. Moses is born in Egypt at a time when the Egyptians are persecuting the Israelites living in their midst. The Pharaoh has decreed that all Israelite male infants are to be killed because the Israelites have grown so numerous that the Egyptian leader is fearful that they pose a threat to the native Egyptian populace. Through some deft action by his mother and sister, Moses escapes this fate and, ironically, grows to maturity in the Pharaoh's palace. Though apparently unaware of his Israelite heritage, Moses is dismayed when he sees an Egyptian maltreating an Israelite worker. In a fit of rage he murders the Egyptian and flees into the wilderness when he learns that his crime has become public knowledge. In the wilderness of Midian he marries Zipporah, a daughter of the Midianite priest Jethro. Some forty years pass which the biblical author passes over in silence. One day, after driving his flock deep into the wilderness, Moses experiences a revelation which propels him back to Egypt in order to liberate the Israelites. In a sequence of events punctuated by repeated miraculous interventions by God, the Israelites leave Egypt and come to congregate around Mt. Sinai. There Moses receives a series of revelations which spell out the obligations of man to his fellowman and to God. These obligations range from the so-called ten commandments to specific legislation involving both the "religious" (e.g., the maintenance of the sacrificial cult, the observance of various holy days) and the "secular" (e.g., the maintenance of the juridical system and the organizing of the army). After about a year, Moses leads the people to the borders of the Promised Land. However, the people are fearful of the native population and refuse to invade Canaan. They are then condemned by God to remain in the wilderness until a new generation is ready to fight the Canaanites. Some thirty eight years of semi-nomadic sojourning ensue. These years are marked by confrontations between Israelites and nation states whose borders the Israelites wish to cross, and by repeated rebellions within the Israelite camp against Mosaic authority. Once more Moses guides the people to the Promised Land where he is informed by God that he will not be permitted to lead the people into the land. Two reasons are given for this at widely separated points in the story. The first has to do with an act of disobedience to God and the second has to do with Moses taking upon himself the responsibility for the sins of the people he leads. Moses installs Joshua as the new leader. Moses then dies on the eastern side of the Jordan River and is buried in an unmarked grave so that "...no one knows his burial place to this day."

While Saul, the first king of Israel, is described as standing head and shoulders above the people, it is Moses, the greatest of biblical Israel's prophets, who stands head and shoulders, in a spiritual sense, over every other character in the Hebrew Bible. It is he who transforms the mixed multitude that leaves Egypt into a united people. To this people, Moses gives a constitution and the wherewithal to invade and conquer the Promised Land. The books of Exodus, Leviticus, Numbers, and Deuteronomy are so dominated by Moses that, along with the book of Genesis, they have come to be known as the books of Moses.

Let us try to begin to understand the story of Moses by placing it in perspective. According to the book of Genesis, in the beginning stages of the human experience mankind was not restrained by law. This changed after the Flood, when God entered into a covenant with man which, among other things, entailed the general prohibition against the shedding of human blood. In the story of Moses, the laws attributed to the great prophet are painstakingly specific. These laws, which differ widely in form and content, are animated by this common factor: God's concern that man will self destruct if he is permitted to live in an environment devoid of legal restrictions. The axiomatic base of these laws is the ten commandments. These laws and the prominent place given to them by the biblical tradition (to say nothing of the postbiblical tradition) testify to one of the most basic propositions of the Hebrew Bible: outside Eden man cannot live without restraint. Man, that is, cannot be trusted to do the "good" thing simply because he knows it to be both "good" and preferable to the "bad." As we saw, the stories in Genesis relate that man, for the most part, will choose the "bad" to his own detriment. Again and again God's words to Cain come back to haunt mankind (Gen. 4:7):

'Surely if you do right
There is uplift.
But if you do not do right
Sin is the demon at the door
Whose urge is toward you,
Yet you can be its master.'

From the Moses story onward in the Hebrew Bible, man's capacity to master "demon sin" is strengthened by legal penalties against wrongdoing.

Thus the importance of Moses can be appreciated by considering the fact that he is the only prophetic lawgiver in the Hebrew Bible. Even in postbiblical Judaism when the Pharisees (around the time of Jesus) expanded on the biblical laws, they always did so in the name of Moses. Which is to say that the Pharisees treated the laws attributed to Moses in the same way the legal system of the United States defers to the founding fathers who authored our Constitution. If anything, the Pharisees were even more deferential because unlike the American legal system which had many framers, Moses alone was reputed to have framed the biblical laws.

Not that the mere presence of the Mosaic constitution prevented wrongdoing. Hardly. The post Mosaic generations are condemned again and again for their immoral behavior. The most trenchant criticism in the Hebrew Bible of the people's behavior is delivered by the prophets who follow Moses.

What characterized these prophets? On the simplest level, the biblical prophet was an individual who bridged the gap between the divine and human realms. The prophet, whatever else he might have been, was God's spokesman. The sayings of the prophets form the very core of the biblical religion. Any inquiry, however, into the nature of biblical prophecy is hindered by the following considerations:

— the Hebrew Bible nowhere sets forth thematically its teaching in regard to prophecy;

— since the Hebrew Bible is the product of individuals with differing interests and perhaps beliefs, it is possible that there is not general agreement as to what constitutes prophecy.

With these reservations in mind we turn now to aspects of the story
of Moses as they relate to the theme of prophecy.

The first revelation in the story of Moses (Exod. 3:1–4:16) is one of
the most curious narratives in all of the Hebrew Bible. Moses, having
lived a shepherd's life in Midian for several decades, one day guides
his flock deep into the wilderness where he is startled to see a bush
burning without consuming itself. He draws near and his incredulity
is heightened when the bush speaks. The voice identifies itself as the
God of the patriarchs of biblical Israel and it tells Moses to return to
Egypt in order to liberate the Israelites. Moses' response is an
expression of his inadequacy: " 'Who am I that I should go to Pharaoh
and free the Israelites from Egypt?' " God assures Moses that he need
not worry: " 'I will be with you, and it shall be your sign that it was I
who sent you; when you have freed the people from Egypt, you shall
worship God at this very mountain.' " Moses, however, is still
unwilling to return to Egypt. He wants to know the name of this God
who is mandating a return to the very land from which he fled.
Generally, as is the case here, to know the name of someone or
something in the Hebrew Bible is to understand that person or
thing's essence; so, for instance, "Adam" means man; Eve means life;
"Abraham" means father of a multitude; "Mahlon" and "Chilion," two
characters in the book of Ruth who die suddenly, mean consumption
and dread disease; and so on. You will recall that Jacob tried
unsuccessfully to learn the name of his mysterious adversary with
whom he wrestled. In our present context Moses, in effect, wants God
to define Himself. It is a bold request. God's rejoinder is, to say the
least, ambiguous. " 'I will be what I will be: tell the Israelites "I will
be" has sent you to them.' " Again the Lord urges Moses to return to
Egypt and to confront the Pharaoh with the demand to free the
people Israel. Moses still wants nothing to do with the mission; he
says: " 'But they will never believe me or listen to me; they will say,
"The Lord did not appear to you." ' " Magnanimously, the Lord gives
Moses the power to perform some extraordinary acts: he is able to
transform his staff into a serpent and then back into a staff; he can
change his healthy hand into a leprous one and then back to a
healthy one; and he is assured that he will be able to convert some of

the water from the river Nile into blood. Incredibly, Moses remains resistant: " 'I have never been a man of ready speech.... I am slow of speech and of tongue.' " Once again the Lord's voice coming from the midst of the burning bush seeks to reassure Moses: " 'Who is it that gives man speech? Who makes him dumb or deaf? Who makes him clearsighted or blind? Is it not I the Lord? Go now, I will be with you as you speak and will tell you what to say.' " Now Moses simply refuses to go. The Lord becomes angry and summarily orders Moses back to Egypt.

Most peculiar in this peculiar episode is Moses' obstinacy in the face of one incredible phenomenon after another. As the story of Moses continues it becomes evident that Moses' behavior is an epitome of the people's behavior: they remain resistant to God in spite of one miraculous event after another. Plagues scourge Egypt; the Red Sea splits; manna showers down from Heaven; rocks gush forth with water; the earth cracks wide open to swallow malefactors, and so on. All this to no avail, as the people persist in their refusal to serve the Lord alone. The Egyptians at least have an excuse, for they do not worship the Lord, God of Israel. The Israelites, who have entered into a covenant with the Lord, remain unbelievably blind to His presence and power. Consider that only a matter of days after witnessing the splitting of the Red Sea, which apparently had made an impression on them (Exod. 14:31: "And when Israel saw the wondrous power which the Lord had wielded against the Egyptians, the people feared the Lord: they had faith in the Lord, and in His servant Moses"), the people complain that they wish they were back in Egypt (Exod. 16:3: "The Israelites said to Moses and Aaron, 'If only we had died by the hand of the Lord in the land of Egypt, when we sat by the fleshpots, when we ate our fill of bread. For you have brought us out into this wilderness to starve this whole congregation to death.' ") When the Lord then sends manna for the people to eat the people complain of thirst. The miraculous appearance of water satisfies them only briefly. And so it continues throughout the story of Moses.

The people's lack of faith in God is symbolized by the fact that it is Moses who ascends the mountain of God (variously called Sinai or Horeb) while the people are not permitted to draw near to the mountain. Moses more and more becomes a man of faith; he becomes, in fact, the greatest of biblical Israel's prophets.

The question we raise now is this: what is it that Moses knows or believes which the people do not? This very question is at the center of one of the most arresting episodes in the story of Moses (Exod. 32–33). Once again the people are shown rebelling against the Lord and His spokesman Moses. They induce Aaron, the brother of Moses, to fashion golden images which will stand in for Moses who has lingered for several weeks on Mt. Sinai. The people proceed to worship these images by eating, drinking, and merrying. Moses, alone on top of the mountain of God, is informed by God that this time the people have gone too far (Exod. 32:7 ff.):

> And the Lord spoke to Moses: 'Go down, for your people whom you led out of Egypt, have acted perversely. They have turned away quickly from the way which I commanded them. They have made for themselves a molten calf and they are prostrating themselves before it and they sacrifice to it, saying, these are the gods Israel who led you out of the land of Egypt.' And the Lord said to Moses, 'I see that this is a stiffnecked people. Now, let Me be, that My anger may blaze forth against them and that I may destroy them, and make of you a great nation.'

Moses intercedes on behalf of the people, "reminding" God of His ancient and enduring promise to Abraham, Isaac, and Jacob that their numerous seed would one day inhabit the Promised Land. The Lord acknowledges this and "...renounced the punishment He had planned to bring upon His people." Moses returns to the camp and shatters the golden images and puts down the rebellion.

Let us now compare Moses' behavior in this context with his behavior in the burning bush episode. In the burning bush tale God first proposes that Moses return to Egypt because it is the just and proper course of action: the Israelites are suffering in Egypt. When this fails, God assures Moses that He will be with him and that, in addition, Moses will return to the very spot where the bush is burning to worship the Lord there with the liberated Israelites. This promise by God has no effect on Moses and it is easy to see why. If Moses had faith that the mission would be successful, he would not have resisted God in the first place. Lacking the requisite faith, no amount of assurance from God is enough for Moses. Then, when in response to Moses' request to know His name, God answers " 'I will be who/what I will be' ", it is again, from Moses' perspective, insufficient. And when God provides Moses with a dazzling magic act, Moses' lack of faith is there for all to see. Moses' complaint, after receiving this magical capacity, that he is not much of a speaker, is virtually a non sequitur. When Moses does return to Egypt it is because God compels him to do so.

Moses' behavior in the Golden Calf sequence is strikingly different. On Mt. Sinai not only does Moses not resist God, he selflessly defends the people and, in effect, reminds God of His obligations (Exod. 32:12 ff.): " 'Turn from your blazing anger, and renounce the plan to punish Your people. Remember Your servants, Abraham, Isaac, and Jacob, how You swore to them by Your Self and said to them: I will make your offspring as numerous as the stars of heaven, and I will give to your offspring this whole land of which I spoke, to possess forever.' And the Lord renounced the punishment He had planned to bring upon his people."

Moses' behavior is reminiscent of Abraham's in the Sodom and Gomorrah episode. There, it will be recalled, the patriarch cautioned God not to kill the innocent along with the guilty. From these two contexts involving the first and the greatest of the prophets, it is evident that the prophet is not simply one who speaks to man for God; the prophet is also one who speaks to God on behalf of the people.

We noted earlier that Jacob's spiritual transformation was framed by two revelations. In the first, Jacob sought to wrest the best possible deal from God. In the second, Jacob sought to wrest the name from his mysterious adversary. As we observed, these two revelations are indicative of Jacob's character change. The second revelation, occurring as it does after more than twenty years have passed in which a cunning boy has matured into a prudent and courageous man, gives witness to the changes that have taken place in Jacob.

Along the same lines, it is to be expected that Moses, who by the time of the Golden Calf episode has emerged as a spokesman for both God and the people he leads, would experience a revelation which is qualitatively different from the one at the burning bush. At the burning bush Moses strove only to evade God's call to return to

Egypt. Now, on Mt. Sinai, Moses intercedes with God for the people (as Abraham had done) and, as Jacob had endeavored to do, Moses seeks to learn God's essence. In the aftermath of having put down the rebellion Moses says to God (Exod. 33:12 ff.):

> And Moses said to the Lord, 'See, You say to me, "lead this people forward," but You have not made known to me whom You will send with me. Further, You have said, "I have singled you out by name, and you have indeed gained My favor." Now, if I have in fact gained Your favor, let me know Your ways, that I may know You and continue in Your favor.... Let me behold Your Presence!'

Moses' bold request is, in a way, met by God. The text continues:

> And He said: 'I will make all My goodness pass before you as I proclaim the name Lord before you: I will be gracious to whom I will be gracious, and I will show compassion to whom I will show compassion. But...you cannot see My face, for man cannot see Me and live.' And the Lord said, 'See, there is a place near Me. Station yourself on the rock and, as My Presence passes by, I will put you in a cleft of the rock and shield you with My hand, until I have passed by. Then I will take My hand away and you will see My back, but My face must not be seen.'

Moses' spiritual growth has brought with it a new awareness of God. From the burning bush the Lord had declared (Exod. 3.14) " 'I will be who/what I will be.' " On Mt. Sinai, in the Golden Calf episode, the Lord expands on this by asserting that His "goodness" is not, in any precise and specific way, predictable: " 'I will be gracious to whom I will be gracious.' " That is, Moses comes to know not only that he does not know the ways of God, but that he cannot know them. One of the key distinctions between Moses and the people is Moses' awareness of his ignorance. His lack of knowledge seems related to the Lord's uniqueness; He is unlike anything or anyone else in Heaven and on the Earth. What we saw in the stories in Genesis remains true in the saga of Moses: the biblical God is essentially incomprehensible. Which is not to say that man knows nothing of God. The manner in which God is pictured creating the Heaven and the Earth (God creates by the power of his "word") suggests that there may be no limit to God's power. In fact, in the Hebrew Bible, whatever limitations exist in God are self-imposed.

The most basic Self-limitation is His allowing man the freedom to create his destiny. The biblical contexts we have thus far examined make it clear that God wants man to fashion his destiny in accordance with the moral norms. That man, nonetheless, so persistently acts immorally causes the biblical writers to express wonderment that this awesomely unique and powerful God continues to care for man.

We saw this caring for man by God, for instance, in the Flood story when God enters into a covenant with mankind in spite of, one might say because of, His knowledge of man's proclivity for evil. Here, in the Golden Calf episode, God's grace filled concern for mankind is spelled out in detail. The gist of God's communication with Moses on Mt. Sinai is the so-called Ten Commandments. Moses shatters the stone tablets on which these commandments were recorded when he, in anger, sees the people worshipping the golden objects. Moses replaces the two stone tablets and carves on them the same God-given words. The text continues (Exod. 34:5 ff.) :

> And the Lord came down in a cloud; He stood with Moses and proclaimed the name Lord. The Lord passed before him and He proclaimed: 'The Lord, the Lord, a God compassionate and gracious, slow to anger, great in loyalty and truth; showing loyalty to the thousandth generation, forgiving iniquity, transgression, and sin; but He does not refrain from all punishments; He visits the iniquity of the fathers upon children and children's children, up to the third and fourth generations.'

Thus, for the biblical God, good deeds have a much more lasting effect than do bad deeds. God's declaration here is a rephrasing of what He said on giving the Ten Commandments (Exod. 20:5):

> 'Do not bow down to them [replications of any natural object] or serve them. For I the Lord your God am a jealous God, visiting the guilt of the fathers upon the children, up to the third and fourth generations of those who reject Me, but showing loyalty to the thousandth generation of those who love Me and keep My commandments.'

God does not reward and punish as does man. In man's system of justice the punishment is to fit the crime. Were God, however, to apply the strict standards of justice to man, man would quickly be wiped off the face of the earth.

God's magnanimous concern for man is at the heart of the book of Jonah, one of the most famous and shortest books in the Hebrew Bible. That book begins with the prophet Jonah disobeying a direct divine command. The Lord orders the prophet east by land to denounce Ninevah, the capital city of Assyria. Jonah forthwith heads west by sea. The biblical writer does not give the reader a clue as to Jonah's motives for disobeying this divine directive. A series of miraculous events (a supernatural storm at sea, the prophet's survival for three days and three nights in the belly of a great fish), convince the reluctant prophet to carry out his prophetic commission. He pronounces Ninevah's doom and then witnesses the repentance of the city's inhabitants and God's subsequent decision to spare the city.

The biblical narrator then discloses what had prompted Jonah to defy God. The narrator relates that when the Lord decided not to destroy Ninevah (4:1–2):

> This displeased Jonah greatly. and he was very angry. And he prayed to the Lord, saying, 'O Lord, is not this what I anticipated when I was still in my native land, therefore I fled to Tarshish. For I know that you are a compassionate and gracious God, slow to anger, with great loyalty, renouncing punishment.'

Jonah paraphrases the two texts in Exodus which we cited above. Those contexts had to do with the biblical God's relationship with the people Israel. The book of Jonah makes clear that God's magnanimity extends to pagan humanity. In fact, in the book of Jonah it is they who exhibit sincere contrition while Jonah, an Israelite prophet, wants them demolished. Unlike Abraham and Moses who, as it were, remind God of His magnanimity, Jonah accuses God of being too soft-hearted. Jonah, by exhibiting a pride filled indignation at God's compassionate concern for the Assyrians, symbolizes everything a prophet should not be. But whatever the differences between Jonah on the one hand and Abraham and Moses on the other, the principle of God's compassionate concern for mankind is the same in all three stories. This principle is one of the overriding themes of the Hebrew Bible.

No human character is allowed to overshadow this principle of God's magnanimity. While Moses, for instance, stands head and shoulders above any other human being in the Hebrew Bible, it is clear that it is not the person of Moses but principles such as God's gracious concern for man which are to endure. Consider how the story of Moses concludes. Near the end of his life the Lord grants him a view of the Promised Land, the land in which the people led by Moses, but not Moses himself, will settle. The narrator then reports the death of Moses as follows (Deut. 34:5 ff.):

> So Moses the servant of the Lord died there in the land of Moab, at the command of God. And He buried him in a valley in the land of Moab opposite Beth-peor, and no one knows his burial place to this day. Moses, at the time of his death, was one hundred and twenty years old; but his eyes were not dimmed nor was his vigor abated.... Never again in Israel did there arise a prophet like Moses whom the Lord knew face to face.

The narrator, be it noted, is careful to point out that "...no one knows his burial place to this day." Moses' burial place will never become a shrine. For Moses is to be remembered, the biblical storyteller suggests, by being true to the values for which he stood. It is not to be wondered at, therefore, that the biblical contexts following the story of Moses rarely refer to him by name. But, as we will see, these contexts emphasize the same values and ideals for which the great prophet lived and died.

As the biblical narrative continues after the death of Moses, it is clear that biblical Israel, for the most part, is not true to these ideals. Although the Israelites succeed in gaining first a foothold in and then dominion over the Promised Land, they almost immediately adopt the idolatrous ways of the Canaanites, the native population which they displace. The first years of settlement are marked by a callous indifference by the tribes to their kinship responsibilities. This leads to one confrontation after another among the Israelite tribes. The virtual anarchy of this period is abandoned eventually in favor of the ordered regimes of kings. But while the monarchs of Israel succeed in bringing a measure of material prosperity to Israel, they are condemned repeatedly by the prophets for undermining the nation's spiritual well-being. It is noteworthy, however, that the Israelite kings sometimes employ prophets who support, and in fact praise their policies.

In an episode recorded in 1 Kings 22 the king's prophets number four hundred while there is but one prophet who stands outside the establishment. We turn to an examination of this episode in order to begin to understand some of the differences between these two kinds of prophets. In this chapter the kings of Israel and Judah confer to decide whether or not to go to war against Syria. The four hundred prophets, who are in the employ of Israel's king, with one voice predict success. The king of Judah, perhaps suspicious in the face of this prophetic unanimity, asks for another prophetic opinion. The Israelite king answers that there is another prophet but " '...I hate him, because he never prophesies anything good concerning me, but only misfortune, [his name is] Micaiah the son of Imlah.' " The Judean king prevails upon the Israelite monarch to fetch Micaiah. The royal messenger implores Micaiah to corroborate what the four hundred have advised. Micaiah's reply is: " 'I will speak only what the Lord tells me.' " When he appears before the kings he declares, his words dripping with sarcasm, that of course they will find success in their military venture. The Israelite king denounces Micaiah and jails him. Micaiah assures the king that his mission will fail and that he will die in battle. The kings do make war on Syria, their forces are routed, and the Israelite king is mortally wounded.

Is a decisive difference between prophets like Micaiah and what we can only call "false" prophets the ability to predict future events correctly? The problem with this criterion is that prophets like Isaiah and Jeremiah, who are obviously considered true prophets of the Lord by the biblical tradition, are frequently wrong in their predictions. Isaiah, for instance, anticipates an eternal reign for the Davidic monarchy. He also foretells, incorrectly, the simultaneous collapse of Syria and the Northern Kingdom. Jeremiah, perhaps the greatest of the prophets after Moses, envisions a time when "northern kings" would erect thrones at Jerusalem's gates. As far as we know, this never happened. He also predicts inaccurately the utter destruction of Anatoth, his hometown. He is certain, too, that a king named Jehoiakim will receive the "burial of an ass," i.e., not be buried at all. This also never happened. Along the same lines, he asserts that King

Zedekiah, who is in fact hauled off to Babylon after having his eyes bored out by the Babylonians, will die "in peace." He believes, moreover, that the Judean exiles in Babylon will be compelled to worship other gods. As far as can be determined, however, the Judeans were able to practice their own religion. And he predicts that the Babylonians will come down and lay Egypt to waste and exile the Egyptians, a prediction never borne out by events.

Aside, however, from the many inaccurate predictions preserved in the books of "true" prophets, there is in the book of Deuteronomy an explicit repudiation of using the ability to foretell the future as a criterion of true prophecy. The text (13:2–6) reads as follows:

> If there should arise in your midst a prophet or dream-diviner and he gives you a sign or portent, and the sign or portent of which he spoke comes to pass, and if he says 'let us serve other gods whom you do not know,' you are not to listen to the words of this prophet or dream-diviner, for the Lord is testing you to determine whether you love the Lord your God with all your heart and all your soul. You are to follow the Lord your God; you are to fear Him; you are to obey His commandments; you are to listen to His voice; you are to worship and cleave to Him. And as for the prophet or dream-diviner [who urged apostasy], he shall be put to death, for he preached falsehood concerning the Lord your God—Who brought you out of the land of Egypt and Who redeemed you from the house of bondage—so that you would stray from the path that the Lord your God commanded you to follow. Thus will you sweep out evil from your midst.

In the above passage from Deuteronomy the supernatural capacity to "see" into the future is not indicative of true prophecy. How then can a "false" prophet accomplish this feat? According to the above citation God sometimes makes it possible for "false" prophets to foretell the future in order to test the faith of biblical Israel. If the individual who displays this extraordinary capacity calls on the people to commit apostasy, which is to say, if that individual attempts to persuade the people to violate the first two commandments, that "prophet" or "dream-diviner" is to be put to death.

The essential criterion which separates the "true" from the "false" prophet is, according to the context in Deuteronomy, observance of the Lord's commands given to Israel by God through the prophet Moses. These commandments spell out the moral stipulations which are to guide mankind's private and societal lives.

The biblical prophets are noteworthy not so much for the correctness of their foresight as for their insight that the be all and end all of human existence is the observance of the moral norms spelled out by the biblical God. Thus the prophets of the Lord detail the moral failings of the people and spell out the fatal consequences of moral backsliding. From the perspective of these prophets, history is a nightmarish amalgam of idolatry and apostasy. Therefore, the prevailing mood of the prophetic utterances in the Hebrew Bible is one of doom. The "false" prophets, conversely, are much more upbeat. While the "true" prophets believe the people are deserving of divine chastisement, the "false" prophets believe that God should reward the people.

A context in the book of Jeremiah (28:1–17) illustrates this last point. There Jeremiah is pictured warning the King that a proposed alliance against the Babylonians can only fail. Another prophet who is present, named Hananiah, predicts success. Of note here is not the accuracy of Jeremiah's prediction (events proved him right), but his conviction that the Israelite people were doomed because of immoral behavior. Here is part of what the prophet says (8:10 ff.):

> For from the least to the most significant,
> They are all greedy for gain;
> Priest and prophet alike,
> They all act falsely.
> They offer false healing
> For the wounds of My poor people,
> Saying, 'peace, peace,'
> When there is no peace.
> They have acted shamefully;
> They have done awful things—
> Yet they do not feel shame,
> They cannot be made to blush.
> But certainly, they will fall,
> They will stumble at the time of their doom.
> So says the Lord.

Then, in chapter twenty three, the prophet contrasts the terrible words he feels compelled to declare to the soothing words of the false prophets (23:9 ff.):

In regard to the prophets.
My heart is broken,
All my bones are trembling;
I have become like a drunken man,
Like one overcome by wine—
Because of the Lord and His sacred word.
...Thus said the Lord of Hosts:
Do not listen to the words of the prophets
Who prophesy to you.
They are misleading you.
The prophecies they speak come out of their own minds,
Not from the Lord....
They declare [in the Lord's name]
'All shall be well with you;'
And to all who follow their willful hearts they say:
'No evil shall befall you.'

We can see, then, that according to Jeremiah the "false" prophets tailor their words for popular consumption. They tell the people, especially the rich and the powerful, what they want to hear. Prophets like Jeremiah, conversely, torment both themselves and the people with their harsh words. It is easy to understand why the "false" prophets were both popular and employable and why prophets like Jeremiah were lone wolves. The people did not like being told that they were behaving in a contemptible fashion. And they certainly did not like hearing that they were about to be visited by the wrath of God.

To repeat: the activities and messages of "true" prophets preserved in the Hebrew Bible suggest that it is not their ability to predict the future or to perform miraculous signs which characterizes biblical prophecy but, rather, the substance of what they said. With very few exceptions, the prophets who have books named after them were not pictured working miracles.

There are, however, a series of narratives in the books of Kings which are filled with a dazzling array of prophetic miracles: revivification, instantaneous cures, the calling down of fire from Heaven, the sustenance of life on meager food supplies, and so on. We turn now to a consideration of some of these narratives in order to see how the miraculous events function in them.

In 1 Kings 13 a "man of God" from Judah journeys, at the behest of the Lord, to the northern shrine at Bethel to foretell the havoc which will be wrought there several centuries later by a king named Josiah. Two wonders attend the pronouncement: the altar cracks wide open, and the arm of the Northern King (Jeroboam), suddenly arrested by paralysis when he seeks to restrain the man of God, is restored to health when the man of God prays to the Lord. A prophet in Bethel learns of the man of God's confrontation with the King and overtakes the man of God as he is returning to Judah. When the man of God refuses to delay his return trip (on the ground of a divine charge not to eat or drink in Bethel and to return immediately to Judah by a route different from that which brought him there), the Bethel prophet declares (v. 18): " 'I am a prophet like you; an angel addressed me with the Lord's charge: "Fetch him back to your home to eat and drink." ' " Now the man of God, believing the prophet, accepts. But while the two of them dine the host prophet receives the word of God which he proclaims to the man of God: because the man of God disobeyed the Lord's express command, he would die enroute home and fail of interment in his ancestral sepulchre. The man of God sets off on an ass provided by his host but is slain by a lion; the possibility of coincidence is precluded by the ass's not bolting and the lion's remaining at the spot, molesting neither beast nor carcass. When the Bethel prophet learns of this he charges his sons that when he dies he is to be buried along with the man of God. The Bethel prophet then declares that the events predicted by the nameless man of God will surely come to pass. This episode ends with the following observation by the narrator (1 Kings 13:33–34):

> After this event, Jeroboam did not turn from his evil way, but continued to appoint priests for the shrines from the ranks of the people [rather than from priestly families]. He ordained as priests of the shrines any who so desired. In this way did the House of Jeroboam incur guilt, to their utter annihilation from off the face of the earth.

One clear message in this episode is the absolute primacy of a personal revelation. The man of God disobeyed a divine directive on the basis of a hearsay report from a prophet who turned out to be lying. Our attention, however, is directed to the role and function of the miraculous in this strange story. There is no doubt that the man of God is a miracle worker; and, of course, the manner of his death is extraordinary. But, and this is the crucial point, there is also no doubting that his miracles are not faith-producing. Consider the following facts:

— the man of God, who performs the miracles, disobeys a directive from God, the very source of his miraculous capacity;

— the Bethel prophet, who heard what the man of God did, and in no way doubted the report, and who, moreover, is himself a prophet, lies to the man of God.

— King Jeroboam, who witnessed the miracles first hand, does not deviate from his evil ways because of the experience.

Whatever other complexities may lurk in this tale, it seems clear that the supernatural events have little or no impact on the characters who perform them, witness them, and hear about them.

Let us now turn to a somewhat more complicated example. The cycle of stories involving Elijah, one of the most famous of biblical prophets, begins (in 1 Kings 17) with the prophet's declaration that it will not rain until he himself announces an end to the drought. The drought is Heaven sent punishment for the pagan ways of Ahab the king of Israel and his Phoenician queen, Jezebel. Two years pass during which famine ravages the land. As for Elijah, he goes into hiding in Phoenicia (present day Lebanon). When he reappears, Elijah proposes to Ahab that there be a prophetic convocation on Mt. Carmel, a bluff in northern Israel overlooking the Mediterranean Sea, to determine whether the Lord, God of Israel, or Baal, a pagan god worshipped by Jezebel, is truly God. That Baal was enormously popular in Ahab's time is made evident by the fact that four hundred and fifty prophets muster for Baal at Carmel while Elijah alone represents the Lord. What follows is worth quoting at length (1 Kings 18:20 ff.):

And Ahab sent orders to all Israelites and assembled the prophets at Mount Carmel. Then Elijah drew near the people and said, 'how long will you keep shifting opinions? If the Lord is God, go after him; if Baal, then follow after him.' But the people did not respond, not even a word. Elijah said to the people: 'I alone am left as prophet to the Lord and the prophets of Baal number four hundred and fifty men. Let two young bulls be given to us. Let them choose one bull, cut it up, and lay it on the wood, but let them not apply fire; I will prepare the other bull, and lay it on the wood, and will not apply fire. You will then call on your god by name, and I will call on the Lord by name; and it will be that the god who responds with fire, that one is God.' And the people answered, 'Very good.' And Elijah said to the prophets of Baal, You choose one bull and prepare it first, for you are the majority; call on your god by name but apply no fire. They took the bull that was given them; they prepared it and called on Baal by name from morning until noon, shouting 'O Baal, answer us!' But there was no sound, and no one responded; so they performed a hopping dance around the altar that had been set up.

When noon came, Elijah ridiculed them saying, 'Yell louder! After all he is a god. But he may be in conversation, he may be detained, or he may be on a journey, or perhaps he is sound asleep and will wake up.' So they yelled louder, and mutilated themselves with knives and spears—as was their custom—until the blood poured all over them. When noon passed, they kept raving.... Still there was no sound, and none who responded or heeded. Then Elijah said to all the people, 'Come closer to me;' and all the people drew nearer to him.... Around the altar he made a trench.... He arranged the wood and he cut up the bull and placed it on the wood. And he said, 'Fill four jars with water and pour it over the burnt offering and the wood.' Then he said, 'Do it again,' and they did it yet another time. The water ran down around the altar, and even the trench was filled with water. When it was time to present the meal offering, the prophet Elijah came forward and said, 'O Lord, God of Abraham, Isaac, and Israel! Let it be known today that You are God in Israel and that I am Your servant, and that I have done all these things at Your bidding. Answer me, O Lord, answer me, that this people may know that You, O Lord, are God; and that You have turned their hearts backward.' And fire of the Lord came down and ate up the offering and the wood and the stones and the dust and the water which ran in the trench. And when the people saw [this] they fell on their faces and they said, 'The Lord, He is God. The Lord, He is God.' And Elijah said to them, 'grab the prophets of Baal, do not let them escape.' They grabbed them and Elijah took them down to the Brook Kishon and slaughtered them there.

On the face of it this episode seems clear enough. In it, Elijah, the one true spokesman for the one true God, wins a great victory which results in the elimination of the Baal prophecy. Not one of the Baal prophets escapes. However, several details in the episode itself, as well as in what follows, obscure what seems to be the explicit point of the narrative.

First of all, why is Elijah the one representative of the Lord, God of Israel, while four hundred and fifty prophets assemble for Baal?

And this within the borders of Israel where Baal is the interloper. Also, what are we to make of the people Israel's silence when Elijah challenges them to declare for either the Lord or Baal? And why do they enthusiastically agree to Elijah's proposal for a contest? What, too, is the meaning of Elijah's beseeching the Lord to send fire from heaven that will demonstrate " '...that You are God in Israel and that I am Your servant...' " and that " '...You have turned their hearts backward' "? Finally, what of the grisly slaughter of the Baal prophets?

These questions can only be answered in the light of what follows this episode. In the very next chapter, Queen Jezebel is shown remaining undaunted following the slaughter of her minions (1 Kings 19:1–2): "When Ahab told Jezebel all that Elijah had done and how he had put all the prophets [of Baal] to the sword, Jezebel sent a messenger to Elijah, saying, 'Thus and more may the gods do [to me] if by this time tomorrow I have not made you like one of them.' " Moreover, the normally intrepid Elijah takes flight into the southern wilderness where he declares that once again he is the lone holdout for the Lord. Elijah, in fact, is so distraught that he longs for death. In the immediate aftermath of his stupendous victory on Mount Carmel he had been filled with such exultation that he was able to run the marathon distance from Mount Carmel to Jezreel before the onrushing chariot of Ahab. Now he is depicted in such despair that he goes off alone into the wilderness to die.

Let us now return to the episode on Mount Carmel. The narrator makes it clear that Elijah is in fact a true prophet of the Lord. If then, as Elijah claims, he alone represents the Lord, it seems reasonable to conclude that Israel has turned its back on the Lord in favor of the pagan god Baal; Israel has thus repudiated its ancient and enduring covenant with the Lord which entailed worship of the Lord alone. When Elijah challenges the people to declare for the Lord or Baal, the people adopt a wait and see attitude. Literally. That is why they so enthusiastically agree to Elijah's proposed contest. For them, seeing will be believing. And after they witness the great miracle wrought by the Lord through Elijah, they do indeed seem to declare for the Lord.

But do the people declare for the Lord in a meaningful fashion and for the right reasons? In a short while that which Jezebel represents, which is to say the worship of Baal, is again dominant. This is evident from the following details in the story:

— Elijah's reason for his flight to the southern wilderness is that he alone represents the Lord;

— when Elijah pleads his case to the Lord he places the blame squarely on the people Israel (1 Kings 19:10): " '...the Israelites have forsaken Your covenant, torn down Your altars, and put Your prophets to the sword. I alone am left, and they are out to take my life.' "

Here, as elsewhere in the Hebrew Bible, Israel's covenant with the Lord is characterized by God's words in Gen. 18: " 'For I have singled him [Abraham] out, that he may instruct his children and his posterity to keep the way of the Lord by doing what is just and right....' "

In the Mount Carmel episode, the people take for convincing evidence not their ancient and enduring covenant with God, whose hallmark is the all importance of moral behavior, but supernatural fire from heaven. From the very moment the people refuse to commit themselves when Elijah demands: " 'If the Lord is God, follow Him; and if Baal, follow him!' " the people have violated the covenant. For worship of Baal in the story of Elijah is synonymous with immoral behavior. Thus the miracle is meant not to push the people towards faith in the Lord but further away from it. And this is exactly what Elijah declares when he calls down the fire from heaven (1 Kings 18:37):

'Answer me, O Lord, answer me, that this people may know that You, O Lord, are God; and that You have turned their hearts backward.'

The miracle not only has no lasting impact on the people; it itself is indicative of the people's lack of faith. The slaughter of the Baal prophets, in which not a one escapes, must surely be a symbolic act. For if none escaped, why is Elijah still alone in representing the Lord? The people mistakenly believe that the problem does not lie in them, whereas according to Elijah in his lament to the Lord, it is the " '...Israelites who have forsaken Your covenant, torn down Your altars, and put Your prophets to the sword.' " In matters of faith, doing, not seeing, is believing. And the doing must be connected with what is just and right.

The same motifs recur in the other episodes in the story of Elijah and that of his disciple Elisha. The two prophets are able to perform one miracle after another, and yet neither prophet is able to win a significant following. In 2 Kings 5, for instance, we are introduced to Namaan, a Syrian general who comes to Israel seeking a cure for his leprosy. The King of Israel is fearful that Namaan's visit is a Syrian ploy to instigate hostilities against Israel when Namaan can find no cure. Elisha sends word to the King that there is nothing to fear because he, Elisha, will cure the Syrian general of his incurable disease. Elisha tells the dubious Namaan to " 'bathe seven times in the Jordan and your flesh shall be restored and you shall be clean.' " Namaan's servants prevail upon him to at least give Elisha's cure a chance. Miraculously, it works. The grateful Namaan, a pagan be it remembered, declares that " '...there is no God in the whole world except in Israel!' " and he urges Elisha to accept a gift. Elisha refuses. But before Namaan has gone on his homeward journey Gehazi, the servant of Elisha, overtakes Namaan and says:

> 'My master has sent me to say: two youths, disciples of the prophets, have just come to me from the hill country of Ephraim. Please give them a talent of silver and two changes of clothing.'

The grateful Namaan is only too willing to do so and urges Gehazi to take two talents of silver rather than just one. Gehazi hides the gift in his home. However, when he goes to Elisha the man of God asserts: " 'Did not my spirit go along when a man [Namaan] got down from his chariot to meet you? Is this a time to take money in order to buy clothing and olive groves and vineyards, sheep and oxen, and male and female slaves?' " Elisha then miraculously afflicts Gehazi with the very same disease that had brought Namaan to Israel.

This episode indicates that not simply were prophets like Elijah and Elisha unable to win a following among the people, but they failed as well to impress those closest to them. Gehazi, in other episodes, has seen his master do extraordinary things. Yet Gehazi does not hesitate to act contrary to his master's will and, what is

more important, contrary to the Power whom his master serves. For
no individual who is deemed worthy of the supreme honorific "man of
God" (as Elisha is here) ever accepts payment for his services. To do
so, of course, would be to reap material benefit from the service of
God.

In this episode the miraculous is no more productive of faith in
Gehazi than it was productive of faith in the Israelite people in the
Mount Carmel tale. Do such stories not teach that miracles cannot, in
and of themselves, either produce or sustain faith in the faithless?
For in these tales, and they are not alone in the Hebrew Bible, the
most extraordinary events make lasting impress only, ironically, on
the pagan Namaan. According to such stories, to those who have faith
in the Lord miracles are unnecessary, and to those who do not have
the requisite faith miracles do not produce lasting belief. Such
miracle stories reaffirm what we learned in the saga of Moses. There
we saw that that which distinguishes the "true" prophet from the
"false" is the content of their messages and not the ability to call
down fire from heaven. And although the prophets do not use the
same words, images, or metaphors, the substance of what each of
them says is identical.

We turn now to an analysis of the essential characteristics of
biblical prophecy. A quality which is shared by so many of the biblical
prophets as to make it a motif of biblical prophecy is the denunciation
of those norms which regulate societal life. Amos, for instance,
accuses the rulers and the powerful of eighth century Israel of the
misuse of their power. He condemns them for crushing the poor and
the weak, for subverting the moral values of biblical Israel's religion
by using the religious institutions to serve themselves rather than
God, and for defrauding and thereby impoverishing the common
people by their corrupt business practices. Read now Amos' own
words (2:4 ff.):

> '...They have rejected the Teaching of the Lord
> And have not followed His laws...
> ...They have sold for silver
> Those whose cause was just,
> And the needy for a pair of sandals.'

(5:7 ff.):

> 'Ah, you who turn justice into wormwood
> And hurl righteousness to the ground!
> ...you put a tax on the impoverished
> And take from them a levy of grain.'

Amos' remedy for the ills of the nation-state is as clear as his indictment (5:14):

> 'Seek good and not evil,
> That you may live...
> Hate evil and love good,
> And establish justice in the gate' [the place of legal inquiries]

Micah, another eighth century prophet, proclaims that the Judah of his day is filled with hypocrites who pretend to worship the Lord but who in fact pay homage only to their pride-filled ambition. Like Amos, Micah laments the fact that evildoers often cloak their injustices in the mantel of the religious ideology of biblical Israel. That is, those whose behavior evinces no real concern for the moral principles on which worship of the Lord depends, dress themselves in fine garb on the religious festivals and appear at the Temple with the required offerings and by so doing pretend or perhaps actually believe that they have fulfilled their religious obligations.

Isaiah compares eighth century Judah to vineyards carefully planted and tended by God which will henceforth produce only briars and thorns because of the immoral behavior of the Judeans. He declares that Jerusalem has degenerated to the level of Sodom, which the Lord leveled because of its immorality. Jeremiah sounds the same refrain: he condemns seventh century Judah because its inhabitants claim to worship a God who demands moral behavior by creating a society in which lying, deceit, treachery, slander, adultery, avarice, and fraud are the order of the day.

The above examples could be multiplied a hundredfold. The prophetic writings overflow with denunciations of the standards which sustain and nourish their societies. The premise which supports these condemnations is that man is not definable strictly in terms of his societal setting. As we noted in the Tower of Babel story, the differences which separate Israelite from non-Israelite are conventional not natural. Societal, national, and racial differences, from the biblical perspective, are no more significant than variations in hair, skin, and eye color. Man, therefore, is not a slave to the norms of his particular time and place. Man can appeal to norms which transcend his time and place in order to evaluate his society. For the Lord, God of Israel, underwrites the moral norms; and the biblical God is not limited by time or space.

This principle finds expression in our own Declaration of Independence: "We hold these truths to be self-evident, that all men are created equal, that they are endowed by their Creator with certain inalienable Rights, that among these are Life, Liberty, and the pursuit of Happiness." As did Jefferson ("...they are endowed by their Creator"), the prophets traced this principle to God. Man's Godgiven capacity to appreciate the good and to act in accordance with that appreciation enabled him to participate in the Divine nature, and it established a common bond among all men, no matter what their national or racial background. We have already seen this at work in the story of David and Bathsheba when David, the greatest of biblical Israel's kings, is unambiguously condemned while the Hittite Uriah speaks and acts for God. Moral behavior and not national, ethnic, or racial origin is the determining factor in evaluating human beings.

In a story in the book of Kings (1 Kings 21) King Ahab proposes to buy a vineyard from a man named Naboth because it abuts the King's property. When Naboth refuses the King's offer, reminding the King in the process that under no circumstances would he consider selling the property on which his ancestors are buried, Ahab returns home in a sullen mood. Jezebel, his pagan wife, moves quickly to procure the vineyard for her husband. She fabricates charges against Naboth and suborns witnesses to testify against him. Naboth and his heirs are executed. As Ahab hurries to take possession of his new toy the Lord sends Elijah to condemn the King's action:

> Thus said the Lord: 'Would you murder and take possession?' Thus said the Lord: 'Since dogs lapped up Naboth's blood, the dogs will lap up your blood too.'

In this episode it is clear that Ahab is not above the law. And the "law" referred to is God's law, given through Moses, which mandates moral behavior. In this story Ahab and Jezebel lie and murder in order to steal Naboth's vineyard. Since the Lord sends the prophet Elijah to Ahab and not to Jezebel we can conclude that Ahab is responsible for his behavior. He has allowed himself to be influenced by his pagan wife. And since in the very first episode of the Elijah story we meet a righteous pagan woman we cannot conclude that what is wrong in biblical Israel is simply attributable to pagans. What is wrong in biblical Israel, from the point of view of the prophets, is that the Israelites are not abiding by the terms of their covenant with God. Which is to say that the prophets do not call for a holy war to eradicate pagans; rather, the prophets call for a change in the direction of the lives of individual Israelites and in the life of the body politic.

The biblical prophets point to human pride as the real source of what is wrong in biblical Israel. In Ahab's case, the king revelled in the power that was his as king and this led him to trample on the inalienable rights of another human being. Ahab, glorying in his own power, in effect worshipped only himself. Worship of self is the inevitable consequence of pride. And worship of self is the indispensable ingredient in the biblical sin of idolatry. Eradicating images of gods other than the Lord will no more stamp out idolatry than liquidating Jezebel would have made Ahab upright. An Israelite who claimed to worship the Lord, who appeared at the Temple on the prescribed occasions, who dutifully followed the religious rituals, would still be guilty of idolatrous behavior if, in fact, he worshipped only himself. The mere stated belief that the Lord is the one true God of the Heaven and the Earth does not itself eradicate idolatry. The belief in the Lord must, according to the prophets, be translated into meaningful action. Idolatry can be uprooted only when mankind worships the Lord properly. And the proper worship of the Lord leads to the erecting and maintaining of just societies. The first two commandments of the Decalogue which proscribe idolatry are comprehensible only in light of the following eight commandments. The first two commandments forbid the worship of that which man himself can make. The last eight commandments order the worship of that which is of divine origin: the moral norms which transcend time and space. That is, the first two commandments assert that only the Lord is to be worshipped, while the next eight indicate how He is to be worshipped. Ahab, in effect, broke four of the ten commandments. He coveted his neighbor's property; he stole; he murdered; and he bore false witness. In the deepest sense of the word, therefore, Ahab was an idolater.

The stories concerning the prophets in the books of Samuel and Kings indicate that the prophets won few converts to their cause of loving God with all of one's heart, all of one's soul, and with all of one's might. The people and their leaders continued to revel in the works of their making. The greatest and most powerful of the kings, David and his son Solomon, are shown breaking virtually every commandment. After Solomon builds the great Temple to the Lord in Jerusalem, he is warned by God that (1 Kings 9:6 f.): " 'if you and your descendants turn away from Me and do not keep the commandments and the laws which I have set before you, and go and serve other gods and worship them, then I will sweep Israel off the land which I gave them....' ' Then little more than a chapter later the narrator relates that in Solomon's old age "...his wives turned away Solomon's heart after other gods...." Again, as in the case of Ahab and Jezebel, the real culprit is not Solomon's pagan marriages but his pagan behavior. And the essence of pagan or idolatrous behavior was self worship. Idolatrous practices penetrated places of worship where pomp and ceremony, pleasing to man, obscured those spiritual concerns which the religious practice was designed to further. Thus the prophet Amos' lament: "Come to Bethel [scene of an important shrine] and transgress, to Gilgal [also the location of a major shrine] and multiply transgression."

In the face of this perversion of the true worship of the Lord, some prophets raised the specter of Israel's exile from the Promised Land. For if the people Israel could not establish a just society how was it to be a "blessing" for the rest of mankind? Some of the prophets warned that divine punishment would be so severe that the people would at last be jolted into the realization that idolatrous behavior is self-destructive. Some of the prophets looked beyond the imminent disaster to a future time when there would be harmony in the human community. This hope apparently was based more on their faith in a loyal and compassionate God than it was in man's capacity to repent. It is worth noting that when last seen in the Hebrew Bible, the people Israel—far from being the spiritual center of mankind—constitute a small and almost completely uninfluential province in the vast Persian empire. And in one of the final ironies recorded in the biblical text, the reader is informed that the pagan Persians must prod the Judeans to rebuild their Temple in Jerusalem.

Why were the prophets unable to exert more influence? The answer may be found in man's headstrong nature. Thus, for instance, when Isaiah receives his "call" to prophetic service, he is told that the people will not heed him (6:10): " 'This people's wits are dulled, their ears are plugged up and their eyes blinded, so that they cannot see with their eyes, nor listen with their ears, nor understand with their wits, so that they could turn and be healed.' " This is reminiscent of Moses' call (Exod. 3:21): "And the Lord said to Moses: 'When you return to Egypt, see that you perform before Pharaoh all the marvels that I have put within your power. I, however, will stiffen his heart so that he will not let the people go.' " As we saw, although the Israelites are finally able to get out of Egypt, neither they nor the Egyptians are converted to the service of the moral norms which lie at the heart of Moses' mission.

However, since so many pages in the Hebrew Bible are devoted to prophets and prophecy, it can be seen that, from the biblical perspective, to fail in the service of the Lord is more deserving of praise than to succeed in the service of man. For the right kind of failure at least points to what is just and proper, while the wrong kind of success merely inflates man's already bloated image of his own self-importance. One of the central affirmations of biblical prophecy is that the most powerful man is as nothing when compared with God whose power is boundless. In the words of Amos (5:8):

> Who made the Pleiades and Orion,
> Who turns deep darkness into dawn
> And darkens day into night,
> Who summons the waters of the sea
> And pours them out upon the earth—

His name is the Lord!

Or consider the words of Isaiah (2:12 ff.):

> For the Lord of Hosts has ready a day
> Against all who is proud and haughty.
> Against all who is high—so that he be brought low:
> ...then man's arrogance should be humbled
> And the pride of man brought low.
> None but the Lord shall be exalted in that day.
> As for idols, they shall vanish completely.
> And men shall enter caverns in the rock
> And holes in the ground—
> Before the terror of the Lord—
> And His awesome majesty,
> When He comes forth to overcome the earth.
> ...Oh, cease to glorify man,
> Who has only a breath in his nostrils!

From the prophetic standpoint, those who exulted most in their strength were in fact the weakest, the most to be pitied. Man is guilty of the worst kind of self-destructive stupidity: he continually trifles with an all powerful God who demands only that man act in his own best interests. Moreover, it is neither baffling nor beyond man's reach. In the last speech of Moses, the great prophet declares (Deut. 30:11–14):

> This commandment which I command you this day is not too wondrous for you, nor is it beyond your capacity. It is not in Heaven, that you should say, 'Who will go up for us to Heaven and get it for us and impart it to us, that we may observe it?' Neither is it beyond the sea that you should say, 'who will cross the sea for us and get it for us and cause us to hear it that we might do it.' No, the thing is very close to you, in your mouth and in your heart, to do it.

Moses and the other biblical prophets appeal to moral norms which are, or should be, clearly recognizable by men. What is clear to the prophets is or should be clear to all men. The prophets speak because they expect to be understood.

The Genesis story of beginnings declared that man was created in the image of God. The Eden tale then elaborated on the meaning of the concept of "image;" in that tale we saw that this concept has to do with the supreme dignity of humankind and the godlike capacity to create. Man is given the extraordinary power to create his destiny for good or for ill. Most biblical narratives are devoted to descriptions of how man misuses this power. The prophets condemned the people because the people were free to act otherwise:

— the people could have chosen the good;

— the people could have protected the rights of the disenfranchised.

The people could have done what is just and proper because to use the words we just quoted from Deuteronomy, the inclination to do the good was in their "mouths and hearts."

The biblical prophets proclaim what their listeners should already know. The prophets do not introduce a new theory of knowledge. They do not introduce arcane concepts. And only in rare instances is their use of the subtleties of rhetoric difficult to fathom. The prophets sought to reveal that godlike capacity in man which, in their estimation, separates man from the beast. In this sense, virtually every biblical narrator is a prophet because they all strove to make the reader sense his godlike capacity. This capacity, while not created by man, can be destroyed by man. This gift from God must be nurtured, and this was the task the prophets of the Hebrew Bible took upon themselves. For the most part, they failed. In a way, however, the failure of the prophets was translated into a victory of sorts by those who created and preserved the biblical record. For it is the prophet and not the tyrant (i.e., Elijah and not Ahab, Moses and not the Pharaoh) whom the Hebrew Bible enshrines. More to the point, it is the good in man and not the bad in man (i.e., the David who confesses his wrongdoing after Nathan's parable and not the David who coldly consigns Uriah to the grave) that the biblical authors glorify. Moreover, from out of the prophetic worldview have emerged three world encompassing religious traditions: Judaism, Christianity, and Islam. And from these traditions has come much of the spiritual base on which Western Civilization rests.

The prophets knew with certainty that God requires moral behavior from man. And the prophets also knew with certainty that if man turns his back on the moral norms he will be punished. The prophets repeatedly articulate these certainties. But one will not find in the prophetic writings a clearcut description of the God who mandates morality. The God who showed Moses only His "backparts" remains mysterious and utterly unique. One can see that this God enters into covenants with men and that He honors these agreements. As we saw, these covenants rest on the certainty that God is compassionate, that good deeds are acknowledged by Him for a thousand generations while bad deeds last but four. But of God's other attributes (or "frontparts") the reader learns almost nothing.

Consider again Isaiah's call to prophetic service in the sixth chapter of that prophetic book:

> In the year that King Uzziah died, I beheld my Lord seated on a high and lofty throne; and the skirts of His robe filled the Temple. Seraphs stood in attendance on Him. Each of them had six wings: with two he covered his face, with two he covered his legs [a euphemism for the pudenda], and with two he would fly. And one would call to the other, Holy, holy, holy! The Lord of Hosts! His presence fills all the earth!' The doorposts would quake at the sound of the one who called, and the place kept filling with smoke. I cried, 'Woe is me; I am lost! For I am a man of unclean lips and I live among a people of unclean lips, yet my own eyes have beheld the King, Lord of Hosts.'

Notice in this passage how little one is able to glimpse of God. Even the attendant Seraphs remain, for the most part, hidden from view. Their function in the passage is to proclaim that God is *Kadosh,* a Hebrew term which means holy in the sense of separate or apart or other than. The Seraph's declaration that God is wholly unique is followed by the paradoxical claim that this unique Being chooses to fill the earth with His presence. God's presence, apart from the majestic orderliness of nature, is at least partially dependent on man's being true to his Godgiven potential. Man's ideal destiny is wholly comprehensible (Isaiah 1:16–17):

> Wash yourselves clean;
> Put your evil doings
> Away from My sight.
> Cease to do evil
> Learn to do good
> Devote yourselves to justice;
> Aid the wronged.

Uphold the rights of the orphan;
Defend the cause of the widow.

Prophets attempted to keep intact the link between God and man by urging man to choose the good over the bad.

Based on our analysis of prophets and prophecy, the following conclusions can be drawn:

— the prophet is a spokesman for God to man, and sometimes is a spokesman for man to God;

— God requires that man be true to the transhistorical moral norms; "transhistorical" because these norms derive from a transcendent God who is above time and space;

— although the substance of the prophetic message is simple and easy to comprehend, most men ignore it, and thereby endanger themselves and their societies;

— prophecy is that rare occasion when God's everpresent address to man (to follow the moral norms) evokes a human response.

We will conclude our remarks on prophets and prophecy by looking at parts of the career of Samuel, a prophet in the time that the monarchy takes hold in biblical Israel. The story of Samuel begins with a description of a favored wife, Hannah, who is barren. Hannah's misfortune is compounded by the taunts of Peninah, also a wife of Hannah's husband Elkanah. Hannah prays to the Lord and vows that if she conceives and bears a son she will dedicate the boy to the Lord all the days of his life. She does conceive and bear a son and when the boy, whom she names Samuel, is weaned she takes him to the sanctuary at Shiloh in accordance with her vow.

The sanctuary at Shiloh is overseen by the priest Eli and his sons Hophni and Phinehas. Eli, though a kindly priest, is unable to control his ne'er-do-well sons who regularly misuse their prerogatives as priests. As bad as are Hophni and Phinehas, that good is Samuel as he grows to maturity at the sanctuary.

Eli is warned by an anonymous man of God that the corrupt activities of his sons will bring down disaster upon Eli's house.

The prophetic career of Samuel begins with a notice that in those days prophecy was a rare phenomenon. Late one night the Lord calls to Samuel who, however, never having "heard" the Lord before, mistakes the voice for Eli's. Twice Samuel asks the old priest what he wants and twice the priest tells him that he has not called. The third time Eli understands that the Lord was calling Samuel. Eli tells Samuel to return to where he sleeps and when he hears the voice to respond as follows, " 'Speak, Lord, for Your servant is listening.' " When the Lord calls again Samuel does respond and listens as God pronounces doom on Eli's house because of the nefarious activities of Hophni and Phinehas. The next morning Samuel tells the aged priest what the Lord has told him. The episode ends with a note to the effect that as time passed Samuel's stature and fame as a prophet grew.

This episode is framed by an opening notice to the effect that prophecy was not widespread and a closing observation that the Lord appeared regularly to Samuel, i.e., that prophecy was no longer a rare phenomenon. In between the frame verses we are treated to what seem to be rigmarole exchanges between God and Samuel on the one hand and Samuel and Eli on the other. Why? This episode marks a turning point in the career of Samuel. No longer will he be an apprentice to the priest Eli; he will henceforth travel the path which will take him to a position of extraordinary power in Israel. Samuel will become the most important figure in pre-monarchical Israel and it will be he who, at God's behest, chooses the king designate and writes the constitution for the new form of government. And it will be Samuel, again at God's directive, who chooses the successor to the first king when that monarch disobeys a divine command. Prior to this episode Samuel is presented as a spiritual son of Eli who, in marked contrast to Eli's flesh and blood sons, acts properly. This episode, then, is not so much a beginning as a continuation of the lad Samuel's development. Samuel's lack of experience in prophetic matters is underlined by his inability to recognize the "voice" as God's. Unlike most of the other biblical prophets to whom we are introduced either in adulthood or mid-career, the young Samuel is still in spiritual matters "wet behind the ears." Thus the narrator observes: "Now Samuel had not yet experienced the Lord; the word of the Lord had not yet been revealed to him."

As for Eli, although he finally understands what it is that Samuel is "hearing," Eli is not himself privy to that "sound." This detail is significant. For Eli is a priest and not a prophet and thus has no direct link with God. The priest oversees the cult; the prophet "hears" the direct word of the Lord. But what is it that Samuel "hears" in this his first revelation? The content of this revelation repeats the substance of what the anonymous man of God had already told Eli. To the man of God Eli made no reply. Here Eli is pictured as resigned to his fate: "...Eli said, 'He is the Lord; He will do what in His eyes is good.' " Eli's passivity is in keeping both with his character and his role. It should be remembered that he was unwilling or unable to discipline his wayward sons. And now with Samuel's increasing power as a prophet-statesman the role of the priest will be diminished greatly.

It is to be expected that there is nothing startlingly new about Samuel's revelation since virtually all the prophets do the same thing: inveigh against impiety and injustice. By repeating much of what the man of God has said, Samuel, in effect, becomes part of the spiritual chain of the prophetic movement. This too stands in marked contrast to the priesthood, the links of which are flesh and blood.

One more detail should be noted. The frame verses indicate clearly that in order for the word of God to be "heard," there must be worthy receivers. The prophetic insistence on man's moral responsibility suggests that a "worthy" receiver would be, above all other things, a good human being who urges his fellow human beings to be good.

As we noted, the third major section of the Hebrew Bible is called simply and appropriately "Writings." We noted, too, that the books which constitute this last section of the Hebrew Bible are very diverse. But however varied the books of this last section may be, the themes we have been tracing in the first two sections are equally visible. Everywhere one finds the conviction that man is responsible for his actions because he is capable of not simply discerning the difference between the good and the bad but of realizing that the good should be valued over the bad. The author of the book of Ruth, for example, assumes that the reader will value Ruth's loyalty. And the aphorisms found in the book of Proverbs are unintelligible unless one accepts the author's premise that wisdom, discipline, and frugality are preferable to stupidity, indolence, and extravagance. The same point can be made regarding books like Lamentations and Psalms where the narrator assumes, as a matter of course, that the reader will share his sympathy for the plight of the downtrodden. And unless one shares with the author of Job the value judgment that it is painful to witness the suffering of the righteous, that book becomes no more than an interesting intellectual debate rather than what it is: a scorching indictment of some pollyannish views of God's providence.

Likewise, almost everywhere in the Writings God is conceived as a Being Who:

— relates loyally and compassionately with man;

— bestows and guarantees the efficacy (if not the triumph) of the moral norms.

Furthermore, the mysteriousness of God, so apparent in the first two sections of the Hebrew Bible, is dramatically evident in Job and Ecclesiastes, two books in the last section which document man's ultimate inability to comprehend the ways of God.

In the book of Job God chooses to test a righteous man's sincerity by subjecting him to harrowing sequences of disasters in which his possessions, his children, and his health are stripped from him. The main portion of the book concerns a series of debates Job has with some acquaintances who insist that Job's suffering is a direct result of his having sinned. These acquaintances articulate many of the arguments men have used through the ages to justify the ways of God:

— since all men are imperfect in contrast to God, even the suffering of the seemingly righteous has its justification;

— suffering can be instructive; it can make a good man better;

— since God's wisdom and power are limitless, limited man is in no position to evaluate the ways of God;

— the suffering of the righteous is shortlived; so too is the prosperity of the wicked.

With equal clarity and with greater conviction (because Job knows, as does the reader, that he has not sinned), Job disputes the acquaintances' contention that God is just in the sense that He rewards the good and punishes the bad. Job knows that he does not deserve what has befallen him. And he is convinced that human experience in general testifies not to God's providential concern for man but rather to His callous indifference to man's fate. As Job sees it, man experiences far too much travail on the way to the grave. And after death there is the shadowy world of Sheol where, as Job puts it, worms and maggots are one's closest kin. In fact, Job seems convinced that, if anything, the wicked live longer, happier lives than do the just.

The discussions between Job and the acquaintances become increasingly abrasive and it becomes apparent that only God can settle the dispute. Job first implores and finally challenges God to appear in order to explain His ways. The reader also wants very much to hear from God since the reader knows what none of the disputants in the book knows, namely, that God is the cause of Job's suffering. Moreover, the reader knows that the acquaintances are simply wrong when they accuse Job of having sinned.

When God does appear, His speeches are a source of great amazement for the following reasons:

— the speeches, while filled with a series of powerful images which depict God's grandeur, seem irrelevant in that God seems not to discuss the issue of justice;

— nonetheless, the speeches apparently satisfy Job who, in effect, apologizes for talking of things which he did not understand.

It is clear that God explicitly rebukes the acquaintances who had striven so hard and, at times so brilliantly, to defend Him (42:7 f.):

When the Lord finished speaking to Job, he said to Eliphaz one of the acquaintances, 'I am angry with you and your two companions because you have not spoken properly in regard to Me, as has My servant Job. So now take seven bulls and seven rams, go to My servant Job and offer a whole-offering for yourselves, and he will make intercession for you; I will certainly show him favor by not being harsh with you because you have not spoken properly in regard to Me as he has.'

God's speeches deserve our close attention because at issue is the relationship between God and man, one of the major themes of our inquiry. Much of what God says is given over to a series of rhetorical questions which are joined to observations about His creation. These questions and observations force Job to view things in a new light. Some of the questions are:

— even if Job were, like God, infinite, would Job have the wisdom to set the universe in order?

— does Job have the power to maintain the harmony of the universe?

— has Job ever done anything to promote the order which permeates the universe?

— has Job investigated the heights and recesses of the earth, let alone the universe?

— does Job have any real comprehension of what death and the aftermath of death consist?

— does Job understand the miracles of conception and birth?

— does Job understand the ways of wild animals and birds?

— can Job control many of the beasts which roam the earth, beasts which display courage and dignity, and which choose to have nothing to do with man?

— and if Job cannot comprehend or even in some ways measure up to these beasts, how can he dare presume to evaluate God, the Creator and Maintainer of the natural universe?

These rhetorical questions (rhetorical because God presumably knows the answers to them) point emphatically to this conclusion: there is a wide chasm separating even the best and brightest human being and God. Moreover, God's mention of and concern for earthly creatures which avoid contact with humankind implies that the earth, to say nothing of the vast universe, does not revolve around the needs and wishes of man. And when God singles out the hippopotamus and the crocodile for special praise, the last point is made forcefully, for:

— neither of these beasts could be called beautiful by man's standards;

— according to God, and who—given the context of the book—should know better than He, both of these beasts are more powerful and more fearless than man;

— if man cannot properly evaluate these earthbound beasts, how is he to appraise God whose reign extends to the Heavens?

What all of this implies is that man's suffering, if it is to be understood properly, must be viewed from God's perspective. Since, however, man is unable to do this, the riddle of human suffering, i.e., why the just so often suffer and the wicked sometimes prosper, must remain unsolved.

But that does not mean that more cannot be said. When God does make His appearance in the book of Job it is to Job, that man who had dared to challenge the belief that God rewards the good and punishes the bad. God, then, clearly prefers Job to those who had tried so hard to prove that God is providentially concerned for mankind. What is it about Job which God esteems? A related question which must be raised is this: why in a book which pivots around the theme of God's justice (or lack of it), and in a book in which the human characters use or refer to the term justice repeatedly, does God not make one reference to the concept or the term in His speeches?

What virtue does Job exhibit which commends him to God? Unlike the acquaintances, Job refuses to suspend his critical faculties in order to justify the ways of God. Job knows by virtue of his own experience and by reasoned observation that there is in fact much undeserved suffering in the world. Job therefore knows that any view of God which affirms that God guarantees moral causality on earth must be erroneous. While Job accuses his visitors of deliberately misperceiving reality in order to affirm the goodness of God, Job himself declares that he will not justify God at the expense of his intellectual integrity. Since God appears to Job and, moreover, explicitly repudiates the acquaintances while He praises Job, it is very probable that, from the author's point of view, God prefers discerning integrity to the acquaintances' apologetic "piety." It is also likely that Job is more correct than are his acquaintances about God's relationship to the earth in general and to man in particular. At issue between Job and the acquaintances is God's role as Rewarder and Punisher. Since God prefers Job to the acquaintances, we are compelled to conclude that in the opinion of the author of the book of Job, God does not guarantee moral causality on earth.

The speeches of God, somewhat indirectly, lead to the very same conclusion. Nowhere in God's speeches (which stretch from 38:1 to 42:10) is there the slightest indication that He does, in fact, reward the just and punish the unjust. What the speeches do emphasize is God's imposition of order on an awesomely complex universe. This thought is repeated so frequently that it is a leit motiv of the speeches.

One purpose of these speeches, and perhaps *the* purpose, is to teach Job and the reader humility. God is certainly successful. In his last speeches Job acknowledges that he is but a man and as such in no position to judge God. Another purpose of God's speeches is to inform the reader that one such as Job who retains his moral and intellectual integrity with no expectation of reward (retains them, in fact, in spite of crushing suffering), is to be preferred (or, as the author puts it, is preferred by God Himself) to those like the acquaintances who insist that the best part of goodness is the reward that it brings.

The speeches of God can be interpreted also as high praise of human freedom. God's speeches reaffirm what the Eden story had indicated: man is free to choose between the good and the bad. In the Eden tale when man took the fruit of the Tree of the Knowledge of the Good and the Bad, he acquired the Godlike capacity to chart his own destiny. The ideal is for man to choose the good in a Godlike fashion, i.e., with no expectation of reward.

With the privilege of freedom comes the responsibility of living with bad choices. If, therefore, aspects of life on earth are hellish, it is at least partially man's own fault. This is not to say, however, that such "accidents of life" as dread disease or natural upheavals are to be viewed as Divine chastisements for human sin. From the perspective of the book of Job, much about life on earth, to say nothing about the workings of the universe, are beyond man's ken.

In a way, God's speeches display only His "back parts." The rhetorical questions which God hurls at Job do not so much provide information about Him as they demonstrate what Job (who is the best of men) does not and cannot know. Thus God begins (38:2 f.):

'Who is this who darkens counsel,
Speaking without knowledge?
Gird your loins like a man;
I will ask and you [endeavor] to answer Me.'

But it quickly becomes apparent that Job is unable to reply to one of God's thunderous questions, for what can Job possibly respond when God asks:

— (38:4): 'Where were you when I set in place the earth's foundations?'

— (38:8): 'Who closed the sea behind barriers When it gushed forth out of the womb?'

— (38:12): 'Have you ever commanded the dawn to break, Assigned the dawn to its place?'

— (38:16): 'Have you penetrated to the source of the sea,
Or walked in the recesses of the deep?
Have the gates of death been revealed to you?
...Have you surveyed the expanses of the earth?
If you know of these, tell Me.'

— (38:33): 'Do you know the laws of heaven
Or impose its authority on earth?'

These and similar questions prompt Job to assert (40:4 f.):

'See, I am of little worth; what can I answer You?
I place my hand on my mouth.
I have spoken once, but will do so no more.

When God, as it were, brushes aside Job's reply and continues the interrogation, Job finally can only say (42:2 ff.):

'I know that You can do everything,

That nothing You propose is impossible for You.
indeed, I spoke without understanding,
Of things beyond me, which I did not know.
...I had heard of You by hearsay,
But now I see You myself;
Therefore, I recant and relent,
Being only dust and ashes.'

Job comes to realize that there is much that he cannot know. But that does not mean that he knows nothing. He knows, for instance, that the good is to be valued over the bad. He knows, moreover, that God values moral and intellectual integrity. And, in light of God's speeches, Job realizes that a human being has no reason whatsoever to expect there to be a relationship between virtue and success. That is to say, the most dread disease will stalk saint and sinner alike; and a storm will in no way distinguish between the good and the bad. Once Job understands this his quarrel with God ends. For Job has questioned why he, a righteous man, should have undergone such suffering. God tells him, in effect, that He never guaranteed moral causality in the world; it simply is not part of the scheme of things. Nevertheless, the pursuit of goodness remains man's ideal destiny. Beyond that, the highest expression of goodness is doing the right thing for the right reason. In the book of Job that would correspond to the pursuit of goodness for its own sake. To act in such a way is to imitate God whose generous treatment of man is not done in expectation of any reward.

The pursuit of goodness for its own sake is an ideal that is set forth in the very first story of the Hebrew Bible. It will be recalled that the Creation story in Genesis is divided into seven parts, each part corresponding to a day. We note now that the seventh day is that day on which God stopped creating and in recognition set that day apart as holy. Thus the first Sabbath (which in Hebrew means to cease or desist) came to be. In the Hebrew Bible the Sabbath is one of the most important holy days. It is, in fact, the only holy day to be prescribed in the Ten Commandments. In Exod. 20:8 ff. we read:

Remember the sabbath day and keep it holy. Six days you shall labor and do all your work, but the seventh day is a sabbath of the Lord your God: you shall not do any work—you, your son or daughter, your male or female slave, or your cattle, or the stranger who lives among you. For in six days the Lord made Heaven and Earth and sea, and all that is in them, and He rested on the seventh day; therefore the Lord blessed the sabbath day and hallowed it.

In Deut. 5:12 ff., where the Ten Commandments are listed again, a different rationale is offered for the observance of the Sabbath:

Observe the sabbath day and keep it holy, as the Lord your God has commanded you. Six days you shall labor and do all your work, but the seventh day is a sabbath of the Lord your God: you shall not do any work—you, your son or daughter, your male or female slave, your ox or your ass, or any of your cattle, or the stranger who lives among you, so that your male and female slaves may rest as you do. Remember that you were a slave in the land of Egypt and the Lord your God freed you from there with a mighty hand and an outstretched arm; therefore the Lord your God has commanded you to observe the sabbath day.

In Exodus 20 one is commanded to abstain from work in imitation of God who on the first seventh day did not work. In Deuteronomy 5 one is commanded to do no work in order to commemorate the liberation from Egypt. In both contexts the order to do no work extends to all of one's household, including even one's domesticated animals. What is the significance of this? And what is the relationship between the two rationales offered for the Sabbath in those two biblical contexts which record the Ten Commandments?

It would seem that both rationales celebrate the concept of freedom. In Genesis 1 God wills to create the Heaven and the Earth; He is free not to create at all or to create a world different from the one we experience. Genesis 1 makes it clear that order permeates our world. And order makes free choice possible. For in a world without order the consequences of any choice would be unknown, Man is placed in a world where choices and the consequences of choices are comprehensible and man is given the freedom to choose. The Sabbath, as a holy day, points to what man should do with his freedom. On the Sabbath man is to do no work and see to it that his household does no work so that for one day out of seven he derives no benefit from his property. In this way, as it were, he "returns" time to God who is the Lord of time. The Exodus context is explicit: it calls on man to desist from work out of imitation of God. And the

Deuteronomy context is no less explicit: the people Israel is to sanctify the seventh day in order to celebrate its freedom from bondage. The Sabbath deals with the question of what one is to do with one's freedom. And the answer is that one is to behave in a Godlike fashion. To behave in a Godlike fashion means to do the right thing not out of need or in expectation of reward, but to do the right thing simply because of the intrinsic merit of that which is right.

The question God asks at the beginning of the book of Job is whether Job is doing the right thing for the right reason. There is no question that Job is behaving properly, that he is a good man. But since he is so prosperous it is possible that Job is good because he believes that virtue leads to success. As a matter of fact, at the beginning of the book Job does believe that God will reward the good man. Thus his consternation when one disaster after another befalls him. He feels that God has betrayed him, but he passes God's test when he refuses to give up his moral and intellectual integrity. Then and only then does God speak so as to inform him that there is no necessary connection between virtue and success. If the good is to be pursued, as it should be, it is to be pursued for its own sake.

It is the acquaintances who persistently maintain that virtue does lead to success and that disaster is a sign that one has sinned. As we have noted, God repudiates their position. However, since much of what has come to be know as a "religious" outlook is in accord with the position developed by the acquaintances, it is perhaps disconcerting to find a book like Job in the Hebrew Bible, for the Hebrew Bible is the spiritual bedrock of Judaism, Christianity, and Islam, and many of the adherents of these religious traditions could not be distinguished from the acquaintances.

If, however, the book of Job is unsettling for some, the book of Ecclesiastes is earthshaking. The author of Job has no trouble finding meaning in life: a life well lived is one in which goodness is pursued for its own sake. The book of Ecclesiastes, however, begins with an assertion that human life is devoid of meaning (1:2–3):

> Utter futility!—said the Preacher.
> Utter futility! All is futile!
> What real value is there for man
> In all the efforts he makes beneath the sun.

Life is essentially futile according to the author of Ecclesiastes because what man wants most is denied him (1:4):

> One generation goes, another comes,
> But the earth remains the same forever.

It is the fact of death which robs life of meaning. This thought is expanded on several chapters later when the narrator asserts that (3:19–21):

> ...in respect of the fate of man and the fate of beast, they have one and the same fate: as the one dies so dies the other, and both have the same lifebreath; man has no superiority over beast, since both amount to nothing. Both go to the same place; both came from dust and both return to dust. Who knows if a man's lifebreath does rise upward and if a beast's breath does sink down into the earth?

Again and again the author returns to the same refrain:

> (8:8): No man has power over the lifebreath; no man can hold back the lifebreath; there is no power over the day of death.

> (9:2): ...The same fate is in store for all: for the righteous and for the wicked; for the good and pure, and for the impure....

> (9:12): ...a man cannot know his time [of death]. As fishes are caught in a fatal net, and as birds are trapped in a trap, so men are caught at the time of trouble, when it comes upon them without warning.

> (11:7–8): How sweet is the light, what a delight for the eyes to behold the sun! Even if a man lives many years, let him enjoy himself in all of them, remembering how many the days of darkness [i.e., death] are going to be. The only future is nothingness.

Nor, according to the author of Ecclesiastes, is life somber and without substance simply because of the unavoidable fact of death. For the author wants us to consider that while man is by nature curious about the ways of God, man lacks the capacity to satisfy this curiosity. God and God's creation are beyond man's comprehension. In his words (8:16–17):

> For I have set my mind to acquire wisdom and to observe the activity that goes on in the world—even to the extent of going without sleep day and night—and I have observed all that God makes happen. Indeed, a man cannot guess the events that occur under the sun. For man tries hard, but fails to guess them; and even if a wise man should think to discover them he would not be able to guess them.

And the more man endeavors to acquire knowledge about the ways of God the more he brings down upon himself despair. For the more he perceives the more does he understand how wretched is man's lot (1:18):

> ...as wisdom grows, distress grows;
> To increase learning is to increase heartache.

The author suggests that he has made the attempt to comprehend and that the attempt has brought him distress. For the attempt brought with it the following somber reflections:

> (2:11): Then my thoughts turned to all the fortune my hands had built up, to the wealth I had acquired and won, and behold, it was all futile and without substance; there was no real value under the sun.

> (7:10, 13–14): Do not say, 'How has it happened that former times were better than these?' For it is not wise of you to ask these questions.... Consider God's doing! Who can straighten what He has made crooked? So in a time of good fortune enjoy the good fortune; and in a time of misfortune, reflect: the one no less than the other was God's doing....

> (8:14): Here is a frustration that occurs in the world: sometimes a just man is repaid according to the behavior of the bad man; and sometimes the bad man is repaid according to the conduct of the just man. I say that all is a frustration.

> (9:11): I have also observed under the sun that
> The race is not won by the swift,
> Nor the battle by the courageous;
> Nor is sustenance won by the wise,
> Nor wealth by the intelligent,
> Nor favor by the learned,
> For the short duration of life renders all successes illusory.

The author of Ecclesiastes claims not to know why God has so arranged things. But he does indicate that man often makes his already bad situation worse. For instance, man refuses to learn from history and thus repeats the mistakes of the past. And man frequently establishes societies in which injustice is commonplace, in which the wicked are honored, in which wrongs are not redressed, in which the worthy do not lead but are led.

What does the author of Ecclesiastes advise his reader to do in the face of such futility? His strongest counsel is to limit one's expectations. If knowledge about the most profound things is beyond us, if we cannot change fundamentally the texture of human existence, if, most of all, we cannot escape the grave, then we should at least strive to do what is within our power. To the best of our abilities we should enjoy ourselves, realizing all the while, however, that a surfeit of the most pleasurable pleasures will not overturn the inherent futility of life. In short, he advises us to make the best of a bad situation. In specific, we are to:

— work well so that we can enjoy the products of our labor (5:17–18): Only this I have found is a real good: that one should eat and drink and get pleasure from all the gains he makes under the sun, during the short span of his life that God has given him; for that is his destiny. Also, whenever a man is given riches and property by God, and is also permitted by Him to enjoy them, he should accept his lot and get pleasure for his gains; that is a gift of God.

— find companionship, for (4:9–12): ...two are better off than one, in that they have greater benefit from their earnings. For should they fall, one can help the other up; but woe unto him who is alone and falls with no companion to raise him! Further, when two lie together they are warm; but how can he who is alone get warm? Also, if one attacks, two can stand up to him....

— take full advantage of youth before a debilitating aging process robs you of vitality (12:1): ...appreciate your youthful vigor in the days of your youth, before the days of sorrow come....

The author of Ecclesiastes ends his work with a vivid and powerful description of the incapacitating effects of the aging process. It is an appropriate ending to a work devoted to the trials and troubles of humankind.

Both in mood and substance the book of Ecclesiastes stands out in the Hebrew Bible. Ecclesiastes does not give primacy to man's moral responsibility which derives from man's having been created in the image of God. For the author of Ecclesiastes the only sensible course of action in a world which seems to him senseless is to eat, drink, and be merry. Also, there does not seem to be one sincere word of praise of God in the book of Ecclesiastes. When the author uses such phrases as a "gift of God" or God's doing or not doing something, they are in reference to what we would call chance or fate. Sometimes the same phrase is used to point to the necessity for man to make the most of his short mortal span by extracting from life what pleasures he can. So, for instance,

— (2:24): There is nothing worthwhile for a man but to eat and to drink and to enjoy himself according to himself. And even that, I observed, comes from God.

— (3:17 ff.): ...God will doom both the good and the bad, for there is a time for every experience and for every event...in regard to the fate of man and the fate of beasts, they have one and the same fate.

— (6:1 f.): There is an evil I have observed under the sun...that God sometimes grants a man riches, property, and wealth...but God does not permit him to enjoy it; instead a stranger will enjoy it.

— (7:13 f.): Consider God's doing! Who can straighten what He has made crooked? So in time of good fortune enjoy the good fortune; and in time of misfortune, reflect: the one no less than the other was God's doing.

Still, in some ways the book of Ecclesiastes is very much in keeping with the other books of the Hebrew Bible. For example, nowhere does the author of Ecclesiastes dispute the belief that man has the capacity to distinguish the good from the bad and to prefer the good. Clearly, too, he prefers enlightenment to ignorance and virtue to vice. He does not, however, believe that individual wisdom and virtue can save one from pain and death. And he apparently refuses to accept the prophetic contention that in the future the community of man will usher in a harmonious epoch by collectively exhibiting wisdom and virtue. Instead, it is the author's belief that man will continue to exhibit the self-destructive tendencies which have thus far characterized his stay on earth. The authors of Job and Ecclesiastes agree that man cannot know the ways of God. And they unite in the conclusion that the world is all too often topsy-turvy in that there is no coherent connection between virtue and success. But their disagreement is as profound as their agreement. The author of Job promotes the belief that the purpose of human existence is to act in conformity with the moral norms. The author of Ecclesiastes proposes that we pursue a life of moderate pleasure. As far as I can determine, the book of Ecclesiastes is unique in the Hebrew Bible in that regard.

Neither in Job nor in Ecclesiastes is a belief in life after death introduced in order to explain undeserved suffering or unrequited evil. This is in keeping with what is by far the dominant afterlife model in the Hebrew Bible. This belief posits a shadowy, murky underworld called Sheol. In Sheol one's soul is at "rest" if one has living male heirs to continue the family line and if these heirs retain possession of the ancestral homestead. Thus land sale in biblical Israel was always conditional on the ability of the original landowners or their kin to buy back their homestead. In fact, once every fifty years (called in the Hebrew Bible the Year of the Jubilee), land which had been sold would revert back to the original owners. Also, the surviving members of a family in which a member died childless would go to extraordinary lengths to provide a son for their dead kinsman. Think again of the story in Genesis 38 where Tamar is compelled to trick her father-in-law into having intercourse with her so that she can provide a son for her dead husband, Er. Or consider, too, the book of Ruth where a similar stratagem is employed to attain the same end, *viz.*, a son for a man who died childless.

The legal framework for providing a son for one who dies without male issue is found in Deut. 25:5 ff.:

> When brothers live together and one of them dies and leaves no son, the wife of the deceased shall not be married to a nonkinsman, outside the family. Her husband's brother shall unite with her and take her as his wife, performing the brother-in-law's duty. The first son that she bears shall be accounted to the dead brother, that his name may not be blotted out in Israel.

Even, however, when a soul is at "rest," existence in Sheol is bleak. Nonetheless, Sheol must not be confused with Hell for at least two reasons. In the first place, in the Sheol model there is no Heaven, and the concept of Hell as it is understood by most requires the positing of Heaven, i.e., a place where the good are rewarded. In the second place, one could live a bad life and still be at "rest" in Sheol if the conditions of male seed and landownership are met. Not that the issue of morality was absent from the Sheol model of afterlife. Hardly, for biblical Israel's tenure in the land was dependent on their moral behavior; exile, of course, would unsettle all the ancestral shades in Sheol since the families of biblical Israel would be forced to leave their ancestral homesteads.

In any case, life under almost any conditions was deemed preferable to the cheerless gloom of Sheol. The author of Ecclesiastes, for instance, certainly cannot be accused of looking at the world through rose colored glasses, and yet he never counsels suicide. Then, too, one can appreciate the depths of Job's despair when, in the early stages of the book, he urges God to dispatch him to Sheol. And one can understand the value placed on longevity in the Hebrew Bible, as well as the need to bear sons. Remember, also, Naboth's horror at the prospect of selling his ancestral homestead to King Ahab. At all costs a family would endeavor to retain possession of the ancestral homestead. Consider, for instance, the following passage in Numbers 27:

> The daughters of Zelophehad...came forward. They stood before Moses, Eleazar the priest, the chieftains, and the whole assembly, at the entrance of the Tent of Meeting, and they said, 'Our father died in the wilderness. He was not one of the faction, Korah's faction [which rose up in unsuccessful revolt against Moses and Aaron, see Num. 16–18; here the daughters of Zelophehad are indicating that their father died of natural causes and not as a result of revolutionary activities] which joined together against the Lord, but died...and he has left no sons. Let not our father's name be lost to his clan just because he had no son. Give us an hereditary portion among our father's kinsmen.' Moses brought their case before the Lord [as there was no legal precedent]. And the Lord said to Moses, 'The plea of Zelophehad's daughters is just: you shall give them an hereditary portion among their father's kinsmen; transfer their father's share to them. Further, speak to the Israelite people as follows: If a man dies without leaving a son, you shall transfer his

property to his daughter. If he has no daughter, you shall assign his property to his brothers. If he has no brothers, you shall assign his property to his father's brothers. If his father has no brothers, you shall assign his property to his nearest relative in his own clan, and he shall inherit it.' This shall be the legal procedure for the Israelites, in accordance with the Lord's command to Moses.

As we can deduce from this procedure, every possible step would be taken to insure that the familial land holdings would remain in the possession of the clan.

However, not even a thousand sons living securely on the ancestral homeland could change what was elemental about existence in Sheol:

— the absence of pleasure

— powerlessness

— murky darkness

— silence

This was the prevalent belief in afterlife in the Hebrew Bible.

Since, however, the Hebrew Bible was composed and compiled over many hundreds of years, it is not surprising that other views concerning afterlife can be discerned in the biblical record. There is, for example, the apparent reference to bodily resurrection in Daniel 12:2: "Many of these that sleep in the dust of the earth will awake, some to eternal life, others to censures, to everlasting disgust." Along the same lines there are passages in Isaiah 26:19 and Ezekiel 37 which also posit a resurrection model. These passages, however, probably refer to a national rather than an individual revival. Also, as we noted, the author of Ecclesiastes apparently believes that only oblivion awaits us beyond the grave. But while the Sheol model is not the exclusive afterlife model in the Hebrew Bible, it is certainly the prevailing one. However, if any belief in afterlife can be said to be the dominant one within Judaism today, it is the resurrection model. How did this system come to displace the Sheol model? To answer this question we will have to examine some facets of the postbiblical Jewish experience.

6

Some Remarks
on Postbiblical Judaism

In an earlier chapter we noted that in the eighth century the Assyrians brought the political independence of Israel, the Northern Kingdom, to an end. Judah, the Southern Kingdom, just barely avoided that fate; however, by the end of the biblical period (the sixth century) Judah was only a small province in the vast Persian Empire. At that time, the population of Judah probably was no more than fifty thousand. The books of Ezra and Nehemiah depict this time as one of internal conflict in Judah and as one of almost complete dependence on Persia. The Persian government apparently sent Ezra to Judah in order to bring a measure of law and order to that troubled province. Ezra expressed great concern over the numerous mixed marriages and over the unwillingness of the Judeans to rebuild the Temple. It was apparently a time of economic, political, and religious dislocation.

We know very little about the period between Ezra-Nehemiah (c. 460–390 B.C.E.) and the Maccabean Revolution (c. 160 B.C.E.) because there are almost no sources in regard to it. The book of Ben Sira (one of the books of the Apocrypha) appears to give us some information about the internal workings of Judean society from about 190–180 B.C.E. The author of this book describes a hierocratic society ruled by a descendant of the line of Aaron, the brother of Moses. But since the book of Ben Sira is devoted to religious matters, there is in it very little sociological information. In order to understand, to the extent that it is possible to understand, this period, we must look at the forces outside Judah which were shaping that tiny nation's destiny.

In 333 B.C.E. the armed forces of Alexander the Great overwhelmed the Persians. When Alexander died in 324, his generals divided up his empire into three main sections. In two of these divisions the rulers (Seleucus in Asia and Ptolemy in Egypt) fought for control over Palestine for the same reason which had prompted the Mesopotamians and Egyptians to fight over it: Palestine's crucial strategic location made it a landbridge between Africa and Asia. Control of Palestine passed back and forth between the Ptolemic and Seleucid forces until 200 B.C.E when the Seleucid ruler Antiochus secured Palestine as part of his domain. Although Judah was initially able to retain control over its civil and religious institutions, its army, such as it was, marched under the Seleucid banner.

During this period a significant number of "Jews" (the name apparently derives from Judean) lived in Ptolemic Egypt. The Egyptian Jewish community produced the first translation of the Hebrew Bible (into Greek), the first part of which was completed about 250 B.C.E. The Jewish community in Egypt was large, fairly prosperous, and intellectually vital.

However, while Jews thrived in Egypt, conditions in Judah under Seleucid rule were deteriorating. The Seleucids, locked in a struggle with the ever-expanding Roman Empire, subjected the Judeans to heavy taxation in order to finance their military ventures. The Seleucid taxation policies brought the first rumblings of revolt to Judah.

In order to strengthen his control over Judah, the Seleucid ruler Antiochus IV sought to diminish the force of Mosaic Law (administered by the Jews) so as to take control of the religious and secular institutions of Judah. The struggle between Antiochus and the Judean leadership came to a head when, in 167 B.C.E., Antiochus desecrated the Temple with pigs' flesh, brought idols into the sanctuary, forbade circumcision, burned copies of the Torah of Moses, and made it virtually impossible for the Jews to observe the traditions of their ancestors. Antiochus killed and imprisoned those Jews who dared to rebel against his Draconian policies.

While many Jews were in favor of introducing more "Greekness" into the political, cultural, and even religious spheres, even the most zealous promoters of "Greekness" among the Jews were incensed by Antiochus' attempt to subvert the Jewish tradition root and branch. The result was that many Jews joined in a revolt led by the Maccabee family. The Maccabees were able to liberate Jerusalem and to reestablish political and religious independence. After the revolution Simon Maccabee was installed as high priest. His son and successor, John Hyrcanus, embarked on an ambitious expansionist policy, and his territorial conquests emboldened him to seek the title of king as well as that of high priest. John Hyrcanus ruled until 104 B.C.E. He so modified the ideology of the Maccabean Revolution, which had been fought in the name of religious freedom, that he sometimes compelled conquered peoples to accept Judaism. One of these conquered peoples, the Idumeans, would one day repay the "favor."

During the Maccabean Revolution political-religious groupings appeared which are never mentioned in the Hebrew Bible. The most powerful of these groups came to be known as the Sadducees and the Pharisees.

It is possible that the name Sadducee is derived from "Zadokite," the designation for a priestly line which traced its origins back to Zadok, one of King David's priests. The leadership of the Sadducees was composed of priests, and this group apparently attracted many aristocratic members. During some administrations the Sadducees were clearly the most powerful political-religious group in Judah.

To assess properly the ideology of the Sadducees, this fact, above all others, must be understood. The Sadducees rejected all laws, customs, and beliefs which were not set forth explicitly in the first five books of the Hebrew Bible. According to the Sadducees, the sum and substance of the Torah, the sacred literature of the Jews, were the books of Genesis, Exodus, Leviticus, Numbers, and Deuteronomy. The Sadducees, therefore, affirmed the Sheol afterlife model, while rejecting the afterlife model championed by the Pharisees, a model which featured bodily resurrection of the dead and heaven and hell.

The name Pharisee may signify either "those who separate themselves from all [ritual] impurity," i.e., a positive designation, or "those who separate themselves from the true way," in which case it would be a disparaging term applied to them by the Sadducees. In their own literature they most frequently refer to themselves as "sages" or "scribes."

The root cause of their ideological dispute with the Sadducees was the Pharisaic claim that, in addition to the first five books of the Hebrew Bible, the Prophets and the Writings as well as an ever expanding "Oral Tradition" constituted the sacred literature of the Jews. This "Oral Tradition," which eventually was written down in works know as the Mishnah, the Talmud, and the Midrash, was a complex and variegated system of legal debates, law codes, legal commentaries, parables, homilies, and so on.

The reason-for-being of the "Oral Tradition" was to interpret the Hebrew Bible. The Pharisees claimed that the "Oral Tradition" was virtually equal in authority to the Hebrew Bible, and on the basis of this claim the Pharisees modified, added to, and occasionally overturned biblical practices and beliefs. Thus, to return to the example of afterlife, the Pharisees could claim that the belief in resurrection and heaven and hell was *the* Jewish model even though this model was nowhere in evidence in the first five books of the Hebrew Bible, and barely mentioned in the Prophets and Writings, because this model was omnipresent in the "Oral Tradition."

The depths of the disputes between the Pharisees and the Sadducees can be appreciated if one considers the fact that the two groups disagreed about what constituted the sacred base of Judaism. And disagreeing on this, the two groups lacked a common base to which to refer and to defer. We are not talking of liberal and strict interpretations of the same sacred constitution, but rather of claims and counterclaims about what was, in fact, the sacred constitution. Which is to say that the Pharisees and the Sadducees lacked a common framework within which to debate their differences.

While priests made up the leadership of the Sadducees, scholar-statesmen constituted the leadership class of the Pharisees. At least from the time of John Hyrcanus onward, the Pharisees appear to have had the support of most of the Judean populace. Saducean authority derived from the sacrificial cult. The Pharisees, however, implemented their interpretations of Judaism in synagogues, an institution which is never mentioned in the Hebrew Bible. The synagogues were primarily places of prayer and of study. In the synagogues, the leading Pharisees displayed their scholarly ability to interpret the sacred literature.

The literature produced by the Pharisees gives witness to the dynamism implicit in their scholarly interpretations. The Pharisees believed that if Judaism was to survive in a relevant fashion, great flexibility would have to be built into it. On occasion, the Pharisees were willing to transform a biblical context. In the words of one of their leaders, "To save the [sacred] law, it is sometimes necessary to break the law." And, as we have noted, the Pharisaic afterlife model in no way conformed to the Sheol model.

However, change within Pharisaic Judaism was not haphazard; rather, change was controlled rigorously by knowledge of the sacred tradition with an eye to the needs of the present. Whereas one was born into the priestly hierarchy of the Sadducees, the Pharisees chose their leaders, some of whom were converts to Judaism, on the basis of scholarly ability. Disputes within Pharisaism were settled by following the will of the scholarly majority.

The following quotations, taken from Pharisaic literature, demonstrate the extent to which the ideal of scholarship was valued by them:

— A man should sell everything in order to have his daughter married to a scholar.

— He who disagrees with his teacher is like one who provoked God. [While this is surely an hyperbole, the effect of this deliberate exaggeration is surely to exalt the worth of the scholar-teacher].

— If a scholar happens to be illegitimate [i.e., born out of wedlock] and a high priest happens to be a fool, the scholar is to take precedence.

— If a person learned that both his father and teacher have lost something, he must [first] help his teacher.

— While the King of Israel takes precedence over the high priest, a scholar takes precedence over the King of Israel.

The best testimony to the Pharisaic reverence for learning is the nature of the literature they produced, a literature which is replete with brilliant interpretations of the Hebrew Bible as well as legal and theoretical debates which are noteworthy for their incisiveness. We will shortly refer to some of them.

Although John Hyrcanus initially supported the Pharisees, in time he turned against them and began revoking their laws. The conflict between John Hyrcanus and the Pharisees apparently was caused by Pharisaic resentment against his increasing power. John Hyrcanus made no friends among the Pharisees when he proclaimed himself King as well as high priest. In today's terminology, the dispute involved a power struggle between the executive (Hyrcanus) and the legislative (the Pharisees) branches of government.

One year after the death of John Hyrcanus (in 104 B.C.E.), his son Alexander Janneas came to power. Janneas ruled from 103–76 B.C.E. He also conferred upon himself the title of King. Much of Janneas' support came from the Sadducees who backed his aggressive foreign policy. Janneas succeeded in expanding Judah's borders by waging wars of conquest. However, the taxes he levied in order to finance these wars brought much civil unrest to Judah. The Pharisees, especially, actively opposed Janneas' aristocratic tendencies and foreign policies. On one religious festival when Alexander Janneas publicly spurned a Pharisaic practice, those in attendance pelted him with fruit. Janneas' bodyguard overreacted, charged into the crowd, and killed many of the spectators. This was but one instance of the strife between Alexander Janneas, a Maccabee, commander-in-chief of the armed forces, high priest, and king, the most powerful individual in all of Judah, and the Pharisees, whose power derived from their scholarship and public esteem.

When Alexander Janneas died, his widow, Alexandra Salome, succeeded him. Perhaps due in part to the fact that she was related to a leading Pharisee, Alexandra Salome turned much of her administrative power over to the Pharisees. The Pharisees immediately began a systematic purge of the Sadducees from positions of power. Once the Pharisees gained control of the legislature they pushed through many much needed reforms, some of which gave greater legal protection to women and which democratized the educational process.

The relative tranquility of Alexandra's regime was shattered at her death when civil strife broke out between the supporters of two of her sons (Hyrcanus and Aristobulus), who both sought to succeed her. Aristobulus initially held the upper hand, but the Idumean Antipater goaded Hyrcanus into renewing hostilities so that a full-fledged civil war raged. When neither side was able to gain a clear advantage, they both appealed to Rome for help. In addition, groups who wanted to rid Judah of Hyrcanus and Aristobulus asked Rome to intervene. The Romans decided to support Hyrcanus; as a result, by 63 B.C.E. Judah was deprived of her political independence and became a province in the growing Roman Empire.

Thus, some one hundred years after the Maccabees began their war of liberation against the Seleucids, the Jewish people so hated and feared the Maccabees that they preferred to be ruled by a foreign power. Certainly one cause of disaffection was the inclination by Maccabean rulers, beginning with John Hyrcanus, to increase their power at any cost. We may recall that, contrary to the ideology of the Maccabean Revolution, John Hyrcanus had forcibly converted some conquered peoples to Judaism. The Idumeans were one of those peoples. And one of them, Antipater, was in a position of great power because of his influence with Rome.

Antipater convinced the Romans to appoint him as "procurator of Judah." Once they did so, Antipater, in turn, appointed his sons as governors over various parts of Judah. Thus did the Idumeans, a people whom John Hyrcanus had conquered and then forced to convert to Judaism, come to rule Judah for the Romans. Herod, one of Antipater's sons, who had been given control of the Galilee (in northeastern Palestine), carefully cultivated Roman favor so that, in 37 B.C.E., he was able to enter Jerusalem and declare himself King.

Herod proved to be a bold and in many ways a capable ruler. He embarked on an extensive building program in an attempt to restore Judah's past grandeur. He married a granddaughter of Hyrcanus and sought to bring back the image of independent self-rule. However, Herod was very erratic. He appeared to believe that many, including those closest to him, were plotting to subvert his authority. The extent of his fear can be seen in the fact that he was driven to execute his wife and his children in the mistaken belief that they were in league with his enemies. Herod's terror tactics turned the people away from him and increasingly toward the Pharisaic leaders. Herod responded to the growing popularity of the Pharisees in what was for him typical fashion. When he was summoned before the Sanhedrin (the legislature) to justify his tyrannical behavior, Herod appeared with a contingent of heavily armed soldiers. The Sanhedrin was forced to back down.

At this time the leading Pharisees were Hillel and Shammai, each of whom headed scholarly academies. Their schools debated all kinds of issues ranging from the secular to the religious. These debates were, for the most part, resolved by the will of the scholarly majority. With very few exceptions, the school of Hillel prevailed. Hillel apparently was the more flexible of the two. He was willing to give more latitude to each age to reinterpret the sacred traditions of Judaism. However, it is important to understand that Hillel insisted that any and all interpretations of the sacred literature be guided both by a deep respect for this literature and by the canons of logic. For example, when Hillel believed that a biblical regulation created excessive hardship, he enacted a legal formulation which had the effect of overturning the biblical ordinance.

Hillel and Shammai continued the Pharisaic effort to preserve the sacred tradition by subjecting it to analysis according to the highest scholarly standards. It was in this way, more than in any other, that they insured the continued relevance of Judaism. The following passage in the Babylonian Talmud (*Yoma* 35b), illustrates Hillel's veneration for scholarship:

...The poor man, the rich man, and the rake appear at the Judgment. When the poor man is reproached for not having studied the Torah and he replies that he has been poor and burdened with work, he is answered: Have you been any poorer than Hillel? It is told of Hillel that with his work he daily earned a few cents of which he gave half to the janitor of the school while using the other half to support himself and his family. One day he found no work, and the janitor of the school did not let him in; so he climbed up and sat down on the skylight to hear the words of the living God from the lips of Shmaya and Ptollion [two great scholars]. It is told that it was on a Friday in the middle of winter, and snow fell on him from the sky. As the dawn came, Shmaya said to Ptollion: Brother Ptollion, on every other day the room is light, but today it is dark, is the day really so cloudy? When they looked up and noticed the shape of a human being in the skylight, they climbed up and found him covered with nine feet of snow. They got him out, washed him and put salve on him, and seated him by the fire, saying that he deserved it and that for his sake one could desecrate the Sabbath [by healing on the Sabbath which, except for extraordinary circumstances, was forbidden].

The central theme of the above story is Hillel's absolute passion for learning. And the context in which the intellectual quest is to take place is the study of the Torah, the sacred literature of the Jews. Hillel's all-consuming urge to study the Torah drives him to spend half of what little money he has to bribe the academy's janitor so that he can gain admittance to the academy. It should be noted, too, that the laws against healing on the Sabbath are superceded by the need to minister to Hillel.

What was it that Hillel and those like him sought in the Torah? There is, perhaps, no simple answer to this question. Or, rather, there is a one word answer which is anything but simple. What Hillel and those like him were seeking in their study of Torah was everything. For Hillel and those like him the Torah was all-encompassing; it was the repository of truth and faith.

Since this was the Pharisaic view of Torah it is hardly surprising that for them the study of Torah was an end in and of itself. It was for them, this study of Torah, a way of life. For the Pharisees, life without Torah was not a life worth living. The following story in the Talmud, concerning Akiba, one of the greatest Pharisees, illustrates this point (*Beruchim* 9a):

...Once the infamous government [Rome] had given an order that the Israelites should no longer concern themselves with the Torah. Then Papos ben Yehudah met Rabbi Akiba as he held public meetings and concerned himself with the Torah. Then he said to him: 'Akiba, are you not afraid of the infamous government?' Akiba replied: 'I shall tell you a parable to which this is comparable. A fox once walked along the bank of a river, and when he saw fish congregating everywhere, he said to them: "what are you fleeing?" They replied: "The nets that men put out for us." "Then might it please you to come on land, and we, I and you, shall dwell together as my ancestors once dwelled together with your ancestors." Then they replied to the fox: "Is it you that is reputed to be the cleverest animal? You are not clever but stupid; if we are afraid even in the element in which we have our life, how much more in the element in which we die!" Thus it is with us too: if it has come to that even now when we sit and study the Torah of which it is written [Deut. 30:20], 'for

it is your life and the length of your days, 'how much more, if we go and withdraw from it!'

The text goes on to relate that a short time later Akiba was imprisoned and tortured by the Romans. It happened that when he was led
to his execution it was time to recite the so-called "*Shema*," the prayer
which reads, "Hear, Israel, the Lord our God, the Lord is one. And you
shall love the Lord, your God, with all your heart, with all your soul,
and with all your might...." This is how his death is described:

> His flesh was ripped off with iron combs, but he took upon himself the yoke of
> the kingdom of Heaven. His students said to him: 'Master, so far?' He replied
> to them: 'My whole life I have pondered over the verse in Scripture, "with all
> your soul and with all your might—"even when He takes your soul; for I
> thought, when shall this opportunity be given to me, and I shall do it. And
> now that it is given to me, I should not do it?' He prolonged the word 'One' so
> long that his soul expired on 'One.'

The study of Torah was Akiba's reason for being. He would not,
under any circumstances, give it up. For Akiba and those like him the
study of Torah was the medium in which one's love of God was expressed. Study of the Torah, for Akiba and those like him, led to imitation of God in the decisive sense of moral behavior, and if it did not
lead to that then it was not proper study of the Torah.

Let us consider one more example regarding the primacy of
morality in the Pharisaic system (*Erubim* 13b):

> For three years the school of Shammai and the school of Hillel argued: one
> said the law was to be decided according to it, the other said the law was to be
> decided according to it. Then a heavenly voice was heard as follows: both rep-
> resent the words of the living God, but the law is to be decided according to
> the school of Hillel. But if both represent the words of the living God, why
> was it granted to the school of Hillel that the law was decided according to it?
> Because it was peaceable and modest and studied not only its own views but
> also those of the school of Shammai; even more, it placed the words of
> Shammai before its own.... This teaches you that when a man humbles him-
> self, the Holy One, Blessed be He, exalts him....

What these examples suggest is that the Pharisees kept alive the
biblical base of Judaism. As we saw, the writers of the Bible insisted,
above all other things, on the primacy of moral behavior. Moreover,

the flexibility of biblical Judaism, which includes worldviews as dissimilar as those of Proverbs and Ecclesiastes, is mirrored in the dynamic textual exegesis employed by the Pharisees. The reverence which both Hillel and Shammai accorded the Torah did not result in agreement. As the last example I cited indicates, it was not only the interpretation which mattered but the manner in which one treated one's opponent. Nowhere, this context suggests, is self-righteous certainty more out of place than in interpretation of the sacred base of Judaism.

Thus, the people had very little difficulty choosing between Herod and Pharisees like Hillel and Shammai. Herod responded to this disaffection by persecuting the Pharisees. Moreover, he ordered that upon his death the leading Pharisees be executed. His order was never carried out. When Herod died, his son Archelaus went to Rome in order to be confirmed as ruler in his father's stead. While he was away civil war erupted. Augustus, the emperor of Rome, decided to divide Judah into three regions, each to be ruled by one of Herod's sons. Augustus' main concern was to stifle outbreaks against Roman rule. When Judah continued to be a breeding ground for dissension and revolutionary activity, Rome (in 6 B.C.E.) chose to annex Judah outright. Now in place of self-rule (however dependent the Jewish rulers were on Rome), were Roman procurators.

Although Rome, in principle, allowed the Jews to manage their own religious and civil affairs, friction between Judah and Rome was probably inevitable. The Roman procurators, far from home, often felt constrained to rule with an iron hand. With few restrictions on how they used (or misused) their power, with Roman troops to back them up, with no real feel for the customs and religion of Judah, procurators like Pontius Pilate (26–36 C.E.) flaunted the power and majesty of imperial Rome. Pilate brought imperial images into Jerusalem, that city set aside as the most sacred by the Jews for the worship of their invisible God. Pilate appropriated Temple funds for his own use. And Pilate had crucified any and all who threatened his authority.

The Judeans did not agree about how to deal with Roman rule of their homeland. Many of the Sadducees supported the Roman occupation of Judah. The Pharisees split sharply over whether dependence on Rome should be welcomed or resisted. Upper class

Pharisees stressed the wealth and stability Roman rule had brought to Judah, and they noted that, in any case, any attempt to throw off the Roman yoke would be futile. Some Pharisees and Sadducees, however, whose lives had been affected adversely by Roman rule, advocated a policy of armed resistance. Still other Pharisees believed that God Himself would intervene dramatically to break the Roman domination of Judah. These Pharisees believed that a Messianic Age was at hand.

The concept of messianism was by no means understood in the same way by all Pharisees. To some it denoted a future age on earth which would be ushered in by man's moral behavior and which would be marked by peace and freedom. To others it represented an immediate and dramatic overturning of conditions which for many were wretched. Some emphasized the role God would play; others insisted that man must take the initiative. Some meant by the concept no more than a political climate in which justice would prevail. Others believed that the so-called Messianic Age had implications not only for earth and the living but for the universe and the dead, some of whom would be resurrected.

Although much remains uncertain, it is possible that the first followers of Jesus belonged to that branch of Pharisaism which stressed the universal implications of messianism. It seems apparent that Jesus himself did not break with the most important features of Pharisaic Judaism. He appeared in synagogues, a Pharisaic institution, where he is pictured interpreting the Bible in a Pharisaic manner. His exalted ethical code is in complete harmony with mainstream Pharisaism. His proclamation, for instance, that "the Sabbath is made for man, not man for the Sabbath," is a premise of the Hillel story we cited above when the rule against healing on the Sabbath is suspended so that Hillel can be ministered to. And Jesus' use of such phrases as "the Kingdom of God" and "sitting at the right hand of God the Father," is congruent with their usage in Pharisaic literature. Moreover, the afterlife model which is everywhere in evidence in the New Testament, a model which features Heaven, Hell, and Resurrection of the Dead, is Pharisaic.

Why then was there a conflict between Jesus and the Pharisees? And why was Jesus not accepted by the Jews as the "Messiah?" The conflict between Jesus and the Pharisees apparently centered on Jesus' claim that he had the authority to speak in his own name without deferring to the will of the scholarly majority. To the Pharisaic leadership Jesus seemed to be saying: "I will make of the law what I want to make of the law because I am the 'Son of Man,' I am the 'Messiah.' " And as the Gospel of Mark states:

> And they were astonished at his [Jesus'] teaching, for he taught them as one who had authority, and not as the scribes [i.e., the Pharisees].

In regard to the issue of Messiah, it should be noted that in the Pharisaic Judaism of Jesus' time, there had arisen a series of related views about the Messiah which centered around the following questions:

— who would the Messiah be?

— when would he come?

— what would he accomplish?

The prevalent Pharisaic view asserted the following:

— the Messiah would be descended from King David;

— the coming of the Messiah would be preceded by the coming of a forerunner usually identified as the prophet Elijah, returned to earth, and by political and cosmic upheavals;

— the Messiah would become the independent king of Judah who would succeed in breaking the power of Rome;

— the Messiah's coming would inaugurate a new age on earth, one of tranquility and prosperity, in marked contrast to the evils and miseries of that age;

— at the Messiah's coming there would be a miraculous ingathering of exiles, living and dead.

The Jewish denial of the Messiahship of Jesus was simply a denial that the Messianic Age on earth had come. Rome continued to rule; no Jewish king had ascended the throne; there had been no ingathering of exiles (miraculous or otherwise); and there was certainly neither tranquility nor prosperity.

The Romans and the Roman sympathizers among the Jews rejected any and all messianic claims, for they carried with them both implicit criticism of Roman rule and a threat to the status quo. The Roman crucifixion of Jesus and others whom the Romans viewed as threats to their rule in Judah did not, however, weaken the forces which opposed Rome. In 66 C.E., many Jews joined in a revolt against Rome. The revolution gained widespread support from the suppressed Judean populace, and it took Rome more than four years to put an end to the revolt.

In suppressing the revolt the Roman legions destroyed the Jerusalem Temple and with it Sadducean Judaism. The Temple, of course, had been the centerpiece of Sadducean Judaism. Out of the ashes, however, a vital Pharisaic Judaism emerged, thanks to Roman support for a Hillelite academy whose function was to order Judean affairs. This academy not only canonized the last section of the Hebrew Bible (the Writings), but continued to breathe new life into biblical ideas and institutions. The biblical holidays, for instance, were freed from their agricultural moorings, and the Temple with its sacrificial praxis overseen by the priestly hierocracy was replaced by the synagogues with their prayer and study and scholarly leadership. The Temple's locale had been Jerusalem; a synagogue would appear wherever there were a sufficient number of Jews to support it.

As for Christianity, once it shed its earlier insistence that the Pharisaic Torah was an integral part of the salvation process, it turned away from Jews and Judaism and towards the Gentile world. In the centuries that followed, Jews and Christians, and Judaism and Christianity, would interact in a wide variety of ways. Sometimes the relationship was marked by cordial reciprocity; all too often, however, there was fear and hostility. There is a terrible irony connected with the fear and the hostility, because both religions are based on the Hebrew Bible, a book which affirms the absolute worth of all human beings. Nothing could be more contrary to the biblical spirit than professing to serve the biblical God by persecuting others.

7

Postbiblical Judaism:
Jews, Judaism, and the Roman Empire

The destruction of the Jerusalem Temple by the Romans in 70 C.E. had an immense impact on Jews and Judaism. Once the Temple was destroyed the Sadducees, whose leadership consisted of priests who depended on the existence of the Temple, disappeared from the scene. This left the Pharisees as the dominant sect and the Pharisaic leadership, whose authority was never rooted in the Temple, moved quickly to shape the institutions and beliefs of Judaism in conformity with mainstream Pharisaic ideology.

The Pharisees were not free to do whatever may have pleased them. On the one hand, Rome was frequently an exacting taskmaster which often promulgated strictures that deprived Jews of the freedom to express themselves as Jews. And on the other hand, many Jews continued to be attracted to the Graeco-Roman ethos as it was expressed in art, philosophy, and literature. As we will see, there is a profound difference between what is arguably the most philosophic book in the Hebrew Bible (Job) and a Platonic dialogue, to say nothing of a treatise by Aristotle. Nor, for that matter, did Cicero's work resonate with the spirit of Mosaic thought, whether theological or legal.

The Pharisees tried mightily to insure the survival of Judaism by interpreting the sacred base of Judaism (the Torah of Moses) so that it was relevant to the existential demands of life under Roman rule. It was no simple task. Every interpretation was charged with political implications.

With the Sadducees no longer a factor, the Pharisees had the *de facto* authority to make the synagogue rather than the Temple the central institution in Judaism. But the Pharisees also had to demonstrate that they had the *de jure* authority. In a celebrated context from the Pharisaic Mishnah (*Pirke Avot*), the Pharisees assert that their authority stretches back in an unbroken chain to no other than Moses, the greatest of prophets. The text is worth quoting in full:

> Moses received the Law from Sinai and committed it to Joshua, and Joshua to the elders, and the elders to the Prophets, and the Prophets committed it to the men of the Great Synagogue. They [the men of the Great Synagogue] said three things: be deliberate in judgment, raise up many disciples, and make a fence around the Law. Simeon the Just was of the remnants of the Great Synagogue. He used to say: by three things is the world sustained: by the Law, by the service, and by the deeds of loving-kindness. Antigonos of Soko received [the Law] from Simeon the Just. He used to say: be not like slaves that minister to the master for the sake of receiving a bounty, but be like slaves that minister to the master not for the sake of receiving a bounty; and let the fear of Heaven be upon you.... Let your house be a meeting-house for the Sages and sit amidst the dust of their feet and drink in their words with trust....Let your house be opened wide and let the needy be members of your household.... Be of the disciples of Aaron, loving peace and pursuing peace, loving mankind and bringing them nigh to the Law....Make your [study of the Law] a fixed habit, say little and do much.... Provide yourself with a teacher.

The Mishnah was apparently the first literary creation of the Pharisees. The Mishnah reached its final form about 200 C.E. and it consists of a vast legal code which interprets, explains, and in some cases revamps biblical law. The passage quoted from above is from *Pirke Avot* ("Sayings of the Fathers"), the one non-legal section of the Mishnah.

The Pharisees also produced the Midrash which like the Mishnah is a multi-volume work and which presents itself as a series of interpretations and explanations of the Hebrew Bible. Like the Mishnah, the Midrash contains legalities, but for the most part it is made up of

THE JEWISH EXPERIENCE 183

homilies, philosophic and theologic speculations, and ethical teachings.

However different in form these two pieces of literature are, they both seek to apply what were taken to be the most fundamental teachings of the Hebrew Bible to the Pharisees' own time. Consider the citation from *Pirke Avot*. It begins by asserting that Pharisaic Judaism is part of a sacred chain stretching back to the Sinaitic revelation. The Pharisees define their task as a continuation and maintenance of this chain by teaching the tradition ("raise up many disciples") and by protecting Judaism's sacred core ("make a fence around the Law").

The selection from *Pirke Avot* proceeds to stipulate some of the theoretical principles and practical consequences of adherence to what was "revealed" to Moses at Mt. Sinai. The preeminent principle is the intrinsic merit of good deeds ("be like slaves that minister not for the sake of receiving a bounty"). Thus behavior comes to be evaluated to the extent that it conforms to or promotes the ideal of decency for the sake of decency. Service to others and deeds of loving kindness become quintessential human standards. In this regard, note how the passage evaluates Aaron, the brother of Moses, who in the Hebrew Bible is the father of the priesthood and, as such, the archetypal Sadducee. The writer of this passage transforms Aaron into a prototypical Pharisee: "Be of the disciples of Aaron, loving peace and pursuing peace, loving mankind and bringing them nigh to the Law." But the "Law" referred to in this passage is the Pharisees' interpretation and expansion of biblical law and not those legal contexts in Exodus, Leviticus, Numbers, and Deuteronomy which feature Aaron and his progeny as high priests. Aaron is nowhere in the *Pirke Avot* context referred to as a priest.

From the destruction of the Temple onwards (that is, from 70 C.E. on), Pharisaism and variegated spinoffs of Pharisaism predominated in the Jewish experience. All the subsequent forms of Judaism (with only rare exceptions) included not only the Hebrew Bible as sacred literature, but the Mishnah, the Midrash, and what is called the Talmud. Although both the Jewish communities of Palestine and Babylonia produced Talmuds, it is the Babylonian Talmud which has exerted the most influence.

The Talmud, like the Mishnah, deals with Jewish law. But unlike the Mishnah, it is much more than a law book. Discussion of legal issues is interspersed with comments which range from personal anecdotes to philosophic ponderings. The Talmud, which in most editions runs to over 15 volumes, has been appropriately compared to the ocean because it is so diverse and sometimes so difficult to fathom.

Let us consider the following example from the Babylonian Talmud which is typical in that it begins with a passage from the Mishnah which is then subjected to discursive analysis. You will note that the Talmudic discussion is guided by the ethical norms which we uncovered repeatedly in one biblical narrative after another. Here is the passage (*Yoma* 82a–82b):

> *Mishnah*...If a woman with child smelt [pork, a forbidden food] she must be given to eat until she is restored. A sick person is fed [pork] at the word of experts [i.e., physicians]. And if no experts are there, one feeds the sick person as much pork as he wants.

In the Mishnah, both cases involve individuals, one pregnant and the other sick, who are fasting on the Day of Atonement, a traditional fast day. Read now how the Talmudic author exegetes the Mishnah:

> *Talmud*...Our Rabbis taught: if a woman with child smelt the flesh of holy flesh [i.e., permissible food], or of pork, we put for her a seed into the juice [of the meat] and place it upon her tongue. If thereupon she feels that her craving has been satisfied [note that it is the woman herself who is to judge], it is well. If not, one feeds her with the juice itself. If thereupon her craving is satisfied it is well; if not one feeds her the fat meat itself, for there is nothing that can stand before [the duty of] saving life, with the exception of idolatry, incest, and bloodshed. Whence do we know about idolatry? [i.e., how do we know that life itself is expendable in a case involving idolatry?] For it was taught: R. Eliezar said: since it is said [that one should love God] '*with all thy soul*': why is it said '*with all thy might*?' [i.e., why does the biblical passage add to what is already obvious?] And since it is said '*with all thy might*'; why is it said: '*with all thy soul*?' [The biblical passage reads like this to tell you that] if there be a man whose life is more cherished by him than his money, for him it is said: '*with all thy soul*'; and if there be a person to whom his money is dearer than his life, for him it is said: '*with all thy might*' [i.e., the biblical text from Deut. 6:5 is in no sense redundant but means to stress the across the board primacy of the command to love God]. Whence do we know about incest and bloodshed? Because it was taught: Rabbi [i.e., *the* Rabbi, referring to Judah the Prince, said to have been the driving force behind the

compilation of the Mishnah] said, *'For as when a man rises against his neighbor, and slays him, even so is this matter'* [the "this" referring to the rape of a betrothed maiden]. What matter do we infer for [the rape of] a betrothed maiden from a murderer? Rather: what was meant to teach...just as in the case of a betrothed maiden it is lawful to save her at the expense of his [the would-be rapist's] life, then also is the case of the murderer. And just as is the case of [an order to] shed blood one should rather be killed oneself than transgress [the prohibition of murder], then also in the case of a [command to rape a] betrothed maiden, one should rather be killed than transgress [the prohibition of violating her]. But whence do we know that the principle applies in the case of a murder? This is reasonable. [This is a crucial remark; what follows is a query, not a proof, because it is assumed that a reasonable reader needs no proof at this point. As for a reader who does not recognize the legitimacy of what is being postulated here, what, it must be asked, would convince him?] For there was a man who came before Raba [one of the most famous of sages] and said to him: the lord of my village told me: kill so-and-so, and if you will not, I shall kill you! He [Raba] answered: Let him kill you, but do not kill! What makes you think that your blood is redder [i.e., more precious] than his. Perhaps the blood of that man is redder than yours?

In a general way it can be said that like the authors of the Hebrew Bible, the Midrash, and the Mishnah, the authors of the Talmud attempt to ascertain the will of God. The above passage from the Talmud amplifies a biblical regulation regarding prohibited foods. Pig flesh was, and is, the most well known of those foods which biblical Israel was to eschew. The biblical regulation reads as follows (Lev. 11:1–8):

And the Lord spoke to Moses and Aaron, saying to them: 'Speak to the Israelite people as follows: these are the creatures that you may eat from among all the land animals: any animal that has true hoofs, with clefts through the hoofs, and that chews the cud—such you may eat. The following, however, of those that either chew the cud or have true hoofs, you shall not eat: the camel—although it chews the cud, it has no true hoofs; it is unclean for you. The daman—although it chews the cud, it has no true hoofs; it is unclean for you. The hare—although it chews the cud, it has no true hoofs; it is unclean for you. And the swine—although it has true hoofs, with the hoofs cleft through, it does not chew the cud; it is unclean for you. You shall not eat of their flesh or touch their carcasses; they are unclean for you.'

From this context in Leviticus it seems that animals whose flesh may be eaten must share two characteristics: cleft hoofs and a capacity to ruminate, i.e., to regurgitate previously swallowed food and to chew it more slowly a second time. Like most biblical regulations, the one above is explicated as the will of the Lord. But why is this particular regulation the will of God? The context in Leviticus gives no rationale as to why biblical Israel was to avoid certain animals as sources of food. As far as I can determine we simply do not know why animals like the pig were considered taboo by biblical Israel.

The passage from Leviticus exemplifies, moreover, the elliptical character of much of the legal material in the Hebrew Bible. The principles which distinguish between permissible and non-permissible animal food sources are stated without elaboration. We are left to conjecture not only about the derivation of these principles but about their application as well.

What is needed is some case law. And that is precisely what the Mishnah and especially the Talmud provide. The texts we have been examining are a good example of this. The terse quality of biblical legal contexts left the door open for great flexibility. In the case which we quoted from the Babylonian Talmud it is clear that the prohibition against eating pork is so qualified that in and of itself the prohibition is not of ultimate primacy. One could say that all things being equal one should abstain from eating pork, but there are instances where it clearly is permissible to eat pork.

The Mishnah qualifies the prohibition, one might say, without qualification. The Mishnah states that if a pregnant woman, on the holiest day of the year when even permissible foods are avoided, yearns for pork, she should be permitted to eat it. Moreover, with or without the word of a medical authority, a sick person should be allowed to do so as well.

While the Talmud expands on the Mishnah's rulings, the same spirit prevails. Thus, if a pregnant woman's yearnings cannot be mollified then she must be given the pork: "...for there is nothing that can stand before [the duty] of saving life." But is it not true that the pregnant woman's life is not at stake? We are dealing with a situation which threatens not life but comfort. And even in such an instance the woman's comfort takes precedence over a biblical prohibition which is not only stated unambiguously but which is set forth in the name of God. So little were the Talmudic interpreters literalists in their reading of Holy Writ!

The Talmud then goes on to discuss those issues which make even life itself of penultimate concern: idolatry, incest, and bloodshed. These things are prohibited absolutely. The prohibition against idolatry is tantamount to an interdiction of indecency since the biblical God, as we have seen repeatedly, commands above all other things decent behavior. As for the injunction against the shedding of blood, it is explained graphically at the very end of the Talmudic context in Raba's observation that "Perhaps the blood of that man is redder than yours."

If Raba's assertion sums up the core principle of this Talmudic passage, then it is accurate to say that the discussion of prohibited foods leads to an attempt to uncover the value judgments which support the prohibition. And the primary value judgment, as stated by Raba, is that one should not do to one's fellow human beings what one does not want done to himself. This would be the consequence of loving God with all of one's heart and all of one's soul.

Since Christianity emerged out of Pharisaic Judaism it is hardly surprising that the assertion to love one's neighbor as oneself is at the heart of biblical Christianity. Leviticus 19:18 states: "Love your neighbor as yourself" and Matthew 5:43 has Jesus state: "You have learned that they were told, 'love your neighbor, hate your enemy.' But what I tell you is this: love your enemies.... If you love only those who love you, what reward can you expect?" Since no text in the Hebrew Bible, the Mishnah, the Midrash, or the Talmud calls for the hatred of one's enemy, it is possible that Jesus is expressing hyperbolically the absolute necessity to treat all human beings as we ourselves would want to be treated.

However that may be, under Roman rule there was much antagonism between the two sister faiths. Some Christians were disappointed that so few Jews came over to the new movement. The disappointment is reflected in some of the Gospel narratives. Consider, for instance, the parable of the vineyard which occurs in three of the Gospels (Mark 12:1–12; Matthew 21:33–46; Luke 20:9–19). The parable goes as follows:

— God, the owner of the vineyard (which is the ideal Israel), leaves it in the hands of tenants [the Jews].

— From time to time God sends servants (the prophets) "to get from them [the Jews] some of the fruit of the vineyard."

— The tenants, however, persecute the prophets so that the owner decides finally to send his son (Jesus).

— The text continues: "...the tenants said to one another, 'This is the heir, come let us kill him and the inheritance will be ours.' And they took him and killed him, and cast him out of the vineyard."

The parable concludes by noting that what the tenants reject will one day become the standard.

This parable is as nothing, however, compared to some inflammatory contexts in the Gospel of John, perhaps the most anti-Jewish of New Testament books. Most scholars believe that John was written after the so-called synoptic Gospels and reflects the growing animus between the two faiths. In the Gospel of John, the entire Jewish people are labeled as killers of Christ and children of the Devil. In the eighth chapter the Gospel writer has Jesus tell "the Jews" that "You are from below, I am from above; you are of this world, I am not of this world. I told you that you could die in your sins, for you will die in your sins unless you believe that I am he." Jesus goes on to indicate that the Jews are of the Devil and that "He who is of God hears the words of God; the reason you do not hear them is that you are not of God."

Such texts in the sacred literature of the Church were sometimes employed to stir up hatred against Jews. Church leaders such as Hippolytus of Rome (third century) and John Chrysostom (fourth century) denounced Jews and Judaism and referred repeatedly to the New Testament. Chrysostom wrote:

Do not be surprised if I have called the Jews wretched. They are truly wretched.... They were called to sonship but they degenerated to the level of dogs.... I know that many have high regard for the Jews and they think that their present way of life is holy. [You will note that that seems to imply a cordial and respect-filled relationship between at least some non- Jews and Jews]. That is why I am so anxious to uproot this deadly opinion.... The synagogue is not only a house of prostitution and a theater, it is also a hideout for thieves and a den of wild animals.... No Jew worships God.... If they are ignorant of the Father, if they have crucified the son, and spurned the aid of the Spirit, can one disclose with confidence that the synagogue is a dwelling place of demons? I am not imagining such things. I know them from my own experience.

One can hope that Chrysostom resorted to such vilifications because many Christians in fact interacted with Jews commercially and socially. One is still left with the disturbing notion that a Church leader the rank of Chrysostom felt compelled to lash out at Jews and Judaism.

Once Christianity became the official religion of the Roman Empire (fourth century), not only were pagan religions outlawed, but things also turned worse for Jews and Judaism. There began a period in the Jewish experience in which the best that Jews could hope for was to be tolerated. In the Roman Empire, the legal system offered the Jews scant protection. In fact, it was decisively weighted against them. Specific prohibitions against Jews and Judaism became part of the legal fabric of the Empire. Jews were prohibited from having Christian slaves; Jews could not proselytize Christians; Jews could not stop other Jews from either converting to Christianity or marrying Christians. Also, Jews were denied access to legal occupations; they were excluded categorically from all civil and military offices and were never to be in a position of authority over a Christian. There were strict regulations against the building of new synagogues or even the repairing of old ones and, as if all of the above were insufficient, the Jews were singled out for a special tax.

In the light of what would happen in later centuries to the Jews, it is well to keep their status in the Roman Empire in perspective. None of the prohibitions or the restrictions resulted in an enforced exile. Nor did any of them call for the extermination of Jews. More than that, some of the most prominent Church leaders sought to moderate the harsh attitudes of those like Chrysostom.

St. Augustine (354–430), for instance, taught that Jews were entitled to life, albeit a subservient one. Augustine's proof-texts of Scripture are instructive. Augustine compared the Jews to the biblical Cain. As Cain killed his innocent brother Abel, the Jews had killed Christ. As Cain deserved to die for his crime so, too, did the Jews. But as God spared Cain, so should the Christians spare the

Jews, for in the fullness of time the Jews would be converted to Christianity. Until then, however, like Cain, the Jews were to be outcasts. Here is some of what Augustine wrote:

> ...not by bodily death shall the ungodly race of carnal Jews perish. For whoever destroys them in this way shall suffer sevenfold vengeance [as in the case of Cain, Gen. 4:15: "The Lord said to him, 'Therefore if anyone kills Cain, sevenfold vengeance shall be taken on him.' And the Lord put a mark on Cain, lest anyone who met him should kill him."], that is, shall bring upon himself the sevenfold penalty under which the Jews lie for the crucifixion of Christ.
>
> ["The Writings Against the Manichaeans," in *A Select Library of Nicene and Post Nicene Fathers of the Christian Church*, 1887, IV (Wm. B. Erdman's Publishing Co., Buffalo, New York), pp. 187 ff.].

While preferable to Chrysostom's vilification of the Jews, Augustine's remarks hardly resonate with good will. You will note that Augustine uses the Cain-Abel story in order to drive home his point that God, for an unfathomable reason, has decreed that the Jews be permitted to live in order that some day they might be converted to Christianity.

However, Augustine's parabolic rendering of the Cain-Abel allegory seems to miss the mark. The Cain-Abel story indicates clearly of what Cain's punishment consists (banishment from his kinship group) and why he is to be spared (so that the reader understands that "Cainness," i.e., that which is egocentric, selfish, jealous, and envious, remains a part of humanity; or, are we not often as guilty as he?). But it is equally clear that human beings will be punished only when they act like Cain (Gen. 4:7):

> 'Surely, if you do right
> There is uplift.
> But if you do not do right
> Sin is the demon at the door,
> Whose urge is toward you,
> Yet you can be his master.'

According to Augustine, however, not only are the Jews guilty who participated in the passion of Jesus, but also Jews of all times and places. Augustine's reasoning is that the very act of remaining Jews is a re-enactment of the original crime. But Cain's crime was murder, i.e., the epitome of indecent behavior. Augustine converts this crime of indecent behavior into affiliation in a religious tradition which, ironically, promotes decency as an ultimate ideal.

What can we say? Was St. Augustine ignorant about Judaism? Or was he indifferent to the truth about Judaism? In either case it is a sad commentary when one of the most influential and acute of the Church Fathers tarnishes his work with this kind of slander.

JUDAISM AND ISLAM

I want now to comment briefly on the early relationship between Judaism and Islam, especially as this relationship can be contrasted to the relationship between Judaism and Christianity. Mohammad, the founder of Islam (which came to be in the seventh century), seems initially to have been favorably disposed toward Jews and Judaism. But, when contrary to his expectations, Jews did not join the new religious movement in significant numbers, Mohammad turned on them with a vengeance. There are instances in which entire Jewish settlements were put to the sword because of their refusal to convert to Islam. As was the case in Christian lands, Jews living in Islamic territories were denied full citizenship and were, therefore, at the mercy of their Islamic hosts.

For the most part, Jews in Islamic lands were treated in the same way as were Christians. At best, this meant that Jews constituted a tolerated minority which was permitted some measure of religious freedom. But even at best there were occupational restrictions imposed on Jews (and Christians) which were very similar to those inflicted by the Christians in their lands.

There was, however, an important difference between Judaism and Islam on the one hand and Judaism and Christianity on the other. We saw that although Christianity emerged out of Pharisaic Judaism, once it became a distinct religious tradition some Christians charged the Jews with rejection of and continued hostility toward Jesus. There were a sufficient number of texts in the New Testament which provided grist for this mill of hatred. To say the least, these charges inflamed the religious sensibilities of many Christians, and particularly in times of economic distress, they provided a convenient rationale for persecuting the Jews.

Islam, however, emerged out of *both* Judaism and Christianity and its founder, Mohammad, and its subsequent leaders proselytized both Jews and Christians. Whereas Jesus lived and died a Jew and whereas his immediate disciples were Jews, Mohammad was born a pagan. Mohammad's conversion experience moved him away from what Judaism and Christianity had already rejected. The common ground shared by Judaism, Christianity, and Mohammad's new religion was not littered with the infighting associated with the beginnings of Christianity.

The Koran, the sacred book of Islam, does not, accordingly, contain anything like the Gospel's sometimes negative rendering of Jews and Judaism. In specific, nothing similar to the charge of deicide can be found in the Koran. Far from it, as the following quotation from the Koran (Sura Two) demonstrates:

> To Moses We gave the Scriptures and after him We sent other apostles. We gave Jesus the son of Mary veritable signs and strengthened him with the Holy Spirit.... We believe in Allah [God's name in Islam] and that which is revealed to us; we believe in what was revealed to Abraham, Isaac, Jacob, and the tribes; to Moses and Jesus and the other prophets. We make no distinction between any of them....

Moreover, to the extent that Jews did not convert to Islam, neither did Christians.

By the middle of the seventh century, the Jews had become a tolerated minority in many Moslem countries. Although the Jews had to pay a special tax, they were allowed to live under their own jurisdiction and, for the most part, worship as they wished. The stronger, more vibrant the economy of an Islamic society, the more fully were Jews allowed and even encouraged to participate in its special institutions. In many Islamic lands, Jews occupied important government positions.

Since Muslim and Christian countries engaged in commercial activities which entailed contact and collaboration, both Muslims and

Christians frequently used Jewish merchant traders as go-betweens. These Jews travelled all over the known world, from the Middle East to the Slavic regions of the north, across Europe to Spain, down into Africa, and out to the Far East.

What I wish to emphasize is that whether in Christian or Muslim lands, Jews as an unarmed minority were often persecuted when economic conditions deteriorated. In good times, both Christian and Muslim rulers were not only willing to exploit Jewish goods and services, but these leaders created a climate in which Jews were accorded extensive rights and privileges. When, however, times were bad, these same leaders had no trouble justifying persecution of the Jews on religious grounds. These rulers had no difficulty in finding "proof-texts" in their sacred literature to justify treatment of the Jews which ranged from granting Jews almost full citizenship to making it impossible for the Jews to step foot outside their ghettos.

8

Halevi, Maimonides, and Spinoza: Postbiblical Judaism and the Bible

The Hebrew Bible has been the lodestar of the Jewish experience. We saw that Rabbinic Judaism produced an extensive body of literature (the Mishnah, Midrash, and Talmud) which is devoted to the principle that the Hebrew Bible constitutes the sum and substance of the truth. The interpretative problem with which the rabbis wrestled was not whether the Hebrew Bible was true but rather how one could get at this truth. For the rabbis this invariably involved discursive analysis.

The rabbis, however, did not simply rely on rational inquiry as a means with which to interpret Holy Writ; many of them also believed that if reason were employed correctly, it could arrive at many of the truths, by dint of its own efforts, which are contained in Scripture. This was equivalent to asserting that God, as it were, created not only the teachings of Scripture but the human mind's capacity to comprehend these teachings in Scripture and elsewhere. Ideally, therefore, there could be no conflict between the conclusions reached by rational investigation independent of the Bible and a valid interpretation of the Bible.

The rabbis were in almost complete agreement that the Hebrew Bible unambiguously affirms the following:

— *The existence of God.* This was not problematic; in its very first line the biblical writer assumes God's existence.

— *The uniqueness of God.* Also not problematic; one need do no more than consider this God's activity in the first chapter of Genesis, to say nothing of this God's unique name.

— *The attribute of God as creator.* Again, one need only refer to the first chapter of the first biblical book.

— *The attribute of God's providential concern for His creation in general and for mankind in particular.* The anthropocentrism of Gen. 1 could hardly be more pronounced. Nonetheless, this attribute which forces us to raise the issue of God's justice is by no means simply and/or easily understood. We have already spoken of the book of Job's treatment of theodicy and there are a sufficient number of biblical texts which bar the way to simplistic generalizations.

By way of example, consider the following tale in 2 Kings 8:7–15:

Elisha arrived in Damascus when Ben-Hadad the king of Syria was ill. The king was told that the man of God had arrived in Syrian territory The king said to Hazael, 'take an offering and go meet the man of God, and through him inquire of YHWH as follows: Will I survive this illness?' So Hazael went to meet him [Elisha], taking such a bountiful gift that it required forty camels to carry it. When he met Elisha he said to him: 'Your servant Ben-Hadad, king of Syria, has sent me to you with this question: Will I survive this illness?' Elisha responded: 'Return to him and say: While you will recover from the illness YHWH has revealed to me that you will certainly die.' Then he stood with his face expressionless until [finally] the man of God broke down and wept. Hazael asked him why he was weeping. He answered: 'because I know the evil you will do to the Israelites: you will set their fortresses ablaze, put their soldiers to the sword, rend fetaled infants limb from limb after ripping open their pregnant women.' And Hazael said: 'But how can your servant, who is but a dog, do this great thing?' Elisha answered, 'YHWH has shown me a vision of you as king over Syria.' So Hazael left Elisha and came to his master [Ben-Hadad] who said to him, 'What did Elisha say to you?' Hazael answered, 'He said to me that you will recover.' And it was that the next day Hazael took a cloth, dipped it in water, and spread it over the king's face [suffocating him]. Thus did Hazael become king in the place of Ben-Hadad.

Consider that Elisha is in Syria at the behest of God (see 1 Kings 19:15) to incite Hazael to murder his master so that as king he can savage the people Israel. For obvious reasons, it is a mission which reduces the great man of God to tears. For our purposes, it is sufficient to ask but one question concerning this tale: what does it reveal about the nature of God's justice? Is it not clear that any discussion of theodicy in the Hebrew Bible would have to take account not only of this tale but of others as well which are equally problematic (see, e.g., Gen. 18:22–32; Judges 11:29–40)?

The text from Kings is complex but the point I wish to make here is simple: the affirmation that Israel's God exists and is unique is of a different order from the assertion that this God is just. Not only was there widespread agreement among the Rabbis that God "is" and is "one" (in the sense of unique) but, moreover, those Rabbis who were attracted to the writing of Plato and Aristotle were reasonably satisfied that it was possible to reconcile the biblical view of God's existence and uniqueness with the views of the great Greek philosophers.

It was important to these Rabbis that there be consistency between Plato and Aristotle and the Hebrew Bible because these Rabbis affirmed that the greatest of philosophers, having employed their reasoning capacities correctly, had arrived at the same conclusions as those enunciated in the Hebrew Bible. But consistency was not so easily achieved when it came to God as creator and God as *the* just judge.

These Rabbis believed they could prove that both Plato and Aristotle posited God's existence and uniqueness. But it was equally clear to them that Aristotle's notion of God precluded the possibility that this God created. For Aristotle, the universe was eternal. And these Rabbis saw clearly that neither the God of Aristotle nor Plato rewards the good and punishes the wicked. The Rabbis understood very well that perhaps Plato and certainly Aristotle had concluded that the universe is governed by fixed and unchangeable laws, a conclusion which left no room for intervention by God, miraculous or otherwise, in nature or history.

While the Rabbis generally could agree with the philosophic tradition that there are immutable laws of nature, they added a proviso that God could at any time interrupt the laws of nature. These interruptions the Rabbis called tokens of God's providential concern for individuals, while God's implanting of immutable laws was for them an indication of God's general concern for His creation. It was on the point of God's freedom and willingness to intervene that the Rabbis, even those who most enthusiastically embraced the way of Plato and Aristotle, separated themselves from the classical Greek tradition. For the Rabbis, God's providential concern was a faith axiom which no argument, no matter how reasoned, could dislodge.

But as to what exactly it meant to affirm God's providence, to say nothing of a host of other matters, there remained within Rabbinic Judaism a question as to the limits of reason, i.e., where reason should stop and faith begin. The Hebrew Bible, for instance, describes certain extraordinary events which some Rabbis took as proof of God's providential concern. However, the Rabbis themselves had not witnessed these events; they knew of them by hearsay. But for them this hearsay was secure because it was contained in the Hebrew Bible, which for them was the most reliable of sources.

Certainly, however, unaided reason cannot corroborate these events. Nor can reason extrapolate these events from current data. That is, the miracles recorded in Scripture were discrete events: manna does not fall from the sky; bushes do not talk and burn without being consumed; seas do not split and then come back together again on cue; and so on.

Again and again the greatest of the Rabbis returned to these questions: what are the limits of reason? What determines these limits, i.e., is it reason or faith which determines when reasonable discourse ceases to be effective? These questions were bound up with another question: how able are we to communicate *with* and *to* others in matters of faith? If we are able to communicate only a very little, then does it not follow that the individual must leave a part of his mind when he enters a sanctuary?

Or, to look at the matter from the side of the religious authorities, should a religious tradition have the right to enjoin reason from going only so far and no further in its investigations? For example, the Church, in the 17th century, compelled the Italian astronomer Galileo to retract his findings that the earth was not the fixed center of the universe, because the Church believed that this conflicted with the explicit testimony of the creation account in Genesis. And in the same century, the Jewish religious leadership of Amsterdam excommunicated Benedict Spinoza after he refused to stop his investigation into the origin and development of Scripture.

Perhaps all of this can be summed up in the following question: how does one proceed when the fundamental beliefs of a religious tradition—beliefs which are based on a divinely revealed source—come into conflict with the findings of rational inquiry—findings which are based on the disinterested quest for truth?

The tension between faith and reason goes to the very heart of a question which permeates the Jewish experience: what is to count as evidence in the elucidation of the nature of Judaism? The issue is one of the highest theoretical importance and it entails practical ramifications which range from the sublime to the absurd.

Perhaps it is Moses Maimonides who, in the Jewish experience, has given these issues the most sublime treatment. His stature is such that both his thought and his life deserve a close look.

Maimonides was born in the southern part of Spain in 1135. His family tutored him in both religious and secular studies. The calm security of his early years was broken in 1148 when an Islamic sect, which would brook no religion but its own view of Islam, conquered much of Andalusia. The Jews of Andalusia were ordered to convert to Islam or emigrate. Many Jews fled northward where there were Christian lands which tolerated Jews. The Jews who decided to stay either converted in fact or in pretense, i.e., while openly practicing Islam these Jews continued in secret to follow the ways of Judaism.

At first, Maimonides' family pretended to convert to Islam while doing what they could to maintain their Jewish ways in secret. Since the penalty for such "heresy" was death, the family always had to be on the move in order to avoid detection. In 1159 Maimonides' family left Spain for Morocco. By this time, the young Maimonides had already written a treatise on logic as well as interpretations of some of the more difficult portions of the Talmud. In Fez, Morocco, Maimonides became involved in a dispute with the religious leadership of the Fez Jewish community over the extent to which a "secret" Jew could publicly practice Islam and still remain legitimately Jewish. The leadership claimed that nothing should be permitted to interfere with the observance of the rituals of Judaism. A Jew, claimed the leaders of the Fez Jewish community, should martyr himself if need be rather than pass himself off as a Moslem if the charade did not permit him to follow every jot and tittle of the Jewish religious praxis. Maimonides' argument, which should remind you of our discussion of the Talmud's treatment of the prohibition against the eating of pork, consisted of two major points:

— since only lip service to Islam was required, no harm was being done;

— life and the preservation of life take precedence over almost all of the commandments.

Maimonides and his family settled into an uneasy routine, one which was broken in 1165 when the chief Rabbi of Fez was executed for allegedly defiling Islamic practice. Maimonides and his family, along with many other Jews, fled.

For a brief time Maimonides and his family stayed in the land which the biblical God had promised to the people Israel. But since there was then no vital Jewish community, and since the country still reeked from the blood spilled during the Crusades, the family, after little more than a year, moved to Egypt. In Egypt there was a large and energetic Jewish community which enjoyed a considerable measure of religious freedom.

In 1168 (Maimonides is now 33) Maimonides' first major work was published. Called the *Commentary on the Mishnah,* it attempted to make the Mishnah more intelligible. It is a difficult work to classify because it reads sometimes like a terse legal work and at other times like a recondite philosophic treatise. In one section, for instance, Maimonides digresses to discuss the concept of immortality. Maimonides ridicules those whom he calls the "vulgar" who:

— believe in corporeal reward and punishment;

— believe in bodily resurrection;

— believe in a supernaturally initiated and maintained messianic age.

Maimonides was well aware that the great majority of Jews believed that which he was rejecting as fatuous. Maimonides goes on to classify Jews into the following three groups:

— The great majority who took the sacred tradition literally and were unaware that there was a deeper, hidden meaning in many biblical texts.

— A smaller group which also took the tradition literally but who, unlike the first group which revered the tradition, had contempt for it.

— A very small number of Jews who understood the sacred tradition as it should be understood.

Maimonides advised those of his readers who belonged to the first two groups to put down *The Commentary on the Mishnah.* In many instances, *The Commentary* makes study of the Mishnah superfluous because Maimonides provides the final legislation. Not surprisingly, *The Commentary* met with opposition from precisely those Jews who did not believe that there were hidden meanings in the sacred literature.

In this early work Maimonides set forth an agendum from which he would never deviate: an insistence that the creators of the sacred tradition of the Jews, especially the Hebrew Bible, were individuals of the highest competence who deliberately framed their teachings in such a way so that both the sophisticated and the naive reader could be enlightened by them.

In 1171 Maimonides and his family left Alexandria for Fostat (present day Cairo). It was then that a crisis in Yemen catapulted Maimonides to the attention of Jews everywhere. In Yemen a fanatical Muslim was relentlessly persecuting Jews. In these awful times a messianic pretender appeared among the Jews promising, while collecting huge sums of money from desperate Jews in the process, to lead them to Palestine. Some of the leaders of the Yemenite Jewish community wrote to Maimonides asking his advice.

Maimonides wrote back advising them to leave Yemen, if necessary, in order to avoid unnecessary martyrdom. Moreover, he wrote that the "messiah" was not to be trusted because he was ignorant of the biblical base of Judaism and its traditional interpretations.

The Jews of Yemen waited out the persecution and threw out the "messiah." In 1174 a more tolerant Moslem regime came to power which granted the Yemenite Jews the same freedoms enjoyed by the Jews in Egypt.

What is of particular interest is Maimonides' repudiation of a messianic claim on the basis of lack of knowledge of the sacred base of Judaism. For Maimonides, one who claimed to be a messiah or, for that matter, a prophet, first of all had to demonstrate the ability to communicate the truths of Judaism. And for Maimonides, the most profound expression of these truths is to be found in the Hebrew Bible.

In 1174 Maimonides' brother, who had been the chief financial supporter of the clan, died at sea, and most of the family's assets went down with him. Maimonides fell very ill and was near death for several months. Years later he would write of this time: "Were not the study of Torah my delight and did not the study of the sciences divert me from my grief, I would have succumbed in my misery."

Maimonides turned to medicine as a means to support his family. During the next decade his fame spread as a healer, a scholar, and an expert on Jewish law. From all over the Diaspora letters came to Maimonides asking for his medical, legal, and philosophic opinions.

In 1180 Maimonides completed his second major work, *The Mishnah Torah*. It is an incredible achievement. *The Mishnah Torah* comprises almost all of the biblical and postbiblical laws and customs extant in his time. Maimonides did not simply repeat and collect these laws and customs; he collated, excised, and reinterpreted them.

Again and again his controlling principle was rationality. Consider, for example, the following:

> While some passages in the Talmud implied that certain stars at the time of the birth of a person exerted an influence upon him, one should not surrender one's reason and accept a belief the falsity of which can be demonstrated by proofs.

Not a few of his contemporaries accused Maimonides of attempting to supplant the entire Rabbinic tradition and make of himself the ultimate arbiter of legal and theoretical disputes. Maimonides himself provided them with ammunition when he wrote in his introduction to

The Mishnah Torah that anyone familiar with the first five books of the Hebrew Bible (where biblical laws are contained) could, after reading *The Mishnah Torah,* have sufficient knowledge of the laws of Judaism so as not to have to consult any other book. Here is how Maimonides put it:

> In our day, when scholars are few and scholarship rare, I am compiling a book on the entire Jewish law, without discussions or debates, wherein all the laws are clearly explained. It will not be necessary, henceforth to consult any other work, but this for a knowledge of Jewish law, therefore I call this book *The Mishnah Torah,* 'The Second Torah.'

When one considers the fact that the Rabbinic literature (i.e., the Mishnah, the Midrash, and the Talmud) comprised part of the sacred base of Judaism, it is easy to understand why he called the work "The Second Torah." And when one considers that these works were part of an authoritative chain of tradition that went back to Sinai (think again of that passage we discussed from *Pirke Avoth*), it is easy to understand why some felt that Maimonides was appropriating for himself too much authority. Some Jews, in fact, condemned *The Mishnah Torah* as heretical.

The Commentary on the Mishnah and *The Mishnah Torah* are breathtaking achievements. We have already noted that the Mishnah, and especially the Talmud are large, variegated, and enormously complex works. Maimonides wrote *The Commentary on the Mishnah* and *The Mishnah Torah* in response to what he perceived as a crisis in Judaism. Maimonides was of the opinion that the immensity of the Jewish legal system which emerged out of the Mishnah and the Talmud and their many interpretations had rendered the system so inchoate that it was difficult to find the final ruling for a specific law, custom, or ritual. Maimonides' treatises made it unnecessary to search through the Mishnah and the Talmud.

There were, and have been, many who took issue with Maimonides for what they took to be tampering with sacred literature. Maimonides' rebuttal took one of two forms. In the first place, he insisted that he did not write either treatise for honor or power, although both came to him as a result of the widespread popularity of both works. And in the second place, he noted that he was prompted to compose the two works so that Jews would no longer be discouraged or perplexed in and by their study of Judaism. The legal system, Maimonides maintained, had to be made more comprehensible.

In 1183 Maimonides married the sister of a secretary to one of the wives of Saladin, the ruler of Egypt. One year later Maimonides became the personal physician of the court of Saladin. This brought prestige to the Egyptian Jewish community because a Jew had been entrusted with the health of the most powerful Muslim in Egypt. But for Maimonides the job was both time-consuming and potentially dangerous. If Saladin fell ill, Maimonides could easily have been blamed if the ruler did not recover.

In spite of his medical duties at the court, made all the more onerous because Saladin apparently had an abnormal anxiety about his health, Maimonides continued his scholarly pursuits. In 1191 (Maimonides is now 56 years old), he completed the work of his lifetime. It is called *The Guide of the Perplexed.* This work is divided into the following five parts:

1. *Epistle Dedicatory*—addressed to one Joseph ibn Aknin who had come in 1185 to study with Maimonides.

2. *General Introduction*—in which are contained some rules for reading *The Guide.*

3. *Part I*—which presents an interpretation of biblical expressions which, if read literally, could be taken to mean that God is in some way corporeal.

4. *Part II*—which presents a proof of the existence of an incorporeal God, wholly different and apart from everything else.

5. *Part III*—which presents an interpretation of the prophet Ezekiel's vision of the Chariot as well as an attempt to find a rational basis for the commandments in Judaism.

Maimonides wrote *The Guide* in Arabic with Hebrew letters. He had written *The Commentary on the Mishnah* in Hebrew and *The Mishnah Torah* in a form of Hebrew which had been unique to the Mishnah. Did Maimonides intend to limit the readership of *The Guide* to only those who knew both Arabic and Hebrew? Be that as it may, *The Guide* was translated into Hebrew during Maimonides' lifetime, apparently with his approval. Then in the thirteenth century it was translated into Latin. Thinkers the stature of Albertus Magnus and Thomas of Aquinas praised *The Guide.* In later years *The Guide* was translated into French, German, and English. *The Guide* has had a powerful and enduring influence not only on Jews and Judaism but on the philosophic tradition as well. We will return to *The Guide* shortly.

Maimonides also wrote extensively in the area of medicine. His fame as a healer, in fact, was so widespread that Richard the Lionhearted wanted Maimonides as his personal physician. It is worth noting that his medical writings are informed by rationality and modesty. He negates guesswork, mysticism, and superstition in the treatment of illness. And he observes repeatedly that he simply does not know the cause and course of a particular disease. He insists that a physician's first priority should be to convince his patient to live moderately, eat sensibly, and exercise regularly. Not surprisingly, some medical schools in our own time invoke a Maimonidean oath at graduation.

In sum, Maimonides' personal life was neither easy nor happy. His youth was spent in mortal fear of fanatical Muslims. In Egypt he was in constant danger from some Muslims and Jews who accused him of being a turncoat. These Muslims viewed him a Jew who converted to Islam only to return to Judaism, while the Jews complained that he had in fact converted to Islam. A daughter died in infancy. His only son was sickly and to Maimonides a disappointment. Some Jews condemned his work, particularly *The Guide,* as heretical. The feuds between his followers and detractors provoked such intensity that some of those who opposed him approached the Dominican order for aid in suppressing *The Guide.* The Dominicans, who had already banned the writings of Aristotle (whom Maimonides praises highly in *The Guide),* agreed, and many copies of *The Guide* went up in flames.

As the years passed, however, Maimonides gained increasing stature. When he died (1204), public mourning was declared throughout Egypt. And there arose about him a saying which attests to his extraordinary importance in the Jewish experience: "From Moses till Moses there arose none like Moses." We have noted the enormous importance of the biblical Moses. Within Judaism none is his equal. But Maimonides comes close.

It should be noted that his two legal works have not supplanted the Mishnah and the Talmud. While a multitude of commentaries have been written on *The Commentary on the Mishnah* and on the *Mishnah Torah,* center stage still belongs to the Mishnah and the Talmud. The attitude towards the *Guide* is somewhat ambiguous. Generally, the *Guide* is not studied with care within traditional Jewish circles. However, the *Guide* has been accorded an important place within the philosophic tradition.

There seems little doubt that from Maimonides' own perspective the *Guide* was his most profound work. In a general way it can be said that the *Guide* attempts to do for the Hebrew Bible what his two earlier works had done for the Mishnah and Talmud. Maimonides' approach to the Hebrew Bible is informed by the principle that there are at least two levels of meaning in Scripture. Put simply, Maimonides was certain that biblical writers deliberately obscured part of their teaching.

According to Maimonides, the biblical authors frequently created what seem to be simple stories which, however, contain deeper levels of meaning. At other times, the biblical authors would employ highly equivocal terms, especially in matters theological. Consider the following quotation from the *Guide:*

> Thus God is sometimes called 'merciful' because in accordance with that order the embryos of animals develop satisfactorily and parents have been endowed with the instinct to protect their children. Or, He [i.e., God] is called 'revengeful' because storms, floods, earthquakes, and the like work destruction.

> [All citations from Maimonides' *Guide* are from the S. Pines translation (Chicago: University of Chicago Press), 1964].

You will note that Maimonides attributes to biblical writers who describe God as "merciful" or "revengeful" a metaphysical intent. This is hardly the way most Jews of his day (or, for that matter, of our day) were reading the Hebrew Bible.

When Maimonides discusses the issue of God's providence, he, in effect, inverts the traditional conception. Mainstream Rabbinic (or

Pharisaic) Judaism asserted that God rewarded the doers of good and punished the doers of evil. That is, for the Pharisees one proves oneself worthy of God's beneficence by virtue of acts of loving kindness, with the proviso, of course, that God brings a large measure of compassion to the bar of justice.

Maimonides' notion of God's providence is seemingly much more oriented to what human beings do. In Maimonides' scheme, it is a human being's intellectual prowess which makes one worthy of God's "attention." God's providence, as it were, protects one according to the degree of that individual's "love" of God, a love which is congruent with how much he knows of God's creation. On the simplest level, and to exaggerate for the purpose of clarification, one who knows about gravity will not hazard a jump from the top of a skyscraper. Maimonides appears to be saying that we live in a universe which, potentially at least, can be comprehended. To the extent that we comprehend we are "protected." It follows, therefore, that God's providence is not equally concerned with all human beings. To put it another way, in Maimonides' view, the reward of virtue is the consequence of virtue, while the punishment of vice is the consequence of vice.

We now will survey Maimonides' interpretation of the book of Job, that biblical book whose chief thematic concern is God's providence. Hopefully, this survey will elucidate further Maimonides' conception of providence as well as the manner in which he searches out the meaning of a difficult biblical book. It is Maimonides' claim that, when first met, Job is preoccupied with a happiness which consists in being healthy, wealthy, and the head of a large family. Thus, when these are taken from him, Job suffers. At this point, Job is not wise, but he is morally perfect. (Thus Job 1:1: "Job was blameless and upright; he feared God and shunned evil.")

According to Maimonides, God educates Job in His revelation from the whirlwind (chs. 38–42). From this revelation Job understands that moral perfection is not the ultimate end of the human being. Rather, Job learns that the ideal human being is one who has actualized his intellect to the fullest extent possible. When this is accomplished, such an individual becomes indifferent to such things as health, wealth, and family. Such things, he realizes, are ephemeral, while the knowing mind, that which is most Godlike in man, is eternal and once actualized will be "protected" by God.

However, and this is a crucial adversative, most human beings, as Maimonides sees it, are incapable of fully actualizing their intellects. But since the Hebrew Bible was intended to meet the needs of all human beings, it must contain something of value for the unwise as well as the wise. Since most people are incapable of understanding profound philosophic thought, if the biblical authors were to speak plainly about such things, the great proportion of humankind would never read the Bible.

Accordingly, the biblical authors framed their teachings so that a reader of the Bible would understand as much or as little as that individual deserved to understand. Thus did the biblical authors imitate God's own model of providence. The more intellectual acumen one brings to the biblical text, the more one will understand. But even the surface level of the text is of benefit to the unenlightened reader, stressing as it does, continually, the need to live a decent life.

To repeat: one gets from the Bible what one deserves to get just as one gets from God what one deserves to get.

Maimonides divides the contents of the Hebrew Bible into four groups. In the first group, Maimonides puts the deepest, the most profound level of Scriptural teaching, that which points to true ideas about God, about creation, and about humankind's true character and fate. Only the most careful, only the most intellectually competent reader will notice the presence and plumb the significance of this level. Into the second group Maimonides puts those texts which stress the importance of compassion and justice. Thus the first group deals with what is true and what is false while the second group deals with what is moral and what is immoral. The third and fourth groups deal respectively with matters of history and ceremony. The last three groups have this in common: to impress the reader with the importance of leading a decent life.

We can infer from these groupings that Maimonides believed that the quintessential human activity, i.e., philosophic speculation, is beyond the reach of most human beings. It is therefore accurate to observe that the great majority of humankind is condemned to a fundamental ignorance concerning the highest truths. More than that, most human beings are unaware completely that they are ignorant. To these people the biblical writers expressed only a portion of what they knew of the truths in as vivid a manner as possible.

For Maimonides, the most perfect expression of religiosity is the quest for wisdom. From his perspective, the goal of the truly religious life is to learn what can be learned, to find a proof for everything which can be proven, for it is only by acquiring knowledge of God's creation that human beings gain knowledge of God. Even for the best of minds, however, our knowledge of God is fragmentary. Maimonides, for instance, readily admits that he has no idea what the ultimate purpose of the universe is.

But the purpose of human life is nonetheless clear to Maimonides: to become as knowledgeable as possible. For "...only wisdom can add to the inner strength and raise a man from low to high estate; for he was a man potentially [before the acquisition of wisdom], and has now become a man actually, and man before he thinks and acquires knowledge is esteemed an animal."

Humanity, therefore, consists of potential and actual human beings. In Maimonides' opinion, the difference between the "potential" and "actual" human being is greater than the difference between humanity as a whole and other kinds of animals. To be sure, it is a grim picture which Maimonides paints. Since the development of an actual human being is very long and difficult, sometimes but one in a generation succeeds. The rest of humankind remains always at various stages of potentiality.

To understand the thrust of Maimonides' thought you must understand that according to him, it is the ability to move from premises to conclusions in a series of logical steps which separates the human being from the beast. Maimonides claims not to know why God created man as He did. This claim is in line with Maimonides' acknowledgment that man has only fragmentary knowledge. In any case, Maimonides presents as the highest ideal the quest to understand things as they are, and not as he might wish them to be. Although Maimonides might wish otherwise, "potential" man exists for the benefit of the "actual" man:

These men [potential human beings] exist for two reasons. First, to serve the one [actual] man: for man has many wants and life is not long enough to learn all the crafts whereof a man has absolute need for living: and when should he find leisure to learn and to acquire wisdom? The rest of mankind, therefore, exists to set right those things that are necessary to man in the commonwealth, for the end that the wise man may find his needs provided for and that wisdom may spread. And secondly, the man without wisdom exists because the wise are very few, and therefore the masses were created to make a society for the wise, that they be not lonely.

At this point it is very important to understand that Maimonides' actual or wise man is not at war with society. If we can assume that Maimonides himself was such a wise man then one need only examine his life which was filled with acts of service to his people. The wise man (and Maimonides himself is a good example of this) lives two lives. In the one, he is engaged in a mostly private quest for wisdom. In the other, he participates in the society which is maintained by the less than wise. In the case of Maimonides, *The Guide of the Perplexed* would represent his guide for the potentially wise while his legal works would be directed to a non-philosophic audience who are engaged in solving societal problems.

The wise man needs society in order to satisfy his elementary needs, as, e.g., companionship, food, and shelter. If the wise man had to attend to these needs he would lack the requisite time and energy to engage in the intellectual quest. In short, the welfare of society is as important to the wise man as it is to the mass of mankind.

We are now in a position to understand Maimonides' attitude toward Judaism in specific and religion in general. According to Maimonides, the true aim of religion is to sustain societal order. As such, the teachings, prescriptions, and proscriptions of religion must be tailored not for the wise few but for the great mass of mankind. Religion is meant to create a climate conducive to societal order. This it achieves by appealing to humankind's baser, more selfish instincts in order to induce philanthropic behavior. Thus, for instance, religion taps into man's selfish proclivity by promising eternal bliss (and by not foreclosing the possibility that this blissful state can be pretty much in line with what the individual wants) in return for a lifestyle which is law abiding. Religion also transmits a system of ritual observances which explicates what in fact it means to be law abiding.

Maimonides believes that it is of the utmost importance for religion to blunt the selfish tendencies of humankind, for if individuals were free to give vent to them society would be torn apart. Religion's ultimate weapon is the warning that God knows not only what all human beings do, but also what they think and feel. Religion's God is the judge who neither slumbers nor sleeps.

By helping to maintain societal order, religion allows for the possibility for one among the many to give himself over to the quest for truth. This quest, of course, is governed by the dictates of reason. The wise man needs religion only in the sense that without it there would not be the societal order which would enable him to pursue his theoretical interests. Religion, therefore, is not "above" reason but "below" it, just as the masses for whom religion was created are "below" the few wise individuals. It is the reasonable few who determine the content of religion; it is the reasonable few who determine whether an individual speaks for God.

Perhaps Maimonides' observations here will remind you of that passage in Deuteronomy (Deut. 13:2–6) in which a miracle worker who violates the law—which for Maimonides would be a rationally conceived law code, the observance of which leads to societal order without repression—is to be put to death. In this biblical passage it is not a supernatural capacity which testifies to the presence of God. In fact, God uses the supernatural to test His people's faith. As Maimonides interprets this passage, the litmus test for religiosity is obedience to a law code conceived of by Moses, the greatest of prophets, whose prophecy is noteworthy for its rationality.

Thus, when Maimonides wrote *The Guide of the Perplexed* his purpose was to uncover (for those of his readers able to see it) the philosophic core of Judaism, particularly as it manifested itself in the Hebrew Bible. As the title suggests, the *Guide* is directed toward those "perplexed" individuals who were torn between what they thought were the conflicting demands of their minds and hearts. These "perplexed" felt that they faced a hard disjunction: one had either to choose the philosophic quest with its emphasis (when all is said and done) on reflective questions, or one chose the way of religion, with its emphasis on answers (i.e., "thus says the Lord...").

Maimonides, in what is surely the most obvious level of the *Guide*, sought to assure those perplexed that it was unnecessary to reject either the philosophic quest or Judaism because, at its core, Judaism was inherently philosophic. In the *Guide*, Maimonides attempted to demonstrate the philosophic nature of the Hebrew Bible, not certainly in its literal but in its metaphorical rendering. Not that all biblical texts are to be interpreted allegorically. But, according to Maimonides, any text which appears to be irrational is to be interpreted in such a way so that its moral is rational.

Maimonides' advice to the perplexed went as follows:

— To thoroughly study the sciences in an orderly fashion.

— To "...not decide every question by the first idea that suggests itself to his mind or at once direct his thoughts and force them to obtain a knowledge of the Creator; he must wait modestly and patiently, and advance step by step. In this sense we must understand the words: 'And Moses hid his face, for he was afraid to look upon God.' "

— To understand, and this is his metaphor, that thought is but a flash in a long night, for man is "in the dark" about most important issues and he will surely never see what light that can be seen unless and until he becomes aware of his ignorance.

— To remain committed to the intellectual quest in spite of the difficulties and imponderables. For while most human beings want to know the truth they want it handed to them on a silver platter; few, that is, have the persistence to remain devoted to theoretical pursuits. In Maimonides' words: "Even the simplest of persons, if you were to wake him up, so to speak, and say to him, would you like to know how many heavens there are, what they are like, and what they contain, what the angels are; how the world was created, what is its purpose and order; what is the soul, and how did it originate in the body, and if so, how, and what is its destiny after separation? He would without doubt say yes. He is eager to know these things. But if you asked him to give up his business for a week, he would refuse, and content himself with vague fancies which appeal to him, and disdain to listen to the man who tells him there are certain matters which cannot be known without much preparation and long study."

I ask the reader to consider again the questions raised by Maimonides in the above quotation. Do they not comprise the sum and substance of the philosophic quest? And is not his assessment of both the eagerness of most people to know the answers to such questions and their unwillingness to spend much time in the search right on the mark?

When Maimonides speaks of what he calls the "great secrets" (i.e., those matters relating to the realm of metaphysics), it is clear that no one in the human community understands them fully and completely. As he puts it, "We are like someone in a very dark night over whom the lightning flashes time and time again." In this context he extends his metaphor and in the process divides humankind as follows:

— Those like Moses for whom the lightning flashes (which would correspond to intellectual enlightenment) are so frequent that it is as if he is in daylight;

— for some few others, the lightning is occasional; Maimonides puts most biblical prophets in this group (you will note that the distinguishing characteristic of Mosaic prophecy is, for Maimonides, its intellectual profundity);

— others only know of the lightning flashes by hearsay; these are individuals who can learn from the great masters but who cannot themselves teach;

— those who never see the light and never hear about it either.

This last group Maimonides refers to as the "vulgar" and he makes it very clear that they will find nothing of value in the *Guide*. The *Guide* is directed at those like Joseph, the addressee of the Epistle Dedicatory. When Joseph came to study with him, Maimonides tested Joseph's intellectual acumen by leading him through a programmatic study beginning with math and leading to astronomy. Joseph had no trouble at this early stage of his studies.

After Joseph next proved himself in logic, Maimonides decided that Joseph: "...was one worthy to have the secrets of the prophetic books revealed...so that you could consider in them that which a perfect man ought to consider." It was at this point that Maimonides' pedagogy changed. Whereas before there had been a direct and orderly progression from the simple to the more complex, now, in regard to the "secrets" Maimonides would only point obliquely to "certain indications." These "indications" are the equivalent of lightning flashes. But here Joseph bridled and demanded that Maimonides tell him, in an unequivocal fashion, about the "deep secrets." When Maimonides refused, Joseph terminated their relationship. Here is how Maimonides puts it:

> Then when God decreed our separation and you betook yourself elsewhere, these meetings aroused in me a resolution that had slackened. Your absence moved me to compose this Treatise which I have composed for you and for those like you, however few they are.

Whatever else it does, the Epistle Dedicatory lays out the virtues necessary for the intellectual quest for truth. It indicates that mental acuity, modesty, a willingness to listen, and patience are necessary to maintain the exhausting marathon run for the truth. Maimonides' *Guide* is meant to help those who are able and willing to make the "run." And if that run is the most exalted activity of which a human being is capable, then it is only a bit of an overstatement to call the *Guide* a salvific aid. Here is how Maimonides ends his Introduction to the *Guide:*

> This [The *Guide*], then, will be a key permitting one to enter places the gates to which were locked. And when these gates are opened, and these places are entered into, the souls will find rest therein, the eyes will be delighted, and the bodies will be eased of their toil and of their labor.

We have already noted that no one has occupied a more important place in the postbiblical Jewish experience than has Moses Maimonides. However, most Jews who revere his name know him for his legal work while scarcely paying any attention to the *Guide.* Moreover, a host of other thinkers were far less inclined than was Moses Maimonides to make reason Judaism's seal of truth. To the extent that this discussion took place within the boundaries of Judaism, it inevitably involved the Hebrew Bible. What, it was asked, did the Hebrew Bible reveal itself to be? Was it, as Maimonides and those who championed his cause claimed, a work which revealed its meaning only upon the most critical scrutiny or was it a relatively simple chronicle of events which were, to be sure, sometimes of the fantastic variety?

Judah Halevi (1075–1141) is representative of those who read the Hebrew Bible not as a philosophic treatise but as an historically accurate account of God at work in history. Halevi's major work is entitled *The Book of the Khazars.* This work takes the form of a dialogue and it appears to criticize the very position which Maimonides later would advance.

The Book of the Khazars (henceforth referred to as the *Kuzari*) presents an imaginary discussion between a Khazar king and representatives of Christianity, Islam, and Judaism, plus a philosopher. The Christian, the Muslim, the Jew, and the philosopher each attempts to convert the king.

The king rejects the views of the philosopher, the Muslim, and the Christian before turning to the Jew who sums up his faith as follows:

> We believe in the God of Abraham, Isaac, and Jacob, who led the children of Israel from Egypt with signs and miracles, who fed them in the desert; and having guided them through the Sea and the Jordan, gave them the land of Canaan for an inheritance. We believe in the God who sent Moses and his Torah, and many thousand prophets after him, exhorting the Jews to keep the Torah, promising high reward to the observant and severe punishment to the disobedient.

Halevi's Rabbi thus looked upon the Hebrew Bible not primarily as a repository of philosophical truth but rather as a chronicle of God's workings in history. To say the least, Maimonides rejected such a conclusion. In the second chapter of his first major section of the *Guide,* in which he recounts a dispute he once had with an unnamed scholar concerning the Garden of Eden story, Maimonides begins his refutation with these caustic words:

> Hear now the intent of our reply. We said: O you who engage in theoretical speculation using the first notions that may occur to you and come to your mind and who consider withal that you understand a book [the Hebrew Bible] that is the guide of the first and last men while glancing through it as you would glance through a historical work....

For Halevi's Rabbi, the truly worthy individual would believe in the Hebrew Bible as a register of God's involvements in history and would, accordingly, observe the commandments found therein as ends in themselves. Maimonides' worthy individual observed the commandments, to be sure, but not as ends in themselves. In Maimonides' view, the commandments create and sustain an environment, both for the individual and the society, in which the quest for knowledge could be conducted. The commandments serve a purely political purpose. The commandments are ends in themselves only to those who are incapable of metaphysical speculation.

Maimonides believes that the Hebrew Bible is not for the most part a chronicle of events so much as it is a road map or guide which can direct one on the quest for wisdom. As we have noted, Maimonides believes that the biblical contexts which prescribe ceremonies or which present factual chronicles either have a deeper philosophic meaning or are intended for those readers who are incapable of speculating about the great secrets.

For Halevi's Rabbi it is otherwise. In fact, Halevi's Rabbi defends Judaism not only against what he understands to be Christianity and Islam, but against philosophy as well. He succeeds in converting the king of Khazars, who initially had been prejudiced against Jews and Judaism, to Judaism. The Rabbi's defense of Judaism hinges on his assertion that the ultimate purpose of Judaism is moral behavior. The Rabbi's role model is the biblical Moses whom he characterizes as a moral exemplar whose wisdom comes not from within (i.e., as the result of theorizing) but from without (i.e., from God).

Of course, Maimonides' role model is also Moses. However, Maimonides' Moses is first and foremost a philosopher who also happens to be a moral human being.

Does Halevi's Rabbi or Maimonides best represent the mainstream position in Judaism? Seemingly, the most accurate answer is that the Jewish experience has found room for not only both, but for virtually every position in between.

On the face of it, the two views appear to be irreconcilable. For Halevi's Rabbi, the highest duty of man is to obey the divine commandments which have as their ultimate purpose the moral life. Halevi's Rabbi seems convinced that philosophy is dangerous for it calls into question the possibility of revelation and therefore it calls into question the unique legitimacy of those commandments said to be given by God. Philosophy thereby undermines not only the unconditional, absolute value of the moral code of Judaism but it leads some of the best minds away from the practice of Judaism.

The proof, for Maimonides, that one is with God is rational reflection; the better the reflection the "closer" one is to God. The proof for Halevi's Rabbi that one is with God is moral behavior.

The two positions represented by Maimonides and Halevi's Rabbi reflect a fundamental tension in Judaism that probably goes back to the very beginnings of the Jewish experience. At the center of the conflict are disparate views not only of human nature but of the Hebrew Bible. For Halevi's Rabbi, the sacred tradition is relatively clear and unambiguous. For Maimonides, the sacred tradition is riddled with ambiguity, and its highest expression must be deciphered in order to be understood.

The practical dimensions of the conflict can be summed up as follows: a life of obedient love versus a life of independent insight. Independent reason thrives on the asking of questions. And to independent reason, revelation is, at best, an uncertain hypothesis. But while reason thrives on questions, a part of man also yearns for answers to these questions. And the more important the question, the deeper the yearning. Moreover, since the possibility of revelation cannot, it would seem, be ruled out, many like Halevi's Rabbi have faith that revelation's concrete expression is in the Hebrew Bible.

Like almost every other fundamental dispute in Judaism, this one too finds its venue in the Hebrew Bible. However, as much as Maimonides and Halevi differ, and the differences appear to be profound, they and their followers agree completely on the absolute and unique importance of the Hebrew Bible for Jews and Judaism.

The all-important place occupied by the Hebrew Bible in the Jewish experience is a point to which we have returned repeatedly. I now want to make this point again by referring you to Benedict Spinoza (1632–1677), the man who is most responsible for effecting a change in the way in which the Bible is read. Keeping in mind Professor Strauss' distinction between "interpretation" and "explanation," it was Spinoza's *Theological-Political Treatise* which shifted the emphasis in biblical scholarship from interpretation to explanation.

In our day, few scholars read the Bible the way Halevi and Maimonides did. In our day, scholars generally read the Bible the way in which they would read any other book. Both Halevi and Maimonides viewed the Bible as a unique book, although they interpreted it differently. Benedict Spinoza declared openly and unambiguously in his *Theological-Political Treatise* that the Bible should be studied as one would study any other book because the Bible, like all other books, is of human origin.

Spinoza was born in Amsterdam of Spanish Jews who had sought refuge in the Protestant Netherlands from the Inquisition. Spinoza's parents provided him with a first class education, both religious and secular. It was not long before Spinoza became one of the "perplexed" for whom Maimonides, centuries before, had written his *Guide of the Perplexed.*

But whereas Maimonides very clearly advised the perplexed to remain loyal to the faith of their forebears (advice Maimonides himself followed), Spinoza was to leave Judaism. More precisely, Spinoza was to be excommunicated. One cause for this difference is clear: Maimonides claimed to find in the Bible sufficient reason to remain a Jew while Spinoza found no such reason.

In the *Theological-Political Treatise* Spinoza has not one good word to say about Moses Maimonides, whose biblical interpretations he dismisses as "...useless and absurd." [All citations are from the Elwes translation of Spinoza's works, Vol. I (New York: Dover, 1951)]. In the *Treatise,* Spinoza also turns against the position advocated by Halevi's Rabbi. Spinoza thus repudiates those like Moses Maimonides who seek to subordinate Scripture to the authority of reason and those like Halevi's Rabbi who seek to subordinate reason to Scripture.

To put this last point another way, Spinoza argues that those like Maimonides seek to make the biblical prophets into philosophers, giving the prophets "...many ideas which they never even dreamed of," while those like Halevi's Rabbi accept mindless superstitions as divine utterances, "...in short, one party runs wild with the aid of reason, and the other runs wild without the aid of reason."

According to his own testimony, Spinoza read and re-read the Bible with great care and he advises his readers to read the Bible as one "reads" nature. One attempts to understand nature by inferring the definitions of natural things from the data supplied by nature herself. One's conclusions are, or should be, independent of what may be just, beautiful, or reasonable. Nature must be allowed to speak for herself.

In the same way, the Bible must be allowed to speak for itself; knowledge of the Bible must be derived from the data supplied by the Bible itself and not at all from consideration of what is reasonable. Spinoza insists that we have no right to assume that the views of the biblical authors conform to the dictates of human reason.

According to Spinoza, nature reveals herself to be consistent and coherent. The Bible, however, does not. Spinoza asserts that the Bible is written in a very obscure style and that, moreover, it is not possible to understand very well the language in which it is written. To quote Spinoza, "The devouring tooth of time has destroyed nearly all the phrases and turns and expressions peculiar to the Hebrews, so that we know them no more." Spinoza concludes:

> If we read a book which contains incredible or impossible narratives, or is written in a very obscure style, and if we know nothing of its author, nor of the time or occasion of its being written, we shall vainly endeavor to gain any certain knowledge of its true meaning.

In substance, therefore, Spinoza is asserting that the Bible is an unintelligible book. Halevi's Rabbi and Maimonides, however much they disagreed on what the Bible teaches, were of one mind in the conviction that the Bible was a most intelligible book.

When Spinoza maintains that his method of interpreting the Bible is identical with the method of interpreting nature, his analogy points to a decisive difference between him and Maimonides and Halevi's Rabbi. Natural science is concerned with the task of establishing objective knowledge. Spinoza believes that "Nature is not bounded by the laws of human reason, which aim only at man's true benefit and preservation; her limits are infinitely wider, and have reference to the eternal order of nature, wherein man is but a speck...." According to Spinoza, God can be known only from the fixed and immutable order of nature; "...nature...always observes laws and rules which involve eternal necessity and truth, although they may not be known to us, and therefore she keeps a fixed and immutable order."

Spinoza's conception of an immutable natural order has no place in it for the miraculous, that is, for the overturning of the natural order. And, in fact, on more than one occasion Spinoza asserts that the miracles recorded in Scripture never happened. He says that the miracles existed only in the superstitious imaginings of those who either thought (mistakenly) they witnessed the extraordinary or who were told of such a happening and believed it.

The many miracles recorded in Scripture testify, Spinoza believes, not only to the text's irrationality but to the naive presence of the view that nature and nature's God are responsive to the needs of humankind. While one biblical poet may proclaim that humanity is the "apple of God's eye," for Spinoza, humanity is but a "speck" in the infinite swirl of the universe. In short, the miracle stories are but one manifestation of what Spinoza calls the "crude speculations" to be found in the Bible. As he puts it, "The Israelite people knew scarcely anything of God;" and later, "Miracles were wrought according to the understanding of the masses, who are wholly ignorant of the workings of nature; it is certain that the ancients took for a miracle whatever they could not explain by the method adopted by the unlearned in such cases...."

We saw that from the point of view of Halevi's Rabbi, the miracle tales in Scripture are to be accepted as factual occurrences which testify to the power and grace of God. For Maimonides, the miracle stories are parables which have within them the highest of prophetic truths. That is, both Maimonides and Halevi's Rabbi, although for different reasons and in different ways, attest to both the excellence and supreme uniqueness of the Bible. Maimonides maintained that, properly interpreted, the miracle stories reveal a philosophic understanding of what he called the great secrets. Moreover, he claimed that since the outside layers of those stories were so simply and beautifully rendered, they were of benefit to the non-philosophic reader as well. Thus did Scripture, perhaps better than any other piece of literature, offer guidance to all shades of humanity.

Halevi's Rabbi, of course, believed that Scripture's miracle stories, as it were, said what they meant and meant what they said when they said (on the external level): God, in fact, sent manna, split the seas, etc. For Halevi's Rabbi, the Bible is first and foremost a record of a time when God regularly walked and talked with humankind.

Spinoza would disagree completely with Halevi's Rabbi on the issue of miracles. Spinoza would insist that miracles did not and do not occur. The miracle stories in Scripture testify to the primitive, prephilosophic nature of the biblical record. Spinoza was certain that miracles like those recounted in the Bible were not reported in his day because his age had a more precise understanding of the workings of nature. He asserted that in the biblical age thought was dominated by imagination, and not ordered by clear and distinct insight and rational planning. The method of argument peculiar to Scripture is not scientific but vulgar. Therefore, the Bible is quite simply not reliable in speculative matters:

> In truth, it is hardly likely that men accustomed to the superstitions of Egypt, uncultivated and sunk in most abject slavery, should have held very sound notions about the Deity....

On one point, however, Spinoza's evaluation of the Bible is similar to that of Halevi's Rabbi. Spinoza holds that the Bible is not to be dismissed out of hand because of its theoretical unworthiness. For the intent of Scripture is not theoretical but practical:

> ...Scriptural doctrine contains no lofty speculation nor philosophic reasoning, but only very simple matters, such as could be understood by the slowest intelligence.... Scripture does not aim at imparting scientific knowledge, and therefore, it demands from man nothing but obedience, and censures obstinacy, but not ignorance.

And it is at this point that we come face to face with a paradox. Halevi's Rabbi and Spinoza would agree that the Bible is to be read literally but they would disagree about the worth of what a literal reading reveals. For unlike Halevi's Rabbi, Spinoza does not equate the love of God with the moral norms enunciated in the name of the biblical God. For Spinoza, love of God, as for Maimonides, is bound up with the intellectual quest for truth. But for Maimonides the Bible is the most invaluable guide in this quest while for Spinoza the Bible is virtually without speculative value.

That Maimonides would agree with Spinoza about the ultimate purpose of human existence, even though Spinoza severed all ties with Judaism, gives witness once more to the central role of the Bible in Judaism. Maimonides claimed to be able to pursue the quest for wisdom by studying the Bible. Spinoza, in effect, ridiculed the intellectual incompetence of the biblical authors.

Moreover, the fact that both Halevi's Rabbi and Maimonides, as differently as they interpreted reality *and* the Hebrew Bible, are nonetheless permanent fixtures in the Jewish experience, testifies again to the diversity of the Jewish experience.

9

The Pre-Modern Experience of the Jews: Paving the Way to the Gas Chamber

In this chapter I am going to trace a broad pattern of persecution of Jews by Christians in pre-modern times. My purpose in doing this is two-fold. In the first place, I want to give the reader some sense of the terrible problem facing Jews as a minority group in societies in which religion was a public rather than a private concern. And in the second place, this pre-modern persecution of the Jews should make it easier for you to understand the how and the why of the Holocaust.

The decisive fact to keep in mind about the experience of the Jews in pre-modern Europe is that, at best, Jews were a tolerated minority: strangers in strange lands. Very few Jews could have protected themselves, as had Father Abraham, by offering a family member as ransom. Pre-modern Europe was for the Jews a much more dangerous place than Canaan had been for the first Israelites. In pre-modern Europe the Jew was consistently denied full-scale citizenship because citizenship was related to religion and there were no Jewish lands. There were Christian lands and there were Muslim lands, but there were no secular nation states in which religion was a private concern. When the Jews were deemed useful by their Christian or Muslim hosts, the Jews often enjoyed a positive existence. When not, the Jews suffered, and sometimes they suffered terribly.

In Germany, France, and England many Jews functioned as international merchants and as large scale money lenders. Both secular and religious leaders used the services of the Jews and for periods of time not only did the Jews achieve positions of power and prestige, but many Jewish communities flourished. However, even in the best of times the Jews realized that at a moment's notice the work of a lifetime could be taken from them. In pre-modern Europe, the Jews were little more than movable property.

The Crusades, for instance, were a disaster for the Jews of Europe. The Church proclaimed that those who took up the Cross in order to expel the Muslims from Christian holy places would be saved. It made sense to many of the Crusaders, the overwhelming majority of whom were ignorant and hungry, to first punish the "enemies of Christ" (i.e., the Jews) in their midst in order to more immediately (and more safely) derive spiritual and material profit.

When not subject to actual persecution, Jews lived always under its threat because of the Church's contention that Jews were to be denied what we would call basic human rights, i.e., life, liberty, and the pursuit of happiness. Pope Gregory VII, for example, in 1081, urged the ruler of Spain to be stricter with the Jews in his domain:

> We admonish your Highness that you must cease to suffer the Jews to rule over Christians and exercise authority over them. For to allow Christians to be subordinate to Jews, and to be subject to their judgment, is the same as to oppress God's church and exalt the synagogue of Satan. To wish to please the enemies of Christ means to treat Christ himself with contumely.
>
> [Quoted in Malcolm Hay, *The Foot of Pride* (Boston: The Beacon Press, 1951), pp. 35f.]

The Pope's preachment could neither be clearer nor potentially more dangerous: the Jews are satanic; they are the enemies of Christ; to treat the Jews with even-handedness is tantamount to insulting Jesus. If from the highest level of the Church, the level in fact which repeatedly came to the aid of Jews, then one can imagine what some of the local priests said and did. Many of these priests described graphically Christ's sufferings and blamed the Jews for it. Jewish communities throughout Europe lived in fear, especially during Holy Week when Christians frequently came out of Easter services primed to repay Jewish perfidy by subjecting Jews to verbal and physical abuse.

Such incidents, however, were as nothing compared to what the Crusaders did to the Jews. The First Crusade (1096) began and ended with massacres of Jews. The great English historian Lord Acton wrote that "the men who took the cross, after receiving communion, heartily devoted the day to the extermination of the Jews." During the course of that Crusade, more than ten thousand Jews were murdered and countless more raped, assaulted, and robbed.

During the Second Crusade, an already volatile situation was made worse by one Ralph, a Cistercian monk, who in the course of his efforts to recruit soldiers, told the Germans that it was their duty first to kill "the enemies of Christ" (the Jews) in their own locales. Bernard, who had been commissioned by the Pope (in 1145) to preach the Second Crusade, had succeeded in adding more recruits by proclaiming that the killing of Muslims in the Holy Land would gain for the Crusaders a place in heaven. Ralph took that preachment and applied it to the Jews, proclaiming that it was equally meritorious (and certainly less dangerous) to kill unarmed Jews. The masses had no difficulty accepting this because for years they had been listening to their priests describe the Jews as the enemies of Christ. As a result of Ralph's preachment, thousands of Jewish men, women, and children were slaughtered.

To his credit, Bernard tried to stop the carnage. He censured Ralph and sent him back to his monastery. But Bernard did not speak the mob's language and, moreover, he was unable to convince the German bishops to intervene on behalf of the Jews. Bernard's failure can probably be attributed to his unwillingness to condemn in no uncertain terms the persecution of the Jews.

Why? On the one hand, Bernard knew that if he did not stop the slaughter of the Jews the Crusaders would lack any motivation to undertake a dangerous journey to meet a well-armed foe. But, on the other hand, he was reluctant to hinder recruiting, nor did he want to imply that Jews should be regarded as normal human beings.

You must understand that St. Bernard was the only one in a high position in the Church who stepped forward to help the Jews. And he was by no means enthusiastic; St. Bernard treated the subject of their having been murdered (and in great numbers) gingerly. Here is some of what Bernard wrote in his encyclical:

> The earth is shaken because the Lord of heaven is losing his land [i.e., Palestine], the land in which he appeared to men, in which he lived amongst men for more than thirty years; the land made glorious by his miracles, holy by his blood.... [He goes on to indicate the sacrilegious ways of the Muslims who control the Holy Land]. Do not hesitate. God is good, and were he intent on your punishment he would not have asked of you this present service [the Crusade]...in return for your taking up arms in his cause, He can reward you with pardon for your sins and everlasting glory...you have a cause for which you can fight without danger to your souls; a cause in which to conquer is glorious and for which to die is gain.... The cost is small, the reward is great...your zeal needs the timely restraint of knowledge. The Jews are not to be persecuted, killed, or even put to flight. Ask anyone who knows the Sacred Scriptures what he finds foretold of the Jews.... The Jews are for us the living words of Scripture, for they remind us always of what our Lord suffered. They are despised all over the world so that by expiating their crime they may be everywhere the living witnesses of our redemption...if the Jews are utterly wiped out, what will become of our hope for their promised salvation, their eventual conversion.

[Quoted in H. Graetz, *History of the Jews,* III (London), pp. 355ff.].

Bernard's reasons for refraining from murdering Jews are rooted not in morality but in pragmatism. He argues that it was a mistake to kill Jews because their existence helped to strengthen Christian faith. Also, if the Jews were treated too harshly they would not convert to Christianity. I direct your attention now to the words with which Bernard ends his remarks on the Jews. In effect, he offers consolation for those who now could no longer kill defenseless Jews. Here is what he wrote:

> But you may demand from them...that all who take up the Cross shall be freed from all exactions of usury.

The Crusaders, that is, did not have to pay off their debts to Jews. That the Jews had to depend on such a "benefactor" underlines how desperate was their plight.

The idea of making the Jews pay for the expenses of the Crusades was used also by one Peter the Venerable who wrote:

> Why should not the Jews contribute more than any one else to the expenses of the holy war? Robbers they be; this is the very reason for compelling them to disgorge. Sacrilegious blasphemers, this is the way to punish their impiety.
>
> [*Ibid.*, p. 360]

For the monk Peter the Venerable, Judaism was synonymous with irreligiosity.

Sadly, it was rare indeed for a Christian religious leader to attack the tradition of anti-Jewishness. Abelard (1079–1142) was one of the few who did. It is of the utmost significance that Abelard attacked this tradition by going to the root of the problem. Abelard asserted that the Jewish people were not responsible for the death of Jesus. He argued that both Jesus and his original disciples were Jews; that the ministry of Jesus was to the Jews; that the Bible of Jesus was the Hebrew Bible; and that, according to the Bible, God's covenant with the Jewish people was eternal. Abelard contended that to hold Jews of all times and places responsible for the death of Jesus was antithetical to the high religious ethic preached by Jesus himself and was therefore disgraceful.

For the most part, Abelard's was a lone voice in the wilderness. Even when, as sometimes happened, the Papacy intervened to stop pillaging of the Jews, the intervention was equivocal. Innocent III, for instance, intervened to caution the Crusaders against slaughtering the Jews in Europe before departing for the Holy Land (as had Bernard in a previous crusade). Innocent proclaimed that the Jews had a right to life but not to a life on an equal footing with their Christian neighbors. The Pope believed that the Jews deserved to live in a state of misery and deprivation.

Pope Innocent III prescribed how Christians should treat Jews and how they should view Judaism. Innocent asserted that:

— Jews were not to be subjected to violence in order to be forcibly converted.

— Christians must not injure, kill, or rob Jews.

— Jews must be permitted to observe their religious tradition without Christian interference.

— Jewish cemeteries were not to be desecrated.

So far so good. But the Pope went on to remark that these pre-scriptions were to apply only to "...those Jews who have not presumed to plot against the Christian faith." [S. Grayzel, *The Church and the Jews in the Thirteenth Century* (Philadelphia, 1933), p.117 f.]

But how was one to interpret this proviso? Many Christians in positions of authority believed that some of the most obvious Jewish observances, such as the dietary laws and some Passover rituals, were in and of themselves anti-Christian. And, of course, many Christians remained convinced that the Jews, by virtue of their re-fusal to accept Jesus as Messiah, were by their very existence as Jews "plotting" against Christians and/or Christianity. Moreover, the Crusaders habitually used the rationalization that Jews were en-gaged in a conspiracy to undermine the Crusades.

In 1205 Pope Innocent III wrote two official letters about Jews and Judaism. One was addressed to the secular ruler of France and the other to the Archbishop of Sens and the Bishop of Paris. The let-ter sent to the Bishops begins with a restatement of the long held principle in the Church that Jews were to be denied the most basic rights "...because they crucified the Lord." It was Christian compas-sion, and not any intrinsic right to life, which was permitting the Jews a continued existence. This toleration which Christians were expected to exhibit toward Jews was yet another indication of the su-periority of Christianity over Judaism, the implication being that were the roles reversed Christians would not fare nearly so well un-der a Jewish majority.

Innocent's letter to the king of France charged the Jews with idolatry, i.e., with worshipping not God but greed. The letter also noted that the Jews took every opportunity to commit gross offenses against Christians and Christianity. The Jews, he asserted, "...take advantage of every opportunity to kill in secret their Christian hosts." Innocent warned the king not to treat the Jews with evenhandedness because rulers who do so "...are exceedingly offensive in the sight of the Divine Majesty who prefer the sons of the crucifiers against whom to this day the blood cries to the Father's ears." Innocent was convinced that if the strict standards of justice were applied the Jews would be wiped off the face of the earth. But while God's decision not to abrogate His covenant with the people Israel was unfathomable, it was nonetheless clear to Innocent that God wanted the Jews to be completely servile to Christians. Innocent urged that economic weapons, ranging from boycotts of Jewish businesses to expulsion from many occupations, be used against Jews.

Ironically, Innocent's two letters would seem to point to two different phenomena. On the obvious level, it is clear that such formal pronouncements only served to intensify a pervasive social ostracism which excluded Jews from sections of town, from all entertainment establishments, from places of culture, and so on. But these letters, and especially the one to the king of France, indicate that some Jews had achieved a measure of power and success which some Christians found offensive.

THE FOURTH LATERAN COUNCIL

In 1215 Innocent convoked the Fourth Lateran Council, four sessions of which were set aside to discuss the treatment of Jews and Judaism. The more than one thousand delegates condemned the practice of usury and pretty much blamed the Jews for it. The delegates did not discuss the fact that in many locales, provincial parishes had borrowed heavily from Jewish money lenders and, moreover, had all too often simply refused to repay the loans. The Fourth Lateran Council provided legal justification for the forgiveness of these debts because, for all practical purposes, the Council defined usurious as any money lent to a Christian by a Jew.

The Council also prohibited the Jews from appearing in public on Christian holidays. And any Jew who was found guilty of "presumptuously blaspheming" was to be arrested and fined. This charge was left so undefined that it came to be applied to Jews who practiced Judaism. Most of the delegates were entirely ignorant about Judaism and in their ignorance assumed that Judaism was by its very nature inherently blasphemous to Christians and Christianity. The most degrading decree which the Council imposed was that which forced Jews to wear a distinctive identifying badge along with criminals and the physically and mentally diseased.

In effect, the Fourth Lateran Council "defined" Judaism only in its relationship to Christianity, and, as such, Judaism was viewed as an affront to Christianity, while Jews were classified as inferior beings. Since these decrees came from the highest level of the Church hierarchy, they engendered terrible excesses among the common people who knew even less about Judaism. In the eyes of many, Jews were deemed to be little more than animals.

As the Crusaders pillaged one Jewish community after another in western Europe, many Jews fled eastward and found a haven in Poland. Although there were periods of persecution and repression, the Polish Jewish community often prospered and, as a result, by the time Hitler came to power there were 3,300,000 Polish Jews. Only 300,000 survived the Holocaust. Initially, the secular powers in Poland welcomed the Jews because many of the Jews had skills which the Polish regime felt it could use. Such Christian kings as Casmir the Great (1333–70), for instance, offered Jews "charters of privilege" as well as protection in return for the Jews' fiscal expertise, ability as administrators, and as urban dwellers.

But even in eastern Europe there was no escaping the edicts of the Fourth Lateran Council. In 1266 the Council of Breslau (a city in southwestern Poland) ordered that Jews were to be segregated from Christians because Christians "...might fall an easy prey to the influence of the superstitions and evil habits of Jews living amongst them." In general, however, the secular powers ignored the Church and gave the Jews protected status.

Jews were often given limited self-rule and they created academies of learning which were the equal of the great Pharisaic schools of the past. However, when Poland was wracked by economic woes in the seventeenth century, the Jews were caught between warring factions and there were horrible slaughters. The point to be made here is that in good economic times the Jews were deemed useful, but woe to them in times of economic dislocation.

Even in the absence of pogroms (i.e., organized oppression of the Jews), prejudice constantly enveloped the Jews in Christian Europe. Since full-fledged citizenship was denied them, the Jews always lived with a measure of fear and alienation. There was only one way for a Jew to stand on equal footing with a Christian and that was to cease being a Jew. That is, if one was not baptized, one was not accepted fully into Christian society. While it is difficult to know how many Jews converted to Christianity, it seems clear that the overwhelming majority of Jews chose not to convert.

Ironically, some of those who did convert turned on their former fellow religionists with a vengeance. In 1239, for example, a convert from Judaism named Nicholas Donin sent to Pope Gregory a stinging attack on the Talmud. Donin, who claimed to be a Talmudic scholar, wrote that the Talmud was filled with superstitious lore and, moreover, that it resonated with hatred of Christians and Christianity. This incredible charge was accepted as credible by the Pope because, if for no other reason, the Pope had never heard of the Talmud. The Pope wrote to bishops throughout Europe that the Jews "...were now following a new [!!!] book called the Talmud, which is full of blasphemy, [it is] abusive and unspeakable."

THE BLOOD-LIBEL CHARGE

Perhaps there is no better example of the perilous nature of Jewish existence in pre-modern Christian Europe than the blood-libel charge. A legend had circulated in medieval Christian Europe that Jews, especially at Passover time, would kidnap Christian children, torture them to death, and then use their blood in the preparation of the unleavened Passover bread (called *matzot*).

The most publicized of such accusations was the alleged ritual murder in Blois (in northern France) in 1171. A Jew was accused of killing a child whose corpse was never found. The Count of Blois, Theobald V, accepted the charge as true, and thirty-one Jews were tortured and then put to death.

Ephraim ben Jacob, a German Jew of the twelfth century, wrote an account of the affair, part of which reads as follows:

> In the year 4931 (1171), evil appeared in France, too, and great destruction in the city of Blois...[for a slight, unintended offense by a Jew, a Christian concocts a story in which a Jew kidnaps and murders a Christian child]...all the Jews of Blois [were] seized and thrown into prison. [Some Christians offered to ransom the Jews out of their trouble, but their offer was refused. A priest continually incited the secular rulers to be as harsh as possible with the Jews. The priest told the Jews the only way they could save themselves was to convert to Christianity. The Jews refused]. At the command of the oppressor they then took the two [Rabbis]...and tied them to a single stake in the house where they were to be burned...they set fire to them and one after another thirty-one Jews were put to the torch.
>
> [L. Poliakov, *The History of Anti-Semitism III* (New York: Vanguard Press, 1977), p.303.]

To keep the blood-libel charge alive, some Christians would hide their own deceased children in Jewish homes, threatening to accuse the Jews of having murdered the children, unless the Jews agreed to pay huge sums of money.

To its credit, the Vatican decreed that in any ritual murder charge against the Jews, the testimony of Christians was not sufficient unless an equal number of Jewish witnesses could be produced. However, in far too many instances, Jews were tortured so that they would implicate other Jews. Thus, in spite of the Vatican's official stand, the blood-libel charge survived into the twentieth century. The Nazis used it in order to stir up hatred against Jews. As we shall see, the Nazis were extremely successful.

As far as can be determined, the blood-libel charge was used against the Jews for the first time in the middle of the twelfth century. A converted Jew named Theobald created this charge out of thin air and an English Benedictine monk named Thomas of Monmouth was the first to commit it to writing. Thomas wrote of a young boy named William whose body had been found in the woods bordering the town of Norwich. Several months passed before Thomas accused the Jews of having murdered the boy. He said that the Jews had kidnapped the boy, tortured him, and then crucified him.

By the end of the twelfth century the tale had spread throughout all of Christian Europe. In one parish after another it was preached that the Jews needed the blood of Christian children in order to practice aspects of their "hideous" religion. In 1182 the king of France drove the Jews out of his country in part because he accepted the truth of the blood-libel charge. It must be added that the royal bureaucracy, the nobility, and the Church profited immensely from the exodus, since the Jews were forced to leave most of their assets behind in France. In effect, the blood-libel charge provided the French with a convenient rationalization to plunder the Jews.

In 1245 Innocent IV published a papal bull (the Papal seal affixed to an official document) which condemned the blood-libel charge. However, that did not stop the bloodletting. Eight years later the Jews of Lincoln (in England) were accused of having crucified a Christian child. The Jews of Lincoln, it was said, kidnapped an eight year old boy named Hugh, fattened him up, and sent invitations to all the Jews of England to be present at Hugh's sacrifice.

The claim was made that Hugh was tortured while the Jews looked on and cheered. Afterwards, so the charge went, Hugh was crucified and disemboweled and what was left of him was thrown into a well, but Christians found the body and one among them was told by "God Himself" that Jews had done this. The Jews of Lincoln were subsequently rounded up and under torture some "confessed" after being assured that those who confessed would not be executed. In fact, eighteen Jews, who refused to confess, were executed.

Hugh was given martyrdom status by the Church and for generations he was venerated as "Little Saint Hugh of Lincoln." Near the spot where Hugh's body was supposedly found, a church was built to which pilgrims came from all over Europe. These pilgrims served to spread further the vicious lie, as they took with them home from Lincoln the story of what the Jews of Lincoln had done to little Hugh.

By now it should not surprise you that there was no evidence that the boy had been killed by anyone, let alone by the Jews for purpose of ritual slaughter. The Jews who confessed did so only under torture, and over half of them subsequently retracted their testimony and were then murdered (Hay, *op. cit.,* pp. 125–130).

All over Europe similar shrines appeared commemorating similar events. In community after community Jews were tortured and murdered without evidence that would be admissible in a court of law. In 1279 some Jews of London were tied to horses and torn to pieces. In Germany (Mainz), in 1283, ten Jews were killed by a mob. In Munich, two years later, a synagogue was torched and 180 Jews burned to death. In 1286 forty Jews were torn limb from limb at Oberwesel.

In each of these incidents the charge was the same: in order to practice Judaism, Jews tortured and murdered Christian children.

The charge persisted. In 1747, at Saslov in the Ukraine, the accused Jews were placed on an iron stake, which slowly cut into their bodies and resulted in slow, agonizing deaths. Other Jews were skinned; others had their hearts cut out; others had their hands and feet amputated; while others were nailed to the gallows. In 1753, in Zhytomir (in the western Ukraine), eleven Jews were beaten to death while other Jews saved themselves from death by accepting baptism. In none of these cases was a child's body ever produced. And in none of these cases was Judaism considered to be anything other than a grotesque religion.

In 1758 Cardinal Ganganelli (who was to become Pope Clement XIV) submitted a report to the Vatican which, in general, exposed the falsity of the blood-libel charge. However, the Cardinal cited as valid the cases of Andrew of Rinn and Simon of Trent. It should occasion no surprise that both of these cases proved to be as fictitious as the rest.

The case of Simon of Trent is particularly instructive. Trent, in northern Italy, was the site of the supposed crime. A Jewish physician was accused of having enticed a 2 1/2 year old Christian child into his office where he crucified the boy, drained his blood, and added it to his unleavened bread. It was said that the Jews had the body for a time until they threw it into a canal. Again, no body was ever found, but under torture some Jews admitted their "guilt." Samuel, the most prominent of the Jews of Trent, was arrested. He was stripped naked, bound hand and foot, and hung by a rope which worked as a pulley, so that his limbs were nearly torn out of their sockets. For three days the rope would be jerked up and down until Samuel lost consciousness. In order to worsen the ordeal, an iron pan containing burning sulfur was held under his nostrils and a piece of wood was tied between his shin bones.

Finally, the torture broke Samuel and he "confessed." But almost immediately he withdrew the confession, whereupon he was again tortured. Again he capitulated and agreed to "confess" but on only one condition, namely, that his torturers would burn him to death rather than continue the torture. On June 23, Samuel was burned at the stake.

Here is a brief postscript. Seven hundred years after Pope Innocent IV's papal bull censured the blood-libel charge, the Nazis (whose leader, Adolf Hitler, had entered into an agreement with the Vatican) published articles substantiating the accusation together with livid depictions of Jews seeking the blood of Christian children. The Nazis wanted the German people to accept the accusation as literally true and the evidence is only too clear that millions of Germans did. But even on a metaphorical level the Nazi message graphically captured the essence of the blood-libel charge: Jews and Judaism were death-dealing parasites.

THE BLACK DEATH

When Jews were expelled from England in 1291, from France in successive waves in the fourteenth century, and from many of the provinces in Germany (at that time Germany lacked the central authority to expel the Jews from all provinces), perhaps Jews understood more clearly the danger and futility of living in societies which made the Christian religion a precondition for full citizenship. At any moment, for any reason, no matter how fantastic or farfetched, the Jews could be subject to persecution or told to leave at a moment's notice.

The so-called "Black Death" of the fourteenth century provided a new excuse for persecuting the Jews. This deadly disease was named for the black spots it caused to appear on the skin. It is now believed that this disease was bubonic plague carried by fleas from infected rats, but at the time it was thought to be caused by water and/or air. Many came to believe that the Jews were systematically poisoning the wells. As the deadly plague ravaged Europe, tens of thousands of Jews were murdered and tens of thousands more were brutalized.

The Jews appealed to Pope Clement VI for help. The Pope issued a bull clearing the Jews of any responsibility for the plague. Moreover, the Pope included in the bull a reaffirmation of the Vatican's stand against the forcible conversion of Jews. But the bull contained no sanctions which would have given it binding force. Nor did the bull in any way imply that the Jews were to be accepted as full-fledged members of the human community. The result was that the bull did not deter Christians from killing Jews. Also, the bull did not effect a change of attitude on the part of Christians toward Jews and Judaism.

THE DESECRATION OF THE HOST

To make matters worse, a new method of stirring up hatred against the Jews appeared. The claim was made that Jews regularly stole the consecrated bread from churches in order to punish the body of Jesus. This charge, of course, was in line with the age old accusation that the Jews had been responsible for the crucifixion of Jesus. Now, it was asserted, the Jews were continuing to "crucify" the body of Jesus in their desecration of the bread of the Eucharist.

Throughout Christian Europe this accusation took hold. Jews, so the charge went, stole the host and mutilated it. Their crime became known when, under torture, Jews admitted not only that they stole and mutilated the holy bread but that they were ready to convert to Christianity (and, of course, they urged other Jews to follow suit) because with their own eyes they had seen the bread bleed. What the Jews supposedly had done to the consecrated bread was in fact done to Jews who frequently were put to an agonizing death. Then the assets of the Jews were confiscated and used in part to build a shrine. Pilgrims would visit this shrine and not only contribute to its upkeep but they would carry home with them the news of Jewish perfidy.

You can understand easily how the "Desecration of the Host" had an advantage, from the point of view of the accusers, over the "Blood-libel" charge. Unlike the libel charge which involved the accusers in having to produce a body, or at least explain why one could not be produced, in the case of the host charges could be brought against the Jews literally out of thin air.

In either case, however, Jewish property was always confiscated. This would appear to be a consistent pattern in both pre-modern and modern anti-Semitism: those who persecuted the Jews almost always profited from it.

We have seen that once Christianity became the official religion of the Roman Empire a process began which led to exclusionary measures, be they religious, political, economic, or social, against the Jews. It was as if the Jews were viewed as animals who were very profitable to hunt. Not surprisingly it was the Nazis who perfected this "sport" of Jew-hunting. The Nazis demonstrated that one could even make use of Jewish carcasses. In one death camp after another the Nazis systematically knocked out gold fillings, hacked off rings from fingers, cut hair off dead women, stripped off the flesh in order to make soap, and used bones to make fertilizers.

The stark fact is that at least from the middle ages to the end of the eighteenth century the Jewish experience has been typified by pervasive persecution. While some Jewish communities would prosper for a time, no Jewish community felt as though it belonged; in no country were the Jews granted equal rights. It is true that in some places the Jews were protected by the secular authorities, and it is equally true that the Papacy sometimes would intervene on behalf of Jews. However, the Jews lived as permanently displaced persons. Perhaps given the political reality wherein there was no separation of church and state, and perhaps given the social reality that people were appallingly ignorant about Jews, and perhaps given the religious reality that people were appallingly ignorant about Judaism, to say nothing of Christianity's stance toward Judaism, the widespread persecution of the Jews was both inevitable and predictable. But it was neither inevitable nor predictable that almost without exception Jews steadfastly maintained their commitment to Judaism, however differently they interpreted what it meant to be a Jew.

THE PROTESTANT REFORMATION

The Protestant Reformation did not usher in a better relationship between Christians and Jews. Martin Luther (1483–1546), the religious genius who initiated the Reformation in Germany, was apparently convinced that the Jews would join him (i.e., convert to his version of Christianity) in his assault on the Church and the old religious order. But when the Jews did not join the new movement, Luther attacked them and their religion in more vitriolic language than the Catholic Church had ever employed. Luther called for the destruction of synagogues, the appropriation of Jewish property, and for their expulsion. His rationale went as follows:

> Verily a hopeless, wicked, venomous and devilish thing is the existence of these Jews who for 1400 years have been, and still are, our pest, torment and misfortune. They are just devils and nothing more.
>
> [H. Grisar, *Luther* (London, 1916), p. 286].

As a writer and speaker, Luther delighted in the use of hyperbole and thus it is possible that his remarks on Jews and Judaism are not to be taken literally. But even as hyperboles, Luther's comments provided grist for mills which were to grind out hatred against the Jews and derision for Judaism.

Consider that while Jewish scholars gave Luther much help in his magnificent achievement of translating the Bible into German, after its completion he declared that the Bible was henceforth a "German book." He told the Jews that the only Bible they had any right to "...is that concealed beneath the sow's tail; the letters that drop from it you are free to eat and drink." Along the same lines, Luther charged that the Jews cursed Jesus on their Sabbath and inflicted harm on Christians whenever the opportunity presented itself. Judaism, Luther evidently believed, was fundamentally diseased: "The Devil with his angelic snout devours what exudes from the oral and anal apertures of the Jews; this is indeed his favorite dish, on which he grows fat like a sow behind the hedge." [J. Janssen, *History of the German People at the Close of the Middle Ages* (London, 1910), pp. 49ff.]

ANTI-SEMITISM IN THE NEW TESTAMENT?

At this point it is appropriate to ask whether the roots of anti-Semitism go back to the very root of Christianity, that is, to the New Testament. Does Christianity, in its very nature, as expounded in its most sacred literature, criticize Jews and/or Judaism? I state at the outset that given the complex and variegated nature of the New Testament such questions cannot be answered by a simple yes or no. And I also want it understood that, as I read it, the New Testament is worthy of the highest praise for the depth, subtlety, and exalted nature of its teachings.

What follows, then, are some fairly simple observations which are restricted to the question at hand. In his letters, Paul excoriates those whom he calls "Judaizers," that is, those members of the new movement who persist in following Jewish rituals and regulations. Paul says very little about Jews as such. There apparently is only one specific accusation of deicide against the Jews in the New Testament writings attributed to Paul. This context (Thessalonians 2:14–16), is thought by some scholars to be an interpolation. Here is the way the passage reads:

> You have fared like the congregation in Judea, God's people in Jesus Christ. You have been treated by your countrymen as they are treated by the Jews, who killed the Lord Jesus and the prophets and drove us out, the Jews who are heedless of God's will and enemies of their fellow-man, hindering us from speaking to the Gentiles to lead them to salvation. All this time they have been making up the full measure of their guilt, and now retribution has overtaken them for good and all.
>
> [New English Bible]

The emphasis in Paul's letters, however, is not on what happened to Jesus. Paul, e.g., never refers to Judas, any more than he mentions the trial of Jesus before the council. Therefore, Paul's polemic is directed not at Jews who never accepted Jesus as the Christ (from the Greek *Christos,* or "anointed one") but rather at those who have accepted Jesus as the Christ and who want to retain their Jewish observances.

The emphasis is different in the Gospel (the first four books of the New Testament) narratives. The Gospel of Mark, for instance, de-emphasizes Roman involvement in what happened to Jesus. Scholars conjecture that this is due to the historical circumstance of not wanting to alienate Rome and the Romans as the new movement spreads. In Mark, Jews of every stripe, whether Sadducee or Pharisee, priest or Herod Antipas, the Sanhedrin or the crowds in the passion narrative, reject Jesus. Even the Jewish disciples do not seem to appreciate what it is that Jesus represents. As for the Jews at large, they are mostly completely blind to the truth and, at times, actively hostile toward Jesus. It seems equally clear that the Jewish disciples fail their Master at decisive moments in the drama. It is to be expected, therefore, that it is a Roman centurion who understands clearly who and what Jesus is (Mark 15:37–39). New Testament scholars suggest that the Gospel of Mark is intended for a Gentile audience without roots in Judaism.

While the Gospel of Matthew is filled with sublime religious sentiments, it is sharply critical of, e.g., the Pharisees about whom it says: "...whatever they do is for show.... They like to have places of honor at feasts and the chief seats in the synagogues...alas, alas for you, lawyers and Pharisees, hypocrites that you are! You shut the door of the Kingdom of Heaven in men's faces...you travel over sea and land to win one convert; and when you have won him you make him twice as fit for hell as you are yourselves...you have overlooked the...demands of the law, justice, mercy and good faith...you are like tombs covered with whitewash; they look well from the outside, but inside they are full of dead men's bones and all kinds of filth. So it is with you: outside you look like honest men, but inside you are brim-full of hypocrisy and crime...you snakes, you vipers' brood, how can you escape being condemned to hell?" (Matt. 23). And then there is the explosive indictment of the Jewish crowd which demands that Pilate have Jesus crucified. The text continues (27:24–25):

> Pilate could see that nothing was being gained and a riot was starting; so he took water and washed his hands in full view of the crowd, saying, 'My hands are clean of this man's blood; see to that yourselves.' And with one voice the people cried, 'His blood be on us, and on our children.'

In the Synoptic Gospels (Mark, Luke, Matthew), the disciples and apostles, for good or bad, are clearly Jews. In the Gospel of John, however, the Jews not only are depicted as outsiders but as opponents of the new movement. Given the absence of a secular nation state, in which religion would be a private concern, the Jews were nothing if not outsiders; it was this image of the Jew which took hold and defined Jewish existence in Christian (and Moslem) lands until the modern period.

10

The Holocaust

The refusal of the Jews to convert to Christianity in large numbers (except, of course, under compulsion) contributed to the hostility some Christians felt towards Jews. Throughout the Middle Ages, especially in times of economic and/or social stress, it was a simple matter to stir up anti-Jewish feelings. As a result, the Jews often became scapegoats; in the last chapter we saw that the Jews were accused of causing epidemics, social and economic dislocations, and the death of Christians in what were described as barbaric Jewish rites.

In German speaking countries (Germany and Austria) there was sometimes an added dimension to anti-Semitism. In these countries, anti-Semitism was more widespread and more "respectable." For centuries in these countries, anti-Semitism was advocated by leading intellectuals and politicians who persisted in using hatred of the Jews to support theories about differences in the human community and in the body politic. Accordingly, there arose in Germany in the nineteenth century a theory about the racial development of humankind. No surprise that one of the basic tenets of this theory was that Jews were to be shunned not only because of what they believed but because of what they were genetically.

It must be understood that the way was prepared for Hitler by centuries of anti-Semitic feeling generated by religious animus, social and economic distress, and by pseudo-intellectual theories about race. Without the long standing anti-Semitic tradition, it is doubtful that Hitler could have pursued successfully what the Nazis called "The Final Solution to the Jewish Problem." Hitler's success also was made possible by the peculiar circumstances in Germany in the wake of the devastating defeat in World War I as well as the devastating terms of surrender which the Allies had forced on the Germans. This certainly made it easier for the Nazis to win the necessary broad based support to carry out their plan to exterminate the Jews.

The Nazi party was founded at the end of World War I in Munich by a locksmith (Anton Drexler) and an engineer (Gottfried Feder). Hitler joined the party seven months later. As it was formulated initially, the party platform had a tone of what has been called strong social radicalism. The platform called for the socialization of private trusts and department stores; it urged industrial profit sharing and widespread land reforms; it demanded confiscation of profits made by any firm during the war. And finally, and most emphatically, the platform called for the exclusion of Jews from the party and, ideally, from the nation.

For the first years of its life, the Nazi party had almost no impact on the political life of Germany. Certainly, its platform was not distinguishable from those of other parties on the political right. In specific, there was nothing distinctive about the party's attitude towards the Jews. George Strasser, one of the party's spokesmen, summed up the party's attitude towards Jews for the 1930 elections as follows:

We desire no persecution of the Jews, but we demand the exclusion of the Jews from human life [how this aim was to be achieved without persecution was left unsaid]. We demand German leadership without Jewish spirit [anti-Semitism was so ingrained in German culture that Strasser felt no need to define "Jewish spirit"], without Jewish wire-pulling and the interests of Jewish capital...we demand protection of our cultural goods against Jewish arrogance and aggression.

Other parties on the far right had expressed and were expressing similar attitudes toward the Jews in much the same way.

What was special about the Nazi party? Why did it succeed where other parties with comparable ideologies failed? Many answers have been given to such questions. Perhaps, given the complexity of the factors involved in the rise of the Nazi party to power, many answers are needed. Some have speculated that the willingness of the Nazis to use violence as a political tool separated them from the pack. It could be said that this willingness is evidence that, to give the Devil his due, the Nazis displayed the courage of their convictions. Of course, given the nature of their convictions, this is equivalent to observing that the Nazis were without scruples. The Nazis, in short, went after the weak and the helpless. In the nine years from 1923–31, for example, the Nazis desecrated 106 Jewish cemeteries and 40 synagogues.

As the party developed and expanded, its guiding principles proved to be very flexible; all of them, that is, with the exception of its anti-Semitic posture. Anti-Semitism thus was the piston that drove the Nazi movement. And since the Nazis proclaimed that the exceptional nature of the "Jewish problem" required an exceptional solution, anti-Semitism was also the driving force behind the concrete expression of Nazi ideology.

According to the Nazis, the Jews had no civilization of their own, i.e., no cultural or ethnic identity *sui generis*. Rather, the Jews were parasites who were bound and determined to destroy legitimate civilizations. The Jews, so claimed the Nazis, took but they did not give and, moreover, they succeeded in hiding their parasitic status by virtue of their domination of the press and high finance.

It probably is unnecessary to note that in post World War I Germany, industry was almost entirely in Christian hands, as were the banking and newspaper enterprises.

The Nazis insisted that since the Jews had no identity as such they lacked any positive aspirations. But what of the centuries old Jewish yearning for a Jewish homeland? According to the Nazis, the longing for a homeland was a subterfuge cloaking the Jewish desire to dominate the world and swindle everyone in it. The "Final Solution" of the so-called "Jewish problem" was, in effect, a radical surgical procedure to excise the "Jewish cancer" from Germany and, eventually, from the world.

But if hands had to be bloodied (and would they ever!) in the process of excision, the promised cure was salvation itself. Again and again the Nazis used religious language to describe their procedure. They declared that the extermination of the Jews was part of a grand plan to attain salvation. And the salvation of mankind depended on the exclusion of the Jews. Thus did the Nazis return to a staple of the pre-modern Jewish experience, but whereas the Jews then had been excluded on the basis of religion, the Nazis proposed that the Jews be denied access to the human community on the basis of race:

> Only those who are our fellow Germans shall be citizens of our state. Only those who are of German blood can be considered as our fellow Germans regardless of creed. Hence no Jew can be regarded as a fellow German.
>
> [A. Bullock, *Hitler, A Study in Tyranny* (New York: Harper and Row, 1964, p. 201.]

This plan to save the human race could only be attained, however, at a very high price. The Nazis started a war in which more than thirty-five million people were killed. This number, which in and of itself is incomprehensible, is made even more unbelievable when one considers the fact that more than half the slain were unarmed civilians.

The war lasted more than two thousand days and brought death to two out of every three European Jews. And had the Nazis won the war not only Europe's Jews, but every Jew everywhere, would have been effaced from the earth's surface. In any case, although some European Jews survived, a way of life, a culture (diverse to be sure, but a culture nonetheless) which had persisted for more than a thousand years, disappeared. Nor is there any reason to suppose that the ethos of European Jewry will ever reappear.

As anti-Semitism was the driving force behind Nazism, so was Hitler the driving force behind Nazism. While much has been written about Hitler and while we have the testimony not only of those who fought with and against him, much about him remains elusive. Apparently, most of the Germans who voted for him did not take his ideas about the Jews at face value. It appears that most responsible people thought that Hitler was using the Jews as a political issue which would make his run for political power more effective. Such a rational explanation, however, cannot explain Hitler's obsessive determination to kill every Jew possible, a determination which in fact hindered not only the war effort but the ability of Germany to make peace. That is, Hitler's "Final Solution" was, from almost any practical perspective, an imprudent disaster. In regard to the Jews, Hitler, a man who had no reservations about lying to friend or foe, meant what he said.

Some scholars have attempted to trace Hitler's anti-Semitic outlook to his upbringing. Hitler was born in 1884 on the Austria-German border. He was the fourth child of Alois and Klara (who was Alois' third wife and twenty three years his junior). Alois was the illegitimate son of a woman named Maria Anna Schcklgruber. As can be imagined, there has been much conjecture about the identity of Hitler's paternal grandfather. More than a few students of Nazism have argued that Hitler's father was part Jewish and that Adolph, knowing this, was so deeply ashamed that he felt compelled to wage an all-out war against Jews. Whatever the psychological plausibility of such a hypothesis, and to me it does not seem plausible, virtually all the genetic evidence is in dispute.

Alois seems to have been disappointed in Adolph because the boy wanted to be an artist rather than a businessman. In 1907 Adolph went off to Vienna to pursue an artistic career. He found no success whatsoever. Years later, one of his teachers described him as "...undisciplined, notoriously cantankerous, willful, arrogant, and bad-tempered." [L. Davidowicz, *The War Against the Jews* (New York: Bantam Books, 1975), pp. 5–28]. But while he found no success as an artist in Vienna, Hitler did find a group which mirrored his emerging belief that the Jews were responsible for many of Germany's problems.

Hitler left Vienna in 1915 and went to Munich. He was twenty-four years old with not much of a past and no prospects for a bright future. World War I changed that, both for him and for Germany. Hitler enlisted and, in the course of the war, was wounded twice. He received the Iron Cross, First Class, a decoration seldom given to a non-commissioned soldier. From all accounts it appears that he was a courageous soldier.

After the war he again gravitated to a group which denounced the Jews, this time for stabbing Germany in the back during the war. By the 1920's Hitler had come to certain and firm conclusions about the Jews. He believed that the Jews constituted a "race." Hitler accepted the quite dubious proposition that the human species could be divided into clearly discernible characteristics. The "semitic" race, that race to which Jews belonged, was parasitic. Jews were clever enough, he believed, to conceal their parasitic nature largely by dominating the world's press. He believed it was vitally important to remove Jews from positions of power and, eventually, from the nation state itself.

Hitler's galvanic speaking style began attracting attention. His theme was a constant one: the "resurrection of Germany" would never be achieved "...without the clearest knowledge of the racial problem and hence of the Jewish problem." The highest expression of humanity was to be found in the "Aryan" race, and its purity had to be safeguarded for only this race could save the world. The political state's reason for being, in fact, was to preserve in as pure a state as possible the Aryan race. For this is what the "Creator of the universe" intended. The Jew, at the opposite end of humanity's racial spectrum, was *the* enemy, a carrier of filth and disease, of death and destruction, a satanic force.

It did not matter to Hitler that the term "Aryan" had no validity whatsoever as a racial designation. This term formerly had specified a family of languages that includes Iranian, Sanskrit, and many of the European languages. Apparently, its use in relation to race was based on the mistaken idea that people who spoke the same or related languages must have had a common racial origin.

But any and all reasonable objections were swept aside by Hitler and his followers who proclaimed a holy war against the Jewish "race." Hitler did not hesitate to announce that he was the "Messiah" who would deliver Germany and the world from the "Jew-Devil." Hitler saw himself as an emissary of God: "Hence today I believe that I am acting in accordance with the will of the Almighty Creator: by defending myself against the Jew, I am fighting for the work of the Lord." (Bullock, *op, cit.*, pp. 23–252).

It seems impossible to overestimate the extent to which the Jews inhabited Hitler's psyche. He was certain that the Jews were the primary cause of evil in the world. Consider that even after he had murdered more than six million of them, the "Jew-Devil" still stalked him. At 4:00 a.m. on April 29, 1945, in a Berlin bunker, the last day of his life, his last words to the German people were:

> Above all I charge the leaders of the nation and those under them to scrupulous observance of the laws of race and to merciless opposition to the universal poisoner of all people, international Jewry.

How could a modern, civilized nation state like Germany have turned its fate over to a man like Hitler, a man who did not belong at the head of a nation so much as he belonged in a hospital for the mentally diseased? Some have speculated that the centuries of anti-Semitism in Germany made Hitler's extreme anti-Semitism palatable. Some have pointed to Hitler's compelling personality as a prime factor. Perhaps both factors were necessary conditions as was the ravaged condition of Germany in the wake of World War I.

Whatever may be the case, Hitler was careful to tailor his speeches to the intended audience. To the dregs of society, Hitler and his henchmen delighted in relating salacious tales about Jews and Judaism. To the upper classes, the Nazis offered pseudo-scientific racial explanations, replete with arcane trappings, of the danger the Jews posed to German society. To the workers, the Nazis served up the tale that the Jews were "capitalistic bloodsuckers." To businessmen, the Nazis identified the Jews as "dirty radicals and communists."

The Nazis succeeded in gaining a broad base of public support. In 1923 the Nazis won 800,000 votes (out of some 45,000,000); by the 1932 election, that number had increased to 14,000,000. Since no party had a clear majority, Hindenberg, the President of the German Republic, sought to end the constitutional crisis by administering the oath of office of chancellor (the presidency was largely a ceremonial office; the real power was in the chancellorship) to Hitler. Hitler, on taking office, swore the following oath:

I will employ my strength for the welfare of the German people, protect the Constitution and the laws of the German people, conscientiously discharge the duties imposed on me and conduct my affairs of office impartially and with justice to everyone.

It is now clear that Hitler never intended to honor this oath, for when he spoke these words he already had decided to do away with the Constitution and anything for which the Constitution stood: democracy, freedom, and impartial justice.

Hitler did not wait long to begin persecuting the Jews of Germany. Barely two months after he came to power, he moved to exclude the Jews from the civil service and from the legal profession. In addition, Hitler made it increasingly difficult for Jewish doctors by cutting them off from all federally sponsored programs.

Then Hitler waited to see how the world would react to these first attacks on the Jews. While he waited there was a period of two years in which he did not put into place any new restrictions against the Jews of Germany. There were many de facto persecutions against the Jews, to which the government gave its tacit approval, but nothing in the way of mandated restrictions.

The summer of 1935, however, saw the beginning of the storm which had been gathering force during the first two years of Hitler's rule. During that summer, Jews were denied admission to movies, to theaters, to swimming pools, to resorts, and to most department stores. There was virtually no resistance in Germany, not from the universities, not from the churches, not from local town councils, to these exclusionary measures. Nor was there any outcry from the western democracies.

Thus was Hitler emboldened to take the next step. In September of 1935 the Nuremberg racial laws were promulgated and adopted unanimously. These laws legitimated racist anti-Semitism and made "the purity of German blood" a legal category. These laws forbade sexual relations between Germans and Jews, whether marital or extramarital, and disenfranchised anyone who had "Jewish blood" from the protection of the laws of the land. These laws related citizenship to race:

Only those who are our fellow Germans shall be citizens of our state. Only those who are of German blood can be considered as our fellow Germans regardless of creed. Hence no Jew can be regarded as a fellow German.

At this point it is appropriate to call to mind—by way of the starkest contrast—these words from our Declaration of Independence:

We hold these truths to be self-evident that all men are created equal, that they are endowed by their Creator with certain inalienable rights, that among these are life, liberty, and the pursuit of happiness. That to secure these rights, governments are instituted among men.

In Nazi Germany, the state's function was not to ensure and to protect individual rights (as is the case in the United States), but to ensure that "legitimate" Germans could disenfranchise "illegitimate" Germans. The criterion par excellence for determining legitimacy was racial. But since the racial theories were, at best, inexact and at worst ludicrous, the state could determine for itself who belonged and who did not belong for any reason it chose. In concrete terms, the Nazi state's primary function was to exterminate Jews. And in this, the Nazis had the support of most Germans.

Consider that when Hitler decided to expunge the mentally and physically disabled from Germany by instituting, as he called it, a program of "euthanasia," the German people reacted so negatively that Hitler was forced to terminate the program. The German people never protested Hitler's murderous policies in regard to the Jews.

Perhaps one can attribute Hitler's all-consuming hatred of the Jews to his demonic personality. However, the German people's support of Hitler's program of extermination of the Jews is much more difficult to comprehend. Jews had been present in the Rhine region as far back as the third century and when permitted to do so, they had participated actively and positively in Germanic culture. For example, of the forty four Nobel prizes awarded to Germans, eight went to Jews and four to half Jews, even though Jews made up less than one percent of the population. Moreover, more than twelve thousand Jews had been killed fighting for Germany in World War I. But in spite of these facts, there was only feeble and sporadic resistance to Hitler's program of genocide.

A large number of measures followed in the wake of the Nuremberg Laws which made it increasingly difficult for the Jews of Germany. For instance, no longer could Jews receive social security benefits or unemployment compensation. Also, special fares and levies were imposed on Jews while Jewish establishments were subjected to boycotts and picketing.

On the night of November 9, 1938, government sponsored violence erupted against the Jews. One hundred and ninety one synagogues were torched and another seventy six were leveled to the ground. This night came to be known as "The Night of Glass" because of all the shattered windows. In addition to the destruction of synagogues, Jewish community centers were plundered and Jewish cemeteries were ransacked. Thousands of Jewish businesses were looted, and thirty six Jews were murdered while hundreds more were injured. It is important to note that both the German population and the western democracies reacted with indifference to "The Night of Glass."

Hitler's successful invasion of Poland in September of 1939 brought the more than three million Jews living in Polish territory under his control. These three million unarmed Jewish civilians faced a well-equipped army of more than a million men who had been inculcated with the belief that the Jews constituted a subhuman race: to these Nazis assigned with rounding up the Jews, every barbarity was considered a salutary deed.

As the Nazis degraded, humiliated, and murdered Jews, the Polish population, almost without exception, stood by and did nothing. Jewish property was confiscated, Jewish girls were raped, and the sacred objects of the synagogues were burned. This irrational hatred begot certain rational consequences. Non-Jews benefited from Jewish property and manpower. Aryan lawyers and doctors profited from the elimination of their colleagues. And boycotts had a favorable effect on competing Aryan businesses.

The concentration camps to which Jews were herded like cattle became a source of enormous profit. Several million were shut up in these camps and all possible labor was extracted from them. But since the ultimate goal of the Nazis was irrational, *viz.*, to murder the Jews after first subjecting them to extreme deprivation, the concentration camps became places of the living dead who could do little work. If there was little economic logic in this, then there was none in the camps which supplanted the concentration camps, camps which were devoted to nothing other than death.

Perhaps it was this total lack of logic which, as much as anything else, trapped the Jews of Europe. The premeditated murder of the Jews had to it so little rationality—economic, political, or philosophical—that the overwhelming majority of Jews refused to believe that this was to be their ultimate fate. And by the time the Jews did realize, it was too late not only to save themselves (for this was almost never an option) but even to choose a death with some dignity. Although, as we have seen, Jewish history in Europe had been riddled with persecution, cold-blooded murder—as an end to itself—had never been the driving force behind the persecution.

Thus, not knowing that it was precisely cold-blooded murder which the Nazis had in mind and, in any case, being incapable of imagining it even after the signs and warnings were everywhere, most of the Jews hoped to wait out this latest wave of persecution, much as they had done in the past. Then, too, the Jews hoped that if they proved to be useful workers that would save them. And the Jews never stopped hoping that the western democracies would intervene on their behalf.

Before the Jews were taken to the death camps (all of which, in contradistinction to the concentration camps, were located in Poland), most of them were concentrated in ghettos or camps all over German-occupied Europe. The Jews had been thrust into ghettos in medieval Christian Europe, but the Nazi ghetto was something quite different. During the Crusades the Jews had lived willingly in separate quarters so as to be better able to protect themselves. Moreover, in the medieval ghetto the Jews were mostly free to come and go in order to conduct their business, just as Christians would enter the ghetto for economic and social purposes. In the medieval ghetto, starvation and disease were almost never the norms, for there was usually sufficient food and adequate sanitation.

But in the Nazi ghetto the food quota was extremely insufficient and only the illegal importation of food into the ghetto held down the number of deaths from starvation. And in the Nazi ghetto, the absence of drainage and sewage facilities caused rampant disease. Finally, in the Nazi ghetto, the Jews were never allowed out, until, that is, the Nazis deported them to the death camps.

Typically, the Nazis first would deport the children and the aged from the ghettos to the death camps. Once this happened, especially in a large ghetto such as the one in Warsaw, it destroyed the small measure of normalcy which the Jews, with such determined heroism, had sought to maintain. In the Warsaw ghetto, before the large scale deportations, there were theaters, schools, and communal organizations which sought to buttress the body and spirit. Incredibly, there was even research. A group of doctors, for example, undertook a study of the pathological aspects of starvation. Perhaps these extraordinary efforts, under the most brutal and brutalizing conditions, are indication of the Jewish resolve not to be broken by the Nazis.

The deportations of the young, the sick, and the elderly, while they led to a disruption of the social life and institutions in the ghetto, made possible a more active resistance because those who remained were mostly the young and able-bodied, and they had nothing to lose.

The revolt in the Warsaw ghetto was unique in that it was the only uprising in occupied Europe that broke out with no relieving forces to count on, no possibility of retreat, and absolutely no chance of success.

The revolt started on August 20, 1942 when members of the Jewish resistance force set buildings on fire to light the way for Russian bombers in the blacked out city. The Germans reacted by staging the largest deportation yet in the ghetto. One hundred thousand Jews were sent off to the death camps, leaving the ghetto some sixty thousand from the original five hundred thousand. The remaining Jews frantically tried to smuggle arms into the ghetto. In January of 1943 the Jews were able to launch their first attack and they caught the Nazis almost completely off guard. Finally, the Jews were spilling Nazi blood.

Heinrich Himmler, the chief of the dreaded Gestapo (the German state police, organized in 1933 to operate against political opposition), ordered that the ghetto be leveled. To the Nazi attack force Himmler said:

> It is necessary that the dwelling space for 500,000 subhumans, which will never be of any use to the Germans anyway, should completely disappear.

The Nazis meanwhile assured the Jews in the Warsaw ghetto that if they would surrender they would be given food and that conditions in the ghetto would be improved. This time the Nazi deception did not work. The leaders of the resistance warned the Jews:

> 'Jews! Don't believe the lies spread by those who are working for the Gestapo.... The time has come to fight. No Jew will mount the transport wagon! If you can't fight, hide!'

On April 19, 1943 the Germans entered the ghetto in force. The Nazi commander was one Juergen Stroop, a forty eight year old Major General in the Waffen S.S., a decorated soldier of wide experience. Stroop had at his disposal one reinforced armored battalion, one cavalry battalion, two German police battalions, Ukranian and Polish auxiliary units, artillery equipment, and sapper demolition squads.

Facing Stroop's force were about one thousand Jews, some of them in their early teens, armed with three light machine guns, a few hundred revolvers, no more than eighty rifles, and a few thousand hand grenades and explosives. Twenty four year old Mordecai Anilewicz was the commander of the Jewish force.

Anilewicz' deputy commander, Yitzchak Zuckerman, was over on the Aryan side of Warsaw in a desperate search for firearms when the fighting started. Anilewicz smuggled out a letter to him, saying:

> Our most daring expectations were surpassed...we attacked the Germans and inflicted heavy losses on them. Our losses were on the whole light. Even this is an achievement...we are forced by circumstances to take recourse to guerilla fighting.... Tonite our groups are starting out...to scent the area and seize arms...we need hand grenades and rifles.... Individuals perhaps will survive. Sooner or later all must fall. In the bunkers where we hide there is not enough air to light a candle.... Perhaps we shall see each other again. The main thing is: the dream of my life has come true.'

That "dream" was vividly concretized in another letter, which was smuggled out of the ghetto, written by a young Jewish woman named Zivia Zuckermann. In part it reads:

> We are happy and laughing. We knew, we felt, that the end of the Germans was near. We knew they would defeat us, of course, but we knew they would pay dearly for it.... It is difficult to describe it.... When we threw our grenades and saw German blood on the streets of Warsaw, after they had been flooded with so much Jewish blood and tears, a truly great joy possessed us.... They, the great fighters, were fleeing from our primitive, homemade grenades.... Of course, they came back....They had ammunition, water and food...all the things we lacked.... They came back with heavy artillery and tanks.... Using Molotov cocktails we set a tank on fire.... They abandoned hundreds of wounded there.... In the ghetto people were embracing and kissing each other, although everyone knew it was almost certain he would fall.... Rabbi Mayzel put his hand on my head and said: 'Bless you, it will be good to die soon. We should have done it earlier.'

On May 4, Stroop asked for and received further aid from the army, and he began to tighten the circle around the embattled Jews. In the ghetto, the day belonged to the Germans, but at night the Jews would come out of their bunkers and strike at German positions. On May 8, the Germans finally were able to locate and encircle the main bunker. The Jews, however, refused to surrender. The Germans lobbed in gas. The Jews then decided to kill themselves rather than surrender to the Nazis. But many of the revolvers were in unworkable condition and the Jews had to line up to wait for death from the hand of a friend. As this helpless scene was going on, someone shouted that one of the entrances to the ghetto had gone undetected. But by this time only a handful of Jews were left. They scrambled out and made it over to the Aryan side where they joined the Polish resistance. Over one hundred perished in the bunker, including Mordecai Anilewicz.

On May 12, Stroop set the whole ghetto ablaze. Three days later he handed in his report on almost a month of fighting. The report began: "There are no longer any Jewish habitations in Warsaw." But there were still some Jews and the shooting continued among the ruins for several more weeks. As late as May 22, Joseph Goebbels (the Nazi minister of propaganda) noted in his diary: "The battle of the Warsaw ghetto continues. The Jews are still resisting." But by June there remained in the ghetto only the dead, silence, and smoke. [See R. Ainsztein, *The Warsaw Ghetto Revolt* (New York: Holocaust Library, 1979)].

The Warsaw ghetto was by no means the only ghetto armed resistance. In central Poland there were 3 armed rebellions, 4 attempted rebellions, and 17 places where armed resistance groups existed. Resistance was more widespread in eastern Poland, however, because of the forests surrounding the ghetto areas. There is evidence of armed underground groups in 91 ghettos in the western Belorussian area alone. And in the Russian ghetto in Minsk, the fourth largest ghetto in Europe, an armed resistance group led by Jewish Communists and supported by the Jewish Council, organized an armed escape into the nearby forest: some 6000–8000 escaped to join the partisans. [Yehuda Bauer, "Jewish Resistance and Passivity in the Face of the Holocaust," *Unanswered Questions: Nazi Germany and the Genocide of the Jews,* ed. François Furet (New York: Schocken Books, 1989), pp. 241–2].

When the German army pushed eastward into Russia, it was followed by special units called "Action Groups." These "Action Groups" were assigned the task of rounding up and exterminating Jews. By the time the Russians had forced the German army to retreat, these "Action Groups" had murdered some two and one half million Jews.

For the most part, these Action Groups were staffed by regular Army police corps. After going into a locale, the Action Groups would round up the Jews, telling them that they were to be deported to a place where they would be put to work for Germany. The Germans assured the Jews that family units would be kept together.

The Germans would stuff the Jews into trucks or railroad cars and take them a few miles out of town. There the Germans unloaded the Jews and stripped them of their money, valuables, and clothing. Then, the Germans methodically shot to death all of them: men, women, and children.

Here is an eyewitness account of one such shooting given by a Latvian guard who had been assigned to one of the Action Groups:

The people from the trucks,—men, women, and children—were forced to undress under the supervision of an S.S. soldier [the S.S. was the Nazi Elite Guard] with a whip in his hand. They were obliged to put their effects in certain spots.... Without weeping or crying out, these people undressed and stood together in family groups, embracing each other and saying goodbye. I watched a family of about eight: a man and a woman about fifty years old, surrounded by their children of about one, eight, and ten, and two big girls of twenty or so. An old lady, her hair completely white, held the baby in her arms, rocking it, and singing it a song. The infant was crying with delight. The parents watched the group with tears in their eyes. The father held the ten year old boy by the hand speaking softly to him. The child struggled to hold back his tears. Then the father pointed a finger to the sky and, stroking the child's head, seemed to be explaining something. At this moment, the S.S. man near the ditch called something to his comrade. The latter counted off some twenty people and ordered them behind the mound. The family of which I have just spoken was in the group. I walked around the mound and faced a frightful common grave. Packed corpses were heaped so close together that only the heads showed. Most were wounded in the head and the blood flowed over their shoulders. Some still moved; others raised their hands and turned their backs to show they were still alive. The ditch was two thirds full. I turned my eyes toward the man who had carried out the execution. He was an S.S. man. He was seated, legs swinging, on the narrow edge of the ditch; an automatic rifle rested on his knees and he was smoking a cigarette. The people, completely naked, climbed down a few steps and stopped at the ordered stop. Facing the dead and wounded they spoke softly to them. Then I heard a series of rifle shots. I looked in the ditch and saw their bodies contorting, their heads already inert, sinking on the corpses beneath.

[Gideon Hauser, *Justice in Jerusalem* (New York: Schocken, 1968), pp. 60–83.]

What is perhaps most frightening about the above description is how routine the procedure was to the S.S. guard. He sits, legs hanging over the edge of this pit of horror, cigarette dangling from his mouth; his body posture suggests a day at the fishing hole.

In fact, the above S.S. officer is emblematic of the vast indifference the members of the Action Groups had towards the fate of the Jews. Twenty two members of the Action Groups were tried at the war crimes trials in Nuremberg. Among the twenty two were a university professor, eight lawyers, a dental surgeon, an architect, an art expert, and even a theologian who had been a parish pastor before the war. All of them pleaded not guilty. Not one expressed any remorse. One after another reiterated that their country was at war and they were acting under orders.

But they did more than profess their innocence. They insisted that they were good, decent, even "religious" men. Witnesses for them stressed their honesty, their familial virtues, their "Christian feelings," and their gentleness of character. If the Germans reacted with a brutalizing, mind-numbing indifference to the Holocaust, then it has been suggested that the Jews went meekly to their deaths like sheep to the slaughterhouse. This simile suggests that the Jews could have and should have offered more resistance. In fact, of course, many Jews did resist. We have noted already that there were armed revolts in many of the ghettos and death camps. In western European countries such as France, Italy, and Yugoslavia, many Jews were members of the general underground movements. Jews were not accepted into the official Polish underground (Armia Krajowa), however; in fact, a number of AK detachments were actively engaged in hunting down and murdering Jews. [Bauer, *ibid.*, pp, 238–245]. Resistance worthy of the name arose among the Jews, however, only when knowledge of the death camps became widespread. And that happened only near the end of the war. [The interested reader is urged to read Steiner's *Treblinka* (New York: Mentor, 1979)]. There are other factors to consider:

— The Germans kept their actions secret and unexpected. For most Jews, the truth became apparent after it was too late to act.

— The Germans used the lie of "deportation" which the Jews were told meant resettlement but which, in fact, meant death.

— There was no precedent for the German plan of genocide. Thus, even when the Jews had advanced warning, they often refused to believe it. The Jews, that is, consistently underestimated the depth of the German insanity.

— There was no place to flee. The Nazis controlled most of Europe and, as we shall see, the western democracies were terrified of being flooded with Jewish refugees.

— Many Jews, with families to protect, hesitated to act, fearful of the awful reprisals any resistance would unleash.

While the Jews were powerless, terrified, and hopelessly confused, the powerful Nazis knew exactly what it was they wanted: to wipe the Jews off the face of the earth. The only question troubling the Nazis was how to most expeditiously accomplish this. I have already noted that the Action Groups were responsible for the murders of some two and one half million Jews. However, the Germans grew disenchanted with the Action Groups because they used too much ammunition, manpower, and time.

Seeking a more efficient method to slaughter Jews, the Germans settled eventually on camps which had extermination as their sole purpose. The Germans experimented with different methods at these camps before settling on death by asphyxiation. At Chelmno, Belzec, Sobibor, and Treblinka the Germans used carbon monoxide. At Maidanek and Auschwitz, prussic fumes were used.

The following testimony by Kurt Gerstein (a German engineer who worked on the theoretical problems of gassing but who upon seeing it used recoiled from it with horror) will perhaps give you some feeling of the death camp situation:

> ...a train arrived...45 cars with more than 6,000 people. Two hundred Ukranians assigned to this work flung open the doors and drove the Jews out of the cars with leather whips. A loud speaker gave instructions: 'strip, even artificial limbs and glasses. Hand all money and valuables in.... Women and young girls are to have their hair cut.' ...then the march began. Barbed wire on both sides, in the rear two dozen Ukranians with rifles. They drew near. Captain Wirth [of the S.S.] and I found ourselves in front of the death chambers. Stark naked men, women, children, and cripples passed by. A tall S.S. man in the corner called to the unfortunates in a loud minister's voice: 'Nothing is going to hurt you! Just breathe deep and it will strengthen your lungs. It's a way to prevent contagious disease. It's a good disinfectant!' They asked him what was going to happen and he answered: 'The men will have to work, build houses and streets. The women won't have to do that, they will be busy with the homework and the kitchen.' This was the last hope for some of these poor people, enough to make them march toward the death chambers without resistance. The majority knew everything; the smell betrayed it. They climbed a little wooden stairs and entered the death chambers, most of them silently, pushed by those behind them. A Jewess of about 40 with eyes like fire cursed the murderers; she disappeared into the gas chambers after being struck several times by Captain Wirth's whip...Wirth ordered 700–800 people in 93 square meters.... [But] the motor would not start. Captain Wirth came up. You could see he was afraid because I was there to see the disaster.... 70 minutes passed and the diesel would not start. The people were waiting in the gas chambers. You could hear them weeping.... The diesel started up after 2 hours and 49 minutes. Twenty-five minutes passed. You

could see through the window that many were already dead.... Jewish workers on the other side opened the wooden doors. They had been promised their lives in return for doing this horrible work.... The people [in the gas chamber] were still standing, like columns of stone, with no room to fall or lean. Even in death you could tell the families, all holding hands.... The bodies were tossed out, blue, wet with sweat and urine, the legs smeared with excrement and menstrual blood. Two dozen workers were busy checking mouths which they opened with iron hooks.... Others checked anuses and genitals looking for valuables. Dentists knocked out gold teeth, bridges, and crowns with hammers.... Then the bodies were thrown into big ditches near the gas chambers...after a few days the bodies swelled and the whole mass rose up 2–3 yards because of the gas in the bodies.... Later they poured diesel oil over the bodies and burned them on railroad ties to make them disappear.

[*Ibid.,* pp. 91f.; cf. pp. 166f., 243, 251, 346, 354, 403, 421.]

For reasons which are as obvious as they are despicable, the Germans frantically sought to remove all traces of the dead. Knowing this, the Jews staged revolts at Sobibor and Treblinka so that a few inmates might escape to tell the world. Having discovered one black truth, *viz.,* that the Germans wanted to annihilate all memories of the Jews, the Jews did not as yet comprehend another awful truth: much of the civilized world already knew in great detail (especially the leadership of the two great western democracies, the U. S. and England) what was being done to the Jews.

Moreover, there was certainly no need to inform the mass of the German populace that their government was systematically murdering Jews. While it is true that very few Germans actually observed the agony in the gas chambers, hundreds of thousands of Germans saw some part of the roundup and delivery of the Jews to the camps. And these Germans surely told other Germans.

Let us consider the matter concretely. There were S.S. contingents which were stationed in the camps themselves; there were the German workers, army units, and officials of the numerous yards and factories in which Jews were worked to death; there were the railroad personnel who were responsible for delivering the Jews to the death camps from all over Europe. These railroad personnel saw the trains returning empty or loaded with used clothes. Moreover, as the war progressed, the press and radio of Hitler's Germany spoke more and more openly of what was being done to the Jews.

Perhaps it is true that only those who did not want to know did not know. Of course, many and profound were the reasons for not wanting to know.

In any case, the Germans certainly knew more than the Jews. As noted, most Jews could not fathom what was happening to them both because nothing like this had ever befallen them and because what was being done to them was inherently incomprehensible. The waves of persecution which had hit the Jews in pre-modern Europe had as their goal not the liquidation of Jews, but of Judaism. That is to say, the onslaught was against Judaism or the Jewish faith. And the Jews, lacking almost any capacity to respond militarily, nonetheless did not, in the greatest number of cases, convert to Christianity in order to save themselves from the fire and the sword. In pre-modern Christian Europe, Jewish faith was attacked by Crusaders, by Inquisitors, by religious fanatics of all stripes, and Jewish faith was rarely found wanting.

The Nazis, however, were not attacking Jewish faith; the Nazis were attacking the Jews themselves. For the Nazis, the "Jewish Problem" consisted of, what was for them, the fact that Jews were subhuman parasites which had to be eliminated. The Nazis never considered conversion to be a solution to the "problem." Thus, even had the Jews wanted to convert, no such option was available to them. It is a telling fact that in the ghettos there were churches for those Jews who had converted (or whose parents had converted) to Christianity. The Nazis considered these Christians to be Jews. For the Nazis, it was not a matter of belief, it was a matter of blood.

So, the Jews were not in a position to save themselves, and the Germans (I am not speaking here of the zealous Nazis) did not much care that the Jews were being liquidated. In 1942, a German who had been a supporter of the old German democracy assessed the attitudes of Germans towards "The Final Solution" as follows:

— 5% enthusiastically approved;

— 69% were indifferent;

— 21% were uncertain and confused;

— 5% categorically disapproved.

The issue I now want to raise has to do not with the attitude of the German people to the slaughter of the Jews but rather with the attitude of the inhabitants of those nations locked in conflict with Hitler's Germany. This is a very complex issue which cuts across individual sensibilities and governmental policies many of the latter of which were and, to some extent, are still cloaked in secrecy. It is also a complex issue because in England and especially in the United States there were a significant number of Jews, some of whom were in positions of power.

Any discussion of these issues should take into account the attitudes of the American public, during the time in question, towards Jews and/or Judaism. A series of polls from 1938 to 1946 dealt with the images Americans had of Jews. The results indicated that more than half of those Americans surveyed thought that Jews were "overly aggressive." [D. Wyman, *The Abandonment of the Jews* (New York: Pantheon, 1984), pp. 14–15, 359; cf. pp. 79, 287, 326f., 405, 416.]

But what did the American public know of Hitler's "Final Solution?" Certain facts are clear. In March of 1942, S. Bertrand Jacobson, just back from two years in Eastern Europe where he worked to aid Jewish refugees, held a press conference. He reported that the Nazis already had systematically slaughtered more than 250,000 Jews in the Ukraine alone. In vivid detail, he described a vast burial site near Kiev in which 7,000 Jews were thrown, some still alive, and covered with dirt. Jacobson reported the words of a soldier who had witnessed the massacre that the field had "heaved like a living sea."

However, of the newspapers in the United States, only the *New York Times* carried the story. And the *Times* omitted the slaughter at Kiev. Also, the *Times* buried the story in the middle of the paper.

In July of 1942, an account of what was befalling the Jews of occupied France reached the United States. The Jews of France were being rounded up and packed into camps to await deportation to the east. The roundup of the Jews included such brutalities as taking Jews from hospital beds. One woman gave birth while police waited to haul off mother and infant. More than 10,000 Jews were crammed into a winter sports arena where there were insufficient food, water, and sanitation facilities. They stayed there for five days before they were transferred to different deportation centers to await shipment to the death camps in Poland. Not even the *Times* carried this report.

In August of 1942, persistent reports came out of Europe that the Nazis had decided to eradicate the Jews and, in fact, had already begun to do so. The State Department dismissed these reports as "fantastic." Moreover, the State Department assured the American public that the mass deportations of the Jews were for the purposes of putting the Jews to work for the Third Reich on labor projects. Thus the State Department was telling the American people exactly what the Germans were telling the Jews who were being deported.

In November of 1942, Rabbi Stephen Wise, one of American Jewry's leading spokesmen, held a press conference in which he offered evidence that the Nazis already had murdered more than two million Jews. He also charged that the State Department knew this and was deliberately suppressing the truth. Wise believed that the Nazis intended to exterminate all Jews under their control. He said that the purpose of his press conference was to galvanize support in the United States and England. Wise urged the two governments to threaten Germany with severe reprisals if it persisted in the wholesale extermination of Jews.

By December of 1942, the exact sites of the death camps in Poland were known to the western allies. Thus seventeen months of systematic, cold-blooded slaughter ran their course between the time the Action Groups started their grisly work in June of 1941 and the time in late 1942 when Stephen Wise and others told the world of Germany's plans to murder the Jews. Even more alarming, however, was the fact that another fourteen months were to pass before the American president, F. D. Roosevelt, would take any action.

Also to be lamented is that even after Wise's press conference, media in the United States continued to ignore almost completely the Holocaust. The *New York Times,* which provided by far the most coverage, in fact covered very little of what was happening to the Jews of Europe, and relegated what it covered to the inside pages. Significantly, such news magazines as *Time, Life,* and *Newsweek* ignored the Holocaust completely.

It also should be noted that the Protestant and Catholic churches in the U. S. remained, for the most part, silent in the face of the Holocaust. So, too, did the Vatican. When the Vatican was asked whether the Pope would be able to make a declaration condemning the extermination of the Jews, the response was that the "...Vatican could not condemn particular atrocities publicly but that it frequently denounced atrocities in general." [*Ibid.*, pp. 29, 49, 75, 237–39, 279, 392].

The official stance of the U. S. government was to deplore the persecution of the Jews but to claim that nothing could be done to stop it while the war continued. Many Americans, both in government and out, insisted that the reports coming out of Europe about the slaughter of large numbers of Jews were gross exaggerations. A Gallup poll, published January 7, 1943, included the following question: "It is said that 2 million Jews have been killed in Europe since the war began. Do you think this true or just a rumor?" 47 percent thought it true; 29 percent thought it rumor; and 24 percent had no opinion. The poll would seem to indicate that there was a sufficiently broad base of public opinion on which to build an organized protest against what was happening to the Jews of Europe.

Meanwhile, a courier from the non-Jewish Polish underground made it to England in January of 1943. He brought with him an eyewitness account of the horrible conditions on the deportation trains bound for the death camps. He also had seen some of the Jewish children who had managed to escape from the Warsaw ghetto so as to avoid deportation to the death camps. These children were attempting to survive in the city streets. He described them:

I shall never forget them. They look less human than like monsters, dirty, ragged, with eyes that will haunt me forever...eyes of little beasts in the last anguish of death. They trust no one and expect only the worse from human beings. They slide along the walls of houses looking about them in mortal fear. No one knows where they sleep; from time to time, they knock at the doors of a Pole and beg for something to eat.

[*Ibid.*, pp. 31–5, 38, 219.]

Shortly thereafter, the Rumanian government, sensing that the war was lost and anxious to gain the good graces of the Allies in the hope of winning favorable terms for peace, offered to transfer 70,000 Jews to any place of refuge chosen by the Allies. In Washington, the British Foreign Secretary, Anthony Eden, said to the American president:

> ...the whole position of the Jews of Europe is very difficult...and we should move very cautiously about offering to take all Jews out of a country like Rumania. If we do that, then the Jews of the world will be wanting us to make similar offers in Poland and Germany. Hitler might well take us up on any such offer and there simply are not enough ships and means of transportation to handle them.
>
> [*Ibid.*, pp. 96–98; cf. p. 239.]

When the United States agreed with the British position, Rabbi Stephen Wise complained that "...if horses were being slaughtered as are the Jews of Poland, there would be now a loud demand for organized action against such cruelty to animals."

It must be concluded that from 1935 onwards, no country was willing to admit the Jews had they been able to leave Nazi Europe. The one exception was the Jewish settlement in Palestine which would have welcomed any and all Jews with open arms. However, the British, who controlled Palestine, refused to allow this for fear of alienating the Arab governments.

To deflect growing criticism, the British and American governments convened in Bermuda a conference on refugees in April of 1943. It is probable that Bermuda was chosen as the site because wartime regulations restricted all access to the island. Thus the two governments could control the coverage of the conference. No Jewish organizations were invited and only five news correspondents were allowed to come to Bermuda.

The conference lasted twelve days and the diplomats were strictly prohibited from placing any special emphasis on Jewish refugees; they were similarly instructed that no steps were to be taken exclusively for Jews. Moreover, the British would not permit any discussion of their Palestine policy, claiming that it was an "internal" matter. The diplomats apparently were so embarrassed by their inaction that they decided to keep their report and recommendation secret. The purpose of the conference was not to help the Jews of

Europe; its purpose was to blunt criticism that the leaders of the two great Western democracies had turned their backs on the Jews.

While the Bermuda Conference was in progress, Samuel Zygielbojm, a Jewish member of the Polish government in exile, committed suicide. Since fleeing to London he had worn himself out trying to generate concern for the plight of the Jews. In despair both over his own failure and the lack of action at the Bermuda Conference, he took his own life. He wrote: "As I was unable to do anything during my life, perhaps by my death I shall contribute to breaking down that indifference."

But England and the United States continued to persist in making it next to impossible for Jewish refugees to obtain visa applications. The U. S. visa application was over 4 feet long and had to be filled out on both sides and in triplicate. That, however, was the least of the problem. In the fall of 1943, two new barriers were set in place. Henceforth, it was stipulated that if a refugee was not in "acute danger," he was not to be admitted. Jews who had managed to reach countries such as Spain, Portugal, and North Africa were not considered to be in "acute danger." Of course, where Jews were in "acute danger," i.e., in Nazi controlled territories, there were no American consuls to issue visas. Also, if one's original visa application was turned down, one could re-apply in six months. But from 1943 onward, it was illegal to inform the refugee why his application had been rejected. The applicant had no way of knowing how to re-write the application.

The results were predictable. Between the Japanese attack on Pearl Harbor (January 7, 1941) and the end of the war in Europe (May 8, 1945), fewer than 20,000 Jewish refugees entered this country. The number was less than 10% of the quota places legally available to people from Axis controlled European countries during those years.

Finally, in March of 1944, F. D. R., by executive order, established the War Refugee Board (W.R.B.) whose express purpose it was to facilitate the entry of refugees into this country. However, from the start the W.R.B was terribly underfunded. In the 16 months of its existence the government contributed only $547,000. The rest of its funds (the W.R B..expended more than 16 1/2 million dollars) came from private Jewish organizations.

The W.R.B. tried desperately to save the 260,000 Jews in Hungary when the Hungarian government, in spite of a host of anti-Jewish regulations, had not delivered its Jews over to the Nazis. But in the early spring of 1944, Hitler sent Adolph Eichmann to Hungary to set in motion the deportation of Hungary's Jews to the death camps. By mid-April, Eichmann had succeeded in concentrating Jews into central locations and by May the trains began rolling to Auschwitz.

The deportation was unspeakably cruel. Jews were crushed into railroad cars without food or water. And before being packed into the trains the Jews had to endure utterly inhumane treatment at the concentration centers. In a brickyard at Kosice, 15,000 Jews were put to await deportation to the killing center at Auschwitz. A woman there smuggled out the following letter:

> I am afraid I cannot stand it for long, for we are suffering beyond description. We lie in the dust, have neither straw-mattresses nor covers, and will freeze to death. The place is sealed. I do not see any way out.... We are so neglected that we do not look human anymore. There is no possibility of cleaning any-thing. We have not taken off our clothes since coming here. Best greetings to all, pray for us that we shall die soon.

Thus, before facing the horrors of the death camp, the Jews were regularly worn down by hunger, abuse, and humiliation.

What follows next indicates that while the Nazis were fully com-mitted to exterminating the Jews, England and the United States were not at all committed to saving them. Consider that by this time the Nazis were pulling back on all fronts and facing terrible shortages of food, munitions, and manpower. But precisely at this time the Nazis diverted trains, which could have carried these items to the front, in order to carry unarmed Jews to Auschwitz. Moreover, the death factories themselves consumed goods and services which could have been used in the war effort.

Each day at least four trains left Hungary for Auschwitz. In each train there were at least 8,000 Jews. Packed so tightly were the Jews that no one was able to sit. They were given no food or water. Thousands died on the way.

It is now a matter of public record that both the governments of the United States and Britain knew that the Nazis were moving to wipe out the Jews of Hungary. The W.R.B. urged Hungary not to hand its Jews over to the Nazis. And the W.R.B. also pressed the Vatican and the five neutral nations (Sweden, Spain, Portugal, Switzerland, and Turkey) to dispatch additional diplomatic personnel to Hungary in order to pressure the Nazis to stop the deportations. Only the Vatican and Sweden did so.

For a time, the W.R.B.'s tactics appeared to work. In July, the Hungarian government put a halt to the deportations. By then, however, about 440,000 Jews already had been deported. But in the capital city of Budapest, most of its 230,000 Jews were intact. Miklos Horthy, the Hungarian premier, offered to permit all Jewish children under ten to emigrate if visas could be provided for them. He indicated further that he would let out any Jews of any age if the British would permit them to enter Palestine.

This offer was made on the seventeenth of July. The W.R.B. assured Horthy that the United States would find havens for all Jews let out of Hungary. But since Horthy's offer had been made to both the United States and Great Britain, the U.S. government said that it would act only in concert with the English. Britain, however, did not want to open up Palestine to the Jewish refugees for fear that the Arab states would shut off the flow of oil. England, therefore, delayed responding.

Finally, and only in response to pressure from church groups in England, the British agreed to issue a joint statement with the U.S. that havens would be provided for any Jews permitted to leave Hungary. By then, however, it was too late. The Nazis had entered Hungary in force, removed Horthy, and installed a puppet regime. The deportation trains had resumed rolling toward Auschwitz. By the time the Russians captured Budapest, less than 100,000 Jews remained there.

Here is a question related to the destruction of most of Hungary's Jews: why did the United States refuse to bomb the gas chambers and crematoria at Auschwitz and the rail lines leading to that death camp? This question was especially pressing in the spring of 1944 because it was then that the Nazis were proceeding to liquidate the Hungarian Jewish community, the last large and concentrated Jewish population in occupied Europe. Moreover, late in April, two escapees from Auschwitz revealed in vivid detail the ghastly procedures at that death camp. This was the fate awaiting the Jews of Hungary. Also, by May, the 15th wing of the American Army Air Force, operating from southern Italy, began bombing Axis industrial complexes in Central and East Central Europe. Thus, Auschwitz and the rail lines leading there were well within the range of the American bombers.

We now know that long before the spring of 1944, the British and American governments had decided not to bomb any of the camps for fear that they would be overwhelmed by refugees. Thus, request after request to bomb Auschwitz and the other death camps in Poland were turned aside. The killing continued at Auschwitz until the Russian army captured the camp on January 27, 1945.

What could America and England have done? The United States could have established the W.R.B. much earlier and it could have funded that agency properly. Also, the United States and Britain could have pressured the Vatican and the neutral governments to work to get Germany to release the Jews. And Britain and the United States could have warned Germany's allies (Rumania, Hungary, Bulgaria, Slovakia) in no uncertain terms not to mistreat their Jews. These satellite states, after 1942, were seeking to make favorable peace terms on their own. At the very least, the western democracies might have issued stern threats of punishment for mistreating Jews.

If, as seems evident, the United States and Great Britain were fearful of being swamped by refugees, then the simplest solution would have been to send those refugees to Palestine. This, however, England steadfastly refused to do. Thus the one place on earth which would have embraced the refugees was closed off to them. For in Palestine there was a significant Jewish population (the *Yishuv*, a Hebrew term for permanent settlement), with a dream, whose hope was made ever more desperate as Jewish suffering escalated, to reestablish a Jewish homeland there.

THE *YISHUV* IN PALESTINE

In order to put the Jewish presence in Palestine in perspective, it is necessary to backtrack a bit in time. One Jewish response to the persistent anti-Semitism was a nationalistic movement which, almost from its beginnings in the 19th century, was called Zionism. The name refers to a hill in Jerusalem on which Solomon's Temple had been built. The very name, therefore, explicitly linked Jewish nationalistic longings with the ancient homeland of biblical Israel.

The specific incidents which gave impetus to Jewish nationalistic feelings were a series of pogroms (1881–1882) in Eastern Europe. The hostility of the governments which sponsored these persecutions, coupled with the vast indifference of the populace, convinced many Jews that they would never be accorded citizenship in these countries.

Other Jews, however, believed that the rise of the secular nation state would end the centuries of Jewish degradation. These Jews were of the opinion that in the secular nation state, where there was a separation between church and state and where, moreover, the bond of society was morality, the Jew would be accepted as a full-fledged citizen. In pre-modern society, religion had been the bond of society; in the modern secular nation state, one's religion, unless it violates civil law, is a private affair which is protected by the state. No modern secular nation state, without doing irreparable damage to its principles, would launch a religious war like the Crusades, whereas the Crusades were perhaps the most characteristic action of the Middle Ages. As we have seen, the Crusades resulted in the murder of entire Jewish communities. For as a religious action, the Crusades inevitably discriminated against those (the Jews and the Muslims) who did not belong religiously.

And, in fact, with the development of constitutionally grounded nation states, the status of the Jews changed for the better in Holland, England, France, and Italy. The situation in Germany was, however, far more ambiguous. Jews were given full political rights for the first time in Germany by the Weimar Republic. But the Weimar Republic had a short existence; it lasted only from 1919–1933. And the Weimar Republic was followed by Hitler's regime which had as its only clear principle the murderous hatred of all Jews.

Prior to Hitler's rise to power, most German Jews believed that they were no less German than Germans of the Christian faith. The Jews believed that the German nation was indifferent to the differences between Christians and Jews. But this principle was affirmed explicitly only during the short lifetime of the Weimar Republic. Therefore, in the 19th century many Jews agreed with Theodor Herzl (1860–1904), the founder of Zionism, that "Who belongs and who does not belong, is decided by the majority; it is a question of power." Herzl, who was not an observant Jew, saw the problem facing the Jews as a political and not a religious one. As a matter of fact, Herzl was not at all intent on locating the new Jewish nation state in the ancestral homeland of the Jews.

What Herzl wanted was to recover Jewish dignity, honor, and pride. Herzl was convinced that this recovery could take place fully only in a Jewish nation state. No matter how liberal the nation state, if the Jews were a minority that state could guarantee only legal equality and not social equality. That is, Herzl's most basic belief was that a minority was always subject to the whims of the majority. The Jewish "problem," as conceived of by Herzl, could be solved only when the Jews had a land of their own, a land in which they could control their own political and social destiny. The geographical location of the land was not of any particular significance for Herzl.

Herzl's purely political slant on Jewish nationalism was transformed when it ran headlong into the central importance of the Bible in the Jewish experience. For the Bible proclaims the essential religiosity of Jewish identity and, moreover, the God Who mandated the manner and form this religiosity was to take also set apart the land of Israel as the once and future site of the Jewish homeland.

Inevitably, therefore, Herzl's political nationalism was transmuted into religious Zionism. And, as such, a Zionist—in addition to the desire to found a Jewish nation state—still would have to wrestle with what it meant to be a Jew. And any Zionist, as a matter of course, would insist that the Jewish homeland be located in the land promised by the biblical God to Abraham and Abraham's progeny.

In 1881 the Jewish settlement in Palestine (the *Yishuv*), numbered no more than 25,000. Almost all of them were elderly Jews, supported by charity; they had gone to Palestine to die rather than to live. The great American writer, Herman Melville, on a visit to Palestine, remarked that these Jews looked more dead than alive and that there was no possibility that Jews had a future there. Events elsewhere would change everything.

In response to the violent pogroms of the 1880s and 90s, the first young Zionist pioneers began coming to Palestine. They set up twenty agricultural settlements. They faced very difficult conditions. The Turkish government (which controlled Palestine until Britain took over after World War I) placed obstacle after obstacle in the path of Jewish immigration and imposed special taxes and levies on the Jews already there. The backward economic conditions and the disease (particularly malaria) induced many of the first settlers to return to eastern Europe. They could not have known that just down history's road were the Nazis.

A sufficient number of Jewish pioneers persisted in Palestine to keep the *Yishuv* alive. A second wave of agricultural pioneers, mostly idealistic young Russian Jews, came between 1904–14. (My maternal grandfather intended to be among them but a mix-up landed him in Philadelphia)! These Jews, like the first Zionist settlers, were determined to make a place for themselves in Palestine.

By 1914 there were 85,000 Jews in Palestine and there were more than forty agricultural settlements. These Jews made every effort to establish an independent lifestyle in direct contrast to the way Jews had lived for centuries in Christian and Muslim lands. There was the beginning of a defense force as well as an emerging new city (Tel Aviv) populated mostly by Jews. There were charitable-aid societies, active political parties, and a free, independent, and multifaceted press. In short, the groundwork had been laid for a modern Jewish nation state.

By 1929 there were 160,000 Jews in Palestine, and ten years later there were 500,000. These Jews consciously and systematically tried to negate the negative stereotype of the Jew which had grown up in medieval Europe. The model adopted by the *Yishuv* was that of an independent individual who lived in an independent land, who was physically strong, and who was willing and able to defend himself. In the light of how the Jews of Europe were to be murdered, it is understandable that the *Yishuv's* model would become an elemental part of Israel's self-image. But I am getting ahead of myself.

The *Yishuv* faced many problems. The British government persisted in trying to heighten tensions between the Jewish and Arab populations in Palestine. This policy apparently was intended to ensure that neither the Jews nor the Arabs would become sufficiently strong to threaten British rule (i.e., divide and conquer). In 1917, the British had issued the Balfour Declaration (named after a former prime minister Arthur Balfour) which stated that the "British government views with favor the establishment in Palestine of a National Home for the Jewish people." But again and again, Britain reneged on this promise as its own imperialistic interests clashed with its promise to establish a Jewish state in Palestine. The ever increasing industrialization in Europe, England, and the United States brought with it an ever increasing dependence on Arab oil. The Arab states, for their part, pressured Great Britain to halt all Jewish immigration into Palestine.

Also, the *Yishuv's* relationship with the Arab population was often tense, sometimes erupting into violent conflict. When, in 1929, Jews and Arabs fought over whether Jews should be allowed access to certain shrines in Jerusalem, Britain reduced Jewish immigration and prohibited Jews from purchasing any additional land in Palestine. In Palestine, all the *Yishuv's* land had been bought legally from Arabs. These moves by Britain were crushing blows to the *Yishuv.*

On one thing Arabs and Jews in Palestine generally agreed, namely, that Palestine would be better off without the British. Not surprisingly, the British insisted that their presence in Palestine was necessary in order to protect Jew from Arab and Arab from Jew. To most Arabs and Jews, however, it was clear that Great Britain wanted to keep a strong presence in the area for its own strategic benefit, and neither the Arabs nor the Jews were yet in a position to do anything about it.

The development of the *Yishuv* had greatly modernized Palestine to the point where it had become the most technologically advanced area in the Middle East. This modernization exacerbated the intersecting tensions involving the Jews, the Arabs, and the British. In

1937 these tensions prompted the British to convoke a Royal Commission to study the problem. After several months of inquiry, the Commission proposed that Palestine be partitioned into a Jewish state, an Arab state, and a British zone. While far from happy with it, the *Yishuv* accepted the proposal. The Arabs, however, rejected it.

Two years later, in 1939, the British government repudiated its own Royal Commission's report, and declared that there would be no partition but that in ten years time Palestine would become an independent state. The British also declared that henceforth Jewish immigration would be limited to an additional 75,000. This was akin to a death sentence to the establishment of a Jewish state in Palestine as it would leave the *Yishuv* a perpetual minority. It was, of course, the minority status of the Jew and the powerlessness which went along with it that caused so many Jews to commit themselves to Zionism in the first place. It was for the Zionists the blackest of ironies that they would be caught in the same trap in the land of their ancestors.

Why were the British acting like this? Apparently, with war clouds gathering, the British were afraid of losing the goodwill of the oil producing Arab states. But whatever the reason, it was clear that the British no longer supported the idea of a Jewish nation state in Palestine.

As we have seen, World War II provided Hitler with the ideal cloak with which to cover his murderous treatment of the Jews. The darkest of nights descended on the Jews of Europe. To put this nightmare in perspective, consider that more than a million and a half Jewish children rode the transport trains to the gas chambers. Almost without exception, these children not only died, but they died hideous deaths. In one camp, the liberating American army found 75,000 pairs of neatly stacked children's shoes. There was not one child left alive in that camp. Depending on what the Nazis decided, these children were shot or drowned or burned or gassed or buried alive or murdered in gruesome medical experiments. And the only rationale offered by the Nazis is that these children were Jews. I repeat that the only clearly discernible principle of Nazism was its murderous hatred of Jews. It mattered not at all to the Nazis what these Jews believed or whether they were young or old or male or female.

The "Final Solution" required for its implementation the cooperation of millions of Germans, Poles, Latvians, Ukranians, and
Russians. Also, the western democracies did little to help the Jews of
Europe. In effect, the Jews who were herded like cattle into the
transport trains, were regarded as little more than cattle by the
world.

In 1945 only 3.1 million Jews were left in Europe out of a pre-war
population of 9.2 million. In only a few lands was there a concerted effort to help the Jews. The Danes, for instance, smuggled more than
6,000 Jews to neutral Sweden in October of 1943. Italy, though ruled
by a Fascist government, refused to cooperate fully with the Nazis
and, as a result, 32,000 of the 40,000 Italian Jews survived the war.
On the other hand, most of the Polish peasants turned fleeing Jews
over to the Nazis, and many partisan movements refused either to accept or aid Jews.

At the Nuremberg Trials in 1945 the following statistics were
compiled which estimate the numbers of Jews murdered by the Nazis.
The numbers speak for themselves in terms of how little most of the
countries were able or willing to do to save their Jews.

	Pre-War	Number Annihilated
Poland	3,300,000	3,000,000
Baltic Countries	253,000	228,000
Germany/Austria	240,000	210,000
Slovakia	90,000	75,000
Greece	70,000	55,000
Netherlands	140,000	105,000
Hungary	650,000	450,000
S.S.R. White Russia	375,000	245,000
S.S.R. Ukraine	1,500,000	900,000
Belgium	65,000	40,000
Yugoslavia	43,000	26,000
Rumania	600,000	300,000
Norway	1,800	900
France	350,000	90,000

Bulgaria	64,000	14,000
Italy	40,000	8,000
Luxembourg	5,000	1,000
Russia	975,000	107,000
Denmark	8,000	0
Finland	2,000	0

While the Jews in the pre-modern period experienced recurrent cycles of persecutions, the "Final Solution" attacked Jews in a uniquely violent manner. The "Final Solution" sought to wipe the Jews off the face of the earth in the service of an ideology which called into question the biblical teaching that all human beings are created in the image of God. For the Nazis, right was not equated with decency but with might, and for the Nazis, only the Aryans were entitled to life, liberty, and the pursuit of happiness.

The wife of a Nazi schoolteacher, both of whom went to Poland to help the war effort, was asked whether there was a difference between Poles and Polish Jews. She answered, "The Poles weren't exterminated, and the Jews were. That's the difference. An external difference." She was then asked if there was an "inner difference." Her response: "I can't assess that. I don't know enough about psychology and anthropology. The difference between the Poles and the Jews? Anyway, they couldn't stand each other." [C. Lanzmann, *Shoah* (Pantheon: New York, 1985), pp. 82f.].

Her remarks perhaps give us a clue as to how the Holocaust happened to the Jews. The Nazis were told to exterminate the Jews and they met no resistance ("...They couldn't stand each other") and they gave the matter no thought ("I can't assess that"). The woman is no brute; she may be called "civilized" and "cultured." But she participated and to this day does not know why, nor does she feel remorse. In the words of Primo Levi, himself a survivor of Auschwitz, "In order to resist, one needs a very solid moral framework." [Primo Levi, *Moments of Reprieve* (Penguin: New York, 1985), p. 171]. On the whole, as Levi notes, mankind resembled Isabella's description of the presumptuous and mortal man in Shakespeare's *Measure for Measure*:

Dressed in a little brief authority,
Most ignorant of what he's most assured,
His glassy essence, like an angry ape
Plays such fantastic tricks before high heaven
As makes the angels weep....

With the above description in mind, consider the following dialogue between Claude Lanzmann, the producer of the film "Shoah," and Franz Suchomel, the S.S. Unterscharfuhrer at Treblinka. Suchomel has been giving a detailed and precise account of the "processing" of Jews at Treblinka (i.e., getting the Jews from the train to the gas chambers as efficiently as possible), when Lanzmann asks: "How was it possible in Treblinka in peak days to 'process' eighteen thousand people?"

Suchomel indignantly protests: "Eighteen thousand is too high."

Lanzmann: "But I read that figure in court reports."

Suchomel: "Sure."

Lanzmann: "To 'process' eighteen thousand people, to liquidate them."

Suchomel: "No Lanzmann, that's an exaggeration. Believe me."

Lanzmann: "How many?"

Suchomel: "Twelve thousand to fifteen thousand. But we had to spend half the night at it. In January the trains started arriving at 6 A.M."

Later Lanzmann asks Suchomel to talk about the cold winter at Treblinka.

Suchomel: "Well, in winter, in December, anyway after Christmas it was cold as hell. Between fifteen and minus four. I know: at first it was cold as hell for us too. We didn't have suitable uniforms." [Lanzmann, *op. cit.*, pp. 105–111].

In the midst of death and suffering which goes far beyond one's ability to comprehend, Suchomel feels sorry for himself: he is working too hard "processing" the Jews and, in addition, he does not have adequate clothes to ward off the cold of winter. Do not Suchomel and the hundreds of thousands like him who followed Hitler's orders match up perfectly with Shakespeare's Isabella's description:

Dressed in a little brief authority,
Most ignorant of what he's most assured,
His glassy essence, like an angry ape
Plays such fantastic tricks before high heaven
As makes the angels weep....

11

Israel and the Diaspora

The "Final Solution" threatened Jews as nothing had before. Inevitably, the Holocaust menaced Judaism also because in the wake of World War II not only the surviving Jews of Europe but the Jews of the free world as well faced squarely the question of whether to remain Jews. For had not the world stood by while almost 70% of European Jewry had been ruthlessly liquidated? Indeed, this fact was clear to anyone with eyes to see. Moreover, it was no less clear that what had happened once could happen again. What was not clear was whether and to what degree the Jews would lose heart. If anything, the opposite seems to have happened. In the aftermath of the "Final Solution," many Jewish leaders have urged their fellow Jews to perpetuate the Jewish heritage precisely in order not to give a posthumous victory to Hitler. This chapter offers a brief survey of the two most vital centers of Judaism today: Israel and the Jewish community in the United States.

During the first years of peace, a quarter of a million Jews who had survived the Holocaust made their way toward Western Europe. Many of them first had attempted to return to their homes in Eastern Europe only to be repelled by the local populace. Jewish property had been appropriated and the new owners were, to say the least, not sympathetic to the idea of returning this property to its original and rightful owners.

Western Europe greeted the Jews by placing them in Displaced Persons (D.P.) camps bordered on all sides by barbed wire. Most of these Jews deeply and desperately had longed to go to Palestine. But the British continued to limit strictly Jewish immigration.

Shiploads of Jews who did manage to get to Palestine, thanks to help from the *Yishuv* and the American Jewish community, in almost all cases were captured by the British who had set up a blockade of Palestine. These Jews, the surviving remnants of the "Final Solution," who had suffered beyond our capacity to imagine, now found themselves interred in D.P. camps on the island of Cyprus or returned to the D.P. camps in Europe.

The British treatment of the survivors as well as the British abandonment of support for a Jewish homeland caused tension to mount in the *Yishuv*. Elements within the Jewish Defense Force (called the *Haganah*), demanded that negotiations cease with the recalcitrant British and that in their stead the Jews begin a campaign of military harassment against the British. These Jews formed a new group known as the *Irgun*, and they proceeded to make life miserable for the British occupying force. For example, when the British captured *Irgun* members and interrogated them roughly, the *Irgun* retaliated by capturing British soldiers and treating them in a like manner. When the British threatened to hang those responsible for what they called acts of terrorism, the *Irgun* warned the British that they would be repaid in kind. When the British did in fact hang *Irgun* members, the *Irgun* immediately captured and hung a like number of British soldiers.

As the negotiation process between the leaders of the *Yishuv* and the British continued to drag along, a great number within the *Haganah* found themselves agreeing with the *Irgun* that since the world did nothing to save the Jews of Europe, and now was doing little or nothing to help the survivors of the Holocaust, it was senseless to count on either the world's good feeling or its pity. The leaders of the *Irgun* and the *Haganah* reasoned that the nation states of the world had demonstrated clearly that they respected those who could protect themselves. Perhaps it was out of this conviction more than any other that the modern nation state of Israel was born.

In the face of an increasingly widespread and effective Jewish resistance, the British capitulated. In April of 1947, the British government turned over the question of Palestine to the United Nations. In November of 1947, the General Assembly of the United Nations voted 33–13 in favor of partitioning Palestine between the Arabs and the Jews.

As soon as the United Nations adopted the partition plan, war broke out in Palestine. Bands of Palestinean Arabs, financed by the Arab states, began to attack Jewish settlements and neighborhoods. The *Irgun* and *Haganah* fought back. Huge sections of the tiny land of Palestine became battle zones, and large numbers of Arabs living next to Jews in these battle zones fled, thus creating the problem of the Palestinean refugees.

Both sides waited for the British to withdraw before launching full scale hostilities. Immediately after the British withdrawal, the armies of Egypt, Transjordan (present day Jordan), Lebanon, Syria, and Iraq invaded the new Jewish state.

Some of the heaviest fighting took place between the *Haganah* and the army of Transjordan which was armed, financed, and advised by the British. In May and June of 1948, Transjordanian units captured the old city of Jerusalem, including the Jewish quarter. But in all other areas the *Irgun* and the *Haganah* (now working in concert) made significant gains. The Israeli forces kept control of the Galilee, the lush valley of Jezreel, the coastal plain, a corridor to Jerusalem, and a part of the Negev.

By the end of the war, in January of 1949, the Israeli army controlled 8,000 square miles in contrast to the 6,200 square miles allotted to the Jewish state in the partition plan drafted by the United Nations.

At the end of 1947, the *Yishuv* numbered 630,000. There followed a great influx of Jews from all over the world. By 1957 there were 1,300,000 Jews in Israel, and by 1980 more than 3 million. By way of comparison, the *Yishuv's* population is similar to that of New Zealand.

The new state of Israel faced a variety of complex and pressing problems. Israel had to handle the task of integrating the great numbers of immigrants who came from both highly developed and backward areas. Moreover, Israel had (and has) a very limited number of natural resources; by almost any standard, Israel is a poor country as measured by its mineral deposits.

Israel's greatest problem, however, was (and is) the ongoing hostility of its Arab neighbors. Only Egypt has established diplomatic relations with Israel while the other Arab states refuse to recognize the right of Israel to exist. Israel's alienation from its Arab neighbors is bound up with its relationship with Arabs living on land conquered by Israel in the wars that have intervened between the birth of the Jewish nation state and the present. While Israel has won each of these conflicts, Israel still remains in a virtual state of siege. The feeling persists in Israel that were the Jewish nation state to lose only one war it would mark the end of its existence. For that is what the Arab states claim that they are committed to.

It is fair to point out that the new state of Israel has not been overwhelmed by these problems. Since 1949, Israel has made significant economic, cultural, and political progress. These advances in part have been made possible by the firm groundwork laid by the *Yishuv,* which from the beginning sought to model the Jewish nation state after the western democracies. Israel today is a parliamentary democracy, consisting of legislative, executive, and judicial branches. All citizens, regardless of race, religion, or sex are guaranteed equality before the law and full democratic rights. Freedom of speech, assembly, press, and political affiliation are guaranteed in Israel's laws and traditions. The high educational level of most Israelis (Israel has one of the lowest illiteracy rates in the world) has enabled Israel both to make use of advanced technology and to create its own high-tech industries. Also, one cannot overestimate the extent to which Israel's special relationship with the United States has helped the Jewish nation state.

The rebirth of the Jewish nation state in the land promised to the patriarchs by the biblical God is surely one of the most dramatic events in the Jewish experience. This land has been one of the focal points of the Jewish experience even in the years when it was largely uninhabited by Jews.

The patriarchs, Abraham, Isaac, and Jacob, sojourned in the land c.1700–1500 B.C.E. Following the stay in Egypt and the wilderness experience, the Bible records that Moses led the Israelites to the eastern bank of the river Jordan c.1300 B.C.E. It was then that Joshua led a strike force into the land and by 1025 B.C.E. the Israelites were in firm control of the land and had established a monarchical form of government. As we have seen, Israel and then Israel and Judah were ruled by kings until the two kingdoms were conquered and their populations exiled by Assyria and Babylon respectively. A restoration took place for some Judeans in the 6th century B.C.E., but except for a brief period of political independence under the Maccabees (165–137 B.C.E.), the land was controlled by other nations (Babylon, Persia, Greece, Rome).

In 66 C.E., the Jews revolted against the repressive rule of Rome. But in 70, after a prolonged siege of Jerusalem, the Roman General Titus breached the city's walls and sacked Jerusalem and destroyed the Temple. The Jews again revolted in 132 and for a time were able to establish an independent Jewish state. But it was short-lived and the final defeat by Rome resulted in Jews being expelled and barred from Jerusalem.

As the Jews spread out into the Diaspora, we have seen that they were beset frequently by persecution. The land of Israel remained in the minds and hearts of Diaspora Jews as a symbol not only of the land of the Bible but of independence and freedom. In addition, the Jewish liturgy was filled with references which bespoke a longing to restore the Jewish nation state in the ancestral homeland. It goes without saying that anti-Semitism increased the longing of the Jews for a homeland of their own. And, of course, wherever Jews went in the Diaspora, they carried with them the Bible; and in numerous biblical texts the land of Israel played a central and important role. In short, in the pre-modern Diaspora, the Jews were denied what the land of Israel represented: religious, political, and social freedom.

While the Jewish presence was sometimes small, there were always Jews in the land. Sometimes the Jewish community was, as in the 16th century, the source of great creativity. Jewish scholars produced important mystic and scholarly writings. For a time, young Jewish scholars came from all over the Diaspora to study in Palestine.

We saw that from the earliest days of civilization in the Middle East, the land of Israel was fought over because of its location at the junction of three continents. Through the centuries successive waves of conquerors battered the land, and Christians and Muslims fought over the land as well.

The Ottoman Empire (1300–1919) stretched for a time from Egypt to Mesopotamia and from Asia Minor west to the Balkans. In the early days of their control over the land, the Turks did considerable building, including the walls which encircle the old section of Jerusalem today. Under the rule of Suleiman the Magnificent (who died in 1566), Jewish life in Palestine thrived. But in the years that followed, the Jewish settlement languished as taxation became as crippling as it was capricious. The great forests of the Galilee and the Carmel mountain range were stripped, and swamp and desert encroached on agricultural land.

It was left to the Zionist pioneers to start the process of the restoration of the land. This restoration went on in spite of the meager resources of the *Yishuv,* as well as the hostility of the Ottoman administration and the difficult local conditions. The difficulties faced by today's Israel spring from the same sources: Israel's meager resources; the hostility of the surrounding nations; and the problem of the Arab refugees.

We already have surveyed the Holocaust, and it suffices to note here that in 1961, Adolf Eichmann, the Nazi official in charge of transporting Jews to the death camps, and who had escaped from allied authorities and had gone into hiding in South America, was captured by the Israeli Mosad (the equivalent of our C.I.A.). Eichmann was spirited out of Argentina and brought to Israel where he was tried, sentenced, and executed for crimes against the Jewish people. This is the only time the death penalty has been carried out in Israel.

THE DIASPORA

The central importance of the land of Israel, both as fact and as symbol, should not obscure the great importance of the Diaspora in the Jewish experience. The Diaspora has nurtured a wide variety of Jews and Judaisms and is no less important than the land of Israel to the Jewish experience.

As early as the destruction of the first Temple in 587 B.C.E., vital Jewish communities were set up by exiles in Babylon and by refugees in Egypt. And as the Greeks and Greek culture spread, Jews settled in all the major cities of the Greek empire. In Alexandria, Egypt, the Jewish community produced the Septuagint, a Greek translation of the Hebrew Bible which, as we have seen, exerted a profound influence on both Judaism and Christianity. In Philo of Alexandria (25 B.C.E. to 50 C.E.) the Diaspora produced an important and creative thinker who sought to find a meeting ground between Jewish and Greek thought. In his extensive writings, Philo tried to prove, for instance, that the first five books of the Hebrew Bible contained the fundamental ideas of Greek philosophy. Centuries later, the great Maimonides, as well as others, would continue this approach which had as its goal the proof that Scripture contained a coherent and sophisticated system of thought.

In an earlier chapter we have already spoken of the Babylonian Jewish community which produced the Babylonian Talmud which has had a much more profound impact on the Jewish experience than has the Talmud produced by the Jews of Palestine. The Babylonian Talmud remains, after the Hebrew Bible, the most sacred of Jewish texts.

The rise and spread of Islam brought many Diaspora Jewish communities under the control of Muslims. In some of these communities Jews were permitted self-rule, and scholarly activity flourished. However, in all but a few Muslim lands the Jews were forced out of agriculture because of a discriminatory land tax which was levied against them. Until the 8th and 9th centuries, the majority of Jews had earned their livings by working their own land. Forced out of agriculture, some Jews became international traders and financiers.

It is inaccurate to generalize about the experiences of Jews under Muslim rule. At certain times and places (e.g., southern Spain from the 9th–12th centuries), there were flourishing Jewish communities which produced religious literature of the first rank. At other times and places, entire Jewish communities were put to the sword.

Since Jews and Judaism both thrived and languished in Muslim lands, it is clear that there was (and is) nothing intrinsic in Islam which produced hostile attitudes toward Jews and/or Judaism. The one constant rule of thumb in the relationship between Jews and Muslims was that when economic conditions deteriorated in Muslim lands, the Jews became convenient scapegoats on which to heap blame for social problems.

The same, of course, was (and is) true of Christianity. Prior to the modern period, the Jews experienced the same highs and lows in Christian lands (and for the same economic reasons) as they had in Muslim countries.

We have seen that in some of the modern nation states Jews, for the most part, were accorded full citizenship. Nowhere was this (and has this been) more true than in the United States. The United States never had to contend with the pre-modern institutions which the European countries had to dismantle in order to create a nation state in which religion was a private affair and in which the citizenry, through its elected officials, controlled the state's destiny. In the United States, there never was a constitutional basis on which to distinguish between the citizen and the "stranger" on the basis of religious affiliation. The Jews in the United States never had to struggle for emancipation as had the Jews in those European countries which first had to eradicate the pre-modern way of doing and looking at things.

As the frontier moved west in the United States, no restrictions were placed on commercial activities of the Jews, and thus many Jews took advantage of the opportunities opening up in this vast land. Then, when the United States went through the process of industrialization, Jews were not excluded from setting up factories or opening department stores.

In short, no Diaspora experience has been as vital as that in the United States. More than five million Jews live in America, and as citizens they, for the most part, have taken advantage of the opportunities afforded them. In the survey which follows you will see that the Jews have developed a variety of communal and scholarly institutions; you will see that American Jews support three major denominations of about equal size (Orthodox, Conservative, and Reform); and you will see that the Jews have been, and are, active in government, politics, business, the professions, and the arts.

In 1776 there were no more than 2,500 Jews in this country. Not surprisingly, the first Jews came in order to escape persecution. Appropriately, the beginnings of American Jewish history go back to the year 1492. While Columbus was preparing for his journey, the Jews of Spain were expelled. Many of these Jews found a temporary haven in Portugal, the very country in which Columbus was forced to seek refuge on his return voyage. The Jews of Portugal, knowing that it was only a matter of time before their situation would worsen, listened with great interest to the reports of the new land on the western shores of the Atlantic Ocean.

While Spain and Portugal began to outfit expeditions to the New World, one Fernao Noronha assembled a group of Jews and proposed a journey to what one day would be called the Americas. He bought a ship and renamed it, appropriately, the *Judea*. Noronha bought four other ships and entered into an agreement with King Manuel involving exploration and settlements in the new land. Noronha agreed to open up at least 600 miles of territory a year and to build forts at various strategic locations. Noronha made his first voyage in 1501 and endeavored to explore the often wild coast of Brazil.

Other Jewish pioneers found their way to South America, to the West Indies, and to Mexico. In the New World the Jews took on vocations as diverse as the lands they were settling. Some owned plantations where they cultivated sugar and tobacco. Some became importers and exporters. There were Jewish merchants, financiers, farmers, artisans, soldiers of fortune, and seamen.

In general, Jews prospered in the New World and as word filtered back, more and more Jews came westward. In many of the Jewish settlements synagogues, cemeteries, and philanthropic agencies appeared. Jews fared better in those South American territories controlled by the Dutch and the English. The Portuguese and the

Spanish often allowed the Office of the Inquisition to set up business. When and where this happened, many Jews moved northward to such places as Virginia, New Amsterdam, and to other seaboard communities in North America.

The Jews did not always receive a warm welcome. Peter Stuyvesant, for one, the governor of New Amsterdam, called the Jewish settlers "godless rascals." Stuyvesant wrote the following letter to the directors of the Dutch West India Company:

> The Jews who have arrived would nearly all like to remain here, but with their customary usury and deceitful trading with the Christians were very repugnant.... We have, for the benefit of the weak and newly developed place and the land in general deemed it useful to require them in a friendly way[!!!] to depart; praying also most seriously in this connection, for ourselves as also for the general community of your worship, that the deceitful race—such hateful enemies and blasphemers of the name of Christ,—be not allowed further to infect and trouble this new colony, to the detraction of your worships and the dissatisfaction of your worships' most affectionate subjects.
>
> [W. Hallo, D. Ruderman, M. Stanislawski, *Heritage: Civilization and the Jews* (New York: Praeger, 1984), pp. 195–96].

You will note that most of the elements of pre-modern European anti-Semitism are present in Stuyvesant's invective: he depicts the Jews as greedy, pushy, and as "blasphemers of the name of Christ." But the conditions in the New World were different, and the directors of the Dutch West India Company decided that the Jews should be permitted to remain. There was a new world to be won, and the Dutch were in fierce competition with England, France, and Spain for this world. The Dutch needed settlers who could deliver goods and services and they were willing to admit any and all who could deliver these goods and services. So the Jews remained and immediately petitioned for a right to buy "a burying place for their nation;" and they began the process of making places for themselves in the New World.

In the 17th and early 18th centuries, Jewish communities (some of them very small) could be found in Massachusetts, New Hampshire, Rhode Island, Connecticut, New Netherlands (New York), New Jersey, Maryland, Virginia, Pennsylvania, North Carolina, and Georgia. Significantly, there were no Jewish settlements in Spanish Florida, for Spain, not yet itself a secular nation state, sought to impose in its colonies a religious litmus test for citizenship. The difference between Spain and England in this regard can be discerned in John Locke's constitution for the Carolinas. Locke was careful to include a clause for the protection of "Jews, heathens, and other dissenters." [*Ibid.*, p. 157]. In a similar vein, in 1649 Roger Williams (the founder of Rhode Island), wrote a pamphlet entitled *The Bloody Tenets of Persecution* which included a plea for toleration of the Jews and Judaism.

The new land generated new ways of looking at things and thus encouraged separation from the ways of Europe. And nowhere was this truer than in matters of faith. Many of the Christians who came to America were themselves fleeing from religious persecution. In the New World what counted most was one's ability to contribute to society and not one's religious preference. In the New World, the bond of society was not religion but decency and the willingness to bear responsibility in the building of a new country. There was a new life waiting for those who were willing to work hard enough to achieve it, and one's work ethic counted for a whole lot more than one's liturgical preference.

Moreover, there were so many diverse forms of Christianity in the New World that the idea of a state church never took root. In America there was no place for a distinction between those who belonged religiously and those who did not. It was just this distinction which in Europe had brought so much suffering down upon the Jews in bad times and social ostracism in more tranquil times.

On the eve of the American Revolution there were Jewish beggars and merchant princes, Jewish unskilled laborers and physicians, Jewish peddlers and shipowners. In the war, Jews served both in the ranks and as officers. This pattern was to be repeated in every war fought by the United States of America.

Not surprisingly, American Jews were strong supporters of the drive for independence from England. The Old World, even at its best, represented that from which the Jews were fleeing. Jews enthusiastically supported Thomas Jefferson's bill establishing absolute freedom of religion, enacted first in Virginia in 1785, and then as part of the United States Constitution as the first amendment:

Congress shall make no law respecting an establishment of religion, or pro-
hibiting the free exercise thereof; or abridging the freedom of speech, or of the
press; or the right of the people peaceably to assemble, and to petition the
government for a redress of grievance.

In a circumstance which was as true to the spirit of the new land
as it was alien to the Old World, the Jews of Newport, Rhode Island
welcomed the first president of the United States with praises of "...a
government which to bigotry gives no sanction, to persecution no as-
sistance." George Washington was quick to respond with the hope
that Jews could find peace and harmony in the new land.

Between 1820 and 1870 more than 150,000 German Jews came to
the United States. Germany was at the time beset by severe economic
problems and many Germans were blaming these problems on the
Jews. The majority of the German Jewish immigrants, rather than
settling on the eastern seaboard, pushed westward into the interior of
the country. Many settled along the Ohio and Mississippi rivers,
while some continued west to California. Jews and others settled in
San Francisco in 1849 as that city sought to keep up with the needs
produced by the gold rush. Among San Francisco's Jews was Levi
Strauss who sold denim overalls ("Levis") to the gold miners.

More than a few of these German Jewish immigrants achieved
great success, even though most of them came here with little more
than they could carry on their backs. Oftentimes, a German Jewish
family could afford to send only its oldest son to the New World, and
when the son had the wherewithal, he would send for the rest of the
family.

These German Jewish immigrants became enthusiastic
Americans and like other Americans exhibited the characteristics of
the local community in which they settled. Thus, when the Civil War
broke out, those Jews in the North supported the Union, while those
in the South supported the Confederacy.

As the Jews exhibited different economic and cultural characteristics which were dictated by local conditions and personal predilec-
tions, so did the Jews display different religious characteristics. Some
German Jews brought with them a liberal form of Judaism which
came to be known as Reform Judaism. The Reformers set about

formulating a Judaism which would be in keeping with the American environment.

Reform Judaism had to compete with the Conservative and Orthodox branches of Judaism for the support of American Jewry. At the present time, each of these three movements has attracted about the same number of adherents. There are great variations in each of the movements, but in a general way they can be distinguished by their attitudes toward change in Judaism. Orthodox Judaism and the more orthodox elements in Conservative Judaism attempt to adhere strictly to the rituals and regulations promulgated in the Bible, Mishnah, and Talmud, while Reform Judaism and the more liberal elements in Conservative Judaism are much more flexible.

To give but one example: the sacred texts do not seem to allow for the possibility of a female Rabbi. Accordingly, Orthodox Judaism permits the ordination only of males while the Reform Movement began ordaining women in 1970. Conservative Judaism began admitting women to their rabbinic school in 1985.

From 1870 to 1890 about 30,000 Eastern European Jews, fleeing from economic hardship and its concomitant, religious persecution, in Russia, Poland, and Rumania, came to the United States. This was the beginning of a large-scale migration of Jews that would, in a few decades' time, make the American Jewish community the most populous Diaspora community in the world. The Jews were a tiny part of the massive waves of migrations that brought tens of millions of immigrants to the United States at the end of the 19th and beginning of the 20th centuries. But though only a very small part of this great movement of human beings, still more than two million Eastern European Jews immigrated to the United States and by doing so changed the make-up of the American Jewish community. In 1880 East European Jews made up about 16% of American Jews; by the end of the migration, the percentage was over 80%.

Most of these Eastern European Jews settled in cities along the Atlantic coast. And most of them, at least initially, lived in terrible poverty. In Eastern Europe, Jews had spoken about the United States as the "Golden Land" where the good life was there for the taking. Few of these immigrants were prepared, therefore, for the harsh conditions which confronted them. Living conditions were dreadfully overcrowded and many of them worked 16 hours a day or more in "sweatshops."

But as bad as conditions were, and they were horrid, very few Jews returned to the Old World because they believed, and they were proven right, that this new land would reward good work and good deeds. Although most endured harsher conditions than the ones from which they had fled, the Jews saw and felt the exhilarating freedom in this country; and they were convinced that their children would know a far better life here than ever would have been possible for them in Eastern Europe.

Conditions were made more bearable in these teeming Jewish neighborhoods by Jewish philanthropic societies which lent money without interest and which offered services which helped ease the acculturation process. Synagogues appeared as well as political and social organizations which nurtured the spiritual, cultural, and intellectual energies of the new immigrants.

Because so many Jews worked in sweatshops, i.e., shops or plants where employees worked long hours at low wages in poor conditions, Jews were in the forefront of the effort to organize unions in order to ameliorate conditions. The deplorable condition at these sweatshops was demonstrated emphatically in 1911 when a fire raged through one of the largest garment shops in New York City. One hundred and forty six workers, most of them young women, died. The following poem by Robert Pinsky [*The New Yorker,* July 3, 1989] captures the horror of this fire and the injustice of the conditions:

Shirt

The back, the yoke, the yardage. Lapped seams,
The nearly invisible stitches along the collar
Turned in a sweatshop by Koreans or Malaysians

Gossiping over tea and noodles on their break
Or talking money or politics while one fitted
This armpiece with its overseam to the band

Of cuff I button at my wrist. The presser, the cutter,
The wringer, the mangle. The needle, the union,
The treadle, the bobbin. The code. The infamous blaze

At the Triangle factory in 1911.
One hundred and forty-six died in the flames
On the ninth floor, no hydrants, no fire escapes—

The witness in a building across the street
Who watched how a young man helped a girl to step
Up to the windowsill, then held her out

Away from the masonry wall and let her drop.
And then another. As if he were helping them up
To enter a streetcar, and not eternity.

A third before he dropped her put her arms
Around his neck and kissed him. Then he held
Her into space, and dropped her. Almost at once

He stepped to the sill himself, his jacket flared
And fluttered up from his shirt as he came down,
Air filling up the legs of his gray trousers—

Like Hart Crane's Bedlamite, "shrill shirt ballooning."
Wonderful how the pattern matches perfectly
Across the placket and over the twin bar-tacked

Corners of both pockets, like a strict rhyme
Or a major chord. Prints, plaids, checks,
Houndstooth, tattersall, madras. The clan tartans

Invented by mill owners inspired by the hoax of Ossian,
To control their savage Scottish workers, tamed
By a fabricated heraldry: MacGregor,

Bailey, MacMartin. The kilt, devised for workers
To wear among the dusty clattering looms.
Weavers, carders, spinners. The loader,

The docker, the navvy. The planter, the picker, the sorter
Sweating at her machine in a litter of cotton
As slaves in calico head rags sweated in fields:

George Herbert, your descendant is a black
Lady in South Carolina, her name is Irma
And she inspected my shirt. Its color and fit

And feel and its clean smell have satisfied
Both her and me. We have culled its cost and quality
Down to the buttons of simulated bone,

The buttonholes, the sizing, the facing, the characters
Printed in black on neckband and tail. The shape,
The label, the labor, the color, the shade. The shirt.

—Robert Pinsky

Incidents like this led to a series of strikes which led to the forma-
tion of labor organizations.

The large majority of the Eastern European Jewish immigrants
lived in neighborhoods made up almost entirely of Jews. At first they
spoke Yiddish (a dialect of German containing elements of Hebrew,
Russian, Polish, etc.), and they clung to the traditions and customs of
the Old World. However, slowly but surely, they became
Americanized. Not that it was easy. In Europe, observant Jews ab-
stained from all work on the Jewish Sabbath and, since European
Jews by and large associated only with other Jews, the strict observance of the Sabbath imposed no financial hardship. The situation
was far different in America. In America, businesses shut down on
Sunday rather than on Saturday; Saturday was a normal business
day. Inevitably, many of the immigrants abandoned strict observance
of the Sabbath, or, for that matter, of any other custom which made it
difficult to live among and compete with other Americans.

However, one deeply ingrained custom of Eastern European
Jewry served the immigrants well in the new land. In Eastern
Europe, Jews had devoted considerable energy to educating their
young. While this education was largely devoted to the interpretation
of the sacred texts of Judaism, this emphasis on education allowed
many of the immigrant children to take full advantage of the
American public school system. And perhaps more than any other
institution, the public schools served to acculturate the immigrants.
In the public schools, the children of the Eastern European Jewish
immigrants learned English and experienced a secular education.

Since it was unthinkable to abandon the study of the sacred literature, the Jews quickly transferred that obligation to the synagogue.
In almost every instance, however, the children channeled most of
their energies into the public school experience. More than any other
factor, it was the public school which accelerated the process of

Americanization. Each day, the children of immigrants spent many hours in the company of students whose traditions and customs differed markedly from those found in the Jewish ghettos of Eastern Europe. The public school, as an institution devoted to the secular pursuit of knowledge, was unthinkable except in a secular nation state. The children brought these experiences home with them and thus did they educate their parents in the ways of America.

At first there were deep differences between the American Jews of German origin and their counterparts from Eastern Europe. But these differences gradually faded as both groups of immigrants moved into the mainstream of American life. Unfortunately, one of the factors which brought the two groups together was an American form of anti-Semitism. Hatred of the Jew in the United States of the late 19th and early 20th centuries emerged for a variety of reasons. To begin with, there was the Depression of 1891 which fed fears that immigrants were taking jobs away from "real" Americans. Also, racial theories, generated in Germany and France, came to these shores and gave birth to the misbegotten idea that a "real" American was a white, Anglo-Saxon Protestant ("W.A.S.P.").

Although anti-Semitism in the United States never attracted the widespread support it had in the Old World, it was, and is, enough of a real threat to unify the American Jewish community. In addition, the fear of persecution in their new country was coupled with reports from Europe that Jews were in fact being persecuted. And these Jews, once the United States virtually shut down immigration in 1921, found themselves trapped in a Europe which shortly was to become a place of suffering and death for Jews on an unprecedented scale. In 1921 an immigration act was passed that limited immigrants from a given country to 3% of the total number of its national residents in the United States as of 1910. Three years later an even more restrictive bill lowered the proportion to 2% of the residents in 1890, and set a maximum of 150,000 immigrants annually from all countries. As a result of these bills, Jewish immigration to this country virtually stopped. Unfortunately, this happened just as the situations in Russia and Poland were deteriorating for the Jews. These Jews were destined to be destroyed in the Holocaust.

As Jewish students matriculated into colleges in numbers way out of proportion to their percentage in the overall population, some universities put quotas in place in order to limit the number of Jews in their institutions. But such roadblocks were so antithetical to the American spirit that they either disappeared or were counterbalanced by the fact that many universities admitted all eligible students.

The result has been that most Jews in the United States feel "at home." After World War II, obstacles to full integration for the Jews all but disappeared. Almost no realm of American life was shut off to the Jews. By the 1970s it was, for all practical purposes, impossible to identify an American Jew by physical appearance, behavior, or lifestyle, unless the American Jew chose explicitly to identify himself as such.

The freedom which so typifies the American way of life presented a problem to the Jewish experience which is almost unique. The Jew in the United States can choose not to be a Jew. Intermarriage, for example, between Jew and non-Jew rose dramatically after World War II. By the mid 1960s about 30% of the Jews who married chose non-Jewish mates. And this figure has continued to rise. This, combined with the freedom to disassociate from Judaism and the low birthrate among Jews has led many American Jewish leaders to express concern that the American Jewish community will eventually disappear.

12

Some Thoughts on Jewish Identity

Of course it is not possible to know what the future holds in store for Jews and Judaism. At the beginning of this century many thought that humanity was on the verge of fulfilling its age old dream of peace and security. Many Jews, certainly, believed that the secular state would offer them a secure haven as well as equality. Instead, this still unfinished century has witnessed more bloodletting than any in human history. And the Jews, in specific, were hounded down almost to extinction by what had been one of the most civilized of secular nation states.

Apart from considerations of the ultimate fate of Jews and Judaism (and, for that matter, of mankind) in a perilous world, there is a whole set of questions which are both more relevant to our concerns and more manageable. These questions have to do with Jewish identity. For example, what does it mean to be a Jew? How can one distinguish Jews from non-Jews and Judaism from other religious traditions?

In biblical days, a Jew was distinguished from non-Jews by virtue of a distinctive nation state and a distinctive language. Perhaps, as well, a host of mores and customs associated with the biblical nation state served to distinguish it from its neighbors. Also, and of far greater weight, the Jews had a religion which alone rejected the basic tenets of paganism. As we have seen, whereas paganism reduces all things, including the gods, to the elemental "stuff," the biblical tradition affirms the radical and unique singularity of its God Who is not of the primordial "stuff." And whereas paganism (with grim irony, since it was human beings proclaiming this) declares that mankind was created to serve the material needs of the gods and consigned a mortal lot because of the selfish wilfulness of the divine community, in its opening pages the Bible grants to mankind the possibility of a high destiny if human beings will serve this God properly. As we have seen, the sum and substance of biblical beliefs, laws, statutes, customs, and mores are designed to expedite the service of God by promoting decent behavior. It is not that the pagans did not value decency. They did. The contrast resides in the fact that the authors of the Bible assert that the ground of all being Himself affirms the primacy of decency, and that, moreover, His loyalty to that one species created in His image brings into play His attributes of justice and compassion. In pagan literature the gods are trigger-happy; in the Bible God is long-suffering in regard to an error prone humanity.

Much appears to have changed since the biblical period. The emergence of Christianity and Islam has meant that Judaism does not stand alone against paganism. Both Christianity and Islam include the Hebrew Bible in their bodies of sacred literature. The fundamental principles of biblical faith, namely, the uniqueness of God, the supreme duty of mankind to adhere to the basic norms of decency promulgated by this God, and the brotherhood of all mankind under the Fatherhood of God are proclaimed with equal fervor and authenticity by Christianity and Islam as well as Judaism. One therefore cannot distinguish Judaism from Christianity and Islam strictly on the basis of its anti-pagan stance.

Should one thus turn, in order to distinguish Judaism from other religious traditions, to the postbiblical developments in Judaism? As we saw, the Pharisees changed many things in biblical Judaism. In the area of practice, the synagogue, prayer, and the Rabbi as religious leader replaced the Temple, the sacrificial offering, and the priest as religious leader. In the conceptual realm, the Sheol afterlife model of biblical Judaism was supplanted by an afterlife model featuring

Heaven, Hell, and bodily resurrection of the dead. We saw, too, that Christianity emerged out of Pharisaic Judaism and that its church and afterlife model correspond not to the Temple and the Sheol model but to the synagogue and the Pharisaic afterlife model.

But what of the multitude of rituals that are enshrined in the literature produced by the Pharisees, *viz.*, the Mishnah and the Talmud? Do these rituals distinguish Jews from non-Jews? The answer to this question would appear to be both yes and no. Yes, much of what Jews do, in terms of prayers uttered, holidays observed, and occasions commemorated, is unique to Judaism.

These practices, however, are not ends in themselves. Rather, they are means to the end of service to God, and the essential quality of that service—decent behavior—is by no means unique to Judaism. I do not mean to suggest that these rituals are unimportant. In fact, Jews have sometimes accepted martyrdom rather than abandon them. But if these rituals are presumed to be efficacious in and of themselves then one attributes to them magical qualities which, it seems to me, would be completely at odds with biblical faith and belong rather to the domain of superstition. Also, the observance of these rituals was (and is) far from uniform. Simply on the basis of observance it would be simplistic to distinguish Jews from non-Jews and equally sophomoric to formulate the characteristics which go to make up a "good Jew."

Perhaps Ruth's words to her mother-in-law Naomi should be our guide: "Your people is my people, your God is my God, and where you die I shall die." Ruth, born a Moabite, embraces Judaism by declaring that she will not abandon Naomi or, more generally rendered, that she will cast her lot with the Jewish people. Should we then use Ruth's heroic words as a criterion for distinguishing Jew from non-Jew? However compelling Ruth's declaration is—and to us it is very compelling—as a distinguishing criterion it faces two obvious problems. In the first place, Jews, who now live in all parts of the world, do not (and have not in the past) experience(d) a common destiny. Consider the different situations of Jews in Russia, the United States, and Israel. Russian Jews are experiencing repressive persecution while American Jews are free to express, or not to express, their Jewishness as they please. And neither of these large Diaspora communities faces the daily dangers that Israelis face. In the second place, Ruth's willingness to identify with the Jewish people is so subjective that it appears to tell us little about objective characteristics which would distinguish Judaism from any other religious tradition. It is clear that Ruth loves Naomi, that this love generates loyalty, and that both love and loyalty are to be highly prized. But to agree that Judaism has an exclusive claim on such virtues is to close one's eyes to other religious traditions.

The very question of who is a Jew is at the heart of a very profound dispute in the modern Jewish nation state of Israel. This dispute has taken two forms at the highest level of Israel's legislative and judicial branches. On the one hand, the Orthodox have insisted that a convert to Judaism must be legitimated by an Orthodox rabbi and, therefore, that no conversion overseen by a Conservative or Reform rabbi is valid. The Israeli Supreme Court has only just recently ruled on this matter and the Court has come down on the side of the more liberal branches (i.e., Reform and Conservative) of Judaism. This decision does little to help one formulate a concise definition of Judaism. In fact, the decision recognizes that diverse claims as to what constitutes a Jew are legitimate.

The second case is more basic and more complicated. This case involves one Brother Daniel who was born in 1922 into a Jewish family. During World War II he was active in the Zionist movement as well as in a Jewish underground group that harassed the Nazis. He was captured by the Nazis but escaped and found refuge in a convent where he remained for the duration of the war. While there, he was converted to Christianity. After the war he became a member of the Carmelite Order and moved to Israel. Once in Israel, he applied for immediate and automatic citizenship, claiming that he was a Jew by nationality and a Christian by religion. When the nation state of Israel came to be, the government had decreed that any Jew anywhere could become an immediate citizen by immigrating to Israel. This was called the "Law of Return." However, the Israeli government denied Brother Daniel's petition. The government stated that anyone who is a Christian cannot at the same time be a Jew.

Brother Daniel appealed the government's decision to the Israeli Supreme Court. In a split decision, the Supreme Court upheld the

government's position. Here, in summary form, are the opinions of
the Court:

> — *the majority opinion:* Whether he is religious, non-religious, or anti-re-
> ligious, the Jew living in Israel is bound, willingly or unwillingly, by
> an umbilical cord to historical Judaism from which he draws his lan-
> guage and its idiom, whose festivals are his own to celebrate and
> whose great thinkers and spiritual heroes nourish his national pride.
> Would a Jew who has become a Christian find his place in all this?
> What can all this national sentiment mean to him? Certainly, Brother
> Daniel will love Israel.... But such a love will be from without—the
> love of a distant brother. He will not be a true inherent part of the
> Jewish world.

> — *the minority opinion:* The tests provided by religious law cannot apply
> to the Law of Return.... In the absence of an objective test provided by
> the Law itself, there is no alternative but to assume that the
> Legislature intended to content itself with the subjective test, that is
> to say that the right to return to Israel belongs to any person who de-
> clares that he is a Jew returning to his homeland and wishes to settle
> there.... The further provision...that the right belongs only to those
> who profess no other than the Jewish religion exceeds...the powers of
> the Government, whose duty it is merely to carry out the Law.

> [W. Hallo, D. Ruderman, M. Stanislawski, *Heritage, Civilization, and
> the Jews: Source Reader* (New York: Praeger, 1984), pp. 292–3].

You will note that both opinions, in effect, apply the standard
enunciated by Ruth, although they interpret this standard differently. The majority opinion questions Brother Daniel's ability to
commit himself with complete love and loyalty to the Jewish people.
It is certainly true that the words Ruth utters (words which are subsequently backed up by her actions) are all-encompassing: "Your people is my people, your God is my God, and where you die I shall die
and be buried." Ruth does not add that while she will live with Naomi
her worship will take a different form. Ruth's declaration leaves no
doubt that her affiliation with the people Israel will be total.

On the other hand, the minority opinion asserts that if Brother
Daniel chooses to live in Israel and thereby to share in the uncertain
destiny of the Jewish nation state, his religious convictions are beside
the point. The minority opinion declares that what is decisive is

Brother Daniel's willingness to be a citizen of Israel. You will note that the minority opinion can find no objective criteria which would allow one to distinguish between Jew and non-Jew. According to the minority opinion, if a person identifies himself as a Jew (which in a sense Brother Daniel does when he says that he is a Jew by nationality), and backs up his declaration with a willingness to live in Israel, that person is, *ipso facto,* a Jew. This, too, is in keeping with Ruth's words which, while all-encompassing, are in no way specific. That is, beyond her love, her loyalty, and her courage, there is nothing concrete in the passage that would allow one to specify what it means to become or be a Jew. I might add here that I agree with the minority opinion. The reader will note that as this chapter continues, it will be clear that I am comfortable with motives such as love and loyalty being at the center of Judaism, and I am in no way troubled that other religious traditions (especially those such as Christianity and Islam which share with Judaism the Hebrew Bible) affirm the same virtues.

For the moment, however, let us focus on the assumption implicit in the majority opinion's ruling. The ruling assumes that there are objective criteria which differentiate Jew from non-Jew and that among these criteria are those which make Brother Daniel's assertion that he is a Jew by nationality and a Christian by religion an oxymoron.

But what are these criteria? At the present time, Judaism manifests itself in three movements: Orthodox, Conservative, and Reform. The differences among these three movements are both real and obvious, theoretical and practical. Orthodox Judaism maintains that the sacred literature of Judaism (Hebrew Bible, Mishnah, Talmud, and Midrash) are of Divine origin. Therefore, the norms, regulations, laws, and rituals found in this literature are to be adhered to strictly. If these regulations conflict with elements of modernity, then it is modernity which must be rejected. However, you should not conclude that all Orthodox Jews agree as to what constitutes the ideal Jewish lifestyle. The Orthodox would be of one mind, though, in rejecting the approach of Reform Judaism. Reform Judaism's stance toward the sacred literature is very different from that of Orthodoxy. Reform Judaism selects those parts of the sacred tradition which it deems relevant to the present situation. In effect, the present situation becomes the standard by which the sacred literature is evaluated. Of course, Reform Jews do not evaluate the present situation in the same way nor do they interpret the sacred literature in the same way. It is fair to say that within both Orthodoxy and Reform the variations—practical and theoretical—are vast.

To compound the issue even more is the matter of Conservative Judaism. In matters theoretical, Conservative Judaism is very close to Reform, especially in regard to a willingness to allow change based on changing historical circumstances. But in matters practical, i.e., ritual practice, many Conservative Rabbis cannot be distinguished from among Orthodox Rabbis.

Let us go to a concrete example. Circumcision has been, and continues to be, a basic and widespread practice among Jews of all stripes. The rite goes back to a text in Genesis (17:9ff.):

> God said further to Abraham, 'As for you, you shall keep My covenant, you and your offspring to come, throughout the ages. Such shall be the covenant, which you shall keep between Me and you and your offspring to follow: every male among you shall be circumcised.... At the age of eight days, every male among you throughout the generations shall be circumcised. Thus shall My covenant be marked in your flesh as an everlasting pact. An uncircumcised male who does not circumcise the flesh of the foreskin—such a person shall be cut off from his kin; he has broken My covenant.'

Although the biblical text sets forth the ritual clearly and unambiguously affirms its importance (i.e., anyone not circumcised is to be "cut off from his brother," which is to say, executed), no rationale is given for the practice. Also, of course, the practice is rooted explicitly in the will of biblical Israel's God. We now know that the practice of circumcision was not unique to biblical Israel. It was, and still is, practiced among peoples all over the world: in Asia, Africa, Australia, and from time to time among the Indian tribes of North, Central, and South America. In the present time, many European and American Christians practice circumcision for reasons of health. It has been estimated that one-seventh of the world's population is practicing circumcision. In biblical days, the people Israel practiced the rite in common with the Phoenicians, the Ammonites, the Moabites, and, surprisingly, the Egyptians. I say surprisingly because the Hebrew Bible generally repudiated the ways of ancient Egypt.

However, while we know in a general way who practiced and practices circumcision, its origins are obscure. There are theories aplenty but, at the present state of our knowledge, none of these theories is confirmed by sufficient evidence.

In the Graeco-Roman world, the Jews frequently were ridiculed for being circumcised. Although the derision intensified in the Middle Ages, the Jews did not stop the practice, nor does any Jewish text contemporaneous to the Middle Ages suggest that Jews should stop the practice in order to lessen the persecution. If anything, the persecution seems to have resulted in expanded importance for the rite. In fact, it was during the Middle Ages that the ceremony was moved from the home to the synagogue where it became a cause for communal rejoicing.

Details of the celebration differed from locale to locale, but everywhere during the Middle Ages the rite was of central importance to Jews. And, I imagine, if you asked a Jew of that time why he was observing this rite, he would have responded that it was mandated in the Hebrew Bible.

The situation changed, however, with the rise of modernity. The founders of Reform Judaism were divided as to whether to continue the practice of circumcision. That controversy ended, for a time, when the medical profession began promoting circumcision for reasons of health. But now the medical evidence is equivocal, and it would be in keeping with the spirit of Reform to stop the practice, while Orthodoxy, because of the unequivocal testimony of the biblical text, would continue to adhere to the practice no matter what.

I refer you now to a somewhat more complicated example. In my analysis of the biblical period we saw that the biblical afterlife model placed great emphasis on the bearing of sons, proper burial, and the retention by the family of the ancestral land holdings on which the family's dead were interred. These concerns were based on a belief, as widespread and as important as any belief in biblical times, that the welfare of the dead depended on the loyalty of the living family, loyalty which was concretized in the above stated factors.

We saw also that with the Pharisees' rise to dominance an altogether different afterlife model came to the fore in Judaism. Whether this afterlife model went back to the earliest days of biblical Israel's existence or whether it postdated the Sheol model is a matter of dispute among biblical scholars. For our purposes, the relative ages of the two afterlife models is of no significance, although the scattered references to the resurrection model in the books of Job, Isaiah, Ezekiel, and Daniel indicate to me that both afterlife models go back to the earliest days of biblical Israel. What is relevant for our purposes is that the Pharisaic afterlife model shifted emphasis away from the linked destinies of the living and the dead to emphasis on the fate of the individual's soul. In the Pharisaic model, salvation did not depend on proper burial or on the loyalty of one's family. Rather, one's salvation in the Pharisaic model would depend on whether and to what degree one had lived in accord with commandments which the Pharisees had promulgated as expressing the will of God. Thus did the rites, customs, and practices connected with death, burial, and mourning assume new aspects. For example, it became a popular belief that the dead would someday be resurrected from their graves in the same clothes in which they were buried, and this led to the practice of burying the dead in the finest clothes. Many religious leaders frowned on this practice because it implied that wealth was a positive determinant of one's fate beyond the grave. The great Rabban Gamaliel urged that everyone be buried in cheap common linen. For a time, at least, this became the general rule.

Also, in Pharisaic times a set schedule for the mourners was set in place. It was stipulated that there be strict mourning for seven days, less severe practices for thirty days, and some observances which would last a full year. Only after twelve months was the state of mourning to end completely. It is probable that this procedure was intended to help the living gradually return to their normal lives.

Rituals whose aim was to allow the mourner to face the fact of death without permitting this fact to crush him represented a shift in emphasis. In the biblical Sheol model, the primary concern was for the welfare of the dead which depended on the continued loyalty of the family. In the Pharisaic model, the dead's fate was, as it were, sealed at death so attention shifted to a concern for the welfare of the living. In biblical days, belief in the Sheol model necessitated that certain things be done on a continuing basis so that the dead could "rest in peace." For example, the sixth commandment of the decalogue reads: "Honor your father and mother, so that you may long endure on the land which the Lord your God is giving you." In other words, the threat of exile looms large for those who do not fulfill obligations to their dead ancestors. And exile, of course, means not only that the dead in Sheol will not rest in peace, but that the generations of the exile, being buried on land to which they cannot hold title, will likewise find no rest. This commandment illustrates vividly the manner in which the Sheol model interlinks the destinies of the living, the dead, and the as yet unborn. The bad deeds which result in exile radiate backwards and forwards in time. The living are cut loose from the land on which the dead are buried and are destined to have children on land which can never be their own.

The crucial difference between these two afterlife models can be summed up in the following way: in the Pharisaic model what a person does in life determines his destiny after death, while in the biblical Sheol model an individual's fate is in flux.

On the face of it, it would appear that the Pharisaic afterlife model is more equitable, emphasizing as it does a firm connection between what an individual does and what happens to that individual. However, appearances to the contrary, a kind of reward and punishment is operative in the Sheol afterlife model. It goes without saying that in the Pharisaic model of afterlife the righteous are rewarded and the wicked are punished beyond the grave. In the Sheol model, on the other hand, it would seem that the worst of individuals who had sired a good number of sons and who was able to leave them a substantial legacy would "rest in peace," while the best of individuals who happened to die childless would be denied security beyond the grave.

However, in the Sheol model, the security of the dead depends on the people Israel's continued residence in the land. If the Israelites defile the land by indecent behavior, they will then, as one biblical prophet after another warns them, be subject to exile. Therefore, rest in Sheol depends not only on an individual's acting properly but on parents inculcating the moral norms in their children. In effect, the Sheol model extends one's area of moral accountability.

But is it fair that children should suffer for the sins of their ancestors? Fair or not, those who believed in the Sheol model could answer that it was an existential fact that the sins of the fathers often are visited upon the children. In our own day we merely need think of the damaging effect of our technology on the environment. For one day, as it were, the bill will come due, and the generation which did not deplete the ozone layer will pay, and a generation which did not pollute the streams, rivers, and oceans of our planet will have to face the consequences.

Whether one accepts the above argument or not, you should understand that an extended moral concern is at the heart of the Sheol model. Consider the following passage in Deuteronomy (6:1 ff.), which is one of the most celebrated of biblical texts:

> And this is the Instruction—the laws and the norms that the Lord your God has commanded to impart to you, to be observed in the land which you are about to cross over and occupy, so that you, your son, and your son's son may revere the Lord your God and follow, as long as you may live, all His laws and commandments which I enjoin upon you, to the end that you may long endure. Do it Israel, willingly and faithfully, that it may go well with you and that you may increase greatly in the land flowing with milk and honey, as the Lord, the God of your fathers, spoke to you. Hear, O Israel! The Lord is our God, the Lord is One. You must love your Lord with all your heart and with all your might. Take to heart these words with which I charge you this day. Impress them upon your children. Recite them when you stay at home and when you are away, when you lie down and when you get up. Bind them as a sign on your hand and let them serve as a mark between your eyes; inscribe them in the doorposts of your house and on your gates.

It is evident that the above biblical text makes residence in the Promised Land depend on the decent behavior of the people Israel. In the text there is the explicit directive to pass on the moral norms, which are the basis of the "Instruction" from one generation to another. It is clear what the biblical God requires of His people, and it is equally clear that the welfare of the people, past, present, and future, depends on the degree to which they abide by the moral norms. The living are obligated to honor the dead by inculcating in their children the love of God.

What I wish to emphasize here is that Deuteronomy 6 does not emphasize an individual's salvation so much as it gives special stress to an individual's responsibility as a link in a chain which extends both backward and forward in time. One's own individual well-being (both in life and afterlife) is bound up inextricably with the behavior and destiny of others. It may be helpful if you recall the Levirate relationship (Deut. 25:5ff.) wherein the individual is urged to imperil his own legacy in order to ensure the well-being of others.

This emphasis on individual responsibility in the Sheol model is in keeping with the biblical notion of decency as a communal virtue. The commandments of the Decalogue (the substratum for biblical moral doctrine), for instance, articulate norms for relational behavior. Interdictions against murder, stealing, adultery, bearing false witness, and coveting stress the requisite virtues in social situations in which the extended family of mankind relates. The honoring of father and mother gives special force to the ideal which is to regulate relationships in the nuclear family. And the Sabbath, the only holiday mandated in the Decalogue, underlines the need to care for the weak and underprivileged.

Thus, it would seem that any attempt to characterize Judaism would need to take account of this great concern with social justice. Whether this makes Judaism unique is not at issue, nor does the observation that the Jewish experience has been marked by a fierce concern with social justice conflict with my repeated insistence that the more than 3000 year experience of the Jews and Judaism has witnessed an extraordinary amount of diversity. The faith that Jews have promulgated, maintained, and defended is almost without exception bound up with the belief that the future depends on what people do, and that the only way to secure the future is to behave decently.

Let me exemplify my point that the core of Judaism is bound up with the primacy of social justice by directing your attention to two pieces of fictional literature, one modern and one ancient.

The modern story, by Philip Roth, is called "Defender of the Faith." ["Defender of the Faith," *Jewish American Stories,* ed. Irving Howe (New York: Mentor, 1977), pp. 373–401]. Roth's story is set in the spring of 1945 just after the end of the war in Europe. The narrator of the story is Nathan Marx, a Sergeant who, after extensive combat in Europe, is stationed at Camp Crowder in Missouri.

One of the new inductees at Crowder, a Private Sheldon Grossbart who like Marx is a Jew, begins dogging Marx in order to get special privileges. Grossbart wants to be excused from a general cleaning of the barracks one Friday night so that he can attend worship services on the Jewish Sabbath. Marx immediately distrusts and dislikes Grossbart, but finds himself defending Grossbart's appeal to the Captain. The Captain asks: "You're a Jewish fellow, am I right, Marx? And I admire you. I admire you because of the ribbons on your chest, not because you had a hem stitched on your dick before you were old enough to know you had one. I judge a man by what he shows me on the field of battle Sergeant."

Marx feels caught between a rock and a hard place. He does not like Grossbart, but the new inductee has guilted him for reasons he does not altogether understand. He sees to it that Grossbart gets permission to attend Friday night worship services. Grossbart thanks Marx effusively, and says that Jews have to stick together because Christians will take every opportunity to mock and harass them. Marx is led to remember his own boyhood:

> I was remembering the shrill sounds of a Bronx playground, where eight years ago.... I had played on long spring evenings, such as this.... It was a pleasant memory for a young man so far from peace and home, and it brought so very many recollections with it that I began to grow exceedingly tender about myself. I indulged myself to a reverie so strong that I felt within as though a hand had opened and was reaching down inside. It had to reach so very far to touch me. It had to reach past those days in the forests of Belgium and the dying I'd refused to weep over; past the nights in those German farmhouses whose books we'd burned to warm us, and which I couldn't bother to mourn; past those endless stretches when I'd shut off all softness I might feel for my fellows, and managed even to deny myself the posture of a conqueror—the swagger that I, as a Jew, might well have worn as my boots whacked against the rubble of Münster, Braunschweig, and finally Berlin. But now...one rumor of home and time past, and memory plunged down through all I had anesthetized and came to what I suddenly remembered to be myself. So it was not altogether curious that in search of more of me I found myself following Grossbart's track to Chapel No. 3 where the Jewish services were being held.

At services, Marx sees that Grossbart never opens the prayer book. Moreover, he hears Grossbart mutter, "Let the *goyim* [a disparaging term for non-Jews] clean the floors!" After services, Grossbart complains to Marx that one of his Jewish friends is gagging over army food because it is not prepared in conformity with Jewish dietary laws. When Marx bridles, Grossbart responds that the Jews of Germany were slaughtered because "...they didn't stick together."

A week later, Marx's Captain, in a fury, tells Marx that Grossbart's father had written his congressman to complain that his son was forced to eat non-kosher food. Marx tries to explain, even though he does not believe it himself, that Grossbart is "very Orthodox." The Captain and Marx go out to a shooting range where Grossbart and the other inductees are practicing. Out of the Captain's hearing, Grossbart, who does not want to be sent to the Pacific (where war is still raging), urges Marx to have Grossbart's orders cut for a post in the states. The Captain comes up and asks Grossbart why he cannot act like Marx:

> 'A year in combat, Grossbart. Twelve goddam months in combat all through Europe. I admire this man...do you hear him peeping about the food?'

When Grossbart implies that Marx is not an observant Jew and, therefore, not a good Jew, the Captain explodes:

> 'Look, Grossbart, Marx here is a good man, a goddam *hero*. When you were sitting on your sweet ass in school, Sergeant Marx was killing Germans. Who does more for the Jews, you by throwing up over a lousy piece of sausage...or Marx by killing those Nazi bastards? If I were a Jew, Grossbart, I'd kiss this man's feet. He's a goddam hero...and *he* eats what we give him.'

After the Captain leaves, Marx learns that Grossbart, not his father, wrote the letter and signed his father's name. Moreover, it is not Grossbart who is troubled by army food, but one of his Jewish friends.

Several days later, another letter to the father's congressman, written by Grossbart, and passed off as his father's, comes to Marx's attention. In it, the "father" thanks the congressman and indicates that his son now realizes that a little unkosher food is insignificant in light of the great war. The "father" writes that his son now sees the light: "...so many millions of my fellow Jews gave up their lives to the enemy, the least I can do is live for a while minus a bit of my heritage so as to help end this struggle and regain for all the children of God dignity and humanity." The letter ends with effusive praise of "Sergeant Nathan Marx" for intervening on his son's behalf.

For a time, Grossbart disappears from Marx's life. Then, one Saturday, as Marx is reading *The Sporting News,* Grossbart reappears. He again asks Marx to intervene so that Grossbart will not be sent to the Pacific, and again Marx rebuffs him. Grossbart next asks for a weekend pass to visit relatives in St. Louis for a Passover dinner. Marx explains that there are no passes during basic training; Grossbart calls him a "goy." It then occurs to Marx that Passover had come and gone weeks before. Undaunted, Grossbart continues to press Marx, saying that his aunt had promised to serve him a good Jewish meal. "Tears came to his eyes. 'It's a hard thing to be a Jew...and it's a harder thing to stay one.' " Marx relents and gives Grossbart a pass and, as an afterthought, asks Grossbart to bring him back some gefilte fish (a traditional dish on Passover).

That same weekend, Marx learns that all trainees, at the end of basic training, will be shipped out to the Pacific. When Grossbart returns from his pass and learns that he is going where bullets are still flying he pleads with Marx to intervene. Marx refuses and Grossbart leaves in a fury, but not before giving Marx an eggroll he had brought back with him from St. Louis. Marx realizes that Grossbart had never intended to have a "Jewish" dinner with relatives but had only wanted a vacation from the base. Marx erupts: "Grossbart, you're a liar! You're a schemer and a crook! You've got no respect for anything! Nothing at all! Not for me, for the truth...you use us all...."

A week later when the orders are cut, Marx sees that of all the trainees, only Grossbart is not going to the Pacific. In fact, Grossbart is to be stationed in Ft. Monmouth, New Jersey. Marx concludes that Grossbart had managed to manipulate a Jewish corporal who works in the dispatching office. Marx calls one of his friends in the dispatching office and assures him that Grossbart is heartbroken that he is not going to the Pacific: "He had a brother killed in Europe and he's hot to go to the Pacific. Said he'd feel like a coward if he wound up stateside."

The next day a livid Grossbart confronts Marx: " 'What do you have against me?... Against my family? Would it kill you for me to be near my father, God knows how many months he has left to him.... There's no limit to your anti-Semitism is there!' " The story ends with Marx fighting back feelings of guilt.

I have devoted so much space to Roth's fine story because it concerns the question of what constitutes Jewishness. That is, who in the story is the "Defender of the Faith?" Grossbart attends religious services, expresses a preference for "Jewish" food, and prefers to associate with other Jews. Marx attends one religious service, and then for reasons that have nothing to do with praying. Moreover, Marx is unconcerned with any of the rituals which have been associated with Judaism, including the dietary restrictions. Marx is non-observant to the extreme. The one time he is pictured reading it is on a Saturday, the Jewish Sabbath, and he is reading *The Sporting News.*

The Captain, who is not a Jew, and who, apart from his awareness that Jewish males are circumcised, knows nothing about the specifics of Jewish practice, clearly prefers Marx as the defender of the faith. He says, " 'Who does more for the Jews, you by throwing up over a lousy piece of sausage...or Marx, by killing those Nazi bastards! If I were a Jew, Grossbart, I'd kiss this man's feet. He's a goddam hero, you know that? And *he* eats what we give him!' " But is the Captain right? In order to determine this, let us take a closer look at Grossbart and Marx.

How would one characterize Grossbart? He seems to be without dignity. He is pushy and/or ingratiating depending on the circumstances. He does not hesitate to lie and what is more, he lies in regard to his parents and his religious tradition. His behavior at services is offensive: he goes to the House of God in order to shirk his responsibilities as a soldier. That is, he uses the realm of the spirit to feather his material nest. The same can be said for the fuss he makes over kosher food. He uses this issue as a wedge against the army. Marx, who has seen Grossbart eat in the mess, says: " 'I've seen you eat like a hound at chow.' " Repeatedly, Grossbart is shown using his "Jewishness" in order to gain an edge. And were it not for Marx's intervention, Grossbart, in fact, would have succeeded in being the only recruit not sent to the Pacific war zone.

The above characterization suggests that what types Grossbart is his complete lack of loyalty. He will sacrifice anything and anyone to get ahead: his parents, his friends, his tradition, his country, and, of course, the truth. You no doubt will recall that over the centuries the enemies of the Jews have been characterizing them as nothing if not disloyal. This charge reached its culmination in Nazi Germany. The Nazis, as we have seen, claimed that the Jews were parasites with loyalties to no one or to nothing but their own craven self-interests. Grossbart, in short, is the Jew whom Jew-haters have pointed to as representing that which is quintessentially Jewish.

Marx, on the other hand, is loyal almost to a fault. I say almost to a fault because while he is obviously loyal to his country, he also feels a sense of loyalty to the likes of Grossbart simply because they both are Jews. Grossbart is able to tap a vein of guilt in Marx, and although Marx confesses that he does not understand it, he knows that the vein runs deep. But whatever Marx does for Grossbart comes back to haunt him because Marx's loyalty to Grossbart is in conflict with Marx's vision not only of reality but of what he, Marx, should be. As the Captain observes of Marx: " 'I admire this man.... Look, Grossbart, he is a good man, a goddam hero.' " The story, it would seem, confirms the Captain's evaluation. Marx has been through hard and extended combat, but through it all he has retained his perspective and his elemental decency. For instance, he had not taken on the role of the swaggering hero; and how tempting it must have been for a young Jewish American soldier as the American army chased the fractured German army across Europe in the last months of the war.

Without question, Marx is a good human being. To argue otherwise is to suggest that such virtues as courage, dignity, modesty, and loyalty are vices. Assuming we agree that Marx is a good human being, we still must ask, given the story, whether he is a good Jew. That is, is he the "Defender of the Faith?"

Throughout the story Marx does nothing which could be construed literally as "Jewish." As noted, he does not observe the dietary laws; he does not attend synagogue; he plays softball on the Jewish Sabbath (when he is not reading *The Sporting News*); he is unaware that Passover (a major Jewish holiday) has come and gone until Grossbart brings up the subject; and he is almost certainly illiterate in regard to the Bible, Jewish history, etc. Moreover, we learn that once he is discharged, Marx has made plans to attend Law School, hardly a profession which is in any way typically "Jewish." The question is, in what way is Marx distinguishable from other decent Americans, or, for that matter, from other decent human beings?

Those of you who have been following the general argument of this book already know the answer to this question. This argument suggests that, to the extent that it is possible to generalize about the Jewish experience, Judaism has featured decency as *the* ideal. Rituals, prayers, practices, laws, and ordinances have, as their reason for being, the fostering of moral behavior. And this is true not only of the rituals but of the institutions which support them and give them concrete expression. The biblical prophets did not hesitate to attack the Temple and the practices associated with it when it was clear to them that the worshippers believed the Temple observances were ends in themselves rather than means to the end of moral behavior. However, no biblical prophet ever questions the belief that morality in and of itself is of ultimate value. And no biblical narrative has as its point of view the notion that morality is of penultimate significance.

It is the notion that decency is of absolute worth that makes Roth's story compatible with the biblical ethos. The "faith" worthy of defense in Roth's story is Marx's decency. If one objects that there is nothing distinctively Jewish about this faith, then consider the following query. Does it matter at all whether any other tradition affirms morality as the ultimate ideal? It matters only in the sense that this is precisely the stated goal of the prophetic visions of the ideal future. The prophet Micah expresses this vision in the following words (Micah 4:1 ff.):

> In the days to come,
> The Mount of the Lord's House shall stand
> Firm above the mountains;
> And it shall tower above the hills.
> The peoples shall gaze on it with joy,
> And the many nations shall go and say:
> 'Come,
> Let us go up to the Mount of the Lord,
> To the House of the God of Jacob,
> That He may instruct us in His ways,
> And that we may walk in His paths.'
> For instruction shall come forth from Zion,
> The word of the Lord from Jerusalem.
> Thus He will judge among the peoples,
> And arbitrate for the multitude of nations,

However distant;
And they shall beat their swords into plowshares
And their spears into pruning hooks.
Nation shall not take up
Sword against nation;
They shall never again know war;
But every man shall sit
Under his grapevine or fig tree
With no one to disturb him.
For it was the Lord of Hosts who spoke.
Though all the peoples walk
Each in the name of its gods,
We will walk
In the name of the Lord our God
Forever and ever.

This vision of the ideal future does not envisage a universal conversion to the religion of biblical Israel in any sense other than the widespread adoption of the moral norms. The "instruction" which will emanate from Jerusalem does not involve any ritual or ordinance; the "instruction" has for its focal point the cessation of strife in the human community. The faith promoted in this passage affirms the hope that social justice will one day be the rule and not the exception.

The very same point of view is present in the opening of the story of Abraham, the first Jew (Gen. 12:1ff.):

The Lord said to Abram, 'Go forth from your native land and from your father's house to the land which I will show you. I will make of you a great nation, and I will bless you; I will make your name great, and you shall be a blessing: I will bless those who bless you, and curse him that curses you; all the families of the earth shall bless themselves by you.'

What is the "blessing" which is to distinguish biblical Israel, in the eyes of God Himself, from among the families of mankind? Six chapters later, as God is preparing to destroy Sodom because of its gross immorality, He is pictured musing (Gen. 18:17ff.):

'Shall I hide from Abraham what I am about to do, since Abraham is to become a great and populous nation and all the nations of the earth are to bless themselves by him? For I have singled him out, that he may instruct his children and his posterity to keep the way of the Lord by doing what is just and right....'

It could not be clearer: the "blessing," the "way of God," is to do what "is just and right." Every ritual, every ordinance, every belief is to be judged as to whether it leads to what "is just and right."

And, so, too, are human beings to be judged. We already have seen this dynamic at work in the David and Bathsheba episode. In that story, it is the Hittite Uriah who is, so to speak, the "Defender of the Faith," i.e., the doer of what "is just and right."

For it is Uriah who displays honesty, courage, and integrity, while David, indisputably the most renowned of biblical Israel's kings, is disloyal to God and country.

Now, of course, Roth could have written a story in which a non-observant Jew acted like Grossbart while the observant Jew behaved like Marx. Roth could have done this and made the very same point about the primacy of ethical behavior by depicting other observant Jews being Grossbart-like. Perhaps Roth made Grossbart the observant Jew in order to bring more sharply into focus his message that the observance of rituals is neither a necessary nor a sufficient cause of decency. The writer of the David story made a similar statement about the insignificance of birth and rank; what counts for both writers is decency, and both are telling us that it can be found in surprising, or, at least, non-conventional places. But wherever it is found, it is to be esteemed.

Let me conclude by referring to one last biblical story which, in a much different way, affirms the same moral as "The Defender of the Faith." The book of Esther appears to be a peculiar book. In the first place, it is the only book in the Hebrew Bible which never mentions God. Also, and more substantively, point of view in the book seems obscure. The book of Esther oscillates, sometimes wildly, among a variety of themes which range from the war between the sexes to palace intrigue and internecine warfare, to the inauguration of a holiday.

The book of Esther, furthermore, has provoked the most diverse reactions among readers. Martin Luther was repelled by the book: "I am so hostile to this book [II Maccabees] and to Esther that I could wish they did not exist at all; for they...have much pagan impropriety." [*Table Talk*, XXIV; cf. Samuel Sandmel's *The Enjoyment of Scripture*, p. 44: "I should not be grieved if the book of Esther were somehow dropped out of Scripture."]. Maimonides, on the other hand, ranked Esther as one of the greatest of biblical books. A look at the current secondary literature on Esther reveals not only the same range of attitudes [see *Studies in the Book of Esther,* ed. Corey A. Moore (New York: Ktav, 1982)] but a profound disagreement over whether the author of Esther intended to write history or fiction; and if history, then what period and if fiction then for what purpose.

We will have occasion to refer to some of these disputes, but let us begin by presenting a synoptic overview of the book itself. Esther opens with a description of an incredibly powerful Persian king (named Ahasuerus) whose domain stretches from India to Arabia (northeastern Africa). This is surely an exaggeration because according to Herodotus [*History* (III, 89)], at the height of Persia's power there were no more than twenty provinces in the empire, while Esther's Persian king is described as having one hundred twenty seven provinces.

This Persian king decides to hold a banquet to end all banquets. He chooses as his site the capital city of Shushan (probably in western Iran) as the focal point of his bash, and there he displays his incredible possessions. For six months the revelers parade past his riches. This is capped by a party at which the wine really flowed: "...the rule for drinking was 'no restrictions!' " (1:8) Shushan is literally awash in "royal wine" served in (what else!) "golden beakers." Since only males were invited to the king's banquet, his Queen (Vashti) held a week long party of her own for women.

On the seventh day of the banquet a soused King Ahasuerus orders the seven eunuchs who attend him to summon Queen Vashti so that she can show off her great beauty. Vashti, however, will have nothing to do with this and her refusal throws the king into a dither. What is worse, the king, for all his enormous power, is unable to make her appear. He consults his seven sages, asking them (1:15): " 'According to the law, what is to be done with Queen Vashti since she did not obey the command of King Ahasuerus conveyed by the eunuchs.' " For this king, the royal "we" apparently is not regal enough; he refers to himself as "King Ahasuerus."

In any case, wise men that they are, the sages extrapolate from the particular to the general: Vashti has committed a grave offense with wide ranging implications (1:17): "...for the Queen's behavior will make all wives take their husbands lightly." The sages have no trouble convincing the king to promulgate a royal edict which will strip Vashti of the royal diadem and give it to one more worthy than she. The edict's intended effect is not only to remove Vashti from the palace but to make wives throughout the king's extensive domain recognize the principle implicit in the edict, namely, that husbands are to rule the roost. "Thus will the judgment executed by Your Majesty resound throughout your realm, vast though it is; and all wives will treat their husbands with respect, high and low alike."

The second chapter opens with a now sober and lonely king thinking of Vashti and longing for female companionship. His servants advise him to conduct an empire-wide search for spectacular young virgins from among whom the king can select a successor to Vashti. The net is thrown out and one of those taken is a Jewess named Esther who is the adopted daughter of Mordecai, a Jew whose family has been in Persia for several generations. The author, for reasons we will discuss, is very careful to give us Mordecai's genealogy ("...son of Jair, son of Shemei, son of Kish, a Benjamite"). As for Esther, her introduction is highlighted by a physical description: Esther is "...shapely and beautiful."

What happens next stretches the imagination, but the narrator manages to keep a straight face. The virgins are put through a year long regimen: six months "with oil of myrrh" and six months with "perfumes and women's cosmetics." Esther manages to win the favor of the eunuch who is in charge of this beauty treatment so that she gets seven maidens to attend her during the cosmetology and perfuming.

What are these women preparing for? Well, a test of sorts. For after twelve months they get to spend a night with the king in order to demonstrate, as it were, whether they are fit to be queen. The current metaphor for this is a one night stand. Esther's turn comes in the seventh year of the king's reign. The eunuch whose favor she had won gives her a top-sided advantage: he tells her what paraphernalia to take. Given the context, these can only be devices to enhance pleasure in intercourse. Esther bowls the king over and he straightaway makes her queen. She is given the royal diadem and honored at a party.

We are informed that up to this point Esther had told no one she was a Jewess, "...for Esther obeyed Mordecai's bidding as she had done when she was under his tutelage." (2:20) Meanwhile, Mordecai learns of a plot by two eunuchs to assassinate the king and passes word of this along to Esther who relates it to the king; Mordecai's good deed is duly recorded in the "King's Chronicles."

In chapter three we are introduced to another major player in the comic opera that is Esther. The king, who to say the least has acted with a singular lack of sobriety, is shown making one Hamen second in power in the realm. As in the case of Mordecai, the author is careful to note Hamen's genealogy; he is the "son of Hammedatha the Agagite." Just as the king has demonstrated a love of power, so too does Hamen, who demands that everyone bow to him face to the ground. Only Mordecai refuses to do so. When Mordecai is asked why he alone refuses to prostrate himself before Hamen, whose power is second only to that of the king, he explains that he is a Jew. As the king had overreacted to Vashti's refusal to display her charms before his drunken merrymakers, so Hamen overreacts to Mordecai's refusal to pay homage to a man drunk on power. A furious Hamen resolves to wipe out all the Jews because they are kin to Mordecai. For Hamen the Jews are guilty by association. Hamen tells the king (3:8), " 'There is a certain people, scattered and dispersed among other peoples in all the provinces...whose laws are different from those of any other people and who do not obey the king's laws; and it is not in Your Majesty's interest to tolerate them.' " It probably is unnecessary to point out that the only "law" any Jew is shown breaking is Mordecai's refusal to put face to ground every time he sees Hamen.

Orders are issued, under the king's seal, to exterminate the Jews and to plunder their possessions. The king gives Hamen a free hand and the altogether unbelievable sum of 10,000 talents of silver (the equivalent of 18 million dollars) to carry out the obliteration of the Jews. As unbelievable as the sum is (in today's dollars one could build a whole fleet of stealth bombers at 500 million a plane and still have enough change left over to send several manned missions to Mars), even more unbelievable is the fact that the decree is announced eleven months before it is to be executed. Moreover, the decree is displayed publicly throughout the realm. One wonders why the Jews would sit around and wait for the sword to fall. No wonder then that this botched plan is used by the king and Hamen as an occasion to celebrate by doing some serious drinking.

Mordecai is devastated when he learns of the decree and dresses in sackcloth and ashes (the biblical attire for mourning). And throughout the provinces the Jews fast and weep. When Esther hears that her uncle is wearing mourning clothes she sends a eunuch to inquire; Mordecai tells the eunuch about the money put in the treasury to finance the destruction of the Jews. Mordecai gives the eunuch a copy of the decree and tells him to show it to Esther so that she, understanding the threat, will go to the king and intercede on behalf of her people.

Esther, however, is most reluctant to go to the king. She explains (4:11):

'All the King's courtiers and the people of the King's provinces know that if any person, man or woman, enters the King's presence in the inner court without having been summoned, there is but one law for him—that he be put to death. Only if the King extends the golden scepter to him may he live. Now I have not been summoned to visit the King for the last 30 days.'

At this juncture, it seems all too clear that Esther is unwilling to risk her life on the chance that she might be able to save her entire people.

Mordecai passes word to Esther that she is deluded if she thinks she will survive the coming purge simply because she is Queen (4:13–14):

'On the contrary, if you keep silent in this crisis, relief and deliverance will come to the Jews from another quarter, while you and your father's house will perish. And who knows, perhaps you have attained to royal position for just such a crisis.'

It should be noted here that Mordecai's threat that Esther's "father's house will perish" makes sense only in the light of the Sheol afterlife model since Esther is an orphan. As we have seen, the dead can be affected for well or for ill in Sheol and Esther's family's wellbeing is dependent on her wellbeing. Also, if ever the avoidance of the word "God" were deliberate in Esther it is in Mordecai's circumlocution that " '...relief and deliverance will come to the Jews from another quarter....' "

With great reluctance, Esther agrees to go to the king, but she implores the Jews to fast on her behalf for three days. Given the fact that during the holiest part of the year (the turn of the year on Yom Kippur) the Jews are required to fast but one day, the hyperbole of the three day fast looms large indeed. All the larger, in fact, because the king receives her with great courtesy (5:3): " 'What troubles you, Queen Esther?...And what is your request? Even to half the kingdom, it shall be granted you.' "

However, Esther continues to be cautious and, rather than intervening for the Jews, she invites the king and Hamen to a banquet where she promises to make known her request. Hamen is beside himself with joy because of the invitation, but his pleasure dissipates immediately when Mordecai again refuses to bow to him. When Hamen returns home he tells his wife of the great honor bestowed on him but ruefully admits that it means nothing to him because of Mordecai's persistent refusal to honor him. His wife has a ready solution: erect a fifty cubit high stake (yet another hyperbole; a cubit is a little more than a foot and a half) and impale Mordecai on it. Hamen considers this a splendid suggestion.

Late that night, unable to sleep, the king has his Chronicles read to him. Even this little detail adds to the ironic depiction of the monarch whose power appears limitless but who is in almost every way a passive character: he doesn't even do his own reading. When the passage concerning Mordecai's exposure of the assassination plot is read to him, the king wants to know how Mordecai was rewarded. He is astonished to learn that nothing was done for the Jew.

Ironically, just at that moment in walks Hamen to ask permission to impale on a ninety foot stake the very individual whom the king has decided to honor. The king asks Hamen (6:5), " 'What should be done for a man whom the king desires to honor?' " Hamen, certain that it is he who is to be honored, proposes that such a man " 'be dressed in royal garb and paraded through Shushan on a royal steed.' "

Hamen, who came to the king to impale a Jew on an unbelievably high stake and who himself is carried upward by the exhilarating (though mistaken) thought that he has been chosen for a special honor, comes crashing down to earth when he learns that it is Mordecai whom the king has decided to single out and, to make matters even worse, it is Hamen who will lead the royal steed bearing Mordecai, all the while proclaiming (6:11): " 'This is what is done for the man whom the king wishes to honor!' "

After leading Mordecai through Shushan, a morose Hamen returns home to his wife's grim assessment: " 'If Mordecai, before whom you have begun to fall, is of Jewish stock, you will not overcome him; you will fall before him to your ruin.' " Hamen's wife's prophecy is on the mark because we soon learn that Hamen has still farther to fall. On the second day of Esther's banquet she tells the king that she and her people are facing destruction and she fingers Hamen as the culprit. The king storms out in a fury and in the process, of course, leaves the queen, a Jewess, alone with an enemy committed to destroying the Jews. This is but another instance of the king's imprudent, irrational behavior.

Hamen, now no longer the hunter but the hunted, begs Esther to save him and prostrates himself on Esther's couch. The irony here is threefold. Hamen, who could not get a Jew to bow before him, finds himself prostrate before a Jewess. Secondly, when the king returns he misconstrues what Hamen is up to (7:8): " 'Does he mean to ravish the Queen in my own palace?' " Finally, it is Hamen whom the king decrees is to be impaled on the stake which Hamen had intended for Mordecai.

As Hamen had taken Mordecai's place so now does Mordecai assume Hamen's place: the king elevates Mordecai to the position formerly held by Hamen. After Queen Esther prostrates herself before the king to plead for the welfare of her people, he countermands the edict which had decreed the destruction of the Jews and confiscation of their property. He gives the Jews permission to protect themselves and their possessions.

If it is true that all is well which ends well, then all is well (8:15): "Mordecai left the king's presence in royal robes of blue and white, with a magnificent crown of gold and a mantle of fine linen and purple wool. And the city of Shushan rang with joyous cries." The Jews throughout the king's realm are thrilled and more than that (8:17), "...many of the people of the land professed to be Jews, for the fear of the Jews had fallen upon them." And for good reason, as the penultimate chapter describes how the Jews systematically slaughtered those who had intended to slaughter them.

The Jews of Shushan were permitted to muster for a second day in order to complete the slaughter, including the killing and impaling of Hamen's ten sons. Some 500 were killed in Shushan and another 75,000 throughout the 127 provinces of King Ahasuerus' realm. In a book where one hyperbole follows another, it is not surprising that not a single Jew lost his life in the battles. Mordecai institutes a holiday (9:22–23): "The same days on which the Jews enjoyed relief from their foes and the same month which had been transferred for them from one of grief and mourning to one of festive joy. They were to observe them as days of feasting and merrymaking, and as an occasion for sending gifts to one another and presents to the poor. The Jews accordingly assumed as an obligation that which they had begun to practice and which Mordecai prescribed for them."

The book of Esther concludes with two brief notices. One tells of the king's imposition of a tribute tax throughout his realm, and the other describes Mordecai's popularity. The imposition of the tax is noteworthy given the opening of the book where the king's possessions are numberless and given the king's ability to give Hamen an unbelievable sum of money to carry out a lamebrained policy.

Scholars have argued about the time frame in which the book of Esther was written as well as the time frame in which it is set. Additionally, scholars have not agreed as to the book's purpose. In seeking answers to such questions, scholars have attempted to trace the personal names in Esther to Persian and/or Babylonian sources. And they have done the same for the holiday Purim which is mentioned only in Esther. The name of this holiday is explained in the book itself (Esth. 3:7, 9:24) as referring to the casting of lots. The extent to which scholars have searched for clues can be seen in the efforts of W.F. Albright, a man who sired a whole generation of biblical scholars, to track down the historicity of the "cosmetic burners" of Esther 2:12 [*Studies in the Book of Esther*, pp. 361–8].

However, even when a scholarly consensus exists as, e.g., in identifying the Persian king of Esther as Xerxes (486–465 B.C.E.), scholars do not know what to do with what to them are the troubling facts that Xerxes never had a queen named Vashti and that Persian queens could be picked from only one of seven noble Persian families (which would certainly disqualify Esther). [See Herodotus' *History* (III, 84, 890).]

Scholars have also puzzled over the numerous differences between the Hebrew and Greek versions of the book of Esther. The Septuagint Esther has 107 additional verses. The differences between the Hebrew and Greek versions, however, go far beyond quantitative or stylistic variations. For our purposes, it is enough to indicate that the term "God," which as we have noted is conspicuous by virtue of its absence in the Hebrew version, appears more than fifty times in the Greek version. It should not surprise you that scholars have devoted considerable energy to the question of which of the versions is the older.

Our analysis of Esther will restrict itself to that version canonized by the Jews, i.e., the Hebrew version. Certainly, the absence of God in a corpus of literature like the Hebrew Bible which is devoted to praise of God is peculiar. And this peculiarity is deepened when one sees that the Persian king is mentioned more than 190 times in 167 verses. This numerical emphasis on the Persian king is all the more peculiar because while Cyrus and his successors are treated positively in the Hebrew Bible (because of their willingness to allow the exiles to return to Judah), the portrait of Ahasuerus is hardly positive. Ironically, in Ezra 1:2 the Persian king issues his edict of return in the name of YHWH "God of Heaven." But in Esther, not the Persian king, not any of the Jews, and not even the narrator mention God. Nor, in Esther, is there any mention of the covenant between God and Israel, of the Torah, the Temple, prayer, or of a ritual like kashrut which Queen Esther clearly ignores. In fact, when it comes to religious practice, fasting is the only one mentioned (Esth. 4:19, 9:31). And, along the same lines, Queen Esther copulates with an uncircumcised male (cf. Gen. 34). Finally, the term "Israel" appears not once in the book of Esther. It seems apparent that such omissions are part of a deliberate rhetorical strategy and it is that premise which will guide our interpretation.

Let us begin with the obvious: the book of Esther is replete with hyperboles and ironic reversals. At the outset we are introduced to a king with extraordinary power (his domain encompasses 127 provinces) and with so many possessions that it takes six months to parade by them. This king gives week long banquets with wine in such abundance that unrestricted drinking (the only rule in regard to drinking is that there are no limits) cannot exhaust the supply. But this king whose authority extends over 127 provinces cannot, ironically, rule his own household. He cannot get Vashti, his queen, to do his bidding.

Vashti's refusal to be treated as just another of her husband's possessions to be put on display leads to another series of hyperboles. The king, who oversees a realm which stretches from "India to Nubia," is mystified as to how to deal with his recalcitrant mate. Thus does he consult with his brain trust (seven sages no less) who come up with a legal statute for a situation which is hardly amenable to legislation. That is, how could a legal stricture compel wives to respect husbands who act as the king acts, which is to say, like a besotted fool? How would one go about enforcing such a regulation? Recall now what it is that gravels the sages (1:16–18): " 'Queen Vashti has offended not only Your Majesty but all of His officials, nay, all of the people of the King's realm. For the queen's behavior will make all wives despise their husbands, as they consider that the King could not make his queen do his bidding. Why this very day the women of Persia will, hearing of the queen's behavior, use it to scorn and to provoke their husbands.' "

To put this another way, why cannot the sages see what is obvious, viz., that the only level-headedness displayed in the opening chapter is Vashti's refusal to be treated like a pet, at best, and an inanimate object at worst? Why should she, or any other woman in her situation, be expected to respect a husband who, after sobering up, is incapable of remorse or sober reflection? For a sober Ahasuerus seeks retribution; he will see to it that his wife and all other wives in the realm are legally subjected.

Nor does the king change with the passage of time. His predilection to treat women as objects (is not the king the prototypical male chauvinist pig?) continues when he initiates a plan to find a replacement for Vashti who, ironically, has been deemed unsuitable for the role of Queen by virtue of her sobriety, sense of dignity, and courage. The net is thrown out and virgins are hauled in like mackerel.

The preparation for a one night stand with the king is rendered so hyperbolically that it is difficult to imagine any reader mistaking the book of Esther for a historical tract. The preening and perfuming continue for a solid year and the process leaves no doubt what the king is looking for: a mate who is physically beautiful and sexually proficient. One young maiden after another is deflowered so the king can find his dream girl. The point of this hyperbole is clear: for 12 months the young women are bathed in oil, saturated with perfumes and cosmetics, and instructed in the ways of the *boudoir* to prepare for the most important of human relationships with a man who is an egomaniac in addition to being a mental and spiritual dullard.

Perhaps the most effective hyperbole in the book of Esther involves the characterization of Hamen. His appetite for power is such that when one Jew will not bow down to him he resolves to wipe all Jews off the face of the earth. This provides a nice counterpoint to the king's determination to punish all wives because of Vashti's refusal to bow to his wishes. Hamen's lust for power reduces him finally to a position of abject prostration before a Jewish woman, an act which, appropriately, is misinterpreted by the king (who misinterprets virtually everything) as an attempted rape, i.e., as an ultimate grab for power. What Hamen wants is power over others; what he gets is humiliation: he has to parade a Jew through the streets of Shushan and he has to plead for his life in front of a Jewess. Hamen ends up in an ironic ascent: he is pinioned to a 50 cubit high stake. His final, unbelievably high, ascent is a "fall."

The exaggerated treatments of the king and Hamen serve to point the way toward what should not be done. Whatever the historical context of the story, its universal dimensions are clear enough. The reader of the book of Esther must never forget that the book's general context is the Hebrew Bible. Therefore, the reader must constantly be on the watch for connections between Esther and other biblical contexts. Among the most general of these connections is that which can be drawn between Esther and the opening chapters of Genesis which proclaim the ultimate worth of all human beings and the sanctity of the male-female relationship. The king and Hamen fail miserably to measure up to the standards set in Genesis. Furthermore, Hamen's blind ambition to evaluate his own strength by his ability to inflict pain on others could not be more antithetical to the biblical ideals set forth so graphically in the Decalogue. Hamen is quite willing to steal; he bears false witness; and he covets. And, of course, it is only his own death which prevents him from conducting a full scale purge of Jews in the king's domain. If the prophet Micah's words represent the right path (6:8 f.): "He has told you, O man, what is good, And what the Lord requires of you: Only to do justice And to love goodness, And to walk modestly with your God.", then it can be said that Hamen and the king are ironic foils to what should be done. They point the way with the backs of their necks.

Before pursuing some of the more specific connections between Esther and other portions of the Hebrew Bible, let us consider the issue raised in the last sentence of the previous paragraph, namely, who it is who speaks for the author in the book of Esther. Esther would seem to be a reasonable candidate. The book is named after her and in many ways she is the book's centerpiece. When Esther is introduced, we are informed that she is "shapely and beautiful." Her physical beauty, while explaining why the king is attracted to her, is not, of course, sufficient reason for the reader to be attracted to her. Nor does the fact that her sexual prowess wins the king's favor mean that the reader should be bedazzled by her. In fact, given the king's track record, whatever he finds positive is almost certain to be negative.

The reader soon learns that, once in the palace, Esther does not divulge her Jewish identity because in this, as in all other things, she obeys Mordecai. Obviously, obedience, in and of itself, need not be a virtue. In fact, in the book of Esther, the first act of disobedience, viz, Vashti's refusal to appear at the king's banquet, is praiseworthy. But, it might be objected, Mordecai is far different from the king. Be that as it may, it is troubling that Esther resists Mordecai's urgings to intercede with the king on behalf of the Jews. Her reluctance is attributed explicitly to her fear for her own safety. While this may be understandable, it does not qualify as heroic behavior. Furthermore, when she finally does go to the king, it is in response to a dire threat by Mordecai that if she does not intervene, Esther will not survive and her "father's house" will be wiped out, the last an allusion to the fact that the dead in Esther's family are dependent on her survival.

While Esther may be preferable to the king and Hamen, there does not seem to be anything exceptional about her. The question to ask of Esther is not whether she measures up to a character like Ruth, for she does not. Think of Ruth's determined and persistent willingness to turn her back on her own self-interest and contrast that to Esther's actions. The question which is more to the point is whether Esther measures up to Vashti who, in a way, never even "appears" in the book and whose non-appearance, rational and heroic as it is, puts Esther to shame.

What then of Mordecai? At first glance, he would seem to be our hero, our "Defender of the Faith." He adopts Esther when her parents die; he uncovers a plot to assassinate the king and, because of this, comes to a position of power which allows him to save the Jewish community of Persia. And it is Mordecai who commemorates the saving by mandating the holiday of Purim. The Jews of subsequent generations are to observe Purim as an occasion for feasting, merry-making, and sending gifts to one another and to the poor.

Still, for all that, Mordecai hardly compares with such biblical worthies as Abraham, Jacob, Joseph, and Moses who, in their stories, reach such great spiritual heights. Nor is Mordecai of the stature of any of the prophets who wear themselves out in the service of God. It is questionable if Mordecai is even the equal of the author of Ecclesiastes (whose spirit permeates the holiday of Purim), who endured mental and emotional torment before observing that the best one can hope for is an earned, moderate pleasure. And of the political giants whom the biblical writers present (as, e.g., Saul, David, Solomon, and Josiah), would anyone seriously want to suggest that Mordecai deserves equal recognition? Even the infamous Ahab is given a splendid death scene when, face to foe and mortally wounded, he fights on.

Mordecai, in short, is lackluster as a character. In fact, his name may be an ironic pun as it apparently is connected with Marduk, the resplendent Babylonian sun god. For all of his efforts, what one is left with is an averted slaughter which is replaced by an actual slaughter and a holiday whose overwhelming emphasis is on eating, drinking, and merriment. Thus does the book of Esther come full circle: it begins with Persians feasting and drinking and ends with the establishment of a holiday which institutionalizes Jewish feasting and merriment.

As noted, when Mordecai is introduced the writer provides us with the following genealogy: "...son of Jair, son of Shimei, son of Kish, a Benjamite." There is a striking similarity here to the genealogy of Saul, the first king of biblical Israel (1 Sam. 9:1 f): "There was a man of Benjamin whose name was Kish...a Benjamite.... He had a son named Saul...." This similarity is strengthened given the genealogy of Hamen, the man Mordecai opposes and replaces. We recall that the writer tells us that Hamen was an "Agagite." Thus does the writer turn our attention to 1 Sam. 15 where King Saul and an Amalekite king named Agag meet in combat. Because of the virtual certainty that this is a deliberate allusion, the context in Samuel needs to be studied for the light it may shed on the book of Esther.

In 1 Sam. 14, Saul, thanks to the heroism of his son Jonathan, wins his first great victory and is shown expanding his military power base. The prophet Samuel directs the king to move against the Amalekites and to destroy them root and branch. The reason? When biblical Israel came out of Egypt, the Amalekites (blood kin of Israel as they are descended from Esau) descended like vultures on the Israelites. Exodus 17:14 reads:

> Then the Lord said to Moses, 'Inscribe this in a document as a reminder, and read it aloud to Joshua: I will utterly blot out the memory of Amalek from under heaven!'

In effect, the prophet is telling Saul that the Amalekite bill has come due. You already know that given the Sheol model of afterlife, the Amalekites who assaulted Israel can themselves be assaulted by striking at their progeny. It is also possible that the author of Esther is directing us to the exodus narrative as well, given the fact that in both Esther and in the drama of the deliverance from Egypt there are the following:

— intrigue at a foreign court;

— a threat against Israel;

— the deliverance of the people Israel;

— the destruction of the enemy;

— the establishment of a festival (i.e., Passover and Purim).

If this is an allusion, what is most striking is the contrast between God's direct and obvious intervention in the story of the exodus and God's absence in the book of Esther. Also, the human characters in the saga of the exodus (Moses, Aaron, Joshua, Miriam) are given the kind of heroic dimensions which are lacking in the likes of Esther and Mordecai.

In any case, in the story involving Saul, the king does proceed to wipe out the Amalekites. Well, almost. He captures King Agag and saves some of the best spoil, this contrary to the direct command of Samuel who had expressly forbidden the saving of life or spoil. When confronted by the prophet, the king insists that the spoil was saved not for anyone's personal benefit but for the purpose of honoring the Lord by offering these animals up in sacrifice. Samuel's response is worth quoting in full (15:22–23):

'Does the Lord delight in burnt offerings and sacrifices
As much as in obedience to the Lord's command?
Surely, obedience is better than sacrifice,
Compliance than the fat of rams.
For rebellion is like the sin of divination,
Defiance, like the iniquity of teraphim.
Because you have rejected the Lord's command
He has rejected you as king.'

Saul admits his wrongdoing but attributes it to his fear of the troops; had he not saved some of the trophies of war (including Agag), his men would have turned on him. But God's own word prevents the prophet Samuel from suspending judgment, and Samuel kills Agag and never again sees Saul. The very next chapter introduces us to the young David, he who will bring Saul's dynasty to an end.

This allusion to the Saul-Agag story does not enhance our appreciation of Mordecai. The genealogy makes Mordecai an analogue not of the prophet Samuel who speaks for God but of King Saul against whom God—through Samuel—speaks. It is Samuel who must lecture the king on loyalty to God and man, and the prophet's references to the superstitious practices of divination and consulting teraphim (apparently household icons) are particularly instructive. For the holiday Purim takes its name from Hamen's superstitious rite of casting lots in order to determine the most propitious time to lay waste the Jews. And it is Saul who will turn later to necromancy (1 Sam. 28).

As a biblical holiday, Purim is askew. Only as an afterthought does the holiday involve the sending of "presents to the poor." The clear focus of the holiday, in contradistinction to every other biblical holiday, is on material pleasure. This is apt in that the entire book of Esther seems out of focus. That which is central in every other biblical holiday and that which is central in virtually every other biblical book, *viz*, the primacy of moral behavior, in the book of Esther becomes little more than an afterthought.

Perhaps that is why there is no mention of God in Esther. There surely is no character who can speak for God, i.e., there is no analogue to the prophet Samuel. At the very beginning of that prophet's ministry (1 Sam. 3:1), the narrator notes that "In those days the word of the Lord was rare; prophecy was not widespread." What is explicit in this passage, namely, that for God's word to be heard there must be a worthy receptacle, is implicit in the book of Esther. Of no character in Esther could the narrator observe what he does of Samuel (1 Sam. 3:19–21): "Samuel matured [as a prophet] and the Lord was with him. He did not leave any of Samuel's predictions unfulfilled. All Israel, from Dan to Beersheba, knew that Samuel was trustworthy as a prophet of the Lord. Thus did the Lord continue to appear...."

The Mordecai-Hamen confrontation, which is framed in the context of the Saul-Agag confrontation, is most noteworthy for what it lacks, namely, Samuel, and therefore the Lord God of Israel. We are now in a position to understand why there is no explicit mention of

God in the book of Esther. For with the possible exception of Vashti, who, after all, never appears on stage, there is no worthy receptacle. There are a number of contexts in Esther in which the avoidance of a reference to God involves the writer in wordy circumlocutions. For instance, when Mordecai warns Esther that she will not be spared if Hamen succeeds, he says (4:13), "...if you keep silent in this crisis, relief and deliverance will come to the Jews from another quarter, while you and your father's house will perish." But if not from God, from what other conceivable quarter could help for the Jews come? Finally, unlike other biblical holidays, the holiday of Purim is not mandated by God.

If God is conspicuous by His absence in the book of Esther, references to the number seven are so numerous in the book as to rule out a random selection by the author. Ahasuerus's banquet lasts for seven days and it is on the seventh day that the king orders the seven eunuchs who attend him to summon Vashti. When Vashti refuses to appear, the king consults his seven sages. And when Esther is preparing for her night with the king, seven maidens attend her. Finally, Esther is summoned to the king in the seventh year of his reign.

You will note that each of these occurrences of the number seven relates to what appears to be *the* major theme of the book, namely, physical merriment. The week long banquet features unrestrained drinking. When Vashti is ordered to appear on the seventh day of the banquet by the seven eunuchs, there is a hint that the king intends that she come clothed only in her royal diadem (1:11): " '...bring Queen Vashti before the king, with the royal diadem, in order to show her beauty to the assemblage,' for she was a beautiful woman." Then when Ahasuerus consults his seven sages, it is to discuss the purely physical side of the male-female relationship. And, of course, the seven attendants who minister to Esther are preparing her for a one night stand.

These repeated references to the number seven in a biblical book which assiduously avoids any explicit mention of God come together to form the book of Esther's most powerful and corrosive irony. I say this because the number seven is of immediate and enduring significance in the Hebrew Bible, but for a purpose which is in direct contrast to the manner in which that number is employed in the book of Esther.

We saw that it was on the first seventh day that God, as it were, put His imprint on creation. For it was on the seventh day that God ceased creating and blessed the seventh day, declaring it to be holy. The seventh day, the day of cessation, is, of course, the Sabbath. And of all biblical Israel's holidays, it is the Sabbath and the Sabbath alone which is mandated in the Decalogue. And we repeat that the Hebrew Bible presents the Decalogue as its supreme revelation. For the Ten Commandments are unique in that they alone are said to be written in God's own script (Exod. 32:16; cf. 34:1): "...the tablets were God's work, and the writing was God's writing, incised upon the tablets."

The Sabbath holiday, which is the only holiday mentioned in the Decalogue, had for its purpose the imitation of God. As God ceased from His "work" on the seventh day, so biblical Israel is to set aside every seventh day. On the first six days of the week (secular time), one is free to use time for one's own benefit. But on the seventh day, one is commanded to return "time" to God by acting God-like, i.e., by aiding the weak, the helpless, and the disenfranchised. To put this another way, on the first six days of the week one is free to tend one's material needs, but on the seventh day one is to devote oneself to the realm of the spirit.

It requires only a moment's reflection to realize that the book of Esther inverts the symbolic significance of the number seven. Worship of the flesh reaches its apex in contexts in which the number seven is employed. Thus does the book of Esther teach indirectly what other biblical books proclaim explicitly: the presence of God in history depends in large part on what human beings do. There is no mention of God in Esther because there is no imitation of God to be found in the world created by Esther's author. That world is dominated by idolatrous behavior because, in effect, the author chose not to introduce a "defender of the faith." Put someone like Roth's character Nathan Marx (to say nothing of the biblical Samuel) in that world and you have the presence of God.

If the Jewish experience can be said to promote a singular ideal, then it is that humankind is to bring God to earth by acts of goodness.

In this sense, the characters in the book of Esther move in a godless world and in this sense, Nathan Marx does more to bring God to earth by playing softball on the Sabbath than does Grossbart by going to religious services.

Suggested Readings

General

Finkelstein, Louis, editor. *The Jews: Their History, Culture, and Religion.* 3rd edition. New York: Harper and Row, 1960.

Golden, Judah, editor. *The Jewish Expression.* New Haven: Yale University Press, 1976.

Jewish Encyclopedia. 12 volumes. New York: Funk and Wagnalls, Inc., 1901–1905.

The Biblical Period

Bright, John. *A History of Israel.* 2nd edition. Philadelphia: Westminster Press, 1972.

Cassuto, U. *Commentary on the Book of Genesis.* 2 volumes. Trans. from the Hebrew by Israel Abrahams. Jerusalem: Magnes Press, 1961–1964.

Kaufmann, Yehezkel. *The Religion of Israel: From Its Beginnings to the Babylonian Exile.* Trans. from the Hebrew and abridged by Moshe Greenberg. Chicago: University of Chicago Press, 1960.

Speiser, E. A., editor. *At the Dawn of Civilization: A Background of Biblical History* (World History of the Jewish People, Vol. I). New Brunswick, N. J.: Rutgers University Press, 1964.

The Rabbinic Period

Goldin, Judah, editor and trans. *The Living Talmud: The Wisdom of the Fathers.* New York: Mentor Books, 1957.

Moore, George Foot. *Judaism in the First Centuries of the Christian Era: The Age of the Tannaim.* 3 volumes. Cambridge, Mass.: Harvard University Press, 1927–1930.

Parkes, Jaime. *The Conflict of the Church and the Synagogue: A Study in the Origins of Anti-Semitism.* New York: Meredian Books, 1961.

Rivkin, Ellis. *A Hidden Revolution: The Pharisees' Search for the Kingdom Within.* Nashville, Tenn.: Abingdon Press, 1978.

Sandmel, Samuel. *A Jewish Understanding of the New Testament.* New York: Ktav Publishing House, Inc., 1974.

The Medieval Period

Abrahams, Israel. *Jewish Life in the Middle Ages.* New York: Atheneum Publishers, 1969.

Baer, Yitzhak. *A History of the Jews of Christian Spain.* 2 volumes. Trans. by Louis Levensohn, Hillel Halkin, S. Nardi, and H. Fishman. Philadelphia: Jewish Publication Society of America, 1961.

Goiten, S. D. *Jews and Arabs: Their Contacts Through the Ages.* New York: Schocken Books, Inc., 1964.

Lowenthal, Marvin. *The Jews of Germany: A Study of Sixteen Centuries.* Philadelphia: Jewish Publication Society of America, 1938.

Roth, Cecil, editor. *The Dark Ages: Jews in Christian Europe, 711–1096* (World History of the Jewish People, Vol. II). New Brunswick, N. J.: Rutgers University Press, 1966.

Trachtenberg, Joshua. *The Devil and the Jews: The Medieval Conception of the Jews and Its Relation to Modern Antisemitism.* New York: Meredian Books, 1961.

The Modern Period

Acosta, Uriel. *A Specimen of Human Life.* New York: Bergman Publishers, 1967.

Blau, Joseph L. *Judaism in America: From Curiosity to Third Faith.* Chicago: University of Chicago Press, 1976.

Chazan, Robert and Marc Lee Raphael, editors. *Modern Jewish History: A Source Reader.* New York: Schocken Books, Inc., 1974.

Dawidowicz, Lucy S., editor. *The Golden Tradition: Jewish Life and Thought in Eastern Europe.* New York: Holt, Rinehart and Winston, 1966.

————. *The War Against the Jews, 1933–1945.* New York: Holt, Rinehart, and Winston, 1975.

Dubnow, Simon. *History of the Jews in Russia and Poland.* Trans. from the Russian by I. Friedlander. New York: Ktav Publishing House, Inc., 1973.

Elon, Amos. *Herzl.* New York: Holt, Rinehart, and Winston, 1975.

Jacob, Walter. *Christianity Through Jewish Eyes: The Quest for Common Ground.* Cincinnati, Ohio: Hebrew Union College Press, 1974.

Howe, Irving. *World of Our Fathers: The Journey of East European Jews to America and the Life They Found and Made.* New York: Simon and Schuster, Inc., 1976.

Levin, Nora. *The Holocaust: The Destruction of European Jewry, 1933–1945.* New York: Schocken Books, Inc., 1973.

Netanyahu, B. *The Marranos of Spain.* New York: American Academy for Jewish Research, 1967.

Poliakov, Léon. *The History of Anti-Semitism.* 3 volumes. Trans. from the French by Richard Howard. New York: Vanguard Press, Inc., 1965–1976.

Strauss, Leo. *Spinoza's Critique of Religion.* Trans. by E. M. Sinclair. New York: Schocken Books, Inc., 1965.

Vital, David. *The Origins of Zionism.* London: Oxford University Press, 1975.